Norman P. Tanner

The Church in Late Medieval Norwich 1370-1532

This study, which is perhaps the closest analysis of religion in a medieval city yet made, is of interest partly because of the importance of Norwich, the city chosen, and partly because of the way in which the subject matter has been treated.

Norwich is of intrinsic interest inasmuch as it was one of the half-dozen leading English cities throughout the late Middle Ages, and probably the second city in the kingdom by the early sixteenth century. Moreover, it was the regional capital of one of the most advanced areas of the country, and geographically and through trade was close to the Low Countries and Rhineland, which were then the most fertile areas for new religious movements north of the Alps – thus raising questions about England's religious connections with the Continent. It was a city in which both the old and the new in the late medieval Church abounded – some fifty parishes, a cathedral, a Benedictine monastery and nunnery, several colleges of secular priests and four friaries; but also hermits and anchorites, several communities of women resembling Continental beguinages, craft guilds and pious confraternities, and a variety of other activities offering a deeper religious life to the laity. One of the most prominent anchoresses of the city was Julian of Norwich, author of *Revelations of Divine Love*, and this book forms a general background to Julian and contains some new information about her life.

The Church is examined primarily as "the people of God," or "the Christian people," rather than as a visible institution; that is, the work is principally concerned with what Christianity meant to and how it was practised by the mass of citizens rather than with the network of buildings and ecclesiastical authorities which made up the outer surface of the local church. A variety of primary sources are used but principally wills, of which a remarkably full collection survives for the city and which help to shed a new kind of light on what might be called popular religion. Apart from its descriptive analysis, the study contains significant conclusions challenging the generally held view that the Church was in a state of marked decline in the late Middle Ages, and suggesting that to some extent the Reformation must be seen as a development from within rather than as a reaction against the late medieval Church.

STUDIES AND TEXTS 66

THE CHURCH IN
LATE MEDIEVAL NORWICH
1370-1532

BY

NORMAN P. TANNER

PONTIFICAL INSTITUTE OF MEDIAEVAL STUDIES

The publishing program of the
Pontifical Institute is supported
through the generosity of
The De Rancé Foundation.

CANADIAN CATALOGUING IN PUBLICATION DATA

Tanner, Norman P.
  The church in late medieval Norwich, 1370-1532

(Studies and texts, ISSN 0082-5328 ; 66)
Bibliography: p.
Includes index.
ISBN 0-88844-066-9

1. Norwich (Norfolk) - Religious life and customs - History.   2. Catholic
Church - England - Norwich (Norfolk) History.   I. Pontifical Institute of
Mediaeval Studies.   II. Title.   III. Series: Studies and texts (Pontifical
Institute of Mediaeval Studies) ; 66.

BR765.N67T36   282'.42615   C83-098713-4

PRINTED BY UNIVERSA, WETTEREN, BELGIUM

Contents

Maps

Acknowledgments

I thank Miss Jean Kennedy, County Archivist of the Norfolk Record Office, for permission to quote from and to publish various records in her care, and also for the unfailing courtesy with which she and her staff have met my numerous requests. Transcripts of Crown-copyright records in the Public Record Office appear by permission of the Controller of Her Majesty's Stationery Office. Appendix 2, from Tanner MS 100, appears by permission of the Keeper of Western Manuscripts at the Bodleian Library, Oxford. I thank the following for permission to quote from their theses: Mr Bruce Burnham, Dr Ralph Houlbrooke, Dr Alison McHardy, Mlle Marie-Simone de Nucé and Dr John Thomson; and Mrs C. Swift for typing the final draft.

Of many other people to whom I am indebted, I wish to thank especially Mr James Campbell of Worcester College, Oxford, for first introducing me to late medieval Norwich and for continuing to provide much information, help and encouragement. In addition, I owe a special debt to the late Dr W. A. Pantin of Oriel College, Oxford, who supervised my doctoral thesis, on which the book is based.

Campion Hall, Oxford   *Norman Tanner*

Notes

Mayors

Unless otherwise stated, all references to men being mayors of Norwich, to the years of their mayoralties and to the names of their wives are based on Basil Cozens Hardy, *The Mayors of Norwich, 1403-1835* (Norwich 1938).

Norwich

The boundaries of the city of Norwich were a much disputed question during the late Middle Ages (see James Campbell, *Norwich*, Historic Towns, ed. Mary D. Lobel [London 1975], p. 23). The usage of this book is that Norwich means the area bounded by the river Wensum and the medieval city walls. Carrow, Trowse, Bracondale, Lakenham, Eaton, Earlham, Heigham, Catton and Thorpe – which lay immediately outside this boundary – are referred to as suburbs of the city.

Quotations

In the transcription of material in the Appendices, the original has been retained except for the introduction of paragraphs, the modernization of punctuation, use of capital letters and division of words (e.g., "before" not "be fore"), the rationalization of the forms i and j, and u and v, the reduction of the form ff to F or f as appropriate, and the expansion of abbreviations except where the contrary is noted by an abbreviation mark ('). In the text of the book quotations have normally been translated into English, where necessary, and the spelling, etc., modernized (with the original being printed in a footnote where necessary). Throughout, matter appearing in square brackets has been supplied.

Wills

References to unpublished wills are followed by the testator's surname in brackets, spelt as it appears in the appropriate published or unpublished index listing the will.

Abbreviations

Ab.C.   London, Lambeth Palace Library, Registers of Archbishops
                    of Canterbury.

A.N.C.   Norwich, Norfolk Record Office, Probate Records, Register-
                    ed copies of wills proved in the Archdeacon of Norwich's
                    Court.

Cal. Close R.   *Calendar of the Close Rolls Preserved in the Public Record
                    Office* (London 1892 –).

Cal. Papal L.   *Calendar of Entries in the Papal Registers relating to Great
                    Britain and Ireland, Papal Letters*, ed. William H. Bliss
                    and Jesse A. Twemlow (London 1893 –).

Cal. Pat. R.   *Calendar of the Patent Rolls Preserved in the Public Record
                    Office* (London 1893 –).

D. and C. Mun.   Norwich, Norfolk Record Office, Dean and Chapter Muni-
                    ments.

D. and C., Reg.   Norwich, Norfolk Record Office, Dean and Chapter Muni-
                    ments, Registered copies of wills proved in the court of
                    the Dean and Chapter (then the Prior and Convent) of
                    Norwich, Register.

D.N.B.   *Dictionary of National Biography*, ed. Leslie Stephen and
                    Sidney Lee, 63 vols. (London 1885-1900).

Emden, *BRUC*   Alfred B. Emden, *A Biographical Register of the University of
                    Cambridge to 1500* (Cambridge 1963).

Emden, *BRUO*   Alfred B. Emden, *A Biographical Register of the University of
                    Oxford to A.D.1500*, 3 vols. (Oxford 1957).

N.C.C.   Norwich, Norfolk Record Office, Probate Records, Register-
                    ed copies of wills proved in the Norwich Consistory
                    Court.

N.C.R.   Norwich, Norfolk Record Office, Norwich City Records.

PROB/11   London, Public Record Office, PROB/11 (Registered copies of
                    wills proved in the Prerogative Court of Canterbury).

REG   Norwich, Norfolk Record Office, Norwich Diocesan Ar-
                    chives, REG (Bishop's Registers).

Reg.   Register

VCH   *The Victoria History of the Counties of England.*

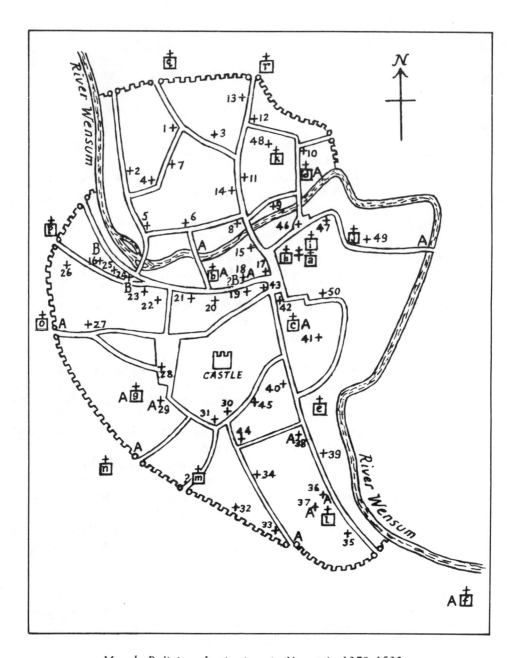

Map 1: Religious Institutions in Norwich, 1370-1532

+ *Cathedral*

+ *Parish Churches*

Northern Ward
1 St Augustine
2 St Martin of Coslany
3 St Botolph
4 St Mary of Coslany
5 St Michael of Coslany
6 St George of Colegate
7 St Olave of Colegate
8 St Clement at Fye Bridge
9 St Edmund
10 St James
11 St Saviour
12 All Saints at Fye Bridge
13 St Margaret at Fye Bridge
14 St Mary Unbrent

Wimer Ward
15 Sts Simon and Jude
16 St Swithin
17 St George at Tombland
18 St Peter Hungate
19 St Michael at Plea
20 St Andrew
21 Holy Cross or St Crowche
22 St John's Maddermarket
23 St Gregory
24 St Laurence
25 St Margaret of Westwick
26 St Benedict

Mancroft Ward
27 St Giles
28 St Peter Mancroft
29 St Stephen

Conisford Ward
30 St John of Timberhill
31 All Saints of Berstreet
32 St Catherine or St Winewaloy
33 St John and the Holy Sepulchre
34 St Bartholomew
35 St Peter Southgate

36 St Etheldreda
37 St Edward
38 St Julian
39 St Clement of Conisford
40 St Peter Permentergate
41 St Vedast
42 St Cuthbert
43 St Mary the Less
44 St Michael of Berstreet
45 St Martin in the Bailey

Liberties of the Cathedral Priory
46 St Martin at the Palace Gates
47 St Matthew
48 St Paul
49 St Helen
50 St Mary in the Marsh

⌂ *Religious Houses and Hospitals*

a   Benedictine Cathedral Priory
b   Dominican Friary
c   Franciscan Friary
d   Carmelite Friary
e   Augustinian Friary
f   Benedictine Nunnery of Carrow
g   College of St Mary in the Fields
h   Carnary College
i   College of Chantry Priests in the
    Bishop's Palace
j   St Giles's Hospital
k   St Paul's Hospital
l   Hildebrond's Hospital
m   Daniel's Alms-Houses
n   Sick-House outside St Stephen's Gate
o   Sick-House outside St Giles Gate
p   Sick-House outside St Benedict's Gate
q   Sick-House outside St Augustine's Gate
r   Sick-House outside Magdalen Gate

A *Anchorage or Hermitage*

B *Community resembling a Beguinage*

Introduction

Erasmus complained in *Sileni Alcibiadis* that "the followers of the world ... call the priests, bishops and popes 'the Church', when in reality they are only the servants of the Church; the Church is the whole Christian people." [1] In recent years ecclesiastical historians have increasingly been paying attention to this second dimension of the Church – the Church as "the Christian people" or "the people of God." [2] The present work follows this new emphasis. In other words, to over simplify, it is not principally concerned with the Church as an institution but rather with what Christianity meant to, and how it was practised by, the mass of Christians. Or to use a scholastic distinction, it is concerned with the Church as *communio fidelium* rather than as a hierarchically governed *regnum*. Special attention is therefore paid to three interconnected questions about the late medieval Church.

First, movement in the Church from below. Most of the surviving records about medieval Christianity are concerned with the administration of the Church as an institution and with what Christians ought to have believed and how they ought to have behaved: for example, papal and episcopal records, the records of ecumenical and local councils, and works of canon law and of theology. Such records may give the impression of a somewhat monolithic Church in which movement came largely from above. Yet movement also came from below through the choices which ordinary Christians made about how they practised their religion. For even within the bounds of orthodoxy a wide range of choices was offered to them, wider indeed than probably appears to most historians today who tend to forget that the fringes of orthodoxy had not

[1] Desiderius Erasmus, *Sileni Alcibiadis*, in *Opera Omnia Desiderii Erasmi Roterodami*, vol. 2.5, ed. Felix Heinimann and Emanuel Kienzle (Amsterdam 1981), p. 174.

[2] The best general survey is Francis Rapp, *L'Église et la vie religieuse en Occident à la fin du Moyen Âge*, Nouvelle Clio, 25 (Paris 1971). For surveys of particular countries, see especially: Bernd Moeller, "Frommigkeit in Deutschland um 1500," *Archiv für Reformationsgeschichte* 56 (1965) 5-31, which has been translated as "Religious Life in Germany on the Eve of the Reformation," in *Pre-Reformation Germany*, ed. Gerald Strauss (London 1972), pp. 13-42; and Jacques Toussaert, *Le sentiment religieux en Flandre à la fin du Moyen Âge* (Paris 1960).

yet been tidied up by the Council of Trent. This book does examine heresy, but it is more concerned with what forms of religion the citizens of Norwich preferred within the wide spectrum of orthodoxy.

Secondly, new movements in the late medieval Church. The latter is often examined in terms of the Reformation which followed. An attempt is made to examine how far the Church in Norwich became ripe for the Reformation, but more attention is paid to examining it as a development from the early and high Middle Ages. Many of the developments in the late medieval Church took place in towns, and special attention is paid to the question of how far Norwich participated in these developments, how far the new movements displaced the religious forms and ideals of the early and high Middle Ages, and how far there was tension between the two.

Thirdly, lay piety. Many of the developments in the late medieval Church offered a deeper religious life to the laity, and much of the movement in the Church "from below" came from the laity rather than from the clergy. This book examines the extent to which the laity of Norwich took advantage of the opportunities offered to them to lead deeper religious lives, how far they were becoming independent of the clergy in the practice of their religion, and the attitude of the laity towards the clergy.

For several reasons the city of Norwich, the subject of this study, is of considerable interest to the student of these questions. It is of intrinsic interest because it was one of the half-dozen most important cities in England throughout the late Middle Ages, and by the 1520s had probably established itself as the wealthiest and most populous city in the kingdom after London,[3] with around ten thousand inhabitants.[4] Furthermore, the religious institutions of the early and high Middle Ages abounded in it. Thus it was an episcopal city and had a Benedictine monastery, four friaries, a nunnery nearby and more parish churches than any other city in England apart from London and possibly Lincoln.[5] At the same time

[3] William G. Hoskins, "English Provincial Towns in the Early Sixteenth Century," *Transactions of the Royal Historical Society*, 5th ser., 6 (1956), 4-5. But see, Josiah C. Russell, *British Medieval Population* (Albuquerque 1948), p. 285.

[4] For no date in the Middle Ages can the population of the city be calculated with precision. Recent estimates for the 1520s, based on the records of the 1525 subsidy, suggest a minimum of about nine thousand and a maximum of thirteen thousand inhabitants, the most likely figure being thought to be around ten thousand (James Campbell, *Norwich*, Historic Towns, ed. Mary D. Lobel [London 1975], p. 18, n. 47; John F. Pound, "The Social and Trade Structure of Norwich, 1525-1575," *Past and Present* 34 [1966] 50). For estimates of the population in the fourteenth century, see below, p. 21.

[5] See pp. 2-3.

Norwich was especially likely to have been in contact with the new religious currents of late medieval Christendom. For, as has been mentioned, towns were principal centres of the new religious movements and Norwich was an important town. It was, moreover, the capital of one of the most advanced regions in the kingdom, and geographically and through trade it was close to the Low Countries and the Rhineland which were then the most fertile areas for religious developments north of the Alps. Julian of Norwich, the anchoress and authoress of *Revelations of Divine Love* (or *A Book of Showings*), provides a glimpse of just how far the citizens of Norwich may have been participating in these developments.

Another reason is that it is over two hundred years since Francis Blomefield first published his monumental survey of Norwich.[6] Since then much work has been done on the Church in this city in the late Middle Ages but no attempt has been made to synthesize the researches. This book, which is based on my doctoral thesis,[7] attempts to make the synthesis.

Finally, wills are the most important source of evidence for this work, and Norwich is one of only three or four cities in late medieval England for which sufficient wills survive to permit studies of this kind.[8] Indeed this is perhaps the first published study of religion in a late medieval English city to make such extensive use of wills, and as such sheds a new kind of light on what might be called popular religion. It is perhaps the closest analysis of religion in a medieval city yet made.

It is important to try to penetrate beneath the surface of the visible Church to what Christianity meant to the mass of Christians, yet the attempt can only hope to achieve a limited success. For religious experience is, to a large extent, indescribable in principle; and in so far as it can be described, the surviving evidence about it is, for the most part, very inadequate. This is particularly true of the Middle Ages because auto-biographical material, such as memoirs or private letters, is so lacking. The picture presented in this book, therefore, is inevitably an impressionistic one. That is to say while, so far as I am aware, all the

---

[6] Francis Blomefield, *An Essay towards a Topographical History of the County of Norfolk*, with a Continuation by the Rev. Charles Parkin (Fersfield and Lynn 1739-1775), vol. 2, which was subsequently published as Francis Blomefield and Charles Parkin, *An Essay towards a Topographical History of the County of Norfolk* (London 1805-1810), vols. 3 and 4.

[7] "Popular Religion in Norwich with special Reference to the Evidence of Wills, 1370-1532" (Oxford University D.Phil. thesis, 1973).

[8] See pp. 113-114.

relevant surviving evidence has been examined, and while an attempt has been made to reach an over-all view of the religion of the citizens, the view is based on evidence that is patchy.

As mentioned, the unusually fine collection of wills is the chief source. Bequests of a religious nature were a principal concern of almost all the wills. Such bequests provide two main kinds of information: first, that some person or thing – for example a book that was bequeathed or a hermit who was named as a beneficiary – existed; secondly, that the donor approved of the beneficiary. The first kind of information and a variety of other sources – chiefly records of visitations, episcopal registers, records of guilds and confraternities and the obedientiary rolls of the cathedral priory – are used in chapters 1 and 2 to describe the religious activities in the city. Chapter 1 discusses what was by the late Middle Ages the old order, that is to say the institutions and ideals that had their origins in the high Middle Ages or earlier – parishes, the secular clergy and religious orders. Chapter 2 discusses movements which, though not confined to the late Middle Ages, were specially characteristic of them – hermits and anchorites, communities resembling beguinages and "lay religious"; craft guilds and pious confraternities; devotion to the saints, pilgrimages and various private devotions; Masses and prayers for the dead; the religious education of the laity. The second kind of information is discussed principally in chapter 3, analysis being made of trends in bequests to various branches of the Church during the period in question. So this chapter returns to most of the persons and institutions discussed in chapters 1 and 2 but looks at them from a different angle, namely from that of what the wills of ordinary citizens tell us about how such persons and institutions were regarded by the mass of citizens. Information of this kind is important because there are so few other medieval records that express directly and in first-person terms what large numbers of ordinary Christians thought about their religion. Finally tensions in the Church in Norwich, including heresy, are discussed in chapter 4.

The year 1370 has been chosen as the opening date largely because wills survive in large numbers from that year and because other records become much more copious at about the same time. It also allows Wycliffe's influence to be considered. To go beyond the early 1530s without continuing to at least 1570 would be unsatisfactory since the new sets of questions arising out of the Reformation would be left hanging in the air without an answer. To continue up to 1570 is not feasible, and a halt has therefore been called at the eve of the Henrician Reformation.

1

The Old Order

At the beginning of the late Middle Ages in most towns the three chief bulwarks of the visible Church were the parochial system, the secular clergy who among other things administered the parishes, and religious orders; they were the principal representatives of what was by then the Church's "old order." Some discussion of this "old order" seems the logical starting-point of this study, and so this first chapter begins with a discussion of the parishes and follows with the secular clergy and religious orders. Both parts have descriptive sections outlining the numbers of people and institutions involved. Thereafter an attempt is made to reach the inner life, though the attempt is of course conditioned considerably by what evidence happens to survive. What the parishes meant to the citizens is therefore discussed in terms of tithes, the sacraments and worship, preaching, burials, clerical involvement in the making of wills, and the laity's control over the parishes. The secular clergy and members of religious orders are examined in terms of their social and geographical origins, their education, various aspects of their material welfare, and their morals. Both parts end with concluding sections.

A. The Parishes

The parish was, according to Canon Law, the primary context within which most Christians were supposed to practice their religion. Their principal religious needs should have been met by the parish and their most tangible religious duties were to it. The parish priest had the official care of the souls of his parishioners, even if the laws of the Church were not always exactly in harmony as to what his duties entailed. He was expected to administer to them the sacraments of Baptism, Penance, the Eucharist, Matrimony and Extreme Unction; to say Mass for them; to instruct them, chiefly through preaching and the confessional; and to visit the sick.[1] For their part lay men and women were normally obliged to hear Mass on Sundays and feast-days in their own parish church,[2] to receive the sacraments of Penance and the Eucharist once a year from their parish priest,[3] and to pay to him what constituted their most onerous financial obligations to the Church – tithes and oblations.

In the countryside, no doubt, the parish was in fact the primary context within which most people practised their religion. But towns possessed other religious institutions which tended to diminish the parish's importance: houses of religious orders and possibly a cathedral where Mass and other religious services could be attended, sermons be heard, the sacrament of Penance be received and people be buried; craft guilds and pious confraternities with their own religious activities; and the private chapels of individual citizens. Norwich abounded in almost all these institutions. So how important to the parishioners was the city's parish system in the late Middle Ages?

i. The Parish Churches

One of the most striking things about late medieval Norwich must have been the number of parish churches. Even today the visitor is amazed at the number still standing within the old city walls. Yet the medieval city possessed roughly as many churches again, churches which were pulled down subsequently or destroyed in an air-raid in 1942. There were at least – and probably exactly – forty-six parish churches in the city in the 1520s.[4] Just as Norwich was then probably the second most populous city in the kingdom with around ten thousand inhabitants,[5] so it was probably exceeded in the number of its parish churches only by London which had slightly more than twice as many churches[6] for five or six times as many people.[7] The number is particularly striking in comparison with those of

---

[1] Peter Heath, *The English Parish Clergy on the Eve of the Reformation* (London and Toronto 1969), pp. xi and 4-8.

[2] *Corpus Iuris Canonici*, Decretales Gregorii ix, 3.29.2; Christopher R. Cheney, "Rules for the Observance of Feast Days in Medieval England," *Bulletin of the Institute of Historical Research* 34 (1961) 145-146.

[3] Charles J. Hefele and Henri Leclerq, *Histoire des Conciles* (Paris 1907-1952), 5: 1350; *Councils and Synods*, ed. Frederick M. Powicke and Christopher R. Cheney (Oxford 1964), 2: 895; David Knowles, *The Religious Orders in England* (Cambridge 1948-1959), 1: 189.

[4] See columns 1 and 2 of Appendix 1 (pp. 173-178).

[5] See p. xvi.

[6] *The Victoria History of London* (London 1909 –), 1: map facing p. 245.

[7] Hoskins, "Provincial Towns," p. 5.

the two major towns nearest to Norwich – Yarmouth and Lynn. Each of these towns had only one parish church for populations in the 1520s of around four thousand and six thousand respectively.[8] Even by European standards the number was high. Venice, probably the largest city in western Christendom, had about seventy parishes; and Bruges, once the largest city in the Low Countries with about forty thousand inhabitants in the 1340s, had only twelve parishes during the late Middle Ages.[9] Nevertheless, by the standards of English provincial capitals as a whole, the number in Norwich was not exceptional for the population. York, for example, had about forty parish churches in the 1520s for some eight thousand people;[10] Lincoln probably had forty-six for a smaller population than York's.[11] The point is that Norwich – like London, York and Lincoln but unlike Yarmouth and Lynn and various other places – was already a major town when, in the eleventh century, parish churches were being built in great numbers thoughout England.

Indeed, the number of parish churches in Norwich even shrank during the late Middle Ages. The high-water mark had been reached certainly by 1300, probably by 1200. By then, in ways and at times that are obscure, the churches and chapels of the Domesday Survey of 1086 (between forty-nine and fifty-four in all) had given way to some sixty parish churches.[12] Between about 1230 and shortly after the Black Death the parish churches of St John the Baptist of Colegate and St Michael of Conisford were absorbed into the Dominican and Augustinian friaries and lost their parochial status;[13] St Margaret's of Newbridge was reduced to the status of chapel-of-ease within another parish;[14] and St Christopher's, St Olave's of Conisford, St John the Evangelist of Conisford and St Ethelbert's were destroyed (the St Ethelbert's built in place of the last

[8] Ibid., pp. 4-5.
[9] Paolo Prodi, "Structure and Organisation of the Church in Renaissance Venice," in *Renaissance Venice*, ed. John R. Hale (London 1973), p. 419; Toussaert, *Sentiment religieux*, pp. 27 and 46. Some parishes may have had more than one church each.
[10] Hoskins, "Provincial Towns," p. 5; *The Victoria History of the County of York, The City of York* (Oxford 1961), p. 365; David M. Palliser, *The Reformation in York 1534-1553* (York 1971), p. 3; David M. Palliser, *Tudor York* (Oxford 1979), pp. 202 and 211-212.
[11] Hoskins, "Provincial Towns," pp. 4-5; James W. Hill, *Medieval Lincoln* (Cambridge 1948), p. 147.
[12] Campbell, *Norwich*, p. 3.
[13] William Hudson, "The Norwich Taxation of 1254," *Norfolk Archaeology* 17 (1908-1910) 104; *Inventory of Church Goods temp. Edward III*, ed. Aelred Watkin, Norfolk Record Society, 19 (no place, 1947-1948), 1: 24; Blomefield, *Norfolk* (1805-1810), 4: 335-336.
[14] Blomefield, *Norfolk* (1805-1810), 4: 474; *Inventory*, ed. Watkin, 1: xiv.

named was a chapel-of-ease to St Mary in the Marsh parish church).[15] There were also several cases of the parishes of two churches being united but with each church retaining its parochial status: St Edward's with St Julian's,[16] Sts Simon and Jude's with St Swithin's,[17] St Michael's of Berstreet with St Martin in the Bailey,[18] St Cuthbert's with, at different times, St Mary in the Marsh and probably St Mary the Less.[19] These processes continued between 1370 and the eve of the Henrician Reformation: St Matthew's and St Cuthbert's parish churches and St Anne's, a chapel-of-ease to the parish church of St Clement of Conisford, were demolished; St Olave's of Colegate, St Margaret's at Fye Bridge and St Catherine's were probably reduced to the status of chapels-of-ease to other parish churches; and St Clement of Conisford parish was joined to the united parish of St Edward's and St Julian's.[20]

Nevertheless the shrinkage does not necessarily imply a decline in the importance of the parish. For between the fourteenth and the early sixteenth century almost every parish church in the city that was not demolished was extensively rebuilt on a grander scale.[21] Larger buildings meant that fewer were needed. Certainly the new churches, as any visitor to Norwich can still see, must have been sufficiently large to cater for communities averaging between two hundred and two hundred and fifty persons each.[22] They appear, moreover, to have been both well equipped for the liturgy and well staffed. There was at least one priest attached to almost every one of them when they were visited by the bishop of Norwich in 1492[23] and on average there were almost two priests attached

[15] Blomefield, *Norfolk* (1805-1810), 4: 54, 65, 102 and 319; Hudson, "Norwich Taxation," p. 107; *The Charters of Norwich Cathedral Priory, Part One*, ed. Barbara Dodwell, Pipe Roll Society, new ser., 40 (London 1974), p. 132; *Inventory*, ed. Watkin, 1: 23.

[16] REG/1, Book 1, fol. 16r; *Inventory*, ed. Watkin, 1: 24.

[17] REG/1, Book 2, fol. 30v.

[18] *Taxatio ecclesiastica Angliae et Walliae auctoritate P. Nicolai IV circa A.D. 1291*, ed. Thomas Astle, Samuel Ayscough and John Caley (London 1802), p. 78; *Inventory*, ed. Watkin, 1: 22-23.

[19] Ernest A. Kent, "Some Notes on the Desecrated Church of St Cuthbert, Norwich," *Norfolk Archaeology* 27 (1939-1941) 94-95; *Charters*, ed. Dodwell, p. 132; *Inventory*, ed. Watkin, 1: 26; see below, p. 187.

[20] See columns 1 and 2 of Appendix 1 (pp. 173-178).

[21] See "Report of the Summer Meeting of the Institute at Norwich, 1949," *Archaeological Journal* 106 (1949) 95-98.

[22] That is to say, in the 1520s, about ten thousand inhabitants (see p. xvi, n. 4) served by probably forty-six parish churches (see p. 2).

[23] See pp. 179-188. St Saviour's and St Mary Unbrent had only one priest between them (see p. 181), as did the churches of the united parish of St Michael of Berstreet and St Martin in the Bailey (see p. 188) and those of the united parish of St Cuthbert's and

to each.[24] And when the archdeacon of Norwich made his visitation in 1368 he found in almost all of them an impressive amount of liturgical equipment and all, or almost all, the service-books which Archbishops Winchelsey and Reynolds had regarded as obligatory for parish churches to possess.[25]

ii. Tithes

Many Christians, no doubt, felt their parish most concretely in their obligation to pay tithes. Yet it is difficult to estimate to what degree they were paid or caused anti-clerical feeling. Professor Constable, in the best recent survey of the question, concluded that they were probably paid by most Christians most of the time and that resistance to them usually centred around such questions as to whom they were owed or on what things they were to be paid rather than the principle of paying them at all. He thought, however, that resistance to paying them increased in the fourteenth and fifteenth centuries.[26]

Certainly there is no evidence to suggest that in Norwich there was widespread and organised resistance to tithes such as existed in late medieval London.[27] It is true that many people in both cities left bequests in their wills to the high altars of their parish churches "for unpaid tithes." [28] But in Norwich, at least, almost all the bequests were small sums, usually between a shilling and 3s. 4d.; and they begin to appear regularly about 1490, replacing bequests left simply "to the high altar" of a parish church. They probably represent a change of fashion in the way scribes phrased wills, or scruples on the part of people close to death that

---

St Mary the Less (see p. 187). No priest was mentioned at St Helen's (see p. 188), but this was also the church of St Giles's Hospital, to which a number of priests were attached (see p. 19). St Clement of Conisford was also without a priest (see p. 187), but this was probably because its rector had died or vacated the benefice shortly before the visitation (REG/7, Book 12, fols. 97v and 163r), and there were three stipendiary priests and a parish chaplain attached to St Edward's and St Julian's (see p. 187), to which St Clement of Conisford was united at least until the death or departure of its rector (see p. 176; REG/7, Book 12, fol. 163r). For non-resident priests, see p. 46.

[24] That is to say, eighty-nine priests for probably forty-six parish churches (see columns 1, 2 and 4 of Appendix 1 (pp. 173-178).

[25] *Inventory*, ed. Watkin, 1: 1-27; *Councils*, ed. Powicke, 2: 1387-1388.

[26] Giles Constable, "Resistance to Tithes in the Middle Ages," *Journal of Ecclesiastical History* 13 (1962) 172-175 and 184-185.

[27] John A. Thomson, "Tithe Disputes in Later Medieval London," *English Historical Review* 78 (1963) 1-2.

[28] For London, see Sylvia Thrupp, *The Merchant Class of Medieval London* (Ann Arbor 1962), p. 185.

they may have been somewhat negligent in paying their tithes, rather than evidence of outright refusal to pay them.

Besides the evidence of wills, information about a number of tithe disputes concerning the city is to be found among the records of the Benedictine Cathedral Priory and of the Norwich Consistory Court.[29] The number is not great and the records of the Consistory Court survive only from 1499, so it is not possible to know whether there were any general developments in the problem during the late Middle Ages. Several points, however, stand out. There is no direct evidence of resistance to the principle of paying tithes; the point at issue in every case was one of fact: whether the tithes had been paid or, more often, in which parish a particular titheable property lay and therefore to whom the tithes were due.[30] Disputes of the latter kind underline the point that the boundaries of at least some parishes in the city were not clear. They show, too, that the disputes were as much within the clerical body as between the clergy and the laity. The institution appearing most frequently was the Cathedral Priory. Since the priory's surviving records are much fuller than those of any other religious body in the city, it is not surprising that it appears to have been the party most involved in the disputes. But because privileges that were liable to provoke tithe disputes were enjoyed by the priory on a much larger scale than by any other institution, so it almost certainly was in fact the party most involved. For the priory was the patron of far more parish churches in the city than any other individual or body[31] and, in the numerous parishes which had the priory as patron of its church but had only a parish chaplain and no priest as rector or vicar,[32] the parishioners probably owed their greater tithes directly to the priory.[33] There is considerable evidence of other quarrels between the priory and various

---

[29] I.e., D. and C. Mun., Box "Disputes and Agreements, v Carrow, v Carmelites," nos. 1582, 1584, 1590, 2418 and 4081-4083, and Box "Disputes, Ecclesiastical Courts, Norwich," nos. 573, 956, 4089 and 4124; *Norwich Consistory Court Depositions, 1499-1512 and 1518-1530*, ed. Edward Stone and Basil Cozens Hardy, Norfolk Record Society, 10 (no place, 1938), no. 115; Norwich, Norfolk Record Office, Norwich Diocesan Archives, ACT/1, Book 1 (1508-1512), fols. 157r-158r. For a discussion of tithe disputes throughout the diocese of Norwich in the sixteenth century, see Ralph Houlbrooke, "Church Courts and People in the Diocese of Norwich, 1519-70" (Oxford University D.Phil. thesis, 1970), chapter 6, and *Church Courts and the People during the English Reformation 1520-1570* (Oxford 1979), chapter 5.

[30] See, for example, p. 159.

[31] See column 3 of Appendix 1 (pp. 173-178).

[32] See column 4 of Appendix 1 (pp. 173-178).

[33] Herbert W. Saunders, *An Introduction to the Obedientiary and Manor Rolls of Norwich Cathedral Priory* (Norwich 1930), p. 61, thought the lesser tithes and offerings went to the parish chaplains.

groups in the city.[34] It would therefore be interesting to know whether the tithe disputes exacerbated these other quarrels and vice versa, but unfortunately there survives no direct evidence to suggest whether this was the case.

Of some significance, too, is the fact that during visitations of the city only one person[35] is known to have been accused of failing to pay tithes.[36] This is not unusual; accusations in the matter also appear to have been fairly rare in the late medieval visitations of Lincoln and Hereford dioceses.[37] It is possible that the lay people who were the delators at the visitations disliked reporting their fellow men and women about a matter in which they too may have been vulnerable; it is even possible that non-payment, or partial payment, was so prevalent as not to merit comment. But it is probably correct to take the rarity of accusations more at face value and to see it as further evidence that tithes were probably paid by most citizens most of the time and did not provoke very much anti-clerical feeling.

iii. Sacraments and Worship

The Council of Trent in 1547 declared the seven sacraments of the Church to be "necessary for salvation." [38] Much information survives about the sacrament of Orders, and what pertains to Norwich will be discussed later.[39] Regarding most of the other sacraments paucity of

---

[34] See pp. 141-162.

[35] Richard Senior (see p. 181).

[36] For the surviving records, of any completeness, of visitations of parishes in the city between 1300 and 1532 see:

    i. Oxford, Bodleian Library, MS Norfolk, Roll 18 (Visitation of Norwich deanery in 1333).

    ii. *Inventory*, ed. Watkin, 1: 1-27 (Visitations of parishes in Norwich, chiefly by the archdeacon of Norwich in 1368).

    iii. D. and C. Mun., Box "Acta et Comperta," Rolls 1, 1a, 3, 4, 6 and 8-10 (Visitations of parishes in Norwich within the peculiar jurisdiction of the Cathedral Priory of Norwich, 1416-1437).

    iv. Appendix 2 below (Bishop Goldwell's visitation of Norwich in 1492).

    v. Ab.C., Reg. Morton 2 (1485-1500), fol. 78r-v (Visitation of four parishes in Norwich in 1499).

[37] *Visitations in the Diocese of Lincoln, 1517-1531*, ed. Alexander Hamilton Thompson, Lincoln Record Society, 33, 35 and 37 (Lincoln, 1940, 1944 and 1947), 3: 288, under "tithes withheld"; "Visitation Returns of the Diocese of Hereford in 1397," ed. Arthur T. Bannister, *English Historical Review* 44 (1929) 284 and 452, and 45 (1930) 446 and 457.

[38] *Enchiridion symbolorum, definitionum et declarationum de rebus fidei et morum*, ed. Heinrich Denzinger and Adolph Schönmetzer, 35th ed. (Freiburg im Breisgau 1973), DS. 1604.

[39] See pp. 18-55.

quantifiable evidence for Norwich, as for the rest of Christendom, makes it difficult to assess whether they held the important position in the lives of Christians which the ecclesiastical authorities hoped they would. The proximity of parish priests and of a bishop left little excuse for children in Norwich not to be baptised and confirmed, and baptismal fonts and vessels for chrism oil were noted as present in many of the parish churches when they were visited by the archdeacon of Norwich in 1368.[40] But the absence of baptismal registers before the sixteenth century makes it impossible to know for certain whether most children were in fact baptized, and recent historians have doubted whether, in Christendom as a whole, the sacrament of Confirmation was conferred with any regularity.[41] There is no direct evidence about Extreme Unction, but the presence of priests as witnesses to wills, and their being named as executors and supervisors of them, suggest that at least some citizens were in close contact with priests as they approached death.[42] As for Matrimony, there is no evidence about the extent to which men and women lived as married couples without troubling to receive the sacrament of Matrimony in a church. Visitation records suggest, however, that infidelity within marriage, as well as other forms of sexual immorality, were fairly common in the city.[43] (Cases involving the clergy will be discussed later.)[44]

Regarding the Eucharist, the central act of worship in the official liturgy of the Church, there is the general evidence which will be discussed later about the laity's support for their parish churches[45] as well as the evidence about private chapels of individual citizens,[46] Masses for the dead[47] and Masses arranged by craft guilds and pious confraternities.[48] There is also the inventory of church goods largely compiled in 1368. Take for example St Peter Mancroft with its very large collection of liturgical items mostly connected with the celebration of the Eucharist: ten complete sets of vestments for a priest, deacon and subdeacon, usually comprising a cope, chasuble, two tunicles and three albs; fourteen other

---

[40] *Inventory*, ed. Watkin, 1: 1-27.

[41] Jean Delumeau, *Le Catholicisme entre Luther et Voltaire*, Nouvelle Clio, 30 bis (Paris 1971), pp. 281-282.

[42] See pp. 14-15. Most wills were made shortly before the testator's death (see p. 116).

[43] See, for example, pp. 180-187.

[44] See pp. 52-53.

[45] See pp. 126-129.

[46] See p. 91.

[47] See pp. 91-110.

[48] See pp. 68-81.

sets of vestments for single priests, five other copes and four capes for boys; nine frontespieces for altars and large quantities of altar linen as well as carpets and pillows; eight chalices, two cups for hosts and a pyx; dishes, cruets, candlesticks, (hand) bells, crosses, four banners, four thuribles, an aspersorium, a vessel for chrism oil, a mitre and a pastoral staff; and various service-books including seven missals, six breviaries and three psalters.[49] Admittedly St Peter Mancroft was the greatest parish church in the city, but its collection was paralleled on a smaller scale by many of the other churches.[50]

But to what extent was this merely the icing on top of the cake? How far did it reflect the feelings of the majority of citizens? This is hard to say, though some information survives about the extent to which the citizens fulfilled their minimal obligations regarding the Eucharist. As mentioned,[51] Christians were normally obliged to attend Mass in their parish church on Sundays and feast-days. At the late medieval visitations of Lincoln and Hereford dioceses many people were accused of not fulfilling the obligation,[52] though mention is not usually made of whether the accusation was proved. For the city of Norwich, too, the evidence does not for the most part relate whether the accusations were proved and it is not always clear whether the person was accused of missing Mass altogether, or simply of not attending it in his own parish church. The picture here too is, however, one of considerable absenteeism. At the visitation of the city in 1492 as many as nine men and women were accused of not attending their parish churches on Sundays and feast-days or simply of being absent from them "at the time of divine service." [53] Three others were accused of keeping taverns open while services were going on[54] and, in a similar vein, it was alleged against one woman that "she observes an evil custom with various people from neighbouring households, who sit with her and drink during the time of service." [55] Accusations of absenteeism were also fairly common at the early fifteenth-century visitations of parishes in the "peculiars" of the Cathedral Priory.[56] More wilful obstinacy was alleged against two men from Catton

---

[49] *Inventory*, ed. Watkin, 1: 1-3.

[50] Ibid., 1: 3-27.

[51] See p. 2.

[52] *Visitations*, ed. Thompson, 3: 286, under "Service, divine, absence from"; "Visitation Returns," ed. Bannister, 44 (1929) 281, 287-288, 445, 448 and 452, and 45 (1930) 92, 101, 445-447, 450, 452, 455, 458 and 460.

[53] See pp. 180, 183, 185 and 187.

[54] See pp. 180 and 185.

[55] See p. 186.

[56] D. and C. Mun., Box "Acta et Comperta," Rolls 1, 1a, 3, 4, 6 and 8-10.

in the suburbs of the city. It was said that "they deride divine service and are unwilling to hear Mass on feast-days, chattering continuously and obstructing the service." Both men denied the charge; one of them successfully purged himself and was dismissed, the fate of the other is not recorded.[57] Even if some accusations were false, it is interesting that the inquisitors at the visitations, who were lay men and women, were far readier to bring charges against their fellow parishioners in this matter than they were in the matter of tithes[58] or in that of the annual reception of the sacraments of Penance and the Eucharist from a parish priest.

Regarding the latter, charges against only two persons are known to have been brought, both men being charged with failure on both accounts.[59] The only recorded reply is interesting inasmuch as the defendant argued that he had received the Eucharist at parish churches other than his own,[60] implying that he was aware of the rather subtle controversy as to whether the sacrament had to be received from the person's own parish priest.[61] Confessors and "ghostly fathers" of testators were mentioned in a fair number of wills, and this suggests that at least some citizens received the sacrament of Penance more frequently than they were obliged to. Some of them can be identified as the parish priests of the testators concerned, a good example being Richard Skypp, the parish priest of David Blake;[62] and a few members of religious orders were mentioned in the same context.[63]

The sacrament of Penance was not only a means of forgiving sins, it was also a means of instructing the laity in their religion.

iv. Preaching

Another important means of instruction was preaching. Its importance would have been diminished if, as has just been suggested, absenteeism from Mass on Sundays and feast-days, and therefore from the sermons preached on those days, was fairly widespread. Its importance depended, too, upon the education of the preachers. This and more particularly the preaching manuals owned by the secular clergy are discussed elsewhere.[64]

---

[57] Ibid., Roll 8 (1430-1433).

[58] See p. 7.

[59] Ab.C., Reg. Morton 2 (1485-1500), fol. 78r; D. and C. Mun., Box "Acta et Comperta," Roll 9 (1432-1437).

[60] Ab.C., Reg. Morton 2 (1485-1500), fol. 78r.

[61] Hefele, Conciles, 5: 1350.

[62] See pp. 14-15.

[63] E.g., D. and C., Reg. 1500-1530, fol. 10r (Spynke); N.C.C., Reg. Multon, fol. 142r (Brigham).

[64] See pp. 28-42.

The most direct evidence about sermons in the city comes from the records of a quarrel between some friars and the monks of the Cathedral Priory. The prior, writing to the monks of Gloucester College, Oxford, in about 1360, said that friars had preached many sermons to the people in the cathedral but the monks had decided to take over the work themselves because, among other things, certain friars had expressed views "against the norm of sound doctrine and the liberty of the Church." He said that the team of monks who took over the preaching was led by Adam Easton (the future cardinal) and that Easton was able to combat the erroneous opinions of the friars.[65] The prior's letter certainly suggests that the sermons of the monks and friars were lively, up-to-date and popular with the laity. Whether the parish clergy provided equally attractive sermons is not known. It is noticeable, however, that the other men from the city known to have enjoyed reputations as preachers came from the regular, not the secular clergy: Thomas Brinton, who was well known as a preacher when he was bishop of Rochester in the late fourteenth century and who had formerly been a monk at the Cathedral Priory of Norwich;[66] and Friar John Brackley, who belonged to the Franciscan friary and had something of a reputation for preaching in the fifteenth century.[67]

It may, however, be wrong to think that popular demand for sermons was as strong as the prior's letter, or *The Book of Margery Kempe*,[68] suggests. For it is noticeable that though the citizens left many bequests of a religious nature in their wills,[69] so that bequests for the preaching of sermons might seem to have been an obvious choice, only three persons from the city are known to have left bequests for this purpose.[70]

v. Burial[71]

Burial was another matter in which Christians had considerable scope to choose between parishes and religious orders. It was a matter that caused conflict throughout late medieval Christendom. The chief

---

[65] *Documents Illustrating the Activities of the General and Provincial Chapters of the English Black Monks, 1215-1540*, ed. William Pantin, Royal Historical Society, Camden 3rd ser., 45, 47 and 54 (London 1931, 1933 and 1937), 3: 28-29.

[66] Emden, *BRUO*, 1: 268-269 (Thomas de Brinton).

[67] Emden, *BRUC*, p. 87 (John Brakley).

[68] Margery Kempe, *The Book of Margery Kempe*, 1: 61-62 and 67-69, ed. Sanford B. Meech and Hope E. Allen, Early English Text Society, 212 (London 1940), pp. 148-152 and 165-167.

[69] See Chapter 3 (pp. 113-140).

[70] N.C.C., Reg. Brosyard, fol. 185r (Felbrigge), and Reg. Haywarde, fols. 124v-125r (Swayn); see p. 94.

[71] Throughout this sub-section see Appendix 3 (p. 189).

contestants were the friars and the parish clergy, the disputes centring around the friars' right to allow Christians to be buried in their churches and cemeteries rather than in those of the persons' parishes, and to receive the money customarily given on such occasions.[72] In Norwich the friars appear to have counted among their adversaries in this matter the Benedictine Cathedral Priory[73] on account of the latter's position as patron of many parish churches in the city.[74] There may, too, have been some tension among the parish clergy inasmuch as a few people chose to be buried in the cemeteries of parish churches other than their own.[75] But wills suggest that most of the tension probably lay between the friars and the parish clergy since almost one in ten of the laity whose wills survive preferred in this matter the churches or cemeteries of friars to those of their parishes.

The parish clergy refined their complaints against the friars by claiming that they acquired a clientele among the well-to-do.[76] The paucity of wills known to have been made by members of the lower ranks of society in Norwich[77] makes it impossible to draw meaningful comparisons between the rich and the poor regarding their choice of place for burial. But the fact that nearly ten per cent of the lay testators looked to the friars for their burial, and that the testators were drawn disproportionately from the upper ranks of urban society,[78] suggests that the parish clergy's claim found some justification in Norwich. The proportion remained fairly constant at around ten per cent throughout the period 1370 and 1517 but dropped sharply to four per cent between 1518 and 1532. The drop corroborates the evidence of testamentary bequests[79] in suggesting that the laity's support for the friaries was declining on the eve of their dissolution.

Regarding burial in the Cathedral or its cemetery, there is some evidence to suggest that it was restricted, among the laity, to the rich. For few lay persons from the city are known to have asked to be buried in them, and most of those who did were prominent citizens who left substantial bequests to the Cathedral Priory. John de Berney is an example. He was a very wealthy merchant and had been a member of

---

[72] Knowles, *Religious Orders*, 1: 184-187.

[73] D. and C. Mun., Box "Disputes and Agreements, v Carrow, v Carmelites," nos. 939, 1898, 3859 and 3866.

[74] See column 3 of Appendix 1 (pp. 173-178).

[75] E.g., N.C.C., Reg. Doke, fol. 111v (Split).

[76] Knowles, *Religious Orders*, 1: 184.

[77] See pp. 115-116.

[78] See pp. 115-116.

[79] See pp. 119 and 222.

Parliament for the city.[80] He left in his will in 1374 over £10 to the Cathedral and the monks of the priory, but even he feared that his request for burial might be refused. He asked to be buried in the Cathedral, in St Anne's chapel, where one of his wives already lay buried, if the prior and monks would allow it. If not, he was to be buried in the parish church of Burgh.[81] In fact the prior and monks granted his request, and the chapel appears to have become a kind of private chapel for the family; at least one other member of the family was subsequently buried in it.[82] The citizens' attitude towards burial in the Cathedral may be another indication of the alienation of the Cathedral Priory from the mass of citizens.[83]

There is, however, no reason to think that tension between the parish clergy and houses of religious orders over the matter of burial was unusually high in Norwich. Various studies suggest that elsewhere, and among other classes of people, the proportion of Christians choosing to be buried outside their parishes was frequently higher than in Norwich. Thus Mlle de Nucé found that between a third and a quarter of some 450 testators from late medieval Toulouse asked to be buried in one of the city's friaries,[84] and Professor Rosenthal has argued that far more of the nobility of late medieval England chose to be buried in religious houses than in parish churches.[85] In addition, many members of East Anglian county families were buried in the friaries of Norwich and especially in the Cathedral;[86] and the latter ties may help to explain why the Cathedral Priory, in its conflicts with the citizens, counted many East Anglian magnates among its allies.[87]

Most of the clerics from the city whose wills survive were probably attached in some way to parish churches.[88] So it is perhaps surprising that proportionally almost twice as many of them as of the laity decided against being buried in a parish church or its cemetery. To some extent

[80] Walter Rye, *Norfolk Families* (Norwich 1911-1913), 1: 43-44; Blomefield, *Norfolk* (1805-1810), 1: 480, 5: 203, 6: 475, 7: 305-306, 10: 175 and 11: 123-124.

[81] N.C.C., Reg. Heydon, fol. 42r (Berney).

[82] *The Register of Henry Chichele, Archbishop of Canterbury, 1414-43*, ed. Ernest F. Jacob (Oxford 1938-1947), 3: 409; Blomefield, *Norfolk* (1805-1810), 4: 38 and 8: 306.

[83] See pp. 141-154.

[84] Marie-Simone de Nucé, "Piété et charité publique à Toulouse de la fin du 13e au milieu du 15e siècle d'après les testaments" (Toulouse University Diplôme d'Études Supérieures, 1961), p. 63.

[85] Joel T. Rosenthal, *The Purchase of Paradise* (London 1972), pp. 82-83 and 92.

[86] Blomefield, *Norfolk* (1805-1810), 4: 7-40, 88-90, 109-111, 335-339 and 417-418.

[87] See p. 147.

[88] See pp. 114-115.

this is to be expected since they were members of the secular clergy[89] and half of those who decided in this way chose to be buried in colleges of their fellow secular priests. Moreover five of the fourteen clerics who looked to the Cathedral Priory were bishops of Norwich and it is not surprising that they wanted to be buried in their cathedral.[90] Even so the fact that a significant proportion of the secular clergy entrusted their burial to friars or to other religious orders shows that relations between the secular and the regular clergy were not altogether strained.[91]

vi. Witnessing and Executing Wills

In some English dioceses the laity were obliged to include their parish priest among the executors and witnesses of their wills.[92] There is, however, no evidence to suggest that such an obligation was in force in the diocese of Norwich. Witnesses to the wills of people from the city of Norwich were not recorded sufficiently consistently to permit statements of statistical significance beyond saying that members of the secular clergy, some of whom can be identified as the testators' parish priests, do appear among the witnesses but by no means in all the cases in which they were recorded.[93] Executors, however, were mentioned in almost all the wills. From 1370 to 1517 between a third and a quarter of the lay testators chose at least one member of the secular clergy as an executor, and here too some of them can be identified as their parish priests. Between 1518 and 1532 the figure was only a sixth.

A few wills throw fuller light on the close ties that might exist between a layman and his parish priest when he was near death and making his will. That of David Blake, a parishioner of St John and the Holy Sepulchre, of unknown occupation, is the best example. It is of interest, too, because it comes at the end of the period in question, when the clergy's influence over the laity is generally thought to have been waning. Blake was within three months of his death when he made his will in July 1518. He asked to be buried in the cemetery of his parish church

---

[89] See p. 114.

[90] Ab.C., Reg. Arundel 2 (1396-1414), fol. 165r (Totington); Register of Chichele, ed. Jacob, 2: 312 (Wakeryng); Ernest F. Jacob, "Two Documents Relating to Thomas Brouns, Bishop of Norwich, 1436-1445," Norfolk Archaeology 33 (1962-1965) 433; PROB/11/6 (Reg. Wattys, 1471-1480), fol. 7 (Lyhert); PROB/11/11 (Reg. Horne, 1496-1500), fol. 35 (Goldwelle).

[91] For some further remarks about burial, see pp. 98-100.

[92] Councils, ed. Powicke, 1: 512 and 2: 1046.

[93] For the wills in question, see section (A) of Appendix 13 (pp. 224-225).

which was the only church to which he left a bequest, and the only witness mentioned in the will was his parish priest, Richard Skypp. The latter was also described as his "ghostly father" and was the only person whom he wanted to help his wife in her role as sole executor of the will.[94]

The laity's choice of members of religious orders as executors or supervisors of their wills was one minor issue in the disputes between religious orders and the parish clergy.[95] It is unlikely to have been a major issue in Norwich since friars were named in these capacities in only about two per cent of the wills of the laity, and members of other religious orders in only about one per cent. Even fewer religious were mentioned as witnesses. In a few cases, however, there is evidence of strong influence being exercised by them, and such cases may have irritated the parish clergy more than their frequency might seem to justify. There is, for example, the case of Christine Savage, which balances that of David Blake. She appointed a Carmelite friar as one of the two executors of her will, sealed her will in a chapel in the Carmelite friary and asked to be buried in the chapel.[96] Or there is the case of Friar John Brackley, the preacher and close friend of the Pastons, who lived at the Franciscan friary in Norwich.[97] He was frequently mentioned as an executor of wills even though members of his order were forbidden to act in such a capacity.[98] He was with Sir John Fastolf when he was dying,[99] apparently influencing him to favour John Paston,[100] and was named as a subsidiary executor in one of Fastolf's wills.[101] Moreover he was one of the executors or supervisors of the wills of Robert Londesdale of Norwich, esquire, and of Thomas At Yates and John Braklee, dyers of the city, the latter probably being a relative of the friar, possibly his father; all three of them cemented their ties by asking to be buried in the church of Brackley's friary.[102]

---

[94] A.N.C., Reg. Cook (1503-1538), fols. 52v-53r (Blake).

[95] Arnold Williams, "Relations between the Mendicant Friars and the Secular Clergy in England in the Later Fourteenth Century," *Annuale mediaevale* 1 (1960) 73.

[96] N.C.C., Reg. Doke, fol. 167r-v (Savage).

[97] Henry S. Bennett, *The Pastons and their England* (Cambridge 1932), pp. 246-247.

[98] "Ordinationes Capituli Generalis Argentinae anno 1362 Celebrati," ed. Gerold Fussenegger, *Archivum franciscanum historicum* 52 (1959) 10-11.

[99] *Paston Letters and Papers of the Fifteenth Century*, ed. Norman Davis (Oxford 1971 –), 2: 186.

[100] Knowles, *Religious Orders*, 2: 203.

[101] *The Paston Letters A.D. 1422-1509*, ed. James Gairdner (London 1904), 3: 165.

[102] Ab.C., Reg. Stafford and Kempe (1443-1454), fol. 138v (Londesdale); N.C.C., Reg. Doke, fols. 103r (At Yates) and 177v (Braklee).

vii. The Laity's Control over the Parishes

Just how far the laity were in control of some parishes in the late Middle Ages has been illustrated by Dr Prodi's study of Venice where "the core of religious life consisted in about seventy parishes administered by parish priests elected by their own parishioners" [103] though he admitted that Venice was very unusual in this respect.[104] Dr Mason has recently argued that in England as a whole the laity were gaining control over parishes well before the Reformation.[105] The little evidence that survives about Norwich suggests rather the opposite.

Certainly the late Middle Ages was the nadir of the laity's influence over presentations to livings in the city. At one end the period was bounded by the eleventh century when, according to Domesday Book, "the burgesses hold forty-three chapels in the borough," [106] and at the other end by the dissolution of monasteries in the 1530s, when a number of advowsons belonging to religious houses passed to laymen. Between 1370 and 1532 the number of advowsons owned by the laity declined slightly and never exceeded half a dozen.[107]

The citizens sometimes criticised the clergy when invited to do so by the ecclesiastical authorities at visitations of parishes.[108] But they do not appear to have had their own machinery for censuring their parish priests. There is evidence of initiative coming from the laity in the repair and rebuilding of parish churches.[109] There are also a few references to parish clerks[110] and to *economi* of parishes,[111] and such men must have held some responsibility. But no churchwardens' accounts survive, and it seems likely that some records would still be extant if there had been many lay officials of this kind. So the parishes of Norwich may well have been among the more conservative ones in English cities in the matter of lay control.

viii. Conclusion

The parish appears to have remained the primary context within which most citizens of late medieval Norwich practised their religion. This

---

[103] Prodi, "Renaissance Venice," p. 419.

[104] Ibid., p. 419.

[105] Emma Mason, "The Role of the English Parishioner, 1100-1500," *Journal of Ecclesiastical History* 27 (1976) 25-29.

[106] *Domesday Book*, ed. Abraham Farley and Henry Ellis (London 1783-1816), 2: 117.

[107] See column 3 of Appendix 1 (pp. 173-178).

[108] See pp. 53-54.

[109] See pp. 126-129.

[110] See p. 115.

[111] See pp. 103 and 129.

conclusion agrees with what Dr Thomson found for late medieval London.[112] Institutions that were largely products of the late Middle Ages, and which were largely independent of parochial structures, will be discussed in Chapter 2. They seem, to anticipate the conclusions of that chapter, either to have made a relatively shallow impression on many citizens, as in the cases of craft guilds and pious confraternities, or to have made a deep impression on relatively few citizens, as in the cases of hermits, anchorites and communities resembling beguinages. Nothing suggests that they supplanted the parishes as the branch of the Church that touched most citizens most closely.

Regarding the laity's choice between their parishes and houses of religious orders, in most important matters it is, as has been said, impossible to know with any certainty how the majority chose. Thus there is very little evidence about the extent to which they attended the liturgy and sermons in their parish churches rather than in the churches of religious orders, or chose their parish priests rather than monks or friars as their confessors. Place of burial may have been a secondary consideration. But the evidence about it is important because it reveals how a large number of the laity chose in the matter, and so indirectly suggests how they may have chosen in matters of greater consequence. Though a significant minority looked to religious orders for their burial, the large majority preferred their parish churches. This finding is supported, broadly speaking, by what has been said about executors of wills and by the evidence that will be discussed in Chapter 3 concerning testamentary bequests.

To say that parishes were more important than any other religious institutions does not necessarily mean that they were, absolutely speaking, of great importance. Perhaps the most quantifiable evidence about the level of religiosity among the mass of citizens is provided by testamentary bequests, and this will be discussed in Chapter 3. What has been said in this section points to rather ambivalent conclusions. On the positive side there is the evidence of numerous well-staffed and well-equipped parish churches and the much less solid evidence that, on the whole, tithes were paid and minimal obligations regarding the annual reception of the sacraments of Penance and the Eucharist were fulfilled. But this must be balanced by the facts that absenteeism from Mass on Sundays and feast-days may have been fairly widespread, and that the laity do not seem to

---

[112] John A. Thomson, "Clergy and Laity in London, 1376-1531" (Oxford University D.Phil. thesis, 1960), pp. 18-19.

have been much interested in exercising control over the affairs of their parishes.

B. The Secular Clergy and Religious Orders

i. Numbers in 1492

The record of Bishop Goldwell's visitation of Norwich in 1492 provides unusually precise information about the number of secular priests in the city that year. All the parishes within the city were visited, and a list of those cited to appear before the bishop was drawn up.[113] The list included chantry and stipendiary priests attached to parish churches as well as parish chaplains and beneficed clergy. It appears to include all the parochial clergy, exclusive of an unknown number of parish clerks[114] who may or may not have been in minor orders.[115] It mentions fifteen rectors,[116] one vicar, twenty-five parish chaplains,[117] two chantry priests and forty-six stipendiary priests. Probably four of the eighty-nine men belonged to religious orders.[118] The others were members of the secular clergy.

The bishop also visited the three colleges of secular priests in the city: the College of St Mary in the Fields, St Giles's Hospital and the Carnary College (called after the charnel-house, for storing the bones of the dead, which it contained).[119] There were a dean (or master), seven prebendaries and six stipendiary priests at the College of St Mary in the Fields.[120] The

---

[113] The record of the visitation is published as Appendix 2 (see pp. 179-188).

[114] For the existence of parish clerks in Norwich, see p. 115.

[115] Heath, *Parish Clergy*, p. 20.

[116] Including John Styward (see p. 188), who was rector of St Mary in the Marsh (REG/6, Book 11, fol. 179r; REG/7, Book 12, fol. 195v); and counting Walter Goos, who was rector of two churches (see pp. 181 and 184), as one person.

[117] Excluding John Owdolff (see p. 181), who was also a rector (see p. 181).

[118] I.e., Brothers Richard Rene, Thomas Somerton, William Davy and Thomas Balbroke (see pp. 181-182, 186 and 188). William Arnold, "canonicus" (see p. 185), and "Dompnus" John Castelacr' (see p. 187) may also have belonged to religious orders.

[119] The college of chantry priests in the Bishop's Palace was dissolved in 1449 (see p. 22). The only evidence for the existence of a college of twenty-four secular priests, sometimes called Beck College, is the description of it given by Blomefield (*Norfolk* [1805-1810], 4: 96). His description suggests that if it existed, which is I think unlikely, its members would have been mentioned, as chantry or stipendiary priests, in the record of the visitation of the parishes, and therefore would not have been additional to the priests that have already been counted.

[120] *Visitations of the Diocese of Norwich, 1492-1532*, ed. Augustus Jessopp, Royal Historical Society, Camden 2nd ser., 43 (London 1888), pp. 11-12. Robert Calton, one of the seven prebendaries, has already been counted in virtue of his other benefice in Norwich, the vicarage of St Stephen's (see p. 185).

record of the visitation does not mention all the priests at the other two colleges;[121] however, there were a master, five priest-fellows and three stipendiary priests at St Giles' Hospital in 1499,[122] and the Carnary College probably comprised a master and three other priests in the late fifteenth century.[123]

To these might be added the bishop of Norwich, the dean of Norwich, the official principal of the Consistory Court,[124] the master of Hildebrond's Hospital,[125] the master of the Grammar School[126] and perhaps the master of the Song School.[127] It is therefore possible to say with some certainty that the secular clergy of the city numbered a bishop and about one hundred and sixteen priests in 1492.

As for the regular clergy, at that time Norwich contained a Dominican, a Franciscan, a Carmelite and an Augustinian friary as well as the Benedictine Cathedral Priory. The priory was visited by Bishop Goldwell in 1492 and forty-six monks were named.[128] They almost certainly included a few monks living in the priory's cells at St Leonard's in the suburbs of Norwich, Lynn, Yarmouth, Hoxne and Aldeby.[129] Saunders calculated that the number of monks resident at the priory in 1492 lay between thirty-eight and forty.[130] As for the friaries, the exact population of none of them is known for any date after the Black Death,[131] but they were probably among the most populous friaries in the country.[132] They probably contained between forty and fifty-three friars each in 1326,[133]

---

[121] *Visitations*, ed. Jessopp, pp. 9-10 and 13.

[122] Ab.C., Reg. Morton 2 (1486-1500), fol. 83r.

[123] Herbert W. Saunders, *A History of the Norwich Grammar School* (Norwich 1932), p. 41.

[124] *Visitations*, ed. Jessopp, p. 1; Bruce Burnham, "The Episcopal Administration of the Diocese of Norwich in the Later Middle Ages" (Oxford University B.Litt. thesis, 1971), pp. 36 and 200.

[125] REG/7, Book 12, fol. 154r.

[126] REG/7, Book 12, fol. 47r.

[127] REG/5, Book 10, fol. 62r.

[128] *Visitations*, ed. Jessopp, p. 8.

[129] Because it appears that the visitations of the cells were not carried out separately but were included in the visitation of the priory (ibid., pp. 72-73 and 320).

[130] Saunders, *Obedientiary Rolls*, p. 161.

[131] The statement in the *Victoria County History* that all the Dominican friars in Norwich were killed by the Black Death is without foundation (*The Victoria History of the County of Norfolk* [London 1901 –], 2: 241; Thomas Tanner and James Nasmith, *Notitia monastica* [Cambridge 1787], Norfolk, 51, nos. 13 and 16).

[132] David Knowles and Richard Hadcock, *Medieval Religious Houses, England and Wales*, 2nd ed. (London 1971), pp. 218, 227, 236 and 242.

[133] Ibid., pp. 218, 236 and 242; Andrew G. Little, *The Grey Friars in Oxford*, Oxford Historical Society, 20 (Oxford 1891), p. 44, n. 1.

and records of ordinations suggest that they were attracting a considerable number of new members in the early sixteenth century. Thus between March 1532 and February 1534 twenty-seven Franciscan, twenty Dominican, sixteen Carmelite and seven Augustinian friars described as "of Norwich" were ordained to one or more major or minor orders;[134] though since only a handful of ordinands were described as belonging to other friaries in the diocese, the ordinands "of Norwich" almost certainly included friars who came to stay at their houses in Norwich for the duration of the ordinations, which were held in the city, as well as those living in Norwich more permanently.[135] Dispensations to hold benefices and to abandon the religious habit suggest that there were a minimum of ten Dominicans, twenty-one Franciscans, fourteen Carmelites and seventeen Augustinians in the Norwich friaries when they were suppressed.[136] Professor Knowles and Mr Hadcock estimated that the number of friars in England and Wales in 1500 stood at about two-thirds of the maximum number before the Black Death and substantially higher than the number in the 1530s;[137] if Norwich followed this pattern, there were probably about one hundred and twenty friars living in the city in 1492.

Allowing for the uncertainty about the size of the population of Norwich at this time,[138] it can therefore be said with some probability that in 1492 between four and six per cent of the male population of the city, and a correspondingly greater proportion of the adult men, were secular priests or members of religious orders.

The available evidence does not permit precise comparisons between Norwich and other English towns in the late fifteenth century. Oxford, which had some 279 friars in 1377,[139] Cambridge and London, whose clerical population in 1381 included 102 rectors and vicars, 513 chaplains

---

[134] Norwich, Norfolk Record Office, Norwich Diocesan Archives, ORR/1 (1531-1561), fols. 1r-20r.

[135] Some of them were probably students at the friaries in Norwich (see pp. 34-35). The only earlier period for which records of ordinations of friars in the diocese of Norwich survive is 18 September 1406 to 17 September 1407. In these records, too, very few friars were described as belonging to houses outside Norwich, and during this period 23 Dominican, 24 Franciscan, 4 Carmelite and 11 Augustinian friars "of the Norwich convent" were ordained to one or more orders (Ab.C., Reg. Arundel 1 [1396-1414], fols. 544r-549v).

[136] *Faculty Office Registers, 1534-1549*, ed. David S. Chambers (Oxford 1966), pp. 149, 160 and 180.

[137] Knowles, *Religious Houses*, pp. 47 and 494.

[138] See p. xvi.

[139] Andrew G. Little, *Franciscan Papers, Lists and Documents* (Manchester 1943), p. 65.

and 75 clerks,[140] formed a group of their own. Norwich lay somewhere in the next group, consisting of several provincial capitals. Lincoln, for example, had over a hundred members of the secular clergy in 1380.[141] Canterbury almost certainly contained more members of religious orders than Norwich[142] but fewer secular priests since it had far fewer parish churches. York, with a large Benedictine monastery, four friaries, a large clerical staff attached to the Cathedral and about forty parish churches in 1500,[143] may have approximated closely to Norwich, though a bequest in a will suggests that there may have been as many as 260 "capellani" in the city and its suburbs in 1436.[144]

ii. Numbers at Other Times

The year 1492 is unique for information about the number of secular priests in late medieval Norwich; for no other year is the number known nearly as accurately. What evidence does exist suggests there was a considerable increase in the number between 1370 and about 1500, but the increase must be seen in the context of two factors. First, the population of the city increased, perhaps twofold, between 1370 and 1525,[145] so that an increase in the number of priests did not necessarily mean an increase in the ratio of priests to lay people. Second, to start at 1370 is to start at a nadir for Norwich, the population then being perhaps no more than half what it had been at its peak before the Black Death.[146] The episcopal registers suggest the epidemic affected the beneficed parish clergy very seriously. Thus institutions to twenty-two parochial benefices in the city were being regularly recorded in the registers, and as many as eleven benefices had new incumbents, three of them having two new incumbents each, during the year ending 24 March 1350.[147] The unbeneficed clergy of the city were also, no doubt, reduced by the plague as well as by the promotion of their members to benefices in the city and

[140] Thrupp, *Merchant Class*, p. 186.
[141] Alison McHardy, "The Crown and the Diocese of Lincoln during the Episcopate of John Buckingham, 1363-98" (Oxford University D.Phil. thesis, 1972), p. 327.
[142] Knowles, *Religious Houses*, pp. 61, 152, 215, 224, 230-231 and 241.
[143] Ibid., pp. 82, 220, 229, 237, 245 and 445; *VCH City of York*, p. 365.
[144] Richard B. Dobson, "The Foundation of Perpetual Chantries by the Citizens of Medieval York," *Studies in Church History*, 4, ed. Geoffrey J. Cuming (Leiden 1967), pp. 37-38.
[145] Campbell, *Norwich*, pp. 16-18.
[146] Ibid., pp. 10 and 16.
[147] REG/2, Book 4, fols. 77r, 86r, 92v, 95r-v, 100r, 102v, 104r, 111r, 113r-v, 116v and 117v. In only one case was the reason for the need to institute a new incumbent recorded.

elsewhere in the diocese. Thus in October 1349 Bishop Bateman obtained a papal dispensation permitting twenty-one-year-olds to hold rectories in the diocese;[148] and during the year ending 24 March 1350 institutions to parochial benefices in the diocese numbered about nine hundred, which was over eleven times as many as the annual average of the preceding five years.[149] However, two tax assessments from the reign of Richard II show that the city of Norwich contained a substantial number of unbeneficed secular priests by the end of the century. Thus under the deanery of Norwich, whose boundaries coincided almost exactly with those of the city, forty-five unbeneficed chaplains were listed in one assessment and fifty-two or fifty-three in the other.[150] Nevertheless these figures are well below the corresponding figure for 1492, especially since the former presumably included unbeneficed clerics attached to the colleges of secular priests as well as those attached to parish churches. In so far as the number of secular priests who made wills that survive is a guide to their total numbers in the city, it is worth noting that the numbers making wills remained constant from 1370 to about 1420, rose sharply during the next decade, remained at this higher level until about 1510 and then declined somewhat.

Any changes there may have been in the number of secular priests must have been largely confined to the parish clergy. For, though numbers within individual colleges of secular priests fluctuated during the period in question, the total number of priests attached to them appears to have remained fairly constant. The episcopal registers show there had been a dean and seven prebendaries at the College of St Mary in the Fields in the second half of the fourteenth century,[151] as there were in 1492.[152] The number of stipendiary priests attached to the college almost certainly grew since five out of six of them in 1492[153] were serving chantries that had been founded after 1370.[154] But bishops of Norwich reduced the college of chantry priests in their palace in Norwich from three to two priests in 1369 and dissolved the college in 1449, alleging in both cases that the endowments of the college did not suffice to pay the priests their

[148] REG/2, Book 4, fol. 118v; *Cal. Papal L., 1342-1362*, p. 331.

[149] Augustus Jessopp, "The Black Death in East Anglia," *The Nineteenth Century* 16 (1884) 930 and 932.

[150] London, Public Record Office, E.179/45/8 and 11.

[151] REG/2, Book 4, fol. 148r; REG/2, Book 5, fol. 62r; REG/3, Book 6, fols. 6r, 18r, 29v, 52v, 74v, 148v and 201r.

[152] *Visitations*, ed. Jessopp, pp. 11-12.

[153] Ibid., p. 12.

[154] See pp. 213-214 and 216-218.

stipends.[155] And the Carnary College, which had comprised six priests soon after its foundation in the early fourteenth century, was reduced to four priests in the first half of the fifteenth century, and to three sometime before it was dissolved in 1548.[156] The number of priests normally at St Giles's Hospital appears to have remained fairly constant at about nine or ten from the early fourteenth century until at least 1526.[157]

As for the regular clergy, the Cathedral Priory was said to contain at least sixty monks in 1309.[158] How many monks were killed by the Black Death is obscure,[159] but the obedientiary rolls of the priory show that the number of monks remained fairly stable at about fifty from 1389 to about 1460, and then declined gradually to thirty-five in 1531.[160] All the relevant evidence about fluctuations in the number of friars has already been discussed.[161]

iii. Numbers of Nuns

Norwich, like the rest of England,[162] had far fewer nuns than secular priests or members of male religious orders. The Benedictine nunnery of Carrow in the suburbs of Norwich was the only house for them in or near the city. Its strength appears to have remained fairly constant at about a dozen nuns throughout most of the period in question, with a minimum of nine and a maximum of seventeen.[163]

iv. Geographical and Social Origins

It seems certain that Norwich contained more secular priests than any other town in the diocese during the late Middle Ages. It also seems certain that far more came from Norwich than from any other town. Thus the registers of the bishops of Norwich or, during vacancies in the see, those of Archbishop Chichele mention the home towns of the large majority of men ordained as secular priests in the diocese between 1413

---

[155] N.C.R., Case 24b, "Writings relating to St Giles Hospital," no. 52.

[156] *Charters*, ed. Dodwell, pp. 152-153; *Cal. Papal L., 1417-1431*, p. 566; Saunders, *Norwich School*, pp. 41 and 46; London, Public Record Office, E.315/68, fol. 325v.

[157] N.C.R., Case 24a, Great Hospital Account Rolls, 1319/20 and 1396/7; Ab.C., Reg. Morton 2 (1486-1500), fol. 83r; *Visitations*, ed. Jessopp, p. 207.

[158] Edward H. Carter, *Studies in Norwich Cathedral History* (Norwich 1935), p. 20.

[159] Saunders, *Obedientiary Rolls*, pp. 146 and 186-187.

[160] Ibid., p. 161.

[161] See pp. 19-20.

[162] Knowles, *Religious Houses*, p. 494.

[163] Walter Rye, *Carrow Abbey* (Norwich 1889), pp. 37-38; *Visitations*, ed. Jessopp, pp. 17 and 273; Josiah C. Russell, "The Clerical Population of Medieval England," *Traditio* 2 (1944) 182-183.

and 1445, and eighty-seven men "of Norwich" were ordained to one or more major orders during these thirty-three years, in the large majority of cases the priesthood being one of the orders conferred. This was almost three times the number from Lynn which was the next most productive town, more than eight times the number from any other town in the diocese, and five percent of the total.[164] It means that Norwich was producing roughly as many secular priests as it was attracting to live in the city.[165]

Chaucer and Langland described London as a magnet attracting priests from outside the city.[166] How far Norwich acted in the same way cannot be known with any accuracy because neither the late fourteenth-century tax assessments[167] nor the records of the vision of 1492[168] mention the home towns of the priests who were then living in the city. (The suggestion that "outlandish" priests were seeking work in the city will be discussed later.)[169] It is clear, however, that a substantial number of the secular clergy of Norwich were natives of the city. For, of the 117 men from Norwich who were ordained between 1413 and 1486,[170] about 27 can be identified with some degree of certainty as men who spent part of

---

[164] John F. Williams, "Ordination in the Norwich Diocese during the Fifteenth Century," *Norfolk Archaeology* 31 (1955-1957) 347-349 and 358. The figure of five per cent assumes that the average number of ordinations per annum was roughly the same between 1413 and 1445 as between 1446 and 1486 (see ibid., pp. 347-349 and 358).

[165] In other words, for a town to produce as many priests as there are living in it, the number of priests who were natives of the town during a period of time equal to the average life of a priest after his ordination, must equal the number of priests living in the town in a given year; or, to express the matter mathematically in a somewhat over-simplified way, this means for Norwich that **116** (i.e., the 87 men "of Norwich" ordained between 1413 and 1445 plus a certain number to allow for ordinands who were in fact natives of Norwich but whose home towns were not mentioned – as I said not all the home towns of ordinands were mentioned – or who were ordained outside the diocese – for the latter see Williams, "Ordination," p. 358) × **1** (i.e., the average life of a priest after his ordination to the priesthood – which I guess to have been roughly thirty-three years – divided by 33 years, namely the time between 1413 and 1445) = **116** (i.e., the number of secular priests living in Norwich in 1492 – see p. 19).

[166] Geoffrey Chaucer, *The Canterbury Tales*, General Prologue, lines 507-511, The Works of Geoffrey Chaucer, ed. Frederick N. Robinson, 2nd ed. (Oxford 1977), p. 22; William Langland, *Piers Plowman*, B Text, Prologue, lines 83-86, ed. Jack A. Bennett (Oxford 1972), p. 3.

[167] See p. 22.

[168] See pp. 179-188.

[169] See p. 109.

[170] I.e., the 87 ordained between 1413 and 1445 plus 30 ordained between 1446 and 1486, when the home towns of ordinands were recorded much less regularly. There survive almost no records of ordinations of secular priests in the diocese before 1413 or between 1487 and 1530.

their lives as priests in their native city. Wills point to the same conclusion.[171]

As for the regular clergy, second names indicate the possible origins of many monks of the Cathedral Priory. They suggest a situation similar to that at Westminster Abbey, where most monks came from outside London and many appear to have been recruited from the abbey's estates.[172] Thus in 1492 three monks of the Cathedral Priory were called Norwich, and most of the others bore the names of other towns and villages in East Anglia, several of which lay near estates of the priory.[173] The names of the obedientiaries, which are known fairly fully from the late thirteenth to the early sixteenth century, suggest that a similar situation existed at the priory throughout the late Middle Ages.[174] If the monks came predominantly from outside Norwich this may help to explain the hostility of the citizens towards the priory.[175] The home towns of only a few friars are known. Some of them can be identified from their parents' wills as sons of citizens of Norwich;[176] and Friar Brackley, the preacher, may have been the son of a dyer of the city.[177] On the other hand John Bale, the Protestant reformer who wrote *Scriptorum Illustrium Maioris Brytannie Catalogus* and became bishop of Ossory and who had once belonged to the Carmelite Friary in Norwich, came from Cove in Suffolk.[178] No doubt, too, more friars than secular priests or monks of the Cathedral Priory came from outside East Anglia because they belonged to centralised orders and could be moved around the country. Indeed, friars even came from abroad to the Franciscan friary.[179]

The wills of the citizens provide interesting evidence about how many of their children pursued religious vocations. Between ten and eleven per cent of the sons mentioned in the surviving wills[180] were secular priests or members of religious orders and two per cent of the daughters were nuns.[181] The figures understate the true situation since they do not include children who became priests or entered religious orders after their parents

---

[171] See p. 27.

[172] Ernest H. Pearce, *The Monks of Westminster* (Cambridge 1916), pp. 36 and 38.

[173] *Visitations*, ed. Jessopp, p. 8; Saunders, *Obedientiary Rolls*, map facing page 1.

[174] Saunders, *Obedientiary Rolls*, pp. 193-201.

[175] See pp. 141-154.

[176] See p. 27.

[177] See p. 15.

[178] Honor McCusker, *John Bale, Dramatist and Antiquary* (Bryn Mawr 1942), pp. 1-2.

[179] See p. 34.

[180] For the wills in question, see section (A) of Appendix 13 (pp. 224-225).

[181] At least one child was mentioned in about fifty-five per cent of the wills of the laity. The average recorded size of families with at least one child was just under two and a quarter children.

made their wills. The parents came predominantly from the upper ranks of urban society.[182] That such a high proportion of the sons of the upper bourgeoisie chose these ways of life in the late Middle Ages is very significant: it shows that the older and more institutional forms of religious life still had considerable appeal for a class of young men who might be expected to have been more than usually anti-clerical. The proportion of sons so choosing showed no sign of declining on the eve of the Reformation; indeed, it was slightly higher between 1490 and 1532 than between 1370 and 1489.

The figures suggest that the wealthier ranks of urban society were producing, in proportion to their numbers, substantially more secular priests than the poorer ranks.[183] Within the will-making population there appears little to distinguish families that produced priests and members of religious orders from those that did not. Only half a dozen wills mentioned families with more than one child pursuing a religious vocation; Anne Blickling, whose three known children comprised two nuns and a monk, was the only testator to mention more than two such children.[184] Usually nothing indicates where the child came in the family; but John Carter, who was a monk at the Benedictine priory of Horsham St Faith in Norfolk and the eldest of several sons of a shearman and bookbinder of Norwich,[185] along with one or two other cases,[186] shows that religious vocations were not confined to younger sons. Excluding from consideration all wills that mention no children, the average size of families with at least one child pursuing a religious vocation was only fractionally larger than that of families without such a child.[187] The occupations of between a third and two-fifths of the fathers in question are known, and they represent a broad spectrum of crafts and trades: there were five weavers, three barkers and one or two men engaged in each of twenty-five other occupations; and they included probably five or six of the forty-five mayors of Norwich who died before 1533 and whose wills survive.[188]

[182] See pp. 115-116.

[183] Compare the minimum of ten to eleven per cent mentioned above, of whom half were secular priests (see p. 27), with the fact that probably a maximum of two and a half per cent of the sons (who survived infancy) of all the citizens were secular priests in the fifteenth century (see pp. 19-20 and 24).

[184] N.C.C., Reg. Hyrnyng, fol. 95v (Blickling).

[185] N.C.C., Reg. Ryxe, fol. 195v (Carter).

[186] N.C.C., Reg. Ryxe, fol. 94v (Kempe); see p. 28.

[187] See p. 25, n. 181.

[188] N.C.C., Reg. Popy, fol. 492r-v (Bewfeld), Reg. Ryxe, fol. 88r (Bowfeld), Reg. Gylys, fol. 2r (Burgh), and Reg. Wylbey, fol. 31v (Wetherby); PROB/11/10 (Reg. Vox,

The sons in question were almost exactly divided between secular priests and members of religious orders. The available evidence suggests that most of them left Norwich but a substantial minority stayed in the city or returned to it. Thus about a third of those who were secular priests are known to have spent a considerable period of their lives as priests in Norwich; and of the sixteen members of religious orders whose houses can be identified, one belonged to the Cathedral Priory,[189] three to friaries in Norwich,[190] eleven to other houses in the diocese[191] and one to Walden Abbey in Essex.[192] Almost half the daughters were nuns at Carrow Priory[193] and the priory's close links with the city no doubt help to explain their choice. For besides being the only nunnery in or near Norwich, it housed a number of lay people including, no doubt, some from Norwich; and girls from the city may have been sent to it to board and to be educated.[194] The other daughters were nuns at other houses within East Anglia.[195]

Wills also provide evidence about men who became priests later in life. Eight secular priests of the city mentioned their wives or children in their wills,[196] though none of the wives is known to have been alive when her husband was ordained. None of them was as eminent as William Canynges, the wealthy merchant and five times mayor of Bristol who became a priest and dean of Westbury College in Gloucestershire after his wife's death.[197] But Thomas Oudolff, the only one of them from Norwich

---

1493-1496), fol. 5 (London), /8 (Reg. Milles, 1487-1490), fol. 4 (Cooke), and /9 (Reg. Dogett, 1491-1493), fol. 17 (Bokenham).

[189] PROB/11/10 (Reg. Vox, 1493-1496), fol. 5 (London); *Visitations*, ed. Jessopp, p. 8.

[190] N.C.C., Reg. Aleyn, fol. 51r (Rash), Reg. Ryxe, fol. 400v (Glanville), and Reg. Spyltymber, fol. 90r (Gedney).

[191] N.C.C., Reg. Brosyard, fols. 85r (Harrowe *alias* Wyghton) and 173v-174r (Farewell), Reg. Ryxe, fols. 195v (Carter) and 202v (Wallis), Reg. Aubry, fols. 26v (Shelton) and 63r (Buckingham), Reg. Hyrnyng, fol. 95v (Blickling), Reg. Doke, fol. 220r (Fader), Reg. Gelour, fol. 230v (Blackdam), Reg. Harsyk, fol. 146r (Renter), and Reg. Betyns, fol. 164v (Derby).

[192] N.C.C., Reg. Harsyk, fols. 294r-295r (Shouldham).

[193] N.C.C., Reg. Brosyard, fols. 159v (Welan), and 350r (Folkard), Reg. Aleyn, fol. 188r (King) and Reg. Wylbey, fol. 31v (Wetherby); PROB/11/9 (Reg. Dogett, 1491-1493), fol. 17 (Bokenham).

[194] Rye, *Carrow Abbey*, pp. 48-52; see p. 67.

[195] N.C.C., Reg. Popy, fol. 492r-v (Bewfeld), Reg. Wight, fol. 2r (Smyth), Reg. Harsyk, fol. 294v (Shouldham), and Reg. Hyrnyng, fol. 95v (Blickling); PROB/11/8 (Reg. Milles, 1487-1490), fol. 9 (Cooke).

[196] N.C.C., Reg. Harsyk, fol. 321r (Clement), Reg. Hyrnyng, fol. 103r (Lomynor), Reg. Surflete, fol. 37v (Hamonde), Reg. Aleyn, fol. 92r (Sampson), Reg. Cobald, fol. 11r (Stalon), Reg. Gelour, fol. 97v (Oudolff), Reg. Multon, fol. 86r (Gilbert), and Reg. Platfoote, fol. 100r (Peket).

[197] *D.N.B.*, 11: 8-10 (William Canynges); Derek Whitfield, "Two Unknown Seals of

about whose background much is known, came from a fairly prominent family. He was one of the five or more children of a wealthy citizen of Norwich[198] and his brother was rector or parish priest of several churches in the city.[199] He mentioned in his will his deceased wife and a daughter.[200] He probably died fairly soon after his ordination[201] and this may explain why he never obtained a benefice. He appears to have died quite a wealthy man since he left in his will bequests worth £20 as well as a tenement and a farm.[202] The other seven men appear to have remained unbeneficed priests, and none of them is known to have studied at a university. The widower who became a priest represents an interesting aspect of lay piety and shows how the latter could become clericalised. Inasmuch as he probably said Masses and prayers for his family, he was also a kind of do-it-yourself chantry. No widow or widower from the city is known to have joined a religious order.

v. Education at the Universities

The level of education achieved by the clergy of late medieval Christendom has been the subject of much debate. Recent writers have argued that the mass of the secular clergy were not grossly ignorant – on the eve of the Reformation as many as a third or a half of them in some dioceses had studied at a university – but their education left them inadequate as priests and for their work as pastors of souls. They studied the wrong things – leading to a preoccupation with the externals of the Church and their own advancement in it rather than to a profound knowledge of theology and its relevance to the human condition – and so were incapable of meeting the spiritual needs of the laity.[203]

Attempts to answer the question of how far the clergy of late medieval Norwich were meeting the spiritual needs of the laity are scattered throughout this book. In general the conclusion is more optimistic than that reached by most writers about the clergy elsewhere. As for their university attainments, the most striking point is the increase of graduates

---

the Bristol Franciscans and a Canynges Deed, dated 1465," *Transactions of the Bristol and Gloucestershire Archaeological Society* 72 (1953) 71, n. 2, and 74.

[198] N.C.C., Reg. Gelour, fols. 92v-93v (Oudolff).

[199] See p. 181; REG/7, Book 12, fol. 137v; *Norwich Depositions*, ed. Stone, no. 115.

[200] N.C.C., Reg. Gelour, fol. 97v (Oudolff).

[201] See the dates mentioned in N.C.C., Reg. Gelour, fols. 92v-93r (Oudolff) and 97v-98v (Oudolff), and *Norwich Depositions*, ed. Stone, no. 115.

[202] N.C.C., Reg. Gelour, fols. 97v-98r (Oudolff).

[203] Rapp, *L'Église*, pp. 125-126; Moeller, "Frömmigkeit," pp. 26-29 ("Religious Life," pp. 28-30); Heath, *Parish Clergy*, pp. 81-82 and 91-92.

among the beneficed clergy after about 1450. Thus, the number of rectors and vicars in Norwich known to have been university graduates rose from 12 out of 158 between 1370 and 1449, to 23 out of 71 between 1450 and 1499, and to 25 out of 60 between 1500 and 1532.[204] The numbers support the claim which Mr Heath has made for England as a whole that between 1450 and 1530 a substantial proportion of the beneficied parish clergy were graduates, and his guess that the figure grew gradually during the eighty years.[205] He found that in the diocese of Norwich the proportion was just over a sixth in the early sixteenth century[206] which means that it was then over twice as high in the city as in the rest of the diocese. Nevertheless, it was much lower in Norwich than in London where 39 out of 52 priests with benefices in 1522 were graduates.[207] The graduates were not evenly spread among the parishes. There were very few of them in the seven livings whose advowsons were in lay hands,[208] and in this respect Norwich followed the national pattern.[209] On the other hand there were unusually sharp increases in their number at St John's Maddermarket and St Michael of Coslany which coincided with the acquisition of their advowsons by New College, Oxford, and Gonville Hall, Cambridge.[210]

As for the unbeneficed parish clergy, the only useful information about the number of graduates among them comes from the record of Bishop

[204] There were rectors or vicars in charge, for all or part of the period 1370 to 1532, of 22 parishes in the city. Unbeneficed parish chaplains were in charge of the other parishes. The rectors and vicars are known chiefly from the records of their appointments in the registers of the bishops of Norwich and, during vacancies in the see, in those of the archbishops of Canterbury. The accuracy of the figures concerning the number of university graduates depends, to a considerable extent, on whether those, and only those, men who were styled "magistri" in the registers were "magistri" in the academic sense. References to university degrees in the registers themselves, as well as other evidence, suggests that the title was in general used consistently in this way. It should be remembered, however, that the "magistri" do not include a probably considerable number of men who only received the degree of B.A. or who spent some time at a university without ever taking a degree (see Emden, *BRUO*, 1: xviii). An incumbent has been considered as belonging to the period within which he was instituted to his benefice when his tenure of office spanned two periods.

[205] Heath, *Parish Clergy*, p. 81.

[206] Ibid., p. 81.

[207] *VCH London*, 1: 245.

[208] I.e., St Botulph's (before about 1450), St Clement of Conisford, St Edmund's, St Margaret of Westwick, St Michael of Coslany (before about 1464), St Michael at Plea and St Peter Hungate (after about 1458) – see columns 1 and 3 of Appendix 1 (pp. 173-176).

[209] Ernest F. Jacob, "On the Promotion of English University Clerks during the Later Middle Ages," *Journal of Ecclesiastical History* 1 (1950) 183.

[210] See pp. 174-175.

Goldwell's visitation of the city in 1492. The record styles as "magister" 1 of the 25 parish chaplains and 4 of the 48 stipendiary and chantry priests attached to the parish churches.[211] It suggests that Mr. Heath's claim, that on the eve of the Reformation graduates among the unbeneficed parish clergy were almost unknown in England outside London,[212] is too pessimistic for Norwich. Nevertheless, the figures are proportionally well below those for the beneficed parish clergy of the city, and there is evidence to suggest that in London a sixth of the unbeneficed clergy in 1522 were graduates.[213]

As for the colleges of secular priests, very few members of the Carnary College, of St Giles's Hospital (apart from the masters of the hospital after about 1430), or of the college of chantry priests in the Bishop's Palace, are known to have been graduates. At the College of St Mary in the Fields the differences mostly paralleled those among the parish clergy. Thus the number of graduates known to have been instituted to benefices (i.e., the deanery and seven prebends) rose from 17 out of 42 between 1370 and 1449 to 38 out of 47 between 1450 and 1532,[214] but none of the unbeneficed stipendiary priests attached to the college is known to have been a graduate.[215]

Professor Jacob argued that the constitution issued in 1421 by the Convocation of Canterbury Province, which urged the promotion of more university clerks to benefices, and its re-issue in 1438 achieved a measure of success.[216] The rise, beginning around 1450, in the number of graduates among the beneficed clergy of Norwich is local support for his argument, though the increase appears to have been longer delayed in Norwich than in some other places.[217] It was about this time, too, that Thomas Gascoigne was urging the need to provide scholarships for young

[211] See pp. 180, 183, 184 and 187.

[212] Heath, *Parish Clergy*, p. 81.

[213] *VCH London*, 1: 245.

[214] Information about the institutions comes chiefly from the episcopal registers.

[215] See *Visitations*, ed. Jessopp, pp. 12, 208 and 270.

[216] Jacob, "Promotion of Clerks," pp. 181-182, despite his apparent endorsement of the view that the constitution was a failure.

[217] Ibid., pp. 181-182. Whether the increase was in any way the direct result of *Cum ex eo* licences for the parochial clergy to go to a university to study, and the support for them given by the Council of Constance in 1418, is impossible to say since during the period in question licences of this kind were not being recorded in the registers of the bishops of Norwich (Emden, *BRUC*, p. xxiv); but it seems unlikely since such licences appear to have been rare throughout the country in the fifteenth century (Roy M. Haines, "The Education of the English Clergy during the Later Middle Ages: Some Observations on the Operation of Pope Boniface VIII's Constitution *Cum ex Eo*," *Canadian Journal of History* 4 [1969] 11-15).

men to go to a university.[218] So it is interesting that the second half of the fifteenth century saw the growth in Norwich of testamentary bequests for priests, or candidates for the priesthood, to study.[219] Most of them were left to present or future members of the secular clergy, rather than to members of religious orders, and usually a university was to be the place of study. An alderman called Philip Curson, for example, said in his will of 1502 that he would pay for his son, if he "will be a priest," to "be found to Cambridge schools to learn that faculty that his mind is most disposed on, till he is bachelor in the law or of art." [220] The bequests are interesting examples of lay people encouraging young men, including their own sons, to become priests and making financial sacrifices to secure a better educated clergy. They must, too, have helped to solve the problem, possibly acute in the fourteenth and early fifteenth centuries,[221] of maintaining students at Oxford and Cambridge. The decline in these bequests after 1517[222] has no apparent explanation.

As for the religious orders the fullest picture once again comes from the Cathedral Priory. In about 1360 the priory had two monks studying at Gloucester College, the Benedictine house at Oxford.[223] However, one of the complaints made at Bishop Goldwell's visitation of the priory in 1492 was that "our monks are not going to the university of Oxford to study, and this is to the great scandal and injury of the monastery." [224] The bishop enjoined that the priory should always have two monks at Gloucester College[225] but complaints of monks not being sent to Oxford were again being made in 1532.[226] The charges give, however, an unbalanced view of the whole: according to Saunders, between one and four monks from the priory were at Oxford or Cambridge every year (except 1492) for which the relevant obedientiary rolls survive between the early fifteenth century, when the names of monks studying at a university began to be recorded, and the dissolution of the priory in 1538.[227]

---

[218] Thomas Gascoigne, *Loci e Libro veritatum*, "Furtum" and "Religio," Passages Selected from Gascoigne's Theological Dictionary, ed. James E. Rogers (Oxford 1881), pp. 112 and 222.

[219] See Appendix 4 (p. 190).

[220] N.C.C., Reg. Ryxe, fol. 386r (Curson).

[221] Ernest F. Jacob, "English University Clerks in the Later Middle Ages: the Problem of Maintenance," *Bulletin of the John Rylands Library* 29 (1945-1946) 313-314.

[222] See Appendix 4 (p. 190).

[223] *Documents*, ed. Pantin, 3: 28-29.

[224] *Visitations*, ed. Jessopp, p. 4.

[225] Ibid., p. 7.

[226] Ibid., pp. 266-267.

[227] Saunders, *Obedientiary Rolls*, p. 185.

The two monks studying at Oxford in about 1360 were the priory's most illustrious products in the late Middle Ages: Adam Easton,[228] later a cardinal and author of *Defensorium ecclesiastice potestatis*, and Thomas Brinton,[229] later bishop of Rochester and a well-known preacher. John Bale, who as a former member of the Carmelite friary in Norwich[230] should have known the local scene, included in his *Catalogus* of writers a remarkable number of other lesser known men who belonged to the priory or to the city's friaries: four monks of the priory besides Easton and Brinton, one Dominican, four Augustinian, five Franciscan and twelve Carmelite friars were included among the writers who flourished between the late fourteenth and early sixteenth centuries.[231] According to Bale and Dr Emden's researches, most of them studied at Oxford or Cambridge. They are powerful proof of the effect of the universities upon the standard of education in a provincial capital. Compared with the twenty-eight members of religious orders, Bale included in his *Catalogus* only one secular priest from the city.[232] It would be interesting to know how far the apparent disparity in intellectual standards influenced the laity in their choice between the secular and the regular clergy in such matters as the confessors they went to and the semons they attended.

As for the choice between Oxford and Cambridge, Dr Emden's researches indicate that the Cathedral Priory sent its monks to both universities,[233] that most of the graduate friars in the city were alumni of Cambridge but a sizeable minority, particularly among the Carmelites, were from Oxford, and that the ratio of Cambridge to Oxford graduates among the secular clergy of the city was about three to one.[234]

vi. *Education outside the Universities*

For Norwich, as for the rest of Christendom, our knowledge of the training of the large majority of secular priests – those who did not study at a university – is very vague. Three schools in Norwich at which prospective priests could get a rudimentary education were the Song School and the Almery School, both of which were attached to the

---

[228] *Documents*, ed. Pantin, 3: 28.

[229] Ibid., 3: 29.

[230] See p. 25.

[231] See Appendix 5 (pp. 191-192).

[232] See p. 192.

[233] Saunders, *Obedientiary Rolls*, p. 184, incorrectly claimed that the priory sent its monks exclusively to Oxford until towards the end of the fifteenth century.

[234] Emden *BRUO* and *BRUC*, passim.

Cathedral Priory, and the Grammar School.[235] In addition boys and clerics who were not priests were attached to St Giles's Hospital and to the College of St Mary in the Fields: they sang in choir and may have been receiving some form of training for the priesthood.[236] Moreover, a few of the testamentary bequests for people to study to become priests[237] seem to have envisaged education at a school rather than at a university. Robert Elys, for example, wanted his wife to "keep little Reynold to the school, if he will abide with her, to the time she knows whether he will be a man of the Church or not." [238] Walter Shane, too, was to be educated outside the universities: in 1496 his master "gladly" (*gratulenter*) dispensed him from his apprenticeship as a grocer so that he could study to become a priest with a cleric called John Russell.[239] Perhaps the most revealing evidence comes from the will of Thomas Bower, who was vicar of St Stephen's from 1501 until his death in 1530.[240] It points to the kind of personal supervision that was probably very common but about which so little is known: he asked to be buried "by the grave of my special master, Doctor Chaumpnes [one of his predecessors as vicar],[241] who brought me up of a child and made me a priest." [242]

Extra-university education was generally more systematic for members of religious orders than for prospective secular priests.[243] The Cathedral Priory of Norwich had a school for its junior monks, though it was said that they were remiss in attending it and that the teaching was in-

[235] Saunders, *Norwich School*, p. 85; Arthur F. Leach, *The Schools of Medieval England* (London 1915), pp. 224-225.

[236] N.C.C., Reg. Doke, fol. 89v (Hunt), Reg. Sayve, fol. 23r (Billern), and Reg. Typpes, fols. 17v and 18v-19r (Smyth); D. and C., Reg. 1461-1559, fol. 74r (Peerse); see p. 122.

[237] See Appendix 4 (p. 190).

[238] Ab.C., Reg. Morton 2 (1486-1500), fol. 23v (Elys).

[239] N.C.R., Case 17d, First Book of Worsted Weavers (1492-1504), fol. 30v; *The Records of the City of Norwich*, ed. William Hudson and John Tingey (Norwich 1906-1910), 2: 154-155.

[240] REG/8, Book 13, second series of folios, fols. 2v-3r; REG/9, Book 14, second series of folios, fol. 9r; N.C.C., Reg. Palgrave, fols. 81v and 82v (Bower).

[241] See p. 234.

[242] N.C.C., Reg. Palgrave, fol. 81v (Bower). Bower appears to have been a university graduate (REG/8, Book 13, second series of folios, fols. 2v and 93r; REG/9, Book 15, fols. 8v and 25v), even though he has not been identified as one by Dr Emden. The passage cannot, however, be referring to an education he received at Gonville Hall, Cambridge, when Chaumpneis was a fellow there since Chaumpneis vacated his fellowship shortly after Bower was born (Emden, *BRUC*, p. 130 [Geoffrey Champeneys]; *Norwich Depositions*, ed. Stone, no. 409).

[243] See: Andrew G. Little, "Educational Organisation of the Mendicant Friars in England," *Transactions of the Royal Historical Society*, new ser., 8 (1894) 49-70; Nicholas Orme, *English Schools in the Middle Ages* (London 1973), pp. 12-21 and 224-243.

adequate![244] The Carmelites of Norwich appear to have trained some candidates from an early age: John Bale entered the friary at the age of twelve[245] and Edmund Ouldhall, bishop of Meath, complained in 1452 that he had been persuaded to take his vows as a friar there at the age of twelve.[246] Indeed, all four friaries in the city appear to have contained schools at which friars could receive at least part of their education for the priesthood.[247]

It is the Franciscan friary, however, about which most is known. An intimate picture of a friar's training there is provided in a letter written by Friar Brackley to John Paston in 1460, a training which combined studies in the house with service of, and supervision by, an older friar – a relationship similar, perhaps, to the one between Bower and Chaumpneis. He recommended the friar delivering the letter as: "my spiritual son – inasmuch as he was brought into the order through me and professed and promoted to the priesthood – who for two whole years now has been my companion and a consoling servant to me during my serious illness, staying up and working day and night, by reason of which he has been much distracted from his studies." [248] In the mid fourteenth century studies at the friary had been well organised. It was one of the order's seven friaries in England established by Pope Benedict xii's ordinance of 1336 as *studia* where theology was to be taught to friars at a pre-university level.[249] The notebook of an Italian Franciscan, Nicholas of Assisi, which contains notes on lectures and disputations which he attended at the friary between 1337 and 1339, shows that it was fulfilling this function shortly afterwards and offering courses of a sufficiently high standard to attract a friar from Italy.[250] Some twenty years later Peter de Candia, the Franciscan friar who later became Pope Alexander v, came from Italy to study at the friary before going on to Oxford University.[251] It appears to have still been attracting friars from abroad in the early fifteenth century since John "of Westphalia," John "of Austria" and Theodoric "of Saxony" were among the Franciscans "of the Norwich convent" ordained in 1406 and 1407;[252] and the large number of

[244] *Visitations*, ed. Jessopp, pp. 77 and 269.
[245] McCusker, *John Bale*, p. 2.
[246] *Cal. Papal L., 1447-1455*, p. 229.
[247] Orme, *English Schools*, pp. 230-232.
[248] *Paston Letters*, ed. Davis, 2: 209.
[249] Victorin Doucet, "Le Studium franciscain de Norwich en 1337," *Archivum franciscanum historicum* 46 (1953) 87.
[250] Ibid., pp. 88 and 95.
[251] Emden, *BRUO*, 1: 346 (Peter de Candia).
[252] See p. 20, n. 135.

Franciscans "of Norwich" ordained in the 1530s[253] suggests it remained a *studium* until its dissolution in 1538.

vii. Education: Books[254]

Some further indications of the education of the clergy are provided by the books they read. The Cathedral Priory possessed one of the finest libraries in England, considerably augmented by some 228 books bequeathed by Cardinal Adam Easton,[255] the former monk of the priory, which were transported from Rome to Norwich in six barrels in 1407.[256] At the dissolution of the priory the library probably contained at least 1,350 volumes.[257] Bale and Leland listed a number of books belonging to the friaries,[258] and the abundance of writers at them[259] suggests they possessed good libraries.

As for the secular clergy, their needs may have been in mind in the will made in 1462 by John Leystofte, vicar of St. Stephen's. He asked that if a library was begun in the city within two years of his death, a book of his called "Repyngton" – probably Bishop Repingdon's *Sermons* – should be given to it.[260] But the library never materialised. It appears, moreover, that the parish churches possessed few books other than service-books and a few standard works of Canon Law.[261] So, except in so far as the libraries of the friaries and the Cathedral Priory were open to them, the secular clergy must have depended upon private collections of books, either their own or those of others willing to lend.

Almost all our information about such collections comes from wills and from the sole surviving inventory of the goods of a priest. The inventory, of the goods of John Baker, provides a very interesting picture of the library of a rector,[262] probably in middle age,[263] who was probably

---

[253] See p. 20.

[254] Throughout this sub-section see Appendix 6 (pp. 193-197).

[255] Henry C. Beeching and Montague R. James, "The Library of the Cathedral Church of Norwich," *Norfolk Archaeology* 19 (1915-1917) 71 and 79.

[256] *Cal. Close R., 1405-1409*, p. 299.

[257] Beeching, "Library," p. 79.

[258] Ibid., pp. 106-116; *Medieval Libraries of Great Britain*, ed. Neil Ker, 2nd ed. (London 1964), pp. 139-140.

[259] See p. 32.

[260] N.C.C., Reg. Brosyard, fol. 272v (Leystofte).

[261] *Inventory*, ed. Watkin, 1: 1-27. See above, p. 5.

[262] He was described simply as a priest in the inventory of his goods (see p. 237). He made his will in August 1518 and had died by 8 September 1518 (see pp. 237-238). He indicated in his will that Richard Baxter and Geoffrey Carter had appointed him to be an executor of their wills (see p. 237), and in each of their wills a John Baker, rector of St John's Maddermarket in Norwich, was named an executor (N.C.C., Reg. Ryxe, fols. 457v

not a university graduate[264] and who lived at a time when printed books were becoming widely available. It mentions 26 books by name and "twenty other small books." [265] About half of those named were legal works, mostly of Canon Law: the *Decrees*, the *Decretals* and *Sext*; "a book, Lynwod" which was presumably *Provinciale*, the work on English ecclesiastical law by William Lyndwood (ca. 1375-1446); the *Institutes*, presumably of Justinian (483-565); "four books of Abbott," probably the commentaries on Canon Law by Panormitanus (1386-1445), the Italian canonist who was often called "Abbas Modernus"; "Casus longi Bernardi," presumably the commentaries on the *Decretals*, called *Casus seu notabilia*, by Bernard of Compostella (?-1267); "W. de Speculat'," probably the *Speculum iudiciale* of William Durandus (ca. 1237-1296), the canonist who was sometimes called "Speculator"; "the third part of *Speculum*," which was probably the third part of the *Speculum iudiciale*, bound separately, since it followed immediately after "W. de Speculat'" in the inventory; and two anonymous works, *Vocabularius iuris utriusque* and *Modus legendi adbrevituras in utroque iure*. There were five collections of sermons: *Sermones Dominicales ... qui ... "Dormi Securæ"... sunt Nuncupati*, usually ascribed to the English Carmelite, Richard Maidstone (?-1396); the anonymous *Sermones parati de tempore et de sanctis*; *Sermones discipuli* by the German Dominican, John Herolt (ca. 1380-1468); *Sermones Vincentii*, probably St. Vincent Ferrer (ca. 1350-1419); and *Sermones magistri Fysher*, presumably John Fisher (1469-1535), bishop of Rochester. The remaining works were *Legenda aurea*, a collection of saints' lives by the archbishop of Genoa, James de Voragine (ca. 1230-1298); "liber Preceptor'," probably the *Expositio decalogi sive preceptorium divine legis* by the German Dominican, John Nider (ca. 1380-1438); an unnamed work of St. Albert the Great

---

[Baxter] and 195v [Carter]). He must therefore have been this John Baker, who was instituted to the rectory of St John's Maddermarket in 1503 and died, still rector, sometime before 27 November 1518 (REG/8, Book 13, second series of folios, fol. 23v; REG/10, Book 16, fols. 48v-49r). The date of his death, and his bequest to the parish church of All Saints (Allhallows) of Berstreet in Norwich (see p. 237), make it almost certain that he was also the John Baker who was instituted as rector of this church in July 1510 and died, still rector, sometime before 22 December 1518 (REG/9, Book 15, fol. 10r; REG/9, Book 14, fol. 150v).

[263] Both his parents were alive when he made his will (see p. 237), and he was a rector for fifteen years (see previous footnote).

[264] He was styled "magister" when his death as rector of All Saints of Berstreet was noted in Bishop Nykke's register (REG/9, Book 14, fol. 150v), but no other known references to him suggest that he was a university graduate, and Dr Emden did not identify him as a student of Oxford or Cambridge.

[265] See p. 239.

(ca. 1200-1280); the Latin-English dictionary called *Ortus* (or *Hortus*) *vocabulorum*, attributed to Geoffrey the Grammarian, the fifteenth-century English Dominican; what was presumably a breviary in two volumes;[266] and a "Bybill," though it cannot be assumed that it was a vernacular Bible since the inventory also recorded the *Decrees*, of which no translation into English is known to have existed, by its vernacular title. Apart from *Casus seu notabilia* by Bernard of Compostella, all the works were in print when the inventory was drawn up, though there are no direct indications as to whether or not Baker's copies were printed books. *Casus seu notabilia* was the only work likely to have been rare at that date: only it, *Speculum iudiciale* and *Legenda aurea* were missing from the day-book of John Dorne, the Oxford bookseller, in 1520.[267] The books indicate conservative tastes and a keen interest in the law of the Church. At the same time the collections of sermons, in particular, suggest a pastorally minded priest and the number of works by foreigners indicate an outlook that was far from insular.

None of the books listed in the inventory of John Baker's goods was mentioned in his will. No doubt, therefore, the books mentioned in other wills of the secular clergy represent only a fraction of the books that they owned. Nevertheless they provide some kind of a general picture of the reading of the secular clergy, at least inasmuch as many of the books not mentioned in the wills may have been similar to the ones mentioned.[268]

Most frequently mentioned were liturgical works, though in some cases it is impossible to know whether the testator was leaving his own book or wanted the book to be bought by his executors and given to the beneficiary. Specially common were missals, processionals, breviaries and psalters. *Rationale divinorum officiorum*, the guide to the liturgy by William Durandus (ca. 1230-1296), appeared in two wills.[269] Of interest too are the "quires with the new service of the Visitation of Our Lady and of the Transfiguration of our Lord God and of the Blessed Name of Jesus" owned by John Barker, rector of St. Margaret of Westwick, who made his

---

[266] MS reads "ij di' (= dimidias?) portuas."

[267] "Day-Book of John Dorne," ed. Falconer Madan, Oxford Historical Society, *Collectanea*, 1 (Oxford 1885), pp. 79-135.

[268] Of books known to have been owned by the clergy of the city but not mentioned in their wills, attention should be drawn to two collections, the contents of both of which are listed by Dr Emden: the forty or so works belonging to Bishop Goldwell (Emden, *BRUO*, 2: 785-786), only three of which were mentioned in his will (see below, p. 38); and the seventy or so books of John Steke (Emden, *BRUC*, p. 553), though Steke's connections with Norwich seem to have been confined to a four year spell as rector of St Laurence's about thirty years before his death (ibid., p. 553).

[269] *Register of Chichele*, ed. Jacob, 2: 313; N.C.C., Reg. Gylys, fol. 83r (Mountford).

will in 1500;[270] for it was during the second half of the fifteenth century that, according to Dr Pfaff,[271] the three celebrations first became generally observed in England as official liturgical feasts.

Legal works were much less common than in Baker's collection. The *Institutes*, presumably Justinian's, appeared in one will.[272] Edmund Wether, Bachelor of Law and master of the Carnary College, owned "all the holy corpus of Canon Law, that is to say the *Decretals*, the *Decrees*, *Sext* and the *Clementines*," when he wrote his will in 1525.[273] A few other priests owned one or more of these four great collections of canons of the Western Church. But Lyndwood's *Provinciale*, the most important work on English ecclesiastical law, did not appear in any will. The only commentaries on Canon Law were Panormitanus's commentary of the *Decretals*[274] and an unnamed work by the French canonist, Henry Bohic (1310-1350), which were left by Bishop Goldwell together with the *Decretals* to the Carnary College where they were to be chained in the library for the use of those working in the Consistory Court[275] and of others wishing to study.[276]

Bibles appeared in four wills,[277] though it is not clear that any of them was in English. Individual books of the Bible were mentioned in several other wills, and extracts from Scripture would, of course, have been included in most of the liturgical works. There were, in addition, quite a wide variety of commentaries on Scripture: "Magister Historiarum," [278] the historical commentary called *Historia scholastica* by "Magister" Peter Comestor (?-ca. 1179), chancellor of Notre Dame cathedral in Paris; several commentaries by the French Franciscan, Nicholas of Lyra (ca. 1270-1340);[279] one or two by the French Dominican, Nicholas of Gorran (1232-ca. 1295);[280] one by Acton,[281] possibly Ralph Acton, the

---

[270] N.C.C., Reg. Cage, fol. 155v (Barker).

[271] Richard W. Pfaff, *New Liturgical Feasts in Later Medieval England* (Oxford 1970), p. 129.

[272] N.C.C., Reg. Johnson, fol. 141v (Hewetson).

[273] N.C.C., Reg. Haywarde, fol. 157r (Wether).

[274] MS reads "Abbas super Decretalibus." See p. 36 for the identification of the book.

[275] The Consistory Court normally met in the Baucham Chapel in the Cathedral (Burnham, "Episcopal Administration," p. 36), and the Carnary College lay within the Cathedral Close.

[276] PROB/11/11 (Reg. Horne, 1496-1500), fol. 35 (Goldwelle).

[277] N.C.C., Reg. Harsyk, fol. 281v (Brown), Reg. Aleyn, fol. 7r (Honingham), Reg. Gylys, fol. 83r (Mountford), and Reg. Wymer, fol. 90r (Buxton).

[278] N.C.C., Reg. Harsyk, fol. 281v (Brown).

[279] *Register of Chichele*, ed. Jacob, 2: 312; N.C.C., Reg. Wymer, fol. 90r (Buxton); see p. 235.

[280] N.C.C., Reg. Brosyard, fol. 272v (Leystofte), and Reg. Doke, fol. 227r (Bernham).

[281] N.C.C., Reg. Aleyn, fol. 12r (Savage).

obscure fourteenth-century Englishman; a commentary on the Canticle of Canticles, wrongly ascribed to Pope Gregory I (ca. 540-604);[282] a commentary on various books of the Old Testament by the fourteenth-century Italian Franciscan, Philip de Monte Calerio;[283] two copies of the "Glossa communis" on the Psalter by Anselm of Laon (?-1117);[284] and a copy of the "Glossa communis" on the five books of Wisdom by an unknown author, with a further gloss by the French Dominican cardinal, Hugh of Saint-Cher (ca. 1200-1263).[285]

Like legal works, collections of sermons were much rarer than in Baker's library: Sermones de sanctis of St. Bonaventure (1221-1274);[286] the "Sermons" of a certain Prior Bartholomew,[287] possibly Bartholomew of Tours, who was prior of the Dominican friary of Saint-Jacques in Paris in the 1260s; two copies of "Repyngton," probably a collection of sermons by the bishop of Lincoln, Philip Repingdon (?-1424);[288] and Bishop Wakeryng's collection of his own sermons.[289] On the other hand manuals of instruction for parish priests, which are missing from Baker's collection, appeared in several wills. The most popular was Pupilla oculi written about 1384 by John de Burgh, chancellor of Cambridge University. It was perhaps the best work of its kind by an Englishman in the late Middle Ages. Qui bene presunt, the manual written by Richard de Leycestria (alias Wetheringsett) about 1230, was mentioned in one will;[290] as was "a book called Pars oculi,"[291] which was the first part of Oculus sacerdotis by William of Pagula, the early fourteenth-century vicar of Winkfield in Salisbury diocese. Legenda aurea (sometimes called Legenda sanctorum), the collection of saints' lives by James de Voragine (ca. 1230-1298), archbishop of Genoa, was exceptionally popular.

Among the other religious books that can be identified with some degree of probability were several works by Fathers of the Church: "some small works of St. Eusebius,"[292] probably Eusebius of Caesarea (ca. 260 - ca. 340); the Confessions and some unanmed works of

---

[282] N.C.C., Reg. Sayve, fol. 23r-v (Billern).
[283] N.C.C., Reg. Aleyn, fol. 24v (Cheese).
[284] Register of Chichele, ed. Jacob, 2: 312; see p. 235.
[285] See p. 235.
[286] N.C.C., Reg. Gelour, fol. 92r (Poringland).
[287] Register of Chichele, ed. Jacob, 2: 313.
[288] See pp. 35 and 235.
[289] Register of Chichele, ed. Jacob, 2: 313.
[290] N.C.C., Reg. Doke, fol. 176v (Reading).
[291] N.C.C., Reg. Jekkys, fol. 255r (Gardener).
[292] N.C.C., Reg. Aleyn, fol. 12r (Savage).

Augustine (354-430);[293] the *Dialogues* of Pope Gregory I (ca. 540-604).[294] In addition there were *Vitae patrum*,[295] a sixth-century collection of writings by and about various Fathers of the Church; "a treatise called *Scintillarum*," [296] the Patristic anthology by the seventh-century Benedictine monk of Ligugé in France called "Defensor"; and "Flores doctorum" [297] which was probably a similar anthology. Also mentioned were *Fasciculus temporum*,[298] a kind of history of the Church by Werner Rolewinck (1425-1502), the Carthusian monk of Cologne; "Formula noviciorum" [299] which was probably the treatise for novices called *De institutione noviciorum* by Hugh of St Victor (ca. 1096-1142); *De claustro anime*,[300] the devotional treatise for monks written by the French Benedictine, Hugh of Fouilloi (?-ca. 1174); some unnamed works of the English Franciscan, Alexander of Hales (ca. 1186-1245);[301] "Credo pacisiens'," [302] which was probably a scribal error for "Credo parisiensis" and so may have been *De fide* by William of Auvergne (ca. 1180-1249), bishop of Paris; two copies of *Dieta salutis*,[303] the treatise on virtues and vices usually ascribed to St Bonaventure but more probably by the French Franciscan, William de Lavicea (ca. 1300); *Oculus moralis*,[304] the treatise on spiritual discernment by the French theologian, Peter of Limoges (?-1306); *Fasciculus morum*,[305] the aid to preaching written by an English Franciscan, most probably Robert Selk, in the late thirteenth or fourteenth century; *Summa predicancium*,[306] the encyclopedia for preachers by the English Dominican, John of Bromyard (?-ca. 1349); "Summa Angelica" [307] which was probably *Summa de casibus conscientie* by the Italian Franciscan, Angelo da Chivasso (1411-1495); and "a book called *Quat' novissimarum*" [308] which was presumably a treatise on the four last things

[293] Ibid.; PROB/11/9 (Reg. Dogett, 1491-1493), fol. 28 (Rightwis).
[294] N.C.C., Reg. Brosyard, fol. 272v (Leystofte).
[295] N.C.C., Reg. Doke, fol. 176v (Reading).
[296] Ibid.
[297] PROB/11/17 (Reg. Fetiplace, 1511-1514), fol. 31 (Stubb).
[298] Ibid.
[299] N.C.C., Reg. Doke, fol. 176v (Reading).
[300] N.C.C., Reg. Aleyn, fol. 24r (Cheese).
[301] N.C.C., Reg. Cooke, fol. 88v (Buckingham).
[302] See p. 236.
[303] *Register of Chichele*, ed. Jacob, 2: 312; PROB/11/9 (Reg. Dogett, 1491-1493), fol. 28 (Rightwis).
[304] *Register of Chichele*, ed. Jacob, 2: 312.
[305] N.C.C., Reg. Jekkys, fol. 255r (Gardener).
[306] *Register of Chichele*, ed. Jacob, 2: 313.
[307] N.C.C., Reg. Johnson, fol. 141v (Hewettson).
[308] N.C.C., Reg. Ryxe, fol. 306r (Waller).

(death, judgment, heaven and hell) and may have been the anonymous *Cordiale quatuor novissimorum*.

There were few books unconnected with Christian theology. Those that can be identified, in addition to the few already mentioned, were "*Cato*," [309] probably the collection of moral precepts called *Disticha* by an unknown author, probably of the second or third century, traditionally called Dionysius Cato; a work of Donatus,[310] presumably the fourth-century grammarian called Aelius Donatus; *De planctu nature*, the dialogue with nature by Alan of Lille (ca. 1120-1202);[311] *Bevis of Hampton*,[312] the thirteenth-century romance; "a book called *Catholicon*" [313] which was probably a dictionary and quite likely the Latin dictionary of that name written about 1285 by John de Balbis, the Dominican friar from Genoa; and Petrarch's (1307-1374) *De remediis utriusque fortune*.[314]

It is surprising that there were so few books of a secular nature. With the possible exception of "Rosarium" [315] which may have been the Lollard treatise of that name and which was owned by the radical vicar of St Stephen's, Geoffrey Chaumpneis,[316] no heretical work was mentioned[317] even though wills up to 1549 have been examined.[318] Petrarch's *De remediis utriusque fortune* was about the only evidence of the "New Learning." Noticeable, too, is the absence of works by late medieval mystics including those from England, which contrasts with their presence in some of the collections of the laity.[319] In some senses, therefore, the books reveal minds that were narrow and conservative, like, according to Professor Dickens, the minds of the early Tudor parish clergy as a whole.[320] On the other hand many of the books were by recent authors or were classics in their fields, and the number of works by foreigners does not indicate minds that were narrow in the sense of

[309] N.C.C., Reg. Hyrnyng, fol. 62r (Eston).
[310] Ibid.
[311] N.C.C., Reg. Spurlinge, fol. 78v (Bevis).
[312] N.C.C., Reg. Brosyard, fol. 113r (Stathe).
[313] N.C.C., Reg. Wylbey, fol. 107v (Excestr).
[314] N.C.C., Reg. Gelour, fol. 92r (Poringland).
[315] See p. 235.
[316] See pp. 124-125 and 234-236.
[317] The two copies of "Repyngton," probably collections of Bishop Repingdon's sermons (see p. 39), are unlikely to have been heretical since, although he had once been a follower of Wycliffe, his published sermons were orthodox.
[318] See p. 193, n. 1.
[319] See p. 112.
[320] Arthur G. Dickens, *The English Reformation* (London 1964), pp. 49-50.

provincial. At the least the books suggest that a fair number of the secular clergy, including those who had not studied at a university, did read and were interested in communicating an intelligent faith to the laity. This and the other evidence mentioned suggest, I think, that in Norwich the secular clergy were not so incapable of responding to the spiritual needs of the laity as some recent writers[321] have thought them to have been in late medieval Christendom as a whole.

The only significant point to emerge about differences in education among the book-owners is that, as might be expected, the proportion of priests owning commentaries on Scripture, works of the Fathers and the heavier theological treatises was much higher among the university graduates than among the non-graduates; and conversely almost all the more popular works such as collections of sermons, manuals of instruction for parish priests and copies of *Legenda aurea* were owned by non-graduates.

As for the introduction of printing, there is little evidence about its effect. Only a handful of books were described as printed, and the proportion of priests mentioning books in their wills did not rise with the advent of printing.

viii. Pluralism and Non-Residence

It might be expected that pluralism was widespread in late medieval Norwich since many of the parochial benefices were worth little[322] and there was an abundance of unbeneficed priests[323] who might have been willing to supplement their earnings[324] by being hired as curates, and since the work of curates in parishes with so few parishioners[325] should have been light.

However, in the returns of pluralists made in 1366 only two priests in the city declared themselves pluralists and neither of them held more than one benefice with the cure of souls: John de Merston said he was rector of St Michael of Coslany parish as well as a prebendary of the College of St Mary in the Fields, and John de Henneye said he was a prebendary of the same college as well as the incumbent of a perpetual chantry in St Peter Mancroft parish church, all in Norwich.[326]

[321] See p. 28.
[322] See columns 5 and 6 of Appendix 1 (pp. 173-178).
[323] See pp. 18-23.
[324] See pp. 108-109.
[325] See p. 4.
[326] *Registrum Simonis Langham Cantuariensis archiepiscopi*, ed. Arthur C. Wood, Canterbury and York Society, 53 (no place, 1956), pp. 9-10.

The returns of 1366 are the last comprehensive returns of pluralists to survive. For the period after that information is less accessible. The records of Bishop Goldwell's visitation in 1492 mention two priests with more than one employment in the city, excluding those with two or more livings that had been officially united:[327] John Oudolff was parish chaplain of St Saviour's as well as rector of St Mary Unbrent,[328] and Robert Calton was treasurer of the College of St Mary in the Fields as well as vicar of St Stephen's.[329] But the records of the visitation do not cover parishes outside Norwich, and so do not reveal how many priests with benefices in the city held others elsewhere in the diocese or outside it. To find this out for 1492, or for any other year, it would be necessary to search systematically through the records of institutions to benefice in the registers of at least all the English bishops.

For graduates there are also the fruits of Dr Emden's researches. The most striking point to emerge is that almost all the graduates holding the deanery or prebends at the College of St Mary in the Fields, or the mastership of St Giles's Hospital, held other benefices concurrently; though as collegial dignities without the cure of souls, tenure of them was canonically "compatible" with that of another benefice, even one with the cure of souls.[330] The right to collate to these benefices lay with the bishop of Norwich,[331] and with no benefices in the Cathedral to confer[332] successive bishops frequently gave them to their officials[333] or to prominent ecclesiastics. Occasionally royal civil servants were appointed, though apparently no foreigner was appointed nor was anybody provided by the pope. Several of the men in question held many benefices concurrently: take, for example, Doctor Nicholas Goldwell, Doctor Thomas Hare and Master John Davyson. The first was appointed dean of the College in 1498 by his brother, Bishop James Goldwell. At the time he was archdeacon of Suffolk, canon of at least four collegiate churches, rector of at least four parish churches and free chapels, and master of St Mary Magdalen Hospital in the suburbs of Norwich.[334] Thomas Hare, a former fellow of All Souls College, Oxford, was collated to the prebend of

---

[327] See column 2 of Appendix 1 (pp. 173-178).

[328] See p. 181.

[329] See p. 185; *Visitations*, ed. Jessopp, p. 11.

[330] The College of St Mary in the Fields obtained a special "motu proprio" to this effect from Pope Boniface IX in 1401 (*Cal. Papal L., 1396-1404*, p. 419).

[331] See REG/3, Book 6, to REG/10, Book 16, passim.

[332] The monks of the Cathedral Priory formed the Cathedral Chapter.

[333] Burnham, "Episcopal Administration," p. 5.

[334] Emden, *BRUC*, p. 263 (Nicholas Goldwell).

chancellor in 1502, and at the time was vicar-general and chancellor of the bishop of Norwich, vicar of one parish and rector of another and shortly afterwards became rector of a third.[335] Finally, Master John Davyson, Keeper of the Hanaper in the Royal Chancery, was presented in 1472 to the prebend of the Mass of St Mary which was in the king's gift because the bishopric of Norwich was vacant. At the time he was dean of St George's Chapel, Windsor, and probably a canon of Salisbury Cathedral.[336]

Pluralism appears to have been considerably less common among the graduates with parochial benefices in the city: among those mentioned by Dr Emden there was a fairly equal division between those who held at least one other benefice concurrently with tenure of a parochial benefice in Norwich and those who did not. None of the parochial benefices in Norwich was very valuable by national standards, but it is noticeable that the pluralists were concentrated among a few of the city's richer livings:[337] St Mary in the Marsh,[338] St Stephen's[339] and St Laurence's;[340] and St John's Maddermarket and St Michael of Coslany, whose advowsons belonged for a time to New College, Oxford, and Gonville Hall, Cambridge,[341] and which were quite frequently held by members of the two colleges in plurality with their fellowships and other benefices.[342]

Known cases of pluralism rose sharply in number after about 1450 among both the collegiate and the parish clergy, but the rise may be more apparent than real, reflecting the increase in the number of graduates after about 1450,[343] since our knowledge of pluralism among the non-graduate clergy is slight.

---

[335] Emden, *BRUO*, 2: 872 (Thomas Hare), and 3: xxvi (Thomas Hare); REG/8, Book 13, second series of folios, fols. 6r-7v.

[336] Emden, *BRUO*, 1: 552 (John Davyson), and 3: xx (John Davyson); *Cal. Pat. R., 1467-1477*, p. 357.

[337] See columns 5 and 6 of Appendix 1 (pp. 173-178).

[338] Emden, *BRUC*, pp. 57 (William Bernham), 220 (John Farewell) and 522 (Peter Shelton). For non-graduate pluralists see: N.C.C., Reg. Spyltymber, fol. 125v (Sharpe); *Cal. Papal L., 1455-1464*, pp. 574-575.

[339] Emden, *BRUC*, pp. 57 (William Bernham), 118 (Robert Calton) and 123 (Thomas Cappe); and, for Master Thomas Bower, REG/8, Book 13, second series of folios, fols. 2v-3r and 93r-v, REG/9, Book 14, folios at end of register, for 1529-1538, fols. 4r and 9r, and REG/9, Book 15, fol. 25v.

[340] Emden, *BRUC*, pp. 20 (William Asshefeld) and 347 (William Lakyngham); Emden, *BRUO*, 3: 1862-1863 (Robert Thompson).

[341] See pp. 174-175.

[342] Emden, *BRUO*, 1: 76 (Thomas Audley), 2: 726 (John Fremantle) and 868 (Edward Hanyngton), and 3: 2099 (John Wyche); Emden, *BRUC*, pp. 38 (John Barley) and 563 (Edmund Stubbes). For a non-graduate pluralist, see above, pp. 35-36.

[343] See pp. 28-30.

As for non-residence, John Davyson may well have spent no time at the College of St Mary in the Fields during his short spell of just over a year as a prebendary.[344] But the level of non-residence at the college does not appear to have been anything like as high as at, for example, the rather larger and grander Cathedral Chapter of Lincoln.[345] The prebendaries who were officials of the bishop of Norwich presumably lived part of the time in the episcopal city, and all the prebendaries were in residence when Bishop Goldwell visited the college in 1492.[346] Moreover, several rather grand ecclesiastics, who held non-parochial benefices in Norwich as well as benefices outside it, are known to have owned houses in the city. For example, the only house mentioned in Nicholas Goldwell's will was his "mansio" in Norwich;[347] so while he was dean of the College of St Mary in the Fields he probably lived in Norwich even if not in his college. And Norwich contained in 1415 the "domus habitacionis" of William Westacre[348] who was then archdeacon of Norwich, keeper of the spiritualities of the bishopric of Norwich during a vacancy in the see and rector of Watlington in Norfolk;[349] and he was living in the same house three years later when he made his will.[350] The house had earlier belonged to John Derlyngton[351] who had held several non-parochial benefices in Norwich in plurality with parochial ones outside the city.[352] Thomas Hare was another case in point.[353] It would be interesting to know how much of the time these men spent in the provincial capital rather than in their country parishes: where they lived would have affected their parishioners in the countryside as well as the quality – intellectual and otherwise – of clerical life in Norwich. But since their parochial benefices lay outside Norwich, it would not have directly affected the cure of souls in the city.

However, the cure of souls in Norwich would have been directly affected if the pluralists with parochial benefices in the city lived outside it. Moreover, if the graduates among them did not live in Norwich, much of the advantage gained by the increase in the number of graduates among

---

[344] Emden, *BRUO*, 3: xx (John Davyson); *Cal. Pat. R., 1467-1477*, p. 357.

[345] Margaret Bowker, *The Secular Clergy in the Diocese of Lincoln, 1495-1520* (Cambridge 1968), pp. 155-159.

[346] *Visitations*, ed. Jessopp, p. 11.

[347] PROB/11/14 (Reg. Holgrave, 1504-1506), fol. 40 (Goldwell).

[348] *Register of Chichele*, ed. Jacob, 3: 351.

[349] Emden, *BRUC*, pp. 629-630 (William de Westacre).

[350] REG/4, Book, 8, fol. 143r (Westacre).

[351] Ibid.

[352] Emden, *BRUC*, p. 185 (John Derlyngton).

[353] See p. 49.

the parish clergy[354] would have been lost. Some of them are known to have lived in the city. Doctor Edmund Rightwis, for example, lived in it for at least some of the time while he was both rector of St Michael at Plea in Norwich and vicar of Bawburgh in Norfolk.[355] Others probably did not reside in it. Doctor John Barley, for example, remained master of Gonville Hall, Cambridge, while he held the Hall's living in Norwich, St Michael of Coslany;[356] and John Fremantle, Bachelor of Canon and Civil Law, was rector of St John's Maddermarket towards the end of his life but probably lived in Chichester, where he had several benefices.[357] These are, however, particular cases. The only more general evidence about the level of non-residence among the parish clergy comes from records of visitations.[358] At Bishop Goldwell's visitation of the parishes of the city in 1492 as many as six priests did not appear: the parish chaplains of St Etheldreda's, St Vedast's and St Martin at the Palace Gates, and the rector of St Mary in the Marsh,[359] for each of which parishes there were no other priests; and two stipendiary priests attached to the united parish of St Edward's and St Julian's.[360] On the other hand it is noticeable that the laity, who felt the effects of clerical non-residence, are known to have complained only once at a visitation that a member of the parish clergy absented himself from his parish: at the visitation of the parish of St Martin at the Palace Gates in 1416, the five lay inquisitors complained that their parish chaplain spent his nights outside the parish.[361]

ix. Upper and Lower Clergy

There was no clear dividing-line between the upper and the lower clergy in the late medieval Church. In so far as tenure of a benefice defined the line for the secular clergy, several points have already emerged

---

[354] See pp. 28-29.

[355] Emden, *BRUC*, p. 481 (Edmund Rightwise); REG/11/9 (Reg. Dogett, 1491-1493), fol. 28 (Rightwis).

[356] Emden, *BRUC*, p. 38 (John Barley).

[357] Emden, *BRUO*, 2: 726 (John Fremantle); *Transcripts of Sussex Wills as far as they relate to Ecclesiological and Parochial Subjects, up to the year 1560*, ed. Robert G. Rice and Walter H. Godfrey, Sussex Record Society, 41-43 and 45 (no place, 1935-1941), 1: 263, 277, 284 and 306-307.

[358] See p. 7, n. 36.

[359] I.e., John Styward (see p. 18, n. 116).

[360] See pp. 186-188. Walter Goos, rector of the united parish of Sts Simon and Jude's and St Swithin's (see p. 175), did not appear for the visitation of St Swithin's (see p. 184) but appeared for the visitation of Sts Simon and Jude's (see p. 181).

[361] D. and C. Mun., Box "Acta et Comperta," Roll 1 (1416).

concerning the situation in Norwich. First, the unbeneficed clergy far outnumbered the beneficed,[362] an inequality that was partly due to the unusual fact that over half the parishes had no rector or vicar but only a parish chaplain.[363] Second, university graduates existed among the unbeneficed clergy[364] but they were far more common among the beneficed clergy[365] and they increased sharply in number among the latter after about 1450.[366] Third, graduates and pluralists were concentrated among the deans and prebendaries of the College of St Mary in the Fields, the masters of St Giles's Hospital and the beneficed clergy of a relatively few of the city's parishes.[367]

There appears to have been remarkably little movement between the ranks of the beneficed and unbeneficed clergy of the city. The evidence suggests that priests either acquired a benefice soon after their ordination to the priesthood and remained members of the beneficed clergy for the rest of their lives, or never acquired one. Thus none of the men known to have lived in Norwich as unbeneficed priests, including those who were graduates, is known to have subsequently acquired a benefice in the city or elsewhere;[368] and over two-thirds of the 289 clerics whose wills survive were still without a benefice in their old age.[369] Conversely, Doctor Richard Poringland appears to have been the only priest to have moved downwards. He came from Norwich and became a fellow of Peterhouse in Cambridge, master of the College of St Michael's Royal in London and vicar of Worstead in Norfolk.[370] Sometime between 1442 and 1457 he was vicar of St Stephen's in Norwich,[371] which was one of the most valuable livings in the city.[372] But he is not known to have held any benefices between 1458 and his death sometime between 1471 and

---

[362] See pp. 18-23.

[363] See p. 29, n. 204, and column 4 of Appendix 1 (pp. 173-178).

[364] See pp. 29-30.

[365] See pp. 29-30.

[366] See pp. 28-30.

[367] See pp. 29-30 and 42-44.

[368] Their subsequent careers outside the city have not been investigated systematically.

[369] See pp. 114-115.

[370] Emden, *BRUC*, p. 458 (Richard Poringland); Blomefield, *Norfolk* (1805-1810), 4: 147.

[371] Neither his institution to the vicarage, nor his vacation of it, were recorded in the episcopal registers, but he was mentioned as vicar in 1448 and 1449 (N.C.C., Reg. Aleyn, fols. 12r [Savage] and 24v [Cheese]; see also Blomefield, *Norfolk* [1805-1810], 4: 147). The last known incumbent had died sometime between 1442 and 1445 (N.C.C., Reg. Doke, fol. 227r-v [Bernham]), and the next known one was instituted in 1457 (REG/6, Book 11, fol. 96v).

[372] See columns 5 and 6 of Appendix 1 (pp. 173-178).

1475,[373] and was described simply as a chaplain when he made his will in 1471.[374]

The lack of inventories of priests' goods makes it difficult to estimate how far the division of the clergy into upper and lower according to the criterion of tenure of a benefice was supported by differences in wealth. The sole surviving inventory, of John Baker's goods, listed "all the goods moveable ... appertaining and belonging in time of ... death" [375] to this probably middle-aged rector.[376] These moveable goods were valued at £21 18s. 1d., exclusive of some clothes and riding-gear whose values were not mentioned. They must have made him a man of fairly comfortable means. His books have already been discussed.[377] He owned two feather-beds and plenty of bed-clothes, and his wardrobe was quite extensive: six gowns, a coat, three tippets, three doublets, two pairs of hose and two shirts. He had enough furniture and table-ware to provide meals in comfort for several persons, and he had presumably owned a horse since he possessed riding-clothes as well as a bridle and two saddles.[378]

The estimated value of Baker's goods was about twice the total value of the bequests in his will.[379] Some testators may, therefore, have been considerably wealthier than their wills suggest. In general, however, there was probably a fairly constant relationship between the value of a testator's bequests and that of his goods. In so far as this was the case, wills suggest that the wealth of the beneficed clergy differed from that of the unbeneficed clergy, but the difference was less than might be expected, and that many of the unbeneficed clergy were comfortably off.

At the top of the pyramid, for the most part in a class of their own, stood the bishops of Norwich. Except Alexander Tottington, each of the five men who died as bishops of Norwich between 1370 and 1532 after reasonably long tenures of the see, and whose wills survive,[380] left in his will, in addition to bequests in kind, bequests in cash worth at least £500.[381] Tottington, who had been a monk and prior of Norwich

---

[373] Emden, *BRUC*, p. 458 (Richard Poringland), discounting his error as to when Poringland was vicar of St Stephen's (see note 371).

[374] N.C.C., Reg. Gelour, fol. 91v (Poringland).

[375] See p. 237.

[376] See pp. 35-36, nn. 262-263.

[377] See pp. 36-37.

[378] See pp. 238-240.

[379] See p. 237.

[380] See p. 14, n. 90.

[381] This and subsequent figures include payments for Masses and prayers calculated at average rates of pay (see pp. 108-109) when testators did not mention sums of money for the Masses and prayers which they wanted to be said.

Cathedral Priory before becoming bishop seven years before his death and so had not had much time to accumulate a large personal fortune, left bequests in cash worth somewhat over £100, many liturgical items and a manor which he thought to be worth £10 a year. The most valuable bequests probably came from Thomas Brown, bishop from 1436 until his death in 1445: bequests in cash worth about £1,250 besides many vestments and household goods, jewels and six horses.

At the next level, in some cases with fortunes comparing with those of some of the bishops, came several priests who held non-parochial benefices in Norwich in plurality with benefices outside the city. Thomas Hare appears to have been the wealthiest of them. The benefices which he held in 1502 have already been mentioned.[382] He was promoted from chancellor to dean of the College of St Mary in the Fields in 1514, remaining dean until his death in 1520. He also remained chancellor of the bishop of Norwich until his death, and vicar-general until at least 1514; and until his death he always held at least two parochial benefices outside Norwich.[383] He appears to have been living in Norwich towards the end of his life.[384] He left bequests worth at least £450 besides a considerable amount of property, including a manor and a hundred and sixty acres of land and a hundred ewes.[385] Archdeacon William Westacre is another example. His benefices have been mentioned[386] and he left bequests worth almost £200 besides vestments and clothes and his house in Norwich.[387] Other men, such as John Rickinghall, dean of the College of St Mary in the Fields and subsequently bishop of Chichester, and John Morton, archdeacon of Norwich and subsequently archbishop of Canterbury, were almost certainly rich men when they held their benefices in Norwich, but their other occupations and benefices make it unlikely that they ever spent much time in the city.[388]

With the possible exception of a few pluralists who are unlikely to have lived in Norwich, no priest with a parochial benefice in the city is known to have been anything like as wealthy as the bishops mentioned, apart from Alexander Tottington, or as Thomas Hare. However, in spite of the poverty of many of the livings,[389] half of the 62 priests between 1370 and

[382] See pp. 43-44.
[383] Emden, *BRUO*, 2: 872 (Thomas Hare); *Visitations*, ed. Jessopp, p. 71; REG/9, Book 14, fols. 113r and 157r (first of two folios numbered 157).
[384] *Norwich Depositions*, ed. Stone, no. 188.
[385] PROB/11/20 (Reg. Maynwaring, 1520-1522), fol. 8 (Hare).
[386] See p. 45.
[387] REG/4, Book 8, fols. 142v-143v (Westacre).
[388] Emden, *BRUC*, pp. 412 (John Morton) and 480 (John Rickinghall).
[389] See columns 5 and 6 of Appendix 1 (pp. 173-178).

1532 who had parochial benefices and whose wills survive[390] – two-thirds of them between 1440 and 1532 – left bequests in their wills worth at least £10, which was roughly the total value of John Baker's bequests or about twice what is thought to have been the average annual wage of a building labourer in southern England in the fifteenth century.[391] Several of them appear to have been rich men. The most valuable bequests came from Roger Medilton, rector of St Peter Mancroft from 1361 until his death in 1375.[392] The rectory, valued at £16 13s. 4d. in 1368,[393] was the richest parochial benefice in the city,[394] and Medilton left bequests worth about £100.[395] Henry Bony, too, appears to have been a rich man. Rector of St Edmund's for fifty years from 1417 until his death in 1467,[396] a living that was valued at only £1 in 1368 and £4 6s. 6d. in 1535,[397] Bony is not known to have held any other benefice, but left bequests worth over £80.[398]

Among the 201 unbeneficed clerics,[399] the proportion leaving bequests in their wills worth at least £10 was between a third and two-fifths, with the figure between two-fifths and a half between 1440 and 1532. The proportion was lower than among the beneficed clergy, but the difference was not as great as might be expected and several unbeneficed clerics left as much as some of the wealthier beneficed clergy. The most valuable bequests came from John Excestre, a cleric in minor orders, once married, who acted as registrar to several bishops of Norwich and who was described in his will as a citizen of Norwich. He left in 1447 bequests worth about £100 besides an unspecified amount of land, tenements and messuages.[400] John Bippis, an unbeneficed priest, left bequests worth over £40 in his will of 1477.[401] Thomas Oudolff was another case in point.[402]

---

[390] See p. 115.

[391] Ernest H. Phelps Brown and Sheila V. Hopkins, "Seven Centuries of Building Wages," *Essays in Economic History*, ed. Eleanora M. Carus-Wilson (London 1954-1962), 2: 177.

[392] REG/2, Book 5, fol. 54v; N.C.C., Reg. Heydon, fol. 54v (Medilton).

[393] See p. 176.

[394] See columns 5 and 6 of Appendix 1 (pp. 173-178).

[395] N.C.C., Reg. Heydon, fol. 54v (Medilton).

[396] REG/4, Book 8, fol. 23v; N.C.C., Reg. Jekkys, fols. 67v-68r (Bony).

[397] See p. 174.

[398] N.C.C., Reg. Jekkys, fols. 67v-68r (Bony).

[399] See p. 115.

[400] N.C.C., Reg. Wylbey, fol. 107r-v (Excestr); *Heresy Trials in the Diocese of Norwich, 1428-1431*, ed. Norman P. Tanner, Royal Historical Society, Camden 4th ser., 20 (London 1977), p. 4.

[401] N.C.C., Reg. Gelour, fol. 154r-v (Bippis).

[402] See pp. 27-28.

Wills suggest that it is unlikely that Norwich possessed a large clerical proletariat living at subsistence level. A large proportion of the secular clergy made wills that survive,[403] and the wills, with some exceptions chiefly before 1440 and chiefly among the unbeneficed clergy, do not give an impression of poverty-stricken priests. How the unbeneficed priests acquired their wealth and spent their time may appear to be something of a mystery. None of them is known to have engaged in trade or in a craft. Some of them were the priests in charge (parish chaplains) of parishes without rectors or vicars,[404] and such men presumably received the lesser tithes and offerings[405] or a stipend from the owner of the benefice. But wills suggest that the answer to the first quesion, though hardly to the second, lies, to a considerable extent, in bequests for chantry services, which offered comparatively good wages to a considerable number of priests without burdening them with much to do.[406] Indeed, free-lancing in this way may well have been more attractive to some priests than acquiring a benefice.

x. Morals

The main sources of information about the morals of priests and members of religious orders are the records of the Norwich Consistory Court, which survive from 1499, and records of visitations. The records do not form a barometer to fluctuations in moral standards: they are insufficiently continuous before 1492 and are, like most such records, heavily dependent upon the moods of the interrogators and the interrogated. However, they throw interesting light upon the minds and behaviour of various people and should be mentioned for the sake of completeness. The records of visitations of religious houses, in which the complaints were made by members of the houses, are indicative of their attitude towards one another and of what kinds of behaviour were thought to be wrong; and those of visitations of parishes, in which the laity could bring complaints against the clergy, are instructive about the attitude of the laity towards their parish priests.

There survive records of seven late medieval visitations of the Cathedral Priory. Bishop Salmon, who visited the priory in 1309, complained that few monks attended the Divine Office and that services in the Cathedral

---

[403] See p. 114.
[404] See p. 29, n. 204, and column 4 of Appendix 1 (pp. 173-178).
[405] See p. 6, n. 33.
[406] See pp. 107-109.

were performed in a slovenly fashion,[407] and Bishop Bateman's injunctions of 1347 were mainly concerned with the priory's finances.
Bishop Bateman also forbade the prior to give lightly dispensations to eat
meat; vagrant and ill-disciplined monks were to be kept in the priory, not
sent to outlying cells;[408] fine or colourful clothes were forbidden; money
given to the monks for personal expenditure was to be cut down; and
women were forbidden to spend the night within the precincts of the
monastery.[409] For the five visitations carried out between 1492 and 1532
there survive the depositions of the monks as well as the injunctions of the
visiting bishops. Sexual faults were prominent: too close contacts with
women were mentioned at all five visitations, the most serious being in
1514 when Brother Robert Worsted was accused of begetting a child by a
girl from the city, and the prior and two other monks were accused of
committing adultery with various women; and in 1526 the third prior
complained that the "wardrober's wife" had suspicious access to the sub-
prior and embraced him in public![410] Most of the other faults seem to
have been problems for the whole English Benedictine Congregation:[411]
wearing clothes and shoes that were regarded as fancy; dancing at night in
the guest-hall; junior monks being idle and too talkative, inssuficiently
devoted to their studies, and players of dice and cards![412] Visitations of
religious houses necessarily involve people accusing their fellow religious.
But even when allowance has been made for this, perhaps the most
striking point to emerge from the last three visitations – those of 1514,
1526 and 1532 – is the bitterness between the two factions into which the
priory seems to have split, largely on the basis of age.[413]

As for the other religious houses in the city, records of visitations are
much less complete and survive only from 1492.[414] Nothing survives for
the friaries. At Carrow Priory complaints were made about the standard
of food and drink, failure to observe various feast-days, failure to pay
various nuns their annual pensions, and the absence of a door, which
allowed the nuns to be seen by the laity and to be approached in choir.[415]

[407] Carter, *Studies*, pp. 19-23.
[408] For the cells, see p. 19.
[409] Christopher R. Cheney, "Norwich Cathedral Priory in the Fourteenth Century,"
Bulletin of the John Rylands Library 20 (1936) 106, 109-110 and 113.
[410] *Visitations*, ed. Jessopp, pp. 74-76, 78 and 200.
[411] *Documents*, ed. Pantin, passim.
[412] *Visitations*, ed. Jessopp, pp. 74-75, 78, 198, 201, 263, 266 and 268-269.
[413] Ibid., pp. 71-79, 196-206 and 262-270.
[414] Ibid., pp. 9-13, 15-17, 145, 206-210 and 270-275.
[415] Ibid., pp. 16-17, 145, 209 and 274-275.

At the colleges of secular priests most complaints concerned the finances of the colleges and other aspects of their material state, the most serious being that Robert Ipswell, a former master of the Carnary College, had absconded with £20 and some jewels belonging to the college![416]

At the visitations of parishes[417] almost all the complaints of the laity against priests and members of religious orders concerned sexual faults. No complaints against them were noted at the visitations of 1333 and 1499, and none of them is known to have been directly[418] accused of sexual immorality in the Norwich Consistory Court. But at five of the nine visitations of parishes within the "liberties" of the Cathedral Priory carried out in the early fifteenth century, at least one priest was said to have committed adultery or fornication.[419] In one parish alone three priests were accused of sexual immorality in one year, 1428.[420] And there were accusations at Bishop Goldwell's visitation in 1492: "Brother John Caster is known to be unchaste with Isabel Chapman, junior";[421] and "Agnes Saunder fosters sexual immorality among priests, women, members of religious orders, canons and all sorts." [422] Whether the accusations were proved is not recorded. If many of them were true, sexual immorality was at least fairly common among the secular clergy at some times. Even if most of them were untrue, it is interesting that the laity were prepared to bring accusations of this kind against priests. It is worth noting, however, that such accusations were far less common than at the 1397 visitation of Hereford diocese.[423]

Only two charges not involving sexual immorality were brought against the clergy at the visitations of parishes: in 1416 the five lay inquisitors of the parish of St Martin at the Palace Gates complained that their rector failed to maintain the lamp in the chancel (presumably the light before the Sacrament)[424] and that, as mentioned earlier,[425] the parish

---

[416] Ibid., p. 10.

[417] See p. 7, n. 36.

[418] Such accusations were indirectly mentioned in a few cases of defamation, namely people charged with defaming various priests' characters by imputations of sexual immorality.

[419] D. and C. Mun., Box "Acta et Comperta," Rolls 1 (1416), 1a (1417), 3 (1421-1423) and 10 (1428 and 1437). For the parishes involved, see pp. 177-178.

[420] Ibid., Roll 10 (1428 and 1437).

[421] See p. 187.

[422] See p. 187.

[423] "Visitation Returns," ed. Bannister, 44 (1929) 279-289 and 444-453, and 45 (1930) 92-101 and 444-463, passim.

[424] D. and C. Mun., Box "Acta et Comperta," Roll 1 (1416).

[425] See p. 46.

chaplain spent his nights outside the parish. In contrast there were
numerous complaints that the parish clergy were neglecting their pastoral
duties at the late medieval visitations of Hereford and Lincoln dioceses.[426]
Perhaps the difference was due to the fact that such neglect was liable to
be felt by the laity much more acutely in country districts than in a large
town like Norwich where there were plenty of priests and churches to
choose from. Finally, the records of the Consistory Court mention two
accusations of clerics interfering with wills: in 1502 the parish chaplain of
St Peter Mancroft was said to have tried, without success, to persuade one
of his parishioners to make a new will and to nominate him as an
executor;[427] and a woman deposed that she had gone to Norwich in about
1512 to try to get her deceased husband's will altered, and having failed to
persuade two clerics to make the alteration, she succeeded in getting a
certain Master Godsalve to do it[428] – very probably Thomas Godsalve,
notary public and registrar of Bishop Nykke, and in which case an
interesting start to a career which later saw him as a great speculator in
Church lands, a close friend of Thomas Cromwell and the subject of a
portrait by Holbein![429]

xi. Conclusion

Any attempt to draw conclusions from this section depends considerably upon how the late medieval Church as a whole is assessed. The late
Middle Ages has traditionally been regarded as a period of decline for the
Church, including the secular clergy and religious orders. To speak of
decline, however, presupposes an original, ideal state from which things
had slipped; and what appears as decline to one historian may be
interpreted as growth by another. Changes in a religious order, for
example, may be interpreted as departures from the rule of the founder or
as developments necessary to meet a new situation. Moreover, much
depends on how far the Reformation is seen as a reaction against the
Church, including the clergy, rather than as a development from within it.

However, no interpretation of the evidence presented suggests that the
clergy of late medieval Norwich was in a state of profound decadence.
There is evidence of many of the abuses that afflicted the clergy of late
medieval Christendom: pluralism, non-residence, excessive wealth,

---

[426] "Visitation Returns," ed. Bannister, 44 (1929) 279-289 and 444-453, and 45 (1930)
92-101 and 444-463, passim; *Visitations*, ed. Thompson, 1: 1-140, and 2: 1-70, passim.
[427] *Norwich Depositions*, ed. Stone, no. 18.
[428] Ibid., no. 188.
[429] *Visitations*, ed. Jessopp, pp. 72 and 263; Kent, "Church of St Cuthbert," pp. 94-95.

ignorance and sexual immorality. But the evidence does not suggest that cases of such abuses in Norwich were, for the most part, on an extravagant scale. That anti-clericalism does not appear to have been widespread among the laity[430] supports this conclusion. How far the clergy rose above a minimal decency is more difficult to say. The number of priests and members of male religious orders suggests that their ways of life remained attractive; though the spacious sites and fine buildings of the religious orders,[431] and the apparent lack of poverty among the secular clergy, suggest this may have been the case as much because their lives were comfortable as because they were pursuing religious ideals. Perhaps the most important indication of development within the clerical body was the increasing interest in education, shown by rises in both the number of priests who were university graduates and the number of testamentary bequests for priests, and candidates for the priesthood, to study. The development did not directly prepare the way for the Reformation. Neither their books, nor the records of heresy trials in East Anglia,[432] nor the teaching at Oxford and Cambridge in the fifteenth century[433] suggests that the clergy of late medieval Norwich were much interested in heresy. Rather, the preparation was indirect; a better education, and perhaps greater financial independence, making the clergy better able to receive the new ideas once they had arrived. But this hypothesis needs testing with research into how the clergy of Norwich behaved during the half century after the closing date of this study.

---

[430] See p. 158.

[431] William Worcestre, *Itineraries*, ed. John H. Harvey (Oxford 1969), pp. 234, 236, 238, 254 and 256; Campbell, *Norwich*, pp. 8 and 11; Blomefield, *Norfolk* (1805-1810), 4: 1-4, 42-46, 85-86, 108-109, 335-341 and 414-422; John Kirkpatrick, *History of the Religious Orders of Norwich* (Yarmouth 1845), pp. 17-178 passim.

[432] See pp. 162-166.

[433] John A. Thomson, *The Later Lollards, 1414-1520* (Oxford 1965), pp. 211-219.

2

New Movements

In the first chapter attention was directed towards what was by 1370 the old order of the Church, and in particular to parishes and to the secular clergy and religious orders. It is now time to look at new movements, and these will be discussed under five headings: first, hermits and anchorites, beguinages and "lay religious"; second, craft guilds and pious confraternities; third, devotion to the saints, pilgrimages and various private devotions; fourth, Masses and prayers for the dead; and finally the religious education of the laity. Of course this is not to suggest that there was a clear dividing-line between the late medieval Church and earlier periods or that the movements were fresh creations of the fourteenth and fifteenth centuries; all of the movements date back to earlier periods. Nevertheless they were all either especially characteristic of the late Middle Ages or received, in various ways, new emphases during this period; many of them being the result of initiatives coming "from below" in the Church and especially from the laity.

A. Hermits and Anchorites, Beguinages and "Lay Religious" [1]

Hermits and anchorites, and lay men and women living in religious communities, were one aspect of the movement in the late medieval Church whereby Christians sought to lead committed religious lives outside (for the most part) the framework of the priesthood and religious orders. For several reasons Norwich is of exceptional interest in this

---

[1] Throughout this section see Appendix 7 (pp. 198-203). The terms "anchor" and "anchoress" have been used to denote male and female recluses who were attached to anchorages. "Hermit" refers to a male recluse who was not attached to an anchorage. "Anchorite" has been used to denote an anchor or anchoress indifferently. This usage follows the general practice of the writers of wills in late medieval Norwich, and their use of the corresponding Latin words "anchor," "anachorissa," "heremita" and "anachorita," though the writers did not draw the distinctions with complete consistency.

matter. First, more hermits and anchorites are known to have lived in Norwich, between 1370 and the Reformation, than in any other town in England. Second, it was perhaps the only town in late medieval England known to have contained communities of lay women closely resembling Continental beguinages. Third, the proximity of Norwich, both geographically and through trade, to the Low Countries and the Rhineland, which were then the most fertile and sophisticated centres outside Italy for religious movements involving the laity, raises the question of Continental influences upon the English Church. Fourth, Norwich possessed in Julian, author of the *Revelations of Divine Love*, one of the most remarkable anchoresses in Christendom.

i. Hermits and Anchorites

The earliest known references to hermits and anchorites in Norwich date from the thirteenth century: John Bonde left bequests to four anchorites in the city in his will dated 1250,[2] and two anchorites were mentioned in the Leet Rolls of Norwich in 1287/88 and 1312/13.[3] After that there is a gap until Julian of Norwich appears at the end of the fourteenth century. There is no obvious explanation for the gap, but Julian is all the more remarkable if she was not the product of a continuous tradition of recluses in the city. During her life the number of hermits and anchorites in Norwich increased from Julian alone to perhaps ten at the same time. There is no direct evidence that she gathered a school of recluses around her, but it seems probable that to some extent she was responsible for the increase. From the 1420s to the 1470s there were probably at least eight hermits and anchorites living in the city at any given time. A will written in 1529 implies that by then they had been reduced to two anchors and four anchoresses,[4] and they seem to have disappeared completely by 1549. Altogether between 35 and 47 hermits and anchorites are known to have lived in the city between 1370 and 1549.

No figures for the whole country have been produced since Miss Clay's incomplete list of almost seventy years ago.[5] She identified 24 of the hermits and anchorites now known to have lived in Norwich between 1370 and 1549;[6] the next most productive towns during the period were,

[2] *Records of Norwich*, ed. Hudson, 2: 358-359.

[3] *Leet Jurisdiction in the City of Norwich*, ed. William Hudson, Selden Society, 5 (London 1892), pp. 6 and 60.

[4] N.C.C., Reg. Palgrave, fol. 67r (Burgh).

[5] Rotha M. Clay, *The Hermits and Anchorites of England* (London 1914), pp. 203-263.

[6] Ibid., pp. 232-237.

she thought, Lynn and London with 14 and 13 recluses respectively and a further five in the suburbs of London.[7]

Of the men, a number were priests or members of religious orders or both. Such were several anchors at the Carmelite friary. They represent an interesting return to the original traditions of the Carmelites, who had formed a primarily contemplative and eremitical order until the modifications to the Rule introduced in the thirteenth century, while Simon Stock was prior-general, changed it into a more active and communitarian one. In addition, "Master" Hugh Kestren, anchor at the Franciscan friary, may have been a priest and a friar; an anchor at the College of St Mary in the Fields was "a monk of a far country"; "Sir" Roger was a recluse at Carrow Priory; a priest called Robert was an anchor attached to St Edward's parish church; and a priest called Master William Clyffe probably lived as a hermit in Norwich for a time. The rest, numbering between 12 and 19, were probably lay men.[8]

The colourful Thomas Scrope is the only one of them about whose origins much is known. He may well have been a grandson, legitimate or illegitimate, of Richard le Scrope, first Baron Scrope of Bolton. He entered the Carmelite friary in Norwich as an ordinary friar but, according to John Bale, left it and was to be seen around 1425 "clad in a hair shirt and a sack and girded with an iron chain, preaching the gospel of the kingdom of God and proclaiming that the new Jerusalem, the bride of the Lamb, was about to come down from heaven and that her spouse would soon be ready to meet her, adding that he himself had already, with much joy, seen her in the spirit." Bale said that his eccentric behaviour angered Thomas Netter, the prior-provincial of the English Carmelites, and a frightened Scrope returned to the friary, this time as an anchor. He remained there as an anchor probably for about twenty years during which time he appears to have written several books. He then reverted to an active life. He went to Rhodes as legate of Pope Eugenius IV, was consecrated bishop of Dromore in Ireland, acted as a suffragan bishop in the diocese of Norwich for twenty-eight years and finally, according to

---

[7] Ibid., pp. 228-233. *VCH London*, 1: 585-588 suggests a somewhat higher figure for London. There were many more recluses in London than in Norwich before 1370 (ibid., pp. 585-588; Clay, *Hermits*, pp. 228-235).

[8] The distinction between anchors and hermits who were lay men, and those who were priests or members of religious orders, has been partly based on the fact that the titles "dominus" and "frater" were used or omitted fairly consistently in the case of each anchor or hermit. Support for the validity of the distinction is provided by the fact that several of those styled "dominus" or "frater," but none of those not so styled, were left money to say Masses.

Bale, spent each Friday of the last years of his life as a barefoot itinerant preacher in the diocese of Norwich, dying in 1492 aged almost a hundred![9]

Of the women, with the possible exception of a certain Alice, none of them is known to have lived as a hermit, unattached to an anchorage, but there were between 12 and 15 anchoresses. "Mistress" Kydman, referred to in 1546 as "sometime anchoress of Carrowe," [10] may well have been the Margaret Kidman who was a nun at Carrow Priory in 1514.[11] Our knowledge of whether others were or had been nuns largely depends on the significance of the title "domina" or "dame." The title, which was often accorded to nuns, was sometimes given to about eight of the anchoresses; and the anchorages of five or six of them were attached to Carrow Priory, or to St Edward's or St Julian's parish churches, whose advowsons belonged to the nunnery.[12] But it cannot be regarded as certain that they were nuns since lay women were also sometimes accorded the title. The point bears on our knowledge of Julian, author of the *Revelations*. On the basis of her writings, Walsh and Colledge regard it as likely that she had been a nun,[13] and the parish church to which her anchorage was attached was St Julian's whose advowson, as just mentioned, belonged to the Benedictine nunnery at Carrow. Moreover Margery Kempe referred to her as "dame." [14] But she was never styled "domina" or "dame" in references to her in wills, and it must remain an open question as to whether she had ever been a nun at Carrow Priory or elsewhere.

A striking feature is the length of time that some of them spent as hermits or anchorites. Thomas Scrope probably spent about twenty years as an anchorite at the Carmelite friary, Richard Ferneys at least twenty years as a hermit, Elizabeth Scott and a certain Agnes about thirty years, and Julian of Norwich probably at least thirty-five years, as anchoresses attached to St Julian's parish church, and Julian Lampett about fifty years as an anchoress at Carrow Priory. Christians were generally supposed to obtain a licence from their bishop before becoming a hermit or

---

[9] *D.N.B.*, 51: 147-148 (Thomas Scrope); John Bale, *Scriptorum illustrium maioris Brytannie catalogus* (Basle 1557), pp. 334 and 629-630; *Handbook of British Chronology*, ed. Frederick M. Powicke and Edmund B. Fryde, 2nd ed. (London 1961), p. 317.

[10] N.C.C., Reg. Wymer, fol. 77r (Waterman).

[11] *Visitations*, ed. Jessopp, p. 145.

[12] See p. 176.

[13] Julian of Norwich, [*Revelations of Divine Love,*] *A Book of Showings to the Anchoress Julian of Norwich*, ed. Edmund Colledge and James Walsh (Toronto 1978), p. 43.

[14] Margery Kempe, *The Book*, 1: 18, ed. Meech, p. 42.

anchorite,[15] and the registers of the bishops of Norwich mention a few cases, all from outside the city, of hermits and anchorites being bound to their ways of life by some kind of formal commitment.[16] But the registers do not provide much detail about the commitments undertaken, and it remains uncertain whether or not recluses in the diocese took vows to remain in their state of life permanently, as happened in some cases in other dioceses[17] and as the author of the *Ancrene Riwle* recommended.[18] Only one or two recluses in the city, before the Reformation, are known to have left their ways of life: Thomas Scrope who left, it might be argued, only at the command of religious obedience;[19] and Richard Ferneys who was described, shortly before his death,[20] in a phrase that could mean either "a former hermit of Newbridge" or "a hermit, formerly of Newbridge," [21] and who may therefore have continued to live as a hermit after his retirement from his bridge. The Reformation saw the end of the last three recluses in the city, in two cases the main reason apparently being the dissolution of the religious house to which the anchorage was attached. In 1546 mention was made of "Mistress Kydman, sometime anchoress of Carrow," and "the chaste woman in St Julian's, sometime anchoress." [22] Two years later the city government granted an annual pension of £1 to Katherine Manne, "late recluse in the house of the black friars," provided she relinquished her rights to the anchorage. The city government had acquired the Dominican friary and evidently wanted to be rid of its last, embarrassing occupant. She is last heard of in 1550 when the city government granted her "free liberty to occupy (*sic*) within this city so long as she shall keep her shop and be sole and unmarried." [23]

Little can be said for certain about how they spent their time. This is true even of those who were Carmelite friars or Benedictine monks or nuns, since their Rules did not specify in detail how members of the order who wished to live as anchorites were to occupy their days.[24] Priority

[15] Clay, *Hermits*, pp. 85-100.

[16] REG/5, Book 9, fol. 112r; REG/7, Book 12, fol. 245v; REG/9, Book 14, fol. 54r.

[17] Clay, *Hermits*, pp. 94-95.

[18] *Ancrene Riwle*, ed. Eric J. Dobson, Early English Text Society, 267 (London 1972), pp. 4-5.

[19] See p. 59.

[20] See p. 233; N.C.C., Reg. Jekkys, fol. 16r (Ferneys).

[21] See p. 233, and ibid. where his successor at Newbridge is mentioned.

[22] N.C.C., Reg. Wymer, fols. 76r and 77r (Waterman).

[23] Clay, *Hermits*, p. 185; Rotha M. Clay, "Further Studies on Medieval Recluses," *Journal of the British Archaeological Association*, 3rd ser., 16 (1953) 79.

[24] *Monumenta historica carmelitana*, ed. Benedict Zimmerman (Larino 1905-1907), pp. 12-189; Benedict of Nursia, *Regula*, cap. 1, Sancti Benedicti Regula Monasteriorum, ed. Cuthbert Butler, 2nd ed. (Fribourg 1927), p. 10.

should have been given to prayer. The *Ancrene Riwle* recommended that anchoresses spend most of the day in a round of liturgical and private prayer, and have one or two maidservants to attend to their external needs so that they might devote themselves more exclusively to the interior life.[25] Certainly the *Revelations of Divine Love* suggest that Julian spent much time in prayer; and she and another anchoress attached to St Julian's parish church, as well as Julian Lampett, anchoress at Carrow Priory, had one or two maidservants each;[26] and Richard Ferneys had a boy as well as a woman whom he described as his guardian (*custos*).[27] None of the recluses is known to have been married. (In a case in the Norwich Consistory Court in 1520 a man was accused of defaming the character of Hugh Kestren, anchor at the Franciscan friary, by declaring that Kestren had a son – the context implies a bastard – but nobody then maintained that the statement was true.)[28] Miss Clay pointed out that hermits frequently kept bridges, repaired roads or performed other civic functions.[29] In Norwich a hermit called Robert Godard was appointed by the city government in 1483 to be keeper of the ditches in the sub-ward of St Stephen's. In return for his work he was given lodgings over St Stephen's (or Needham) Gate, and so he may have also acted as a part time gate-keeper.[30] The hermits of St Giles Gate, Bishopsgate and Berstreet Gate may, too, have acted as gate-keepers, and the hermits of Newbridge may have looked after the bridge of that name. Hermits, however, were not confined to particular places in the way that anchorites were bound to their anchorages. How they might wander abroad is well illustrated by a bequest to Richard Ferneys from Robert Baxter, a former mayor. He left Ferneys £40 in his will dated 1429 "to make a pilgrimage for me to Rome, going round there fifteen times in a great circle, and also to Jerusalem, doing in both places as a true pilgrim does." [31] And Robert Farnell, a hermit from Norwich, was among the pilgrims at the English Hospice in Rome in the spring of 1514.[32]

As for their education and guidance, some could rely on the religious orders to which they belonged. Even among those who were not

[25] *Ancrene Riwle*, ed. Dobson, pp. 15-38 and 311.

[26] *Register of Chichele*, ed. Jacob, 3: 413; N.C.C., Reg. Gelour, fol. 91v (Poringland).

[27] See p. 233.

[28] *Norwich Depositions*, ed. Stone, no. 216.

[29] Clay, *Hermits*, pp. 57 and 71.

[30] N.C.R., Case 16d, Proceedings of the Municipal Assembly, Book 1 (1434-1491), fol. 122r.

[31] N.C.C., Reg. Surflete, fol. 86v (Baxter).

[32] George Hay, "Pilgrims and the Hospice," *The Venerabile* 21 (1962) 142.

members of religious orders, some probably relied on priests and nuns at the religious houses and parish churches to which their anchorages were attached. For example, when Emma Stapleton was received as an anchoress at the Carmelite friary, Thomas Netter, the prior-provincial of the English Carmelites, appointed the prior, the sub-prior and three other members of the friary to instruct her.[33] Little is known for certain about the books they read, or had read to them. Tyndale's translation of the New Testament and his *Obedience of a Christian Man* were presented to Katherine Manne, anchoress at the Dominican friary;[34] and the psalters bequeathed by Richard Ferneys[35] were the only books mentioned in their wills.[36] The most intriguing case is that of Julian of Norwich. As mentioned, there appear to have been no recluses in the city immediately before her to instruct her, and it is uncertain that she had been a nun. She said she was "unlettered"[37] and received her revelations directly from God,[38] but Walsh and Colledge are convinced that she was a very learned woman.[39] She may have instructed other recluses in the city.[40] Richard Ferney's bequests to various other hermits and anchorites[41] also suggest contacts among recluses — a kind of "recluse society" similar, albeit in a minor key, to the clerical society of the city.

Prayer was, no doubt, the chief means by which they hoped to make an impact on society. Its effects are difficult to measure. Testamentary bequests to them, about which more will be said later,[42] show that in Norwich they enjoyed considerable support from both clergy and laity. Partly this may have been support for the work of hermits as gate-keepers and guardians of bridges and ditches. Also people seem to have expected recluses to act as counsellors: King Henry v consulted an anchorite at Westminster Abbey at a critical moment in his life[43] and Margery Kempe consulted Julian of Norwich.[44] But counselling and helping with the

---

[33] Clay, *Hermits*, p. 137.

[34] See p. 164.

[35] See pp. 233-234.

[36] The other surviving wills are Thomas Bassett's (N.C.C., Reg. Spyltymber, fol. 169r-v) and John Levot's (ibid., fol. 224v).

[37] Julian, *Revelations*, Long Text, chapter 2, ed. Colledge, p. 285.

[38] Ibid., Long Text, chapters 2 and 4, ed. Colledge, pp. 285 and 294.

[39] Ibid., ed. Colledge, pp. 41-51.

[40] See p. 58.

[41] See p. 233.

[42] See pp. 130-131.

[43] Kenneth B. McFarlane, *Lancastrian Kings and Lollard Knights* (Oxford 1972), p. 124.

[44] Margery Kempe, *The Book*, 1: 18, ed. Meech, pp. 42-43.

upkeep of the city were secondary roles. Their principal task was to lead a life of private prayer; and the number of them in the city, as well as the number of bequests left to them in wills, suggest that such a life was valued.

As men and women trying to lead religious lives outside the normal framework of the priesthood and religious orders, anchorites and hermits were in a sense an anti-order. However, in Norwich there is little evidence of conflict between them and the ecclesiastical authorities. Thomas Scrope quarrelled with his prior-provincial, but before he became an anchor. Katherine Manne alone is known to have been suspected of heresy.[45] As for Julian's *Revelations*, Dr Molinari has argued at length for its orthodoxy.[46] It is true that the book shows little interest in the institutional Church, but a mystical treatise can scarcely be expected to, and Julian praised obedience to the teaching of the Church.[47] There were never sufficient anchors and hermits in the city to affect seriously the number of priests and male religious; but the community at Carrow Priory, which was the only nunnery in or near Norwich, might have been considerably affected both by its own nuns becoming anchoresses and by possible recruits to the nunnery becoming anchoresses instead. Yet far from showing hostility towards anchorites, the nunnery and several of the religious houses of men appear to have encouraged them by providing anchorages both for lay men and women and for priests and religious.

ii. Communities Resembling Beguinages

As a form of religious life outside the priesthood and the established religious orders, the solitary life of a hermit or anchorite was much more popular in late medieval England than life in a community. In Continental Europe, on the other hand, especially in the Low Countries and the Rhineland, beguinages and similar communities appear to have enjoyed the greater popularity.

Norwich is of special interest in this matter since it was perhaps the only town in late medieval England known to have contained communities of lay women closely resembling beguinages.[48] Information about them is, however, tantalizingly slight and barely extends beyond

---

[45] See p. 164.

[46] Paolo Molinari, *Julian of Norwich* (London 1958), p. 197.

[47] Julian, *Revelations*, Long Text, chapters 46 and 80, ed. Colledge, pp. 494 and 707-708.

[48] It should be noted that the communities in Norwich were never called beguinages in the records referring to them.

knowledge of their existence. Two groups flourished briefly in the mid fifteenth century. An unknown number of women, variously described as sisters living together[49] and as sisters dedicated to chastity,[50] dwelt in a tenement of a certain John Pellet (or Pyllet) in St Swithin's parish from about 1427 to 1444. Three women in a second group were living in a tenement in St Laurence's parish shortly before the first group disappeared from trace. The second group had been reduced to two sisters by 1457 and disappeared from trace after 1472. The women were described as sisters[51] or poor women,[52] dedicated to chastity[53] or under a vow of chastity,[54] and dedicated to God.[55] According to Blomefield and Taylor, who did not quote their sources, a third group of sisters were living together under a religious vow at an unknown date in a house in the churchyard of St Peter Hungate parish.

The tenement inhabited by the second group of women had belonged to a certain John Asger. Asger was then a very uncommon name in Norwich and throughout East Anglia.[56] It is therefore very possible that the owner of the tenement was one of the only two John Asgers known to us: either John Asger, merchant of Bruges and mayor of Norwich in 1426 and who died in 1436; or his son, also called John, who was born in Zeeland in the Low Countries, was a citizen of Norwich and died in the same year as his father.[57] The year 1436 was six years before the group is known to have existed. But the fact that the house was constantly referred to as "a tenement recently belonging to John Asger"[58] suggests that there may have been a connection: either that the group had in fact existed earlier and had been given the tenement by one of the Asgers, or that one of them had left it to be given to such a group if it were formed. So it may well be that the communities in Norwich had a least a tenuous link with the Low Countries, the heart of the beguine movement.

---

[49] "Sorores pariter comorantes" (N.C.C., Reg. Hyrnyng, fol. 153v [Wilby]), "sorores simul comorantes" (N.C.C., Reg. Surflete, fol. 86r [Baxter]).

[50] "Sorores castitati dedicate" (N.C.C., Reg. Surflete, fol. 55r [Christian]).

[51] "Sorores" (N.C.C., Reg. Aleyn, fol. 59r [Veautre]).

[52] "Mulieres paupercule" (N.C.C., Reg. Brosyard, fol. 160r [Child]).

[53] "Castitati dedit'" (N.C.C., Reg. Aleyn, fol. 59r [Veautre]).

[54] "Votum castitatis emittentes" (N.C.C., Reg. Aleyn, fol. 112r [Estwegt]), "votum castitatis admittentes" (N.C.C., Reg. Aleyn, fol. 123r [Horsley]).

[55] "Deo dedicate" (N.C.C., Reg. Doke, fol. 177v [Braklee]).

[56] *Index of Wills Proved in the Consistory Court of Norwich, 1370-1550, and Wills among the Norwich Enrolled Deeds, 1298-1508*, ed. Margaret A. Farrow, Norfolk Record Society, 16 (1943-1945), p. 13.

[57] Hardy, *Mayors of Norwich*, p. 20; *Cal. Pat. R., 1429-1436*, p. 112.

[58] N.C.C., Reg. Wylbey, fol. 13r (Dunston), and Reg. Aleyn, fols. 15v (Alcock), 61r (Dyra), 112v-113r (Estwegt) and 123r (Horsley).

The communities in Norwich resembled Continental beguinages inasmuch as they appear to have begun as informal communities of women living religious lives outside the framework of the established religious orders. They differed from the latter in several ways. They appeared several centuries after beguines first appeared on the Continent, and at a time when most beguinages were becoming institutionalised, developing into convents or charitable institutions such as hospitals and almshouses. The communities in Norwich never became institutionalised in this way, and may perhaps be seen as a brief return to the primitive spirit of the beguine movement. On the Continent ecclesiastical authorities brought pressure to bear on beguinages either to become clearly defined institutions, with a definite Rule and so on, or to dissolve;[59] but there is no evidence that pressure of this kind was brought to bear on the communities in Norwich, and there is nothing to suggest that they incurred the suspicions of heresy that plagued beguines on the Continent. Why they faded away is not clear. Lack of recruits would appear to be the most likely reason, but lack of financial support may have been a contributory factor.[60]

iii. "Lay Religious"

Hermits and anchorites, and communities resembling beguinages do not appear to have come into much conflict with the ecclesiastical authorities in Norwich. They represent, nevertheless, a movement away from the established structures of the Church. Some of the laity sought the status of what might be called "lay religious" in the opposite direction, namely by associating more closely with a religious order while remaining in the lay state. Some of the means taken are discussed elsewhere: burial in the church or cemetery of a religious house;[61] founding a chantry in a religious house;[62] belonging to a confraternity attached to a religious house.[63] In addition, some citizens were confraters of the houses themselves, positions that admit of no clear definition but which normally gave participation in the rewards gained by the prayers and good works of the members of the house in return for some kind of benefaction or for observing the Rule of the house in a mitigated form. Margaret East, for

---

[59] Richard W. Southern, *Western Society and the Church in the Middle Ages* (Harmondsworth 1970), pp. 329-331; Ernest W. McDonnell, *The Beguines and Beghards in Medieval Culture* (New Brunswick 1954), pp. 521, 563 and 573.
[60] See p. 131.
[61] See pp. 12-13.
[62] See pp. 96-97, 107-108 and 212-219.
[63] See pp. 73-74 and 208.

example, was described as a sister of the Franciscan friary[64] and Agnes Thorpe, the widow of an alderman, mentioned her letters of confraternity with the London Charterhouse.[65] Others hoped to become confraters posthumously. Thomas Trowse, for example, left money to the Cathedral Priory so that the priory might in return write his name in its martyrology, keep his anniversary in perpetuity and "do for him as they would for one of their own deceased brethren." [66] Some of the laity went so far as to live in the religious houses, though their motives may have been economic, or the desire for a comfortable retirement, more than religious. John Molicourt, for example, was said to be living in the Carmelite friary when he made his will, though his wife was still alive and it is not clear whether she was allowed to live with him; and Sir Robert Norwich was said to be living with the prior of the Cathedral Priory when he made his will, and he begged the prior and monks to receive him as a brother of their chapter.[67] The Close and Patent Rolls show that the priory granted corrodies to a number of lay men and women, though it appears to have given them against its own wishes and under pressure from the Crown.[68] Others preferred the Benedictine nunnery of Carrow. Thomas Fyncham and his wife, for example, had a dwelling within the nunnery and in 1445 it passed to a former mayor and his wife, Thomas and Margaret Wetherby, whose daughter was a nun there.[69]

The measures taken show, in various ways, that the laity's search for a deeper religious life did not express itself exclusively in a flight away from the established institutions of the Church.

B. Craft Guilds and Pious Confraternities[70]

Craft guilds and pious confraternities entered their Golden Age in the late Middle Ages, growing dramatically in number and importance

---

[64] N.C.C., Reg. A. Caston, fol. 203v (East).

[65] See p. 125.

[66] N.C.C., Reg. Heydon, fol. 20r (Trowse).

[67] N.C.C., Reg. Jekkys, fol. 206r (Molicourt), and Reg. Doke, fol. 5r (Norwich).

[68] *Cal. Pat. R., 1345-1348*, p. 539; *Cal. Pat. R., 1446-1452*, p. 134; *Cal. Close R., 1461-1468*, p. 164; *Cal. Pat. R., 1476-1485*, p. 307.

[69] *Cal. Pat. R., 1441-1446*, p. 366; N.C.C., Reg. Wylbey, fol. 31v (Wetherby).

[70] Throughout this section see Appendix 8 (pp. 204-210). Contemporary documents did not distinguish consistently between guilds and confraternities. The following distinction has been used in this book in order to avoid confusion: (pious) confraternity signifies a confraternity that was chiefly religious in nature but was not connected with a craft or a trade; (craft) guild signifies the guild of a craft or trade. It should be remembered

throughout Europe.[71] Their growth challenged the old order in the
Church, partly because they cut across the structures and boundaries of
parishes and partly because most of them were controlled by the laity
rather than by the clergy.

The returns made by English guilds and confraternities in 1389, in
response to the Guild Ordinance of the previous year,[72] list 19 guilds and
confraternities in Norwich. Only Lynn with 51, London with 41 and
Lincoln with 30 had more.[73] Few of them in England, according to the
returns, had been founded before the fourteenth century.[74] In Norwich
only one or two confraternities were said to have been founded before this
date, though other evidence shows that four guilds had existed in the city
in the late thirteenth century. Confraternities and the religious activities of
guilds were, for the most part, brought to an end by act of Parliament in
1547.[75] The present study therefore covers much of the period during
which they are of interest to the ecclesiastical historian.

i. Craft Guilds

Seven of the 19 returns coming from Norwich in 1389 were made by
craft guilds: those of the barbers, candlemakers, carpenters, peltiers,
tailors, artificers and operators, saddlers and spurriers. The returns give
the appearance that the seven guilds, like those of other English towns,[76]
were organisations whose chief functions were religious rather than the
exercise of economic or political control over crafts and trades. The chief
function of each guild was said to be the performance of various religious
activities on its annual guild-day, usually the celebration of a guild-Mass

---

that in Norwich, as in other English towns, the distinction between a craft or trade and its
guild was frequently blurred. At times there appears to have been a fairly clear distinction
between a guild as an institution and the craft or trade which it represented, though even
here it is often unclear as to whom membership of the guild was open; at other times the
terms "craft" and "guild" were used virtually synonymously, along with words such as
"mystery" or "occupation." Moreover the distinction between guilds as institutions and
"ad hoc" activities of crafts and trades was also frequently unclear.

[71] Rapp, L'Église, pp. 128-129; Étienne E. Delaruelle, Edmond-René Labande and
Paul Ourliac, L'Église au temps du Grand Schisme et de la crise conciliaire, Histoire de
l'Église, ed. Augustin Fliche and others, 14 (Paris 1962-1964), pp. 666-668.

[72] Cal. Close R., 1385-1389, p. 624.

[73] Herbert F. Westlake, The Parish Guilds of Mediaeval England (London 1919),
pp. 167-174, 180-188, 192-200 and 236-238.

[74] Ibid., pp. 138-238.

[75] John D. Mackie, The Earlier Tudors (Oxford 1952), p. 465; Philip Hughes, The
Reformation in England (London 1950-1954), 3: 152.

[76] Westlake, Parish Guilds, pp. 36-48 and 149-238.

and the offering of one or more votive candles to the church in which the Mass was said. Two of the guild-Masses were celebrated in the Cathedral and one each in Carrow Priory, the Carnary College, the College of St Mary in the Fields and St Michael's Chapel, a non-parochial chapel in the suburbs of the city attached to a cell of the Cathedral Priory. It is noticeable that none of them was celebrated in a parish church. Some of the guilds said they provided funerals, Requiem Masses and other religious services for deceased members, and the peltiers' guild said it maintained two chaplains "serving God" in the Cathedral.[77] Some of them claimed to provide financial assistance to members who had fallen into poverty. But pageantry and feasting, which later became so important, were mentioned in only one return: at the annual Mass of the peltiers' guild, which was dedicated to St William, the boy from Norwich allegedly murdered by the Jews of the city in the twelfth century, "a knave child, innocent, bearing a candle that day weighing two pounds" was to be "led between two good men, tokening the glorious martyr"; and the members of the guild were to have a feast together.[78]

It is doubtful, however, whether the guilds were in fact the almost exclusively religious organizations that their returns suggest. The Guild Ordinance of 1388, which ordered the returns, was issued by the king on the authority of the Cambridge Parliament of that year.[79] The parliament, according to the continuator of Higden's *Polychronicon*, wanted to suppress guilds and use their goods for the war against France.[80] For this reason, and given the general atmosphere of civil disturbance in the 1380s, it is not surprising that they claimed to possess little wealth and barely mentioned their political importance or their economic role in regulating crafts and trades.[81] Moreover the returns may well understate the number of guilds since there was little incentive for them to make returns apart from the risk of detection by the central government. But even if their number has been understated, as well as their political and economic importance, with which this study is not directly concerned, there is no reason to think that the returns do not give a more or less accurate description of the religious activities of at least some of the guilds.

[77] See p. 212.

[78] *English Guilds*, ed. Toulmin Smith, Early English Text Society, 40 (London 1870), pp. 30-31.

[79] *Cal. Close R., 1385-1389*, p. 624.

[80] *Polychronicon Ranulphi Higden*, ed. Churchill Babington and Joseph R. Lumby, Rolls Series (London 1865-1866), 9: 191.

[81] Westlake, *Parish Guilds*, pp. 36-48 and 149-238.

After 1389 the fullest descriptions come from two sets of ordinances for crafts issued by the city government in 1449 and 1543.[82] As ordinances they describe how the city government wished guilds to function, but in so far as they were codifications of existing customs they also provide a description of how the guilds were functioning in practice. They indicate that the guilds were by these dates primarily economic bodies regulating particular crafts, but they mention most of the religious activities which featured in the returns of 1389. Both sets of ordinances ordered crafts to provide for each member who died a Dirge and a Mass which living members were to attend, and those of 1543 ordered people practising a particular craft to attend a Mass for all the living and dead members on some day after the guild-Mass was celebrated. The ordinances of 1449 ordered crafts to keep an annual day "of solemnity in worship of their avow," and those of 1543, together with a list of guild-days that follows,[83] provide a fuller description of the religious services that were to be performed on the guild-days. Sixty-one crafts, singly in the cases of the tanners and the worsted-weavers, but otherwise in small groups, were to hold their guild-days annually on the Thursday before Pentecost, the feast of Corpus Christi and thirteen Sundays between Pentecost and the end of October. On the appointed day the wardens of the guild or guilds in question were to offer lights to burn before the Sacrament in St John's Chapel in the Common Hall,[84] and the members were to attend a guild-Mass which in most cases was to be celebrated in the Common Hall but in some cases was to be in the Cathedral and in the case of the tanners in St Swithin's parish church. The ordinances of 1543 also provided for the support of a chantry: each member of each craft was ordered to pay a penny a year to support a chantry priest who was to "sing" in the Common Hall for the king and queen, the prince and the king's council, the living and dead members of the guilds and for the prosperity of the city of Norwich.

The ordinances of 1449 also mentioned processions. "All those persons that shall be clad in the clothing of crafts ... shall at all times be charged to all walkings and ridings to the worship of the avow of the craft on the principal day" (presumably the craft's annual guild-day). And crafts were to be ready to process in their livery to the Cathedral, with the mayor, sheriffs and aldermen of the city, or to any other place as the mayor

---

[82] *Records of Norwich*, ed. Hudson, 2: 278-310.

[83] Ibid., 2: 310-311.

[84] The Common Hall (not to be confused with the Guild Hall) had been the church of the Dominican friary until the latter was dissolved in 1538.

should direct, on the feasts of All Saints, Christmas and the Epiphany. By about 1489, possibly as early as 1449, thirty-two crafts were also processing to the College of St Mary in the Fields on the feast of Corpus Christi. The crafts, each with its banner, were preceded by torchbearers, surrounding the Sacrament, and followed by the sheriffs and the mayor, with the aldermen, with books or beads (presumably rosary beads) in their hands, bringing up the rear. By 1543 over seventy crafts were taking part in this procession, which then started and finished at the Common Hall.[85]

It was out of a procession on Whit Monday that the mystery plays performed by the guilds appear to have developed. In 1527 St Luke's guild, which was described in 1543 as composed of pewterers, braziers, plumbers, bellfounders, glaziers, stainers and members of other, unnamed occupations,[86] claimed that it had performed every year "of long time past" on Whit Monday "many disguisings and pageants of the lives and martyrdoms of many holy saints as well as of many other light and feigned figures and pictures of other persons and beasts ... at the time of the procession then making a great circuit of the said city." The guild claimed that many people from the surrounding countryside came to watch the pageants, but the cost of producing them fell on the guild alone and had ruined it. In order to relieve itself of the burden the guild asked the mayor, the sheriffs and the Common Council to order each craft to produce a pageant for the procession; to which they agreed, no doubt remembering the economic value of the pageants as a tourist attraction.[87] Once again the city government appears to have been partly responsible for the expansion of the religious activities of the guilds. It was probably as a result of the agreement that there came to be compiled a list of crafts and the plays performed by them which can be dated to about 1530 and which is to be found among the records of the city government. Sixty-three crafts were listed under twelve plays: Creation of the World; Hell Cart; Paradise; Abel and Cain; Noah's Ship; Abraham and Isaac; Moses and Aaron with the Children of Israel and Pharaoh with his Knights; Conflict of David and Goliath; The Birth of Christ with Shepherds and the Three Kings of Cologne; The Baptism of Christ; The Resurrection; The Holy Ghost. The plays were probably performed on Whit Monday,[88]

---

[85] *Records of Norwich*, ed. Hudson, 2: 312-313, where "c. 1453" should read "c. 1543" (see ibid., 2: 312, n. 1).

[86] Ibid., 2: 311.

[87] *Non-Cycle Plays and Fragments*, ed. Norman Davis, Early English Text Society, Supplementary Text 1 (London 1970), pp. xxvii-xxviii.

[88] Ibid., pp. xxxi-xxxii.

following the city government's decision, rather than on the feast of
Corpus Christi which was the more usual day in England for the
performance of such plays.[89] Since they were to take place "at the time of
the procession then making a great circuit of the said city," they were
probably performed on moveable floats as was frequently the custom in
England.[90] Indeed "Paradise" was described as "a pageant ... on a four-
wheel cart." [91]

"Paradise" is the only one of the twelve plays whose text is in any way
still known,[92] but plays corresponding to all of them except the "Conflict
of David and Goliath" are to be found in other cycles.[93] The plays form a
complete cycle, though an unusually short one, containing only half as
many plays as the Chester cycle, the shortest of the four great ones (York,
Towneley, Chester and Coventry). The Norwich cycle was unusual, too,
in that the proportion of Old to New Testament plays was two to one
whereas the proportion in each of the four great cycles was less than one
to three. The absence of a play about the Passion of Christ is also most
unusual since this is so central to the Christian message and cycles of
mystery plays developed in part at least out of the liturgical representation
of the Passion at Holy Week and since, moreover, each of the four great
cycles contained several plays about it.[94] Still, we have here evidence
for Norwich of this form of popular education in the Christian faith
combined with celebration, coming to a climax, interestingly enough,
after the Reformation had already begun on the Continent; though it may
well be that some of the plays, or similar ones, had existed considerably
earlier, before they were gathered into a cycle and so brought to the
attention of historians.

It may be said, in conclusion, that the growth in the economic
importance of guilds in Norwich during the late Middle Ages was
accompanied by an expansion, not a decline, in their religious activities.
Thus, most of the religious activities mentioned in the returns of 1389
appear to have continued until the Reformation; the number of crafts

[89] Edmund K. Chambers, *The Medieval Stage* (Oxford 1903), 2: 138; Hardin Craig,
English Religious Drama of the Middle Ages (Oxford 1955), pp. 127-132.

[90] Chambers, *Medieval Stage*, 2: 95-96; Craig, *English Religious Drama*, pp. 121-125
and 301.

[91] *Non-Cycle Plays*, ed. Davis, p. xxxv.

[92] The text, in so far as it is now known, is printed in ibid., pp. 8-18.

[93] Chambers, *Medieval Stage*, 2: 407-436; Craig, *English Religious Drama*, pp. 300-
301.

[94] Chambers, *Medieval Stage*, 2: 408, 410-411, 413-414 and 417-418; Craig, *English
Religious Drama*, pp. 131-132 and 301.

known to have held annual guild-days grew from 7 to 61 between 1389 and 1543; and guilds became involved in processions and plays. The guilds were composed of, and controlled by, the laity; they were largely independent of the parochial system; and part of the initiative in the expansion of their religious activities appears to have come from the city government. But their importance in the religious life of the city, and the extent to which they challenged the old order of parishes and religious houses, should not be exaggerated. They needed the clergy for some of their religious activities and some of their services were held in churches. They did not compare in importance with the livery companies and craft guilds of fifteenth-century London,[95] still less with the "Scuole" of Renaissance Venice.[96] Nor do they appear as impressive, or as having as many charitable or ceremonial activities, as the craft guilds of Coventry or York, provincial capitals of similar standing to Norwich. Thus several guilds in York, unlike any in Norwich, had their own halls and managed alms-houses or hospitals;[97] while the greater importance of guilds in Coventry may have been because the paucity of parish churches in the city (only two) created a vacuum which the guilds were able to fill.[98] The processions, the mystery plays and the annual guild-days with their mixture of feasting and religious services were colourful events which must have made an impression on religion in Norwich and helped to cement Christianity into the social life of the city. But the activities were confined to a few days of each year, and nothing suggests that guilds supplanted parishes as the single most important religious institution in the lives of most citizens.

ii. Pious Confraternities

Late medieval Norwich contained many pious confraternities that were not connected with crafts or trades. They fall into two main categories: those connected with parishes and those connected with religious houses or non-parochial churches. A few confraternities are not known to have been connected in either of these ways, though this may simply be the result of lack of evidence.

[95] George Unwin, *The Gilds and Companies of London*, 4th ed. (London 1963), pp. 155-217.

[96] Brian Pullan, *Rich and Poor in Renaissance Venice* (Oxford 1971), pp. 33-193.

[97] *VCH City of York*, pp. 96 and 481-482; David M. Palliser, "The Trade Gilds of Tudor York," in *Crisis and Order in English Towns 1500-1700*, ed. Peter Clark and Paul Slack (London 1972), pp. 96 and 110.

[98] Charles Phythian-Adams, "Ceremony and the Citizen: The Communal Year in Coventry," in *Crisis and Order*, ed. Clark, pp. 57-85.

Twelve of them made returns in 1389 in reply to the Guild Ordinance of 1388. Three of the twelve will be discussed separately: the confraternities of Corpus Christi,[99] the Annunciation of St Mary[100] and St George.[101] Regarding the other nine, the chief duty of their members was said to be attendance at the confraternity's annual Mass. Most of them said they maintained one or more votive lights in the church in which they celebrated their Mass, offered alms to members who fell into poverty and provided various religious services for those who died. St Catherine's and St Christopher's confraternities had a few other customs: each of them held an annual feast; quarrels among members of St Catherine's were to go before other members before being taken to a Common Law court; and the return of St Christopher's contains an interesting prayer indicating popular interest in the recovery of the true Cross and in healing the Schism, which the aldermen and brethren of the confraternity were to say whenever they met together: they were to pray for the pope, the king and most other ranks of secular and ecclesiastical society – including the patriarch of Jerusalem – for the Holy Land and "the holy Cross, that God of his might and his mercy bring it out of heathen power into the rule of holy Church, and that God of his mercy make peace and unity in holy Church." [102]

Wills provide almost all our information about the nine confraternities after 1389. They also provide most of our information about some 36 other confraternities known to have existed in the city at various times during the late Middle Ages. One of them, the Bachelery confraternity, will be discussed separately.[103] Of the others, 19 or 20 were attached to parishes, eight to friaries, one or two to Carrow Priory and one to the Cathedral; and about five are not known to have been connected with any such institutions. Most of these 44[104] confraternities appear to have had a short life. None of them is known to have existed throughout the late Middle Ages, and only four of them are known to have enjoyed a continuous existence approaching a hundred years. But far from their number declining as the Reformation and the dissolution of confraternities approached, it reached a peak in the early sixteenth century: 12 or 13 existed at some time between 1370 and 1400, 10 between 1440 and 1470, 21 between 1510 and 1532.

---

[99] See pp. 75-76.
[100] See pp. 77-78.
[101] See pp. 78-81.
[102] *English Guilds*, ed. Smith, pp. 21-23.
[103] See p. 78.
[104] I.e., 9 + 36 − 1.

Nobody from Norwich rivalled Degenhard Pfeffinger, the councillor of the elector of Saxony, who belonged to at least 35 confraternities at his death in 1519![105] But in so far as a bequest to a confraternity in a will is an indication that the donor was a member of it, then a fair number of citizens belonged to more than one confraternity, including some in other parts of the country. By far the most popular of the latter, in terms of testamentary bequests, was Our Lady's confraternity at Boston in Lincolnshire,[106] a popularity no doubt explained partly by the town's connections with Norwich through the wool and cloth trades. The furthest afield was St Christopher's confraternity in York, to which a mercer called John Fraunces left a bequest;[107] and Dr Hammer discovered a citizen of Norwich among the members of St Thomas's confraternity in Oxford.[108] Membership of at least many confraternities in Norwich appears to have been open to both clergy and laity, men and women. How far the clergy controlled the confraternities is not clear, though at least in some cases a confraternity attached to a parish appears to have counted the parish priest among its members,[109] and so presumably he had some influence over it. Nor is it clear whether the activities mentioned in the returns of 1389 were adopted, or added to, by later confraternities. Further information is limited to a few suggestions that members of some confraternities were expected to attend various religious services when a member died[110] and evidence about their chantries.[111]

Corpus Christi, or the Priests', Confraternity. The confraternity of Corpus Christi – also called the priests' confraternity – said in its return of 1389 that it had been founded in 1278.[112] This was only fourteen years after Pope Urban IV had established Corpus Christi as an official feast of the universal Church,[113] and if the claim was correct the confraternity was, so far as is known, the oldest one in England dedicated to this

---

[105] Theodor Kolde, *Friedrich der Weise und die Anfänge der Reformation* (Erlangen 1881), pp. 15 and 74-75.

[106] E.g., N.C.C., Reg. Gylys, fol. 77r (Bisby), and Reg. Gelour, fol. 92r (Poringland).

[107] PROB/11/12 (Reg. Moone, 1500-1501), fol. 7 (Fraunces).

[108] Carl I. Hammer, "The Town-Gown Confraternity of St Thomas the Martyr in Oxford," *Mediaeval Studies* 39 (1977) 473.

[109] E.g., N.C.C., Reg. Harsyk, fol. 115r (Buckingham), and Reg. Palgrave, fol. 81v (Bower).

[110] E.g., N.C.C., Reg. Robinson or Fedymontt, fol. 6r (Swan).

[111] See p. 94.

[112] "The Hitherto Unpublished Certificates of Norwich Gilds," ed. John Tingey, *Norfolk Archaeology* 16 (1905-1907) 300.

[113] *Corpus iuris canonici*, Clementis Pape V constitutiones, 3.16.1.

mystery[114] and the oldest of all the confraternities in Norwich with the possible exception of the Annunciation of St Mary's.[115] It was unique in Norwich in that all its members appear to have been clerics (both beneficed and unbeneficed).

According to the return[116] the members of the confraternity held an annual procession at the College of St Mary in the Fields on the octave day of the feast of Corpus Christi and afterwards attended the Mass of Corpus Christi in the college chapel. This was followed by a dinner which was said to be for the sole purpose of fostering the participants' love for each other! They were to attend Exequies the same evening and a Requiem Mass the following morning, and they were expected to attend various religious services when a member died – a practice that wills show continued until the Reformation.[117]

Wills prove that the confraternity had a continuous existence until 1546[118] and it appears to have been revived briefly during the reign of Mary.[119] Its membership appears to have remained exclusively clerical; thus it was frequently described in wills as the priests' confraternity and none of the laity is known to have left a bequest to it. It said in its return of 1389 that it had been founded by the chaplains of the College of St Mary in the Fields[120] and its religious services were held in the college. These connections with the college, together with the fact that none of the regular clergy is known to have been a member,[121] suggest that it was the preserve of the secular clergy, and, assuming again that people normally left bequests only to confraternities to which they belonged, it looks as though a good proportion and a wide cross-section of all the secular priests of the city were members of it, with a quarter of those whose wills survive[122] and were written between 1440 and 1489 leaving a bequest to it, a half between 1490 and 1532. It appears to have been a kind of craft guild for priests, and was another aspect of clerical society in the city.

---

[114] Westlake, *Parish Guilds*, p. 49.
[115] See pp. 208-210.
[116] "Hitherto Unpublished Certificates," ed. Tingey, pp. 300-302.
[117] E.g., N.C.C., Reg. Jekkys, fol. 142v (Bolytowth).
[118] N.C.C., Reg. Wymer, fol. 6r (Pennyman).
[119] "Hitherto Unpublished Certificates," ed. Tingey, p. 285.
[120] Ibid., p. 300.
[121] It is just possible that the absence of the regular clergy is more apparent than real, due to the fact that the membership of the confraternity is known almost exclusively from wills, and the regular clergy did not make them (see p. 114).
[122] See pp. 224-225.

The Confraternity of the Annunciation of St Mary. The confraternities of the Annunciation of St Mary, of the Bachelery and of St George are of special interest partly because they appear to have succeeded each other as the most important confraternity in the city and partly because they enjoyed close connections with the city government.

The confraternity of the Annunciation of St Mary claimed in its return of 1389 to have been founded in time out of mind. Like the confraternity of Corpus Christi, it said that on a certain day each year it celebrated Mass and the service of Exequies in the College of St Mary in the Fields, and on the following morning a Mass for deceased members, and that it held an annual procession. The procession started and finished at the college and was held on the feast of Corpus Christi – perhaps an indication of its precedence over Corpus Christi confraternity's procession which had to be content with the octave day of the feast – and during it the brothers and sisters of the confraternity, carrying lighted torches, were to surround the Sacrament on its journey. (It may well have been out of this procession that there developed in the fifteenth century the very similar procession of crafts on the same day.)[123] In 1389 the wardens of the confraternity were Walter Bixton and Henry Lomynour who were among the most prominent inhabitants of the city, both having been several times bailiffs of Norwich and members of Parliament for the city. Moreover John of Gaunt, duke of Lancaster, seems to have been considered a member. If the size of its undertakings as well as of its fees and fines is anything to judge by, its other members (who included women) must in general have been fairly wealthy. At this time, too, it was claiming to employ two chantry priests to say Mass and the Divine Office in the College of St Mary in the Fields for the king and the duke of Lancaster and their ancestors, and for the living and dead members of the confraternity, and a Carmelite priest to do likewise in the Carmelite friary.[124] Although basically a lay confraternity, it does not appear to have been in conflict with the clergy. Indeed, it said in its return that it had been founded to support the College of St Mary in the Fields, the employment of two chantry priests being part of this support, and it annually offered a chalice or a book or a vestment to the college.[125]

The confraternity disappears from trace after 1402.[126] It may have become absorbed into the Bachelery confraternity, which begins to appear

[123] See p. 71.
[124] See p. 213.
[125] "Hitherto Unpublished Certificates," ed. Tingey, pp. 274-278 and 288-300.
[126] N.C.C., Reg. Harsyk, fol. 294r (Shouldham).

in records shortly after this date and which was also connected with the College of St Mary in the Fields. Possibly the two confraternities were identical, as Hudson and Tingey thought.[127]

The Bachelery Confraternity. The Bachelery confraternity was first mentioned in 1414 when it was described as a group of citizens, allied by oath with the oligarchs of the city, who prevented the commons from freely electing the mayor and sheriffs and damaged the city's Worsted Seld by diverting business away from it to the private houses of members of the confraternity.[128] It was again involved in the politics of the city in the 1440s, this time on the side of the majority of the citizens against an alliance of ecclesiastics and a faction in the city government led by Thomas Wetherby.[129] And in 1443 it was described, in its defence, as a meeting of citizens immemorially held on certain days in the College of St Mary in the Fields in honour of St Mary the Virgin.[130] Despite the paucity of surviving evidence about the confraternity, it was clearly an important – perhaps the most important – confraternity in the city during at least part of its apparently brief existence, though it seems to have been more a political and social body than a religious one. No more is heard of it after 1443. Hudson and Tingey thought it was probably absorbed into St George's confraternity.[131]

St George's Confraternity. St George's confraternity claimed to have been founded in 1385,[132] and it was the only confraternity in the city known to have survived the Reformation. After changes in its constitution in about 1547[133] it survived as the Company of St George into the eighteenth century.[134] Its return of 1389[135] suggests that at that time it was similar to most other confraternities in the city and lacked the special status of the confraternity of the Annunciation of St Mary. In 1417, however, it became the only confraternity in late medieval Norwich to acquire a royal charter[136] and it seems to have taken over, together with

---

[127] *Records of Norwich*, ed. Hudson, 2: xlii.
[128] Ibid., 1: 72 and 74-75.
[129] Ibid., 1: 341; see below, pp. 146-151.
[130] Ibid., 1: 341-342.
[131] Ibid., 1: c, and 2: cxlii.
[132] *English Guilds*, ed. Smith, p. 17.
[133] *Records of the Gild of St George in Norwich, 1389-1547*, ed. Mary Grace, Norfolk Record Society, 9 (no place, 1937), p. 25.
[134] Benjamin Mackerell, "Account of the Company of St George in Norwich," *Norfolk Archaeology* 3 (1852) 372-374.
[135] *English Guilds*, ed. Smith, pp. 17-18.
[136] *Records of St George*, ed. Grace, pp. 28-29.

the Bachelery confraternity for a time, the position of eminence among the confraternities of the city. It is unique, too, in the extent of its surviving records: its account-rolls survive for many years between 1420 and 1547,[137] and the minute-book of its assemblies from 1451 to 1547.[138] The records show that it conducted, for the most part on a rather more exalted scale, almost all the religious and other activities that are to be found scattered among the other confraternities of the city. They also show that its activities changed little between 1420 and 1547.

The charter of 1417 stated that the confraternity had maintained a chantry priest in the Cathedral for the last thirty years, and the chantry survived into the 1540s.[139] Moreover it claimed in its return of 1389 to provide various religious services for members who died and alms for those who fell into poverty,[140] and its records suggest that both obligations were met. In some cases the alms were substantial: two men and "Father Clifford," members of the confraternity said to have fallen into poverty, were each granted sixpence a week for a year in 1533;[141] and Robert Clifford, another member said to have fallen into poverty, received sixpence a week for three years between 1530 and 1533.[142]

The confraternity's annual festivities comprised a mixture of religious services, feasting and pageantry centred around the feast of St George, or some other day if the feast fell near Easter.[143] On that day members were to attend Mass in the Cathedral, and various religious services on that and the following day, for the benefactors and dead members of the confraternity and for King Henry v who had granted the charter in 1417.[144] The charter gave the confraternity the right to hold an annual dinner, and this took place after the Mass in the Cathedral. At first it was held in the Dominican friary but in 1473 it was decided to seek a move to the Bishop's Palace and it was held there on at least a few occasions. It was evidently an elaborate and costly meal: the four members whose duty it was to bear the cost of it in 1533 were prepared to pay up to £9 among them to be discharged from the obligation.[145] By the early fifteenth

[137] N.C.R., Cases 8e and 8f, Account Rolls of the Guild of St George, 1420/1 to 1546/7.
[138] *Records of St George*, ed. Grace, pp. 43-157.
[139] See p. 212.
[140] *English Guilds*, ed. Smith, pp. 17-18.
[141] *Records of St George*, ed. Grace, p. 134.
[142] N.C.R., Case 8f, Account Rolls of the Guild of St George, 1530/1 to 1532/3.
[143] *Records of St George*, ed. Grace, p. 15.
[144] Ibid., pp. 18-19.
[145] Ibid., pp. 18-19, 28, 72, 86 and 90; N.C.R., Case 8f, Account Rolls of the Guild of St George, 1532/3.

century the confraternity was also conducting an elaborate procession on its feast-day. The centre-piece was a pageant depicting the exploits of the saint, which included a man on horseback as St George and another in a model dragon, sometimes made more fiery by the use of gunpowder! A maiden on horseback was added in 1532. Also in the procession were the mayor and aldermen of the city, the members of the confraternity mounted on horses and clothed in its livery, and twenty-four priests, twelve in red copes and twelve in white ones; and throughout the proceedings the bells of the Cathedral were to be rung![146]

The confraternity was conspicuous for both the number and the social standing of its members. They numbered at least 120 in 1468/69 and nearly 200 in 1521/22, and on average 23 persons were entering the confraternity each year between 1430/31 and 1434/35.[147] Most members, no doubt, came from Norwich; but a considerable number of them are known to have come from East Anglian county families, including William de la Pole, earl of Suffolk, Sir John Fastolf, Sir Thomas Erpingham and several members of the Paston family.[148] Miss Grace noted that members of humble trades became members of the confraternity's Common Council despite an apparent attempt, sometime between 1452 and 1463, to exclude craftsmen and persons of humble rank from membership of the confraternity, or at least from its government.[149] (The failure of the attempt may explain why the entrance fee to the confraternity came down from half a mark to 1s. 6d. about that time.)[150] But the earlier entrance fee, the cost of the annual dinner which members met by turns out of their own pockets,[151] and financial contributions that were presumably expected of members in order to pay for various other activities, suggest that the confraternity was principally for wealthier citizens. It appears to have been governed exclusively by laymen, but its members included a number of clerics, including several bishops of Norwich,[152] several members of the Carmelite friary,[153] an anchor attached to the friary – probably Thomas Scrope[154] – and some women.[155]

---

[146] *Records of St George*, ed. Grace, pp. 16-18.
[147] N.C.R., Cases 8e and 8f, Account Rolls of the Guild of St George, 1430/1 to 1434/5, 1468/9 and 1521/2.
[148] *Records of St George*, ed. Grace, pp. 23-24.
[149] Ibid., pp. 13 and 23.
[150] N.C.R., Case 8e, Account Rolls of the Guild of St George, 1447/8 and 1461/2.
[151] *Records of St George*, ed. Grace, p. 18.
[152] Ibid., p. 24.
[153] Ibid., p. 24.
[154] N.C.R., Case 8e, Account Rolls of the Guild of St George, 1445/6; see p. 198.
[155] E.g., ibid., 1432/3 and 1433/4.

Its pre-eminence among the confraternities of Norwich was sealed in 1452 when it was united with the city government. The reasons for the union are not clear. It happened at a time when several conflicts involving the city were easing.[156] There is no direct evidence that the confraternity as a body was involved in the disputes, as the Bachelery confraternity appears to have been,[157] but some – probably many – of its members were involved as individuals.[158] The union may, therefore, have formed part of the settlement to the disputes. It enacted that the outgoing mayor of Norwich should automatically become the alderman of the confraternity the following year – a provision that is known to have been observed – that the aldermen of the city should automatically become members of the confraternity, and that common councillors should have the right to become members if they so wished; dismissal from the office of alderman or common councillor of the city was to bring automatic dismissal from the confraternity, and conversely dismissal from the confraternity was to bring loss of the city's liberties.[159] The confraternity became, in a sense, a department of the city government.

Conclusion. Lack of information makes it difficult to compare Norwich with other English towns. Probably the number of confraternities in Norwich was large, except in comparison with London. Thus 48 confraternities in Norwich, of which some 25 are known to have been attached to parishes, compares with 68 confraternities attached to parishes found by Unwin in late medieval London,[160] but only about 15 confraternities of various kinds known to have existed in late medieval York,[161] a provincial capital of similar standing to Norwich. With the notable exception of the confraternity of Corpus Christi, they were largely composed of, and probably largely controlled by, the laity. But they do not appear to have been fundamentally opposed to the clergy and the older religious institutions. They depended upon the clergy inasmuch as almost all of them had links with a particular parish or religious house and they needed priests for the performance of most of their religious activities. Despite their number, and with the exception of St George's confraternity and perhaps a few others, their activities do not appear to have been extensive and it seems probable that records would have survived if they had been

---

[156] See pp. 152-153.
[157] See p. 78.
[158] See *Records of St George*, ed. Grace, pp. 12 and 23-24.
[159] Ibid., pp. 13-14 and 39-43.
[160] Unwin, *Gilds of London*, pp. 367-370.
[161] *VCH City of York*, pp. 482-483.

so. Like the craft guilds, they were important but secondary features in the religious scenery of the city.

C. Devotions to Saints, Pilgrimages and Private Devotions

Various devotions to the saints enjoyed great popularity in the late Middle Ages and appear to have reached a climax on the eve of the Reformation.[162] At the same time many aspects of them were criticised by orthodox reformers as well as by those regarded as heretics. The official teaching of the Church encouraged devotion to the saints, as well as to the Persons of the Trinity, and to some extent specified the forms of such devotion, for example regarding the liturgy, relics and pilgrimages. Christians enjoyed, nevertheless, considerable freedom both as to which persons they wished to honour and as to the forms in which they expressed their devotion.

i. Christian Names, Patron Saints and Votive Lights

Devotion to a saint presumably influenced some parents in choosing names for their children. John, the name of the Baptist and of the Evangelist, appears to have been much the most popular male name in Norwich throughout the late Middle Ages.[163] Almost a third of the men whose wills survive bore it. William followed in popularity, being chosen for about fifteen percent. Both names enjoyed an international popularity,[164] William also being the name of the boy from Norwich who was venerated as a saint after allegedly being crucified by the Jews of the city in 1144. Each of Thomas and Robert were chosen for over eleven per cent, Richard for over five per cent. This means that the remarkably high proportion of three out of four men were called by one of only five names. Nicholas, Edmund and Henry, which was popular well before the death of King Henry vi, were each chosen for about three per cent. The pattern in Norwich appears to have been similar to that in the country as a whole in the thirteenth and fourteenth centuries except that many more in Norwich were called Edmund, the name of the ninth-century East Anglian king and martyr, and substantially fewer were called Roger.[165]

---

[162] Delaruelle, *L'Église*, p. 787; Roger Aubenas and Robert Ricard, *L'Église et la Renaissance*, Histoire de l'Église, ed. Augustin Fliche and others, 15 (Paris 1951), p. 344.

[163] See Appendix 9 (p. 211).

[164] See Nicole Hue, "Les noms de personnes à Castres à la fin du xive siècle," in *Onzième congrès d'études de la Fédération des Sociétés académiques et savantes Languedoc-Pyrénées-Gascogne, 11-13 juin 1955* (Albi 1956), pp. 198 and 200.

[165] Emden, *BRUO*, 3: 2233-2242; Emden, *BRUC*, pp. 689-695.

Regarding the women, there was no single name of outstanding popularity; but Margaret was chosen for about eighteen per cent, each of Johanna or Joan, Agnes and Alice for between twelve and thirteen per cent, Elizabeth or Isabel for about nine per cent and Catherine for about seven per cent. Julian, the name of the anchoress from the city and author of the *Revelations of Divine Love*, was chosen for only one woman. More surprising is that no testator was called Mary, perhaps the result of hyper-devotion, just as boys are not called Jesus in most countries today.

Testators from Norwich followed the custom of beginning their wills with various clauses commending their souls to God, to St Mary and to all the saints. St Mary and all the saints did not drop out of the clauses during the period in question, as happened in the diocese of York in the 1540s.[166] But the description of Mary as a virgin disappeared from the clauses for the most part after about 1490. The disappearance more or less coincided with the change from Latin to English as the language of the wills, and may be the result of the change more than of doubts about Mary's virginity. Towards the end of the fifteenth century an increasing number of testators mentioned other saints by name. Those most frequently mentioned were, in descending order, Peter, Michael, Martin, George, Lawrence, John the Baptist, Stephen, Gregory, Margaret, Andrew, Paul and Clement.[167] (Of their names only John and Margaret were especially popular as Christian names.) In most cases, however, the saint chosen appears to have been the patron saint of the testator's parish church, so their inclusion in the commendatory clauses may simply represent another change of fashion in the way scribes phrased wills – the patron saint of the testator's parish church being more or less automatically included – rather than the devotion of testators to particular saints.

No scope was offered for choosing patron saints of parish churches since no new parish churches were established in the city during the late Middle Ages.[168] St Mary was the most popular patron of craft guilds and pious confraternities, eight guilds and nine confraternities being dedicated to her. This was more than the number dedicated to Christ and to the Trinity. Three or four were dedicated to St Augustine, three to St Anne and two each to St Barbara, St Margaret, St James and St William (the peltiers' guild being dedicated to St William of Norwich).[169]

---

[166] Arthur G. Dickens, *Lollards and Protestants in the Diocese of York, 1509-1558* (Oxford 1959), p. 172.

[167] This and subsequent statements in this sub-section are based on the sample of 904 wills used in chapter 3 (see pp. 114-116 and 225).

[168] See pp. 3-4.

[169] See pp. 205-210.

Lights before images of saints received an ever increasing number of testamentary bequests from the citizens during the late Middle Ages.[170] The bequests give an idea of the amazing number of statues and paintings there must have been in some of the city's parish churches.[171] St Mary was much the most popular saint in this form of devotion, lights dedicated to her receiving over four times as many bequests as those dedicated to the next most popular saint, St John (whether the Baptist or the Evangelist was not usually specified). Enjoying a more modest cult were, in descending order, Saints Anne, Margaret, Christopher, Thomas, Peter, Catherine, Clement, George and Michael. All these saints, except St Christopher, were popular as patrons of guilds and confraternities, as saints to whom people commend their souls in wills or as saints whose names were common as Christian names. Very few bequests were left to lights before images of St William or St Edmund; none to lights before images of the other East Anglian saints – Felix, Wulstan, Etheldreda and Withburga. The lack of enthusiasm for East Anglian saints, partly excepting St Edmund and St William of Norwich, contrasts with the numerous representations of them in the stained-glass windows and on the walls, pulpits and rood-screens of East Anglian churches. Regarding other saints, wills from Norwich generally support the iconographic evidence of East Anglia. Both kinds of evidence agree on the pre-eminent popularity of St Mary. The only important difference is that St Edward appears more frequently in iconography than in wills.[172]

A number of bequests were left to lights in honour of Christ. They were variously described as sepulchre lights, rood or "perk" lights, lights of St Saviour, lights before the Sacrament or before the body of Christ. The normal custom in late medieval England appears to have been for the Sacrament to be suspended over the high altar in some form of a hanging pyx,[173] so most of the bequests were probably to lights burning before such pyxes. Bequests of this kind, however, numbered only slightly more than those to lights dedicated to St Mary.

[170] See pp. 118 and 222.

[171] For example, see p. 230.

[172] W. W. Williamson, "Saints on Norfolk Rood-Screens and Pulpits," *Norfolk Archaeology* 31 (1955-1957) 299-346; Ernest W. Tristram, *English Wall Painting of the Fourteenth Century* (London 1955), pp. 295-302; Christopher Woodforde, *The Norwich School of Glass-Painting in the Fifteenth Century* (Oxford 1950), pp. 228-229; Montague R. James, *Suffolk and Norfolk* (London 1930), pp. 232-236.

[173] Gregory Dix, *A Detection of Aumbries* (London 1942), pp. 28 and 40-41.

ii. *Pilgrimages*

Opposition to pilgrimages was a charge frequently levelled against suspected Lollards,[174] including many of those from the diocese of Norwich brought before Bishop Alnwick between 1428 and 1431.[175] Moreover many orthodox reformers were sceptical of their value.[176] Nobody from Norwich is known to have given departure on a pilgrimage as the reason for making his will, as happened often in late medieval Toulouse.[177] But of the wills that survive,[178] 31 contained bequests for people to make pilgrimages on behalf of the testators concerned to various shrines outside the city or, in a few cases, bequests to the shrines themselves.

Over twenty shrines in East Anglia were mentioned in this way. Not surprisingly Our Lady of Walsingham, the most famous shrine in the area, was much the most popular. Some testators wanted several shrines to be visited. Thomas Oudolff, for example, instructed his executors to hire one man to go "naked in his shirt" to the Holy Rood of Beccles and another to go barefoot to Our Lady of Walsingham.[179] Gregory Clerk, mayor in 1505 and 1514, wanted pilgrimages to be made on his behalf to the Holy Cross of Bromholm, the Holy Rood at "Recclys," [180] Our Lady of Walsingham, Our Lady of "Redybone," [181] Our Lady of "Armeburghe," [182] Our Lady of Grace at Ipswich, Our Lady of Grace at Cambridge, Our Lady of the Mount at Lynn, St "Tebald" and St "Wandred," [183] St "Hede" of "Cremyngham," [184] St Audry of Ely and St Philip's arm at Castle Acre.[185] Alice Winter stated in 1448 that she wanted a man to be hired to make a pilgrimage, for her soul and the souls of the people to whom she was bound, to the cross at Newton,[186] the cross at Reydon, the cross at Terrington and St John's chapel at Terrington, the

---

[174] Thomson, *Later Lollards*, pp. 245-246; Jonathan Sumption, *Pilgrimage* (London 1975), pp. 196, 258-259, 270 and 272-273.

[175] *Heresy Trials*, ed. Tanner, pp. 13-14.

[176] Sumption, *Pilgrimage*, pp. 273-274, 290 and 301-302.

[177] Nucé, "Piété et charité" (1961), pp. 9 and 134.

[178] See Appendix 13, section A (pp. 224-225).

[179] N.C.C., Reg. Gelour, fol. 97v (Oudolff).

[180] *Sic* in MS – probably a scribal error for Beccles.

[181] *Sic* in MS – probably Redbourne in Lincolnshire or Redbourne in Hertfordshire.

[182] *Sic* in MS – place unidentifiable.

[183] *Sic* in MS – no place(s) mentioned, presumably a St Theobald and St Wandrille or St Wandru.

[184] *Sic* in MS – probably a scribal error for Cressingham, presumably St Hedda.

[185] PROB/11/18 (Reg. Holder, 1514-1517), fol. 28 (Clerk).

[186] Three places in Norfolk alone were called Newton.

Holy Trinity and All Saints of Lynn and St Margaret of Lynn, St Felix of Babingley, St Leonard of Norwich and Our Lady of Walsingham, as well as to the cross "of the north door, London,"[187] and to St Thomas of Canterbury.[188] Other East Anglian shrines mentioned were St Nicholas of Tibenham and the image of Sts Peter and Paul at Sustede.[189] Numerous small shrines, frequently dedicated to saints of only local fame, were, according to Mr Sumption, a feature of fifteenth-century Christendom.[190] Many small shrines were chosen by testators from Norwich, but most of them were dedicated to widely known saints (e.g., St Mary) or to general objects (e.g., roods and crosses) rather than to local people.

The cult of St Thomas of Canterbury appears to have been in decline in England as a whole in the late Middle Ages.[191] Nevertheless the saint's tomb was the shrine in England outside East Anglia that was most popular with testators from Norwich. Seven of them sent pilgrims or left bequests to it. Margaret East was one of them: in 1484 she reminded her cousin, a shoemaker in the city, of his promise to make a pilgrimage on her behalf to St "Wandrede"[192] and to St Thomas of Canterbury, and to pray for her at the shrines so that she might be released from the vows she had made of making pilgrimages to them herself. She also left money to her cousin to extend his journey to the tomb of King Henry vi at Chertsey Abbey.[193] The bequest is further evidence that the king was venerated as a saint soon after his death,[194] but it was unique among testators from Norwich. The Holy Blood of Hailes in Gloucestershire[195] and St Anthony of Camber in Sussex[196] were the other English shrines mentioned.

Testators who provided for pilgrims to be sent to shrines abroad illustrate from one angle how English Christians transcended their national church. Twelve of them left money for their executors to hire men – usually priests – to make pilgrimages on their behalf to Rome. The priests were usually instructed to "sing (presumably Masses) and pray" there for the souls of the testators and of various other people. Some of

---

[187] Possibly the preaching-cross in the cemetery of St Paul's Cathedral.

[188] N.C.C., Reg. Wylbey, fol. 150v (Winter).

[189] N.C.C., Reg. Surflete, fol. 25v (Sistede), and Reg. Cobald, fol. 10v (Veer).

[190] Sumption, *Pilgrimage*, p. 269.

[191] Ibid., pp. 150, 160 and 268-269.

[192] *Sic* in ms – no place mentioned, probably St Wandrille or St Wandru.

[193] N.C.C., Reg. A. Caston, fol. 203v (East).

[194] *D.N.B.*, 26: 67 (Henry vi).

[195] N.C.C., Reg. Wolman, fol. 223v (Osborn).

[196] ms reads "Camberton" and "Caumb'rston" in Sussex (N.C.C., Reg. Cage, fol. 112r [Aylemer], and Reg. Gylys, fol. 99r-v [Thursby]).

them were instructed to make the Stations of Rome or to say Mass at the specially indulgenced altar of Scala Caeli.[197] Besides pilgrims sent by testators, sixteen people from the city were among some seventeen hundred pilgrims from England known to have stayed at the English Hospice in Rome in the years for which records survive, namely 1479-1484, 1504-1507 and 1514.[198] Pilgrimages to Rome were expensive and time-consuming. The citizens of Norwich who travelled there themselves, or sent others, are interesting examples of a residual attachment to the papacy on the eve of England's break with it and at a time when the papacy apparently had little that was attractive to offer Englishmen. Robert Baxter's bequest to a hermit to make a pilgrimage on his behalf to Rome and Jerusalem has been mentioned.[199] Edmund Brown, a merchant who made his will in 1446, also provided for ambitious pilgrimages abroad. Besides being told to hire a man for seven shillings to go on foot to St Thomas of Canterbury, his executors were instructed to hire a man for five marks to make a pilgrimage to St James of Compostella during the next Year of Grace and to hire another man, for a sum of money to be negotiated with him, to travel "to Zeeland or beyond, over the sea, to the pilgrimage of the blood of our Lord Jesus Christ, called the Holy Blood of Wihenhak," [200] which was probably the Precious Blood at Wilsnack in Germany to which Margery Kempe had once travelled.[201]

Nobody from Norwich is known to have left money in his will for somebody to be sent on a crusade. But Henry Sharpe, rector of St Mary in the Marsh in Norwich and of St Mary of Fulmodestone in Norfolk, bequeathed six shillings and eightpence in 1507 "to the Christian wars against the unfaithful Turks." [202] And the records of the worsted-weavers mention a vow made by two of the citizens to go on a crusade: John Ocle and John Davy vowed to God, St Mary and all the saints to go to the Holy Land, under the protection of King Henry VII, to fight God's enemies.[203] This was made in 1499 and so the two men were probably responding, rather belatedly, to Pope Innocent VIII's call for a crusade which the king had ordered to be proclaimed throughout England some ten years

---

[197] E.g., see p. 101.
[198] Hay, "Pilgrims," pp. 109-144.
[199] See p. 62.
[200] N.C.C., Reg. Wylbey, fols. 116r-117r (Brown). "Wihenhak" *sic* in MS.
[201] Margery Kempe, *The Book*, 2: 4-5, ed. Meech, pp. 232-235.
[202] N.C.C., Reg. Spyltymber, fol. 126r (Sharpe).
[203] *Records of Norwich*, ed. Hudson, 2: 156-157.

earlier.[204] They seem to have had the approval of both the secular and the ecclesiastical authorities since their vow was supervised by the rector of one of the parish churches and witnessed by the mayor, the two sheriffs and two aldermen of the city.[205]

Norwich itself, principally the Cathedral, was also an important centre for pilgrimages. Margery Kempe came to the city to "offer at the Trinity"[206] before and after her journey to the Holy Land.[207] Money given by other donors was listed in the account-rolls of the sacrist of the Cathedral Priory, though they unfortunately contain few details about who, or how many, the donors were.[208] The priory had obtained from Rome in 1291 an indulgence remitting a year and forty days of penance to penitents who visited the Cathedral on certain days,[209] and offerings to its high altar fluctuated between about £20 and £50 a year from the late thirteenth century, when the surviving account-rolls begin, to the late fourteenth century,[210] and between £55 and £85 a year from the 1390s to the 1440s[211] except for three years at the turn of the century. During each of the three financial years between 1399 and 1402 they were increased to about £120 by offerings made to the Cathedral on its patronal feast-day, Trinity Sunday. An unspecified indulgence, perhaps connected with the Jubilee Year of 1400, had been acquired for the feast-day during the three years and each year between £49 and £85 was received on the day.[212] The offerings must have formed an important source of income for the priory since the peak of £120 represents over twelve per cent of its taxed income, or about six per cent of what Saunders calculated to be its actual income exclusive of receipts in kind.[213] Offerings to the high altar declined rapidly in value in the 1450s and 1460s to about £20 a year, remaining at this level until the 1520s and 1530s when they fell to about £5 a year.[214] In the late fifteenth and early sixteenth centuries the priory again obtained special indulgences for certain days. The first was acquired in 1473 by

[204] *Cal. Papal L., 1484-1492* (vol. 14), pp. 52-53; Bernard Andreas, *Historia regis Henrici septimi*, ed. James Gairdner, Rolls Series (London 1858), p. 54.

[205] *Records of Norwich*, ed. Hudson, 2: 156-157.

[206] I.e., the Cathedral, which was dedicated to the Trinity.

[207] Margery Kempe, *The Book*, 1: 26 and 43, ed. Meech, pp. 60 and 102.

[208] For testamentary bequests to the Cathedral, see pp. 120-121 and 222.

[209] *Cal. Papal L., 1198-1304*, p. 540.

[210] D. and C. Mun., Obedientiary Rolls, nos. 210-248.

[211] Ibid., nos. 249-289.

[212] Ibid., nos. 252-254.

[213] Saunders, *Obedientiary Rolls*, pp. 29-30.

[214] D. and C. Mun., Obedientiary Rolls, nos. 290-334.

Bishop Goldwell from Pope Sixtus IV and granted remittance of twelve years and twelve "quadragene" of penance to those who, having confessed their sins, helped towards the repair of the Cathedral and visited it on the feasts of the Trinity and of the Annunciation.[215] The second was the indulgence "De Portiuncula," and offerings connected with it were first recorded in 1505.[216] The two indulgences, however, did not have the attraction of the one granted a century earlier. Offerings connected with them totalled £21 in 1473/74,[217] the first year of the indulgence acquired by Bishop Goldwell, but in no other year did they exceed £7.

The sacrist of the Cathedral Priory recorded offerings at many other shrines in the Cathedral, and the keeper of the account-rolls of St Leonard's, a cell of the priory in the suburbs of the city, recorded offerings to several shrines at the cell. The most valuable were those left to an image of St Leonard at the cell and, in the Cathedral, to a shrine of St William (presumably St William of Norwich whose shrine in the Cathedral had flourished in the twelfth century[218]), to St Mary's chapel, to some unspecified relics and to a cross. Offerings to each of them exceeded £10 in some years[219] but declined in value in the fifteenth century, rather sooner than offerings to the high altar of the Cathedral. The decline contradicts, in so far as the offerings were made by pilgrims, the view of Aubenas and Richard that pilgrimages retained their popularity throughout Christendom during the century before the Reformation[220] and indicates, in so far as the shrines were dedicated to saints, a decline in one form of devotion to them.

There were two shrines of local men in the Cathedral besides that of St William. Offerings in a trunk "at the head of Bishop John" began to be recorded in the sacrist's account-rolls the year after the death of John Salmon, bishop of Norwich from 1299 to 1325,[221] and offerings in a trunk "at the head of Bishop Walter" (presumably Walter Suffield, bishop of Norwich from 1244 to 1257) began to be recorded in the late thirteenth century.[222] The offerings were sufficiently large for a time to suggest a

---

[215] REG/7, Book 12, fol. 206r-v.

[216] D. and C. Mun., Obedientiary Rolls, no. 317.

[217] Ibid., no. 303.

[218] Ronald C. Finucane, *Miracles and Pilgrims: Popular Beliefs in Medieval England* (London 1977), pp. 118-121 and 161-162.

[219] W. T. Bensly, "St Leonard's Priory, Norwich," *Norfolk Archaeology* 12 (1893-1895) 193; D. and C. Mun., Obedientiary Rolls, nos. 224-225, 239, 244 and 246.

[220] Aubenas, *L'Église*, p. 345.

[221] D. and C. Mun., Obedientiary Rolls, no. 231.

[222] Ibid., nos. 216 and 219-220.

popular devotion to the two men, but it does not appear to have been maintained since the offerings disappear from record in the second half of the fourteenth century. Their cults bear some resemblance to those of Bishops Grosseteste and Dalderby of Lincoln.[223] There is, however, no evidence of a posthumous cult in the late Middle Ages to the anchoress Julian of Norwich, despite the reputation for holiness she appears to have enjoyed during her lifetime.[224] Pilgrimages to the grave of Richard Caistor, vicar of St Stephen's in the early fifteenth century, and other evidence of his cult are discussed in the introduction to his will.[225]

iii. Objects of Piety and Private Chapels

The objects of piety owned by the citizens cannot be described at all fully because the inventories of the goods of only two of them survive.[226] "Saint John's head in alabaster" [227] belonging to John Baker was the only object of this kind, apart from religious books,[228] to be mentioned in the two inventories. Many citizens, however, bequeathed pious objects in their wills. Their bequests give some idea of the kinds of objects in private ownership and say something about the religious devotions of the citizens.

About five per cent of the citizens whose wills survive[229] bequeathed one or more rosaries.[230] Some owned many: a chaplain called John Stathe, for example, bequeathed ten in 1451 and a goldsmith called William Underwood bequeathed six in 1470.[231] A few citizens left Agnus Deis, Paxes and crucifixes. Several left images of saints, usually on cloth or on rings and most frequently of St Mary, or representations of scenes from the life of Christ, most frequently of his crucifixion. Mabel Maloysel, for example, bequeathed in 1383 a gold ring "with a stone called a diamond with an image of Saint Mary of Walsingham" and William Harbald, parish chaplain of St Martin at the Palace Gates, bequeathed in 1468 "a

---

[223] *D.N.B.*, 13: 384 (John Dalderby); Dorothy M. Owen, *Church and Society in Medieval Lincolnshire*, History of Lincolnshire, ed. Joan Thirsk, 5 (Lincoln 1971), p. 126; Eric W. Kemp, "The Attempted Canonization of Robert Grosseteste," in *Robert Grosseteste, Scholar and Bishop*, ed. Daniel A. Callus (Oxford 1955), pp. 243-246.

[224] See pp. 58 and 63.

[225] See pp. 231-232.

[226] See pp. 35 and 111, n. 367.

[227] See p. 239.

[228] See pp. 36-37.

[229] See Appendix 13, section A (pp. 224-225).

[230] The usual terms were "par precarum," "par precularum," "pair of beeds" or simply "beeds."

[231] N.C.C., Reg. Brosyard, fol. 113r-v (Stathe), and Reg. Jekkys, fol. 182r (Underwood).

stained cloth, with a crucifix in the middle and two images, namely of Saint Mary and Saint John." [232] Catherine Kerr was one of the very few who left relics or things that had touched holy objects: she left a gold ring that had touched Christ's grave "as it is said." [233]

One in six or seven of the clerical testators bequeathed items needed for saying Mass, mostly vestments and chalices. So did some of the laity, though in most cases it is not clear whether the donor owned the object or rather wanted it to be bought after his death and given to the beneficiary. Papal indults to possess portable altars were acquired by two unbeneficed priests and eight lay men and their wives. [234] A few other citizens are known from other evidence to have possessed altars [235] and Elizabeth Drake, married first to a vintner and then to a mercer, as well as William Norwich and Gregory Clerk, both former mayors, had private chapels in houses of theirs which probably lay in Norwich. [236] Such chapels must have made them considerably independent of their parish churches. In York it appears to have been fairly common for citizens to employ one or more priests as private chaplains. [237] In Norwich, however, there is evidence of only one or two families possibly retaining priests in this way: Agnes Segrym, the wife of a former mayor, left a bequest to a man whom she called "my priest" but who was not her parish priest; [238] and Richard Waller was called "my priest" by alderman Robert Thorpe and his wife when they wrote their wills; [239] he was later, perhaps already, the priest of the chantry founded by the alderman. [240]

D. Masses and Prayers for the Dead

The value of Masses and prayers, in alleviating the suffering of souls in Purgatory, was solemnly proclaimed in the creed prepared by Pope

---

[232] N.C.C., Reg. Heydon, fol. 213v (Maloysel), and Reg. Jekkys, fol. 127v (Harbald).

[233] N.C.C., Reg. Multon, fol. 90v (Kerr).

[234] *Cal. Papal L., 1396-1404*, p. 568; *Cal. Papal L., 1404-1415*, pp. 15, 345 and 406; *Cal. Papal L., 1417-1431*, pp. 300 and 450; *Cal. Papal L., 1427-1447*, pp. 128-129; *Cal. Papal L., 1431-1447*, p. 243.

[235] For example, see below, p. 229.

[236] N.C.C., Reg. Spyltymber, fol. 68v (Drake *alias* Davy); PROB/11/5 (Reg. Godyn, 1463-1468), fol. 30 (Norwich), and /18 (Reg. Holder, 1514-1517), fol. 28 (Clerk).

[237] Dobson, "Chantries of York," p. 37.

[238] N.C.C., Reg. Gelour, fols. 81r-82r (Segrym); REG/6, Book 11, fol. 162v; REG/7, Book 12, fol. 136r.

[239] PROB/11/12 (Reg. Moone, 1500-1501), fol. 19 (Thorpe), and /13 (Reg. Blamyr, 1501-1503), fol. 26 (Thorpe).

[240] N.C.C., Reg. Ryxe, fol. 305r (Waller); see p. 218.

Clement ɪᴠ for Emperor Michael ᴠɪɪɪ Palaeologus and recited in the emperor's name at the second Council of Lyons in 1274: "We believe that the intercessions of the faithful who are living help to relieve their pains [i.e., of the souls in Purgatory], that is to say Masses, prayers, alms and other works of piety, which have customarily been performed by the faithful, on behalf of others of the faithful, according to the approved practices of the Church." [241] The doctrine was repeated in 1439 when the Council of Florence proclaimed union with the Greek Church in the bull "Laetentur Caeli." [242]

The multiplication of Masses for the dead, especially through chantries, was a characteristic of late medieval Christianity. Chantries were also an aspect of lay piety: unlike houses of religious orders, they offered their founders considerable control over the services to be performed and the clergy performing them, and they lay within the financial means of the middle class. At the same time the doctrine of Purgatory, and the value of Masses and prayers for the dead, were principal targets for the Reformation. Even orthodox reformers criticised the multiplication of Masses.

The following topics will be discussed: the number and types of Masses and prayers requested, the mentality behind the requests, and their social and economic effects.

i. The Requests: Perpetual Chantries [243]

No houses of religious orders or colleges of secular priests were founded in Norwich after the first third of the fourteenth century. Thereafter perpetual chantries, requiring more or less daily services of a priest in perpetuity, were the most ambitious religious foundations made in the city or by its inhabitants elsewhere. Some thirty individuals, groups of individuals or corporate bodies are known to have tried to found about forty such perpetual chantries after 1369. In some cases it is not clear that the desired foundation was realised, several chantries do not appear to have survived until the dissolution of chantries, and in two cases[244] two foundations appear to have been united by the monks of the Cathedral Priory into single chantries. Before 1370 about twenty-six perpetual chantries are known, with varying degrees of certainty, to have been

---

[241] *Enchiridion symbolorum*, ed. Denzinger, ᴅs. 856.

[242] Ibid., ᴅs. 1304.

[243] Throughout this sub-section see Appendix 10 (pp. 212-219).

[244] See pp. 94 and 96.

founded in the city, all after 1240.[245] Two-thirds of them were included in the foundations of three colleges of secular priests: the Carnary College, St Giles's Hospital and the college of chantry priests in the Bishop's Palace. Several of these older chantries, too, were later united into fewer ones or were dissolved. Thus, as mentioned, the inadequacy of the endowments was the alleged reason why the college of chantry priests in the Bishop's Palace, founded by Bishop Ayremine (1325-1336), was reduced from three to two priests in 1369 and dissolved in 1449.[246] It was also the alleged reason why the two chantries founded by Lettice Payn of Norwich in 1313 were united into a single chantry sometime before 1369,[247] though this survived until the general dissolution of chantries;[248] and it probably helps to explain why the priests celebrating in the Carnary College for the souls of their founder, Bishop Salmon (1299-1325), and of various other people, were reduced from six to four in the first half of the fifteenth century and to three sometime before the dissolution.[249] Inadequacy of endowments for many chantries in Norwich after 1350, and the resulting need to unite them into fewer chantries or to dissolve them, were local examples of problems which were widespread in late medieval Christendom and seem to have resulted chiefly from the fall in value of incomes from endowments and, at least in England, from the rise in chaplains' wages after the Black Death.[250]

The number of perpetual chantries in Norwich did not approach the number in London. There the "Valor Ecclesiasticus" listed 44 chantries in St Paul's Cathedral alone and 186 chantries in 65 parish churches.[251] Even in York, a city similar in size and importance to Norwich, about 140 perpetual chantries are known to have been founded.[252] Norwich was unusual, however, in that it did not suffer the decline in new foundations

[245] Blomefeld, Norfolk (1805-1810), 3: 512, and 4: 48, 55, 57, 125, 163, 174, 201, 381 and 386-387; Kirkpatrick, Religious Orders, p. 136.
[246] See pp. 22-23.
[247] Cal. Pat. R., 1313-1317, p. 31; Inventory, ed. Watkin, 1: 19.
[248] London, Public Record Office, E.315/67, fol. 647v.
[249] See p. 23; Cal. Papal L., 1417-1431, p. 566; Saunders, Norwich School, pp. 50 and 70-72.
[250] Auguste Molinier, Les obituaires français au Moyen Âge (Paris 1890), p. 149; Kathleen L. Wood-Legh, Perpetual Chantries in Britain (Cambridge 1965), p. 93.
[251] Valor ecclesiasticus temp. Henr. VIII, ed. John Caley and Joseph Hunter (London 1810-1834), 1: 367-369 and 378-384. All or most of them were, almost certainly, perpetual chantries. I have counted what were listed as single chantries, but were served by two or more (full-time) priests, as two or more chantries.
[252] Dobson, "Chantries of York," p. 24.

after 1400 which occurred in the country as a whole, including in London and York.[253]

The founders after 1369 fell into five groups – first, craft guilds and pious confraternities. Chantries founded by craft guilds and by the confraternities of St George and of the Annunciation of St Mary have been discussed.[254] Three other confraternities had chantries: the confraternity of Our Lady, attached to St Stephen's parish church, was employing a chantry priest in the church from at least 1524, probably earlier; the confraternity of the Mass of Jesus, attached to St Peter Mancroft parish church, maintained a chantry of the Mass of Jesus in the church from about 1458; and the confraternity of the Mass of Jesus, attached to the Cathedral, maintained a similar chantry in the Cathedral from about 1466.[255] In addition, there are a few references in wills in the 1520s and 1530s to a Mass of St John in St Peter Mancroft parish church, a Mass of Jesus in St Gregory's parish church and a Mass of Jesus probably in St Stephen's parish church. These votive Masses were probably maintained by confraternities attached to the churches, or by the parishes themselves. It is doubtful whether they were said daily.

Bishops formed the second group. Of those who died as bishops of Norwich after 1369 after reasonably long tenures of the see, five tried to found perpetual chantries.[256] Thus each of bishops Tottington (1406-1413), Wakeryng (1415-1425), Brown (1436-1445) and Lyhert (1445-1471) provided in his will for a priest, usually a monk of the Cathedral Priory, to say Mass daily in the Cathedral, in most cases near his tomb, for his soul and the souls of various other people. Bishop Wakeryng's was the only foundation known with certainty to have been realised, and it was probably united with Sir Thomas Erpingham's sometime in the early sixteenth century. Bishop Lyhert stipulated that his chantry priest was to preach to the people of the diocese every year during Lent and Advent. This was one of the very few provision in wills for preaching.[257] The fifth

---

[253] Ibid., pp. 32-33; Rosenthal, *Purchase of Paradise*, pp. 32-35; *VCH London*, 1: 205; Alan Kreider, *English Chantries: The Road to Dissolution* (Cambridge Mass. 1979), pp. 72, 75 and 86-90.

[254] See pp. 69-70, 77 and 79.

[255] The Mass was sometimes called the Mass of the Name of Jesus, and correspondingly the confraternities which managed chantries celebrating this Mass were sometimes called confraternities of the Mass of the Name of Jesus or simply confraternities of the Name of Jesus. For the Mass, see Pfaff, *New Feasts*, pp. 62-83.

[256] In addition to Bishop Thomas Percy, who died in 1369 but whose executors obtained a licence to found a perpetual chantry for his soul in 1373 (see below, p. 212).

[257] See p. 11.

bishop was James Goldwell (1472-1499). Directly or through the executors of his will he was the most prolific of all the founders in question. Between 1475 and about 1505 he and his brother Nicholas, who was one of his executors, established a perpetual chantry in their home town, Great Chart in Kent; his executors founded another chantry for him and his brother in 1502 in their former college, All Souls at Oxford; and in 1503 they contracted with the master and priest-fellows of St Giles's Hospital for the hospital to find three more chantry priests to celebrate for his soul. It is interesting that instead of keeping all the chantries for itself, the hospital immediately sub-contracted one of them to the Cathedral Priory and another to the College of St Mary in the Fields. At least the former as well as the chantries at Great Chart and All Souls College survived until the Henrician Reformation. Five chantry priests would have sufficed to establish a college. It is perhaps surprising that neither Bishop Goldwell nor anyone else from Norwich during the period in question founded such a college or even grouped priests of existing chantries into one as Thomas Thoresby, for example, did at Lynn in the early sixteenth century.[258] They preferred to attach their chantries to existing institutions.

Other clerics from the city formed the third group. Unlike the bishops, none of them chose the Cathedral. In his will of 1489 John Smyth, master of St Giles's Hospital, left property to the hospital for eighty years provided it had chantry services for his soul performed for eighty years or, if it could obtain a licence for alienation in mortmain, it could keep the property for ever on condition that the services were performed in perpetuity. There is no evidence that the licence was obtained. The chantry for the soul of John Derlyngton was also entrusted to the hospital. He too had been its master. How far he was responsible for the foundation is not clear. However, that the hospital paid £60 in 1410 to obtain a licence for the establishment of the chantry suggests it was probably realised.[259] John Wygenhale chose the College of St Mary in the Fields, of which he had been dean, for his chantry. The foundation deed was a tripartite indenture by which the college bound itself to pay £10 a year to the mayor and commonalty if it failed to perform the chantry services, and in the event of such a failure the mayor and commonalty pledged themselves to get the services performed with the money.[260] Miss Wood-Legh cited many cases of the laity using civic authorities as guarantors of

---

[258] *VCH Norfolk*, 2: 455.
[259] *Cal. Pat. R., 1408-1413*, p. 187.
[260] N.C.R., Case 3i, Private Deeds, Box 7, "Chapel Field College."

their chantries.[261] John Wygenhale is an interesting case of a cleric doing it, against failure on the part of his former college. There is, however, no evidence that the guarantee was tested and the college was still maintaining the chantry in 1492, thirty-two years after its foundation. Wygenhale, Derlyngton and Smyth were prominent ecclesiastics.[262] Ralph Churchman, the last man in the group, is not known to have held a benefice and was simply described as a cleric and citizen of Norwich. He chose the College of St Mary in the Fields for his perpetual chantry in 1391, but it did not appear among the chantries listed at the visitation of the college in 1492[263] and may have never been founded.

The fourth group comprised members of the East Anglian gentry who chose their provincial capital for their chantries. Four of them chose the Cathedral: Dionysia de Tye, widow of Sir Peter de Tye, in about 1375; Sir Thomas Erpingham sometime before 1429; Justice William Paston in 1444; and Elizabeth Clere, widow of Sir Robert Clere of Ormesby, in 1478. Although their main interests lay outside Norwich, Dionysia de Tye and Sir Thomas Erpingham are known to have owned town houses in the city,[264] Erpingham and William Paston asked to be buried in the Cathedral,[265] and the Clere family owned the advowson of St Edmund's rectory in Norwich.[266] Tye's two chantries were probably united into a single one, but this survived until the Reformation. So did Erpingham's chantry, though it was probably united with Bishop Wakeryng's. Elizabeth Clere was one of the few founders to specify additional prayers to be said by the priest outside of his daily Mass. Moreover she instructed him, or his cleric, to remind the congregation that they could gain an indulgence if they said an Our Father and a Hail Mary for her soul and for the souls of her husband and of all Christians during the Mass. It is interesting that a congregation was expected at a chantry Mass. William Paston's chantry services appear to have been performed daily only for a short time because the money deposited in the Cathedral Priory as payment was smuggled out, allegedly by his eldest son John![267] The group also included two other members of the gentry with town houses in

---

[261] Wood-Legh, *Perpetual Chantries*, chapter 7.

[262] Emden, *BRUC*, pp. 185 (John Derlyngton), 534 (John Smyth) and 655 (John Wygenhale *alias* Saresson).

[263] *Visitations*, ed. Jessopp, p. 12.

[264] N.C.C., Reg. Heydon, fol. 95r (Tye); John H. Druery, "The Erpingham House," *Norfolk Archaeology* 6 (1864) 144.

[265] *Register of Chichele*, ed. Jacob, 2: 380; *Paston Letters*, ed. Davis, 1: 21.

[266] See p. 174.

[267] *Paston Letters*, ed. Davis, 1: 46, and 2: 609-611.

Norwich:[268] Sir Edmund Bokenham of Snetterton and Sir John Wodehous, one of the chamberlains of the Exchequer. Bokenham chose the
College of St Mary in the Fields for his chantry in 1479, and it survived
for at least thirteen years. Wodehous obtained a licence in 1421 to found a
perpetual chantry in the Carnary College, though Saunders doubted
whether it was established.[269] His instructions for the foundation are
interesting for several reasons. He intended to present the priests to the
chantry himself during his life, but subsequently they were to be
presented by his successors as chamberlains,[270] not by the Carnary
College. Moreover, he gave them unusually heavy duties, especially
before nine o'clock in the morning, and he hoped to obtain the prayers of
poor people attending the daily Mass in return for offering them alms. The
Augustinian friary was chosen for three chantries by Sir Thomas
Kerdeston of Claxton in 1446 and for one chantry in about 1516 by Sir
James Hobart of Hales Hall near Loddon, an attorney of Henry VII.

The last group chiefly comprised prominent lay men of Norwich. In
contrast to the other foundations by private individuals, a much smaller
proportion of theirs were entrusted to religious houses. None of them was
entrusted to the Cathedral Priory whereas four of the country gentry's
were. This may reflect the hostility between the citizens and the priory,[271]
contrasting with the much better relations that seem to have existed
between the priory and the country gentry.[272] The chantry founded in
1412 by William Setman, a wealthy mercer who later became mayor, was
entrusted to the College of St Mary in the Fields. The daily Mass was to be
said on alternate weeks in the college and in St Peter Mancroft parish
church, of which the college was patron. The chantry was guaranteed by
the mayor and commonalty in the way Wygenhale's was.[273] So was the
chantry established in the college between 1406 and 1422 by John
Alderford and others.[274] The college was also chosen in 1388 by William
Appleyard, who later became mayor several times, the college binding
itself to forfeit a sum of money to the bailiffs and commonalty if it failed to
perform the chantry services.[275] The executors of the wills of Richard
Brown and Ralph Segrym, both former mayors, founded a chantry for the

[268] N.C.C., Reg. A. Caston, fol. 38r (Buckingham); *Register of Chichele*, ed. Jacob, 2:
442.
[269] Saunders, *Norwich School*, pp. 42-43.
[270] *Cal. Pat. R., 1416-1422*, p. 377.
[271] See pp. 141-154.
[272] See pp. 13 and 147.
[273] N.C.R., Case 3i, Private Deeds, Box 7, "Chapel Field College."
[274] Ibid.
[275] Ibid.

souls of the two men and of various other people in the Guild Hall in
1472. The priest was also to act as a kind of chaplain to those imprisoned
there. The management of the chantry was entrusted to the master and
priest-fellows of St Giles's Hospital, the hospital binding itself to forfeit a
sum of money to the mayor and commonalty if it failed in its obligations.[276] It is noticeable that all the chantries guaranteed (in one way or
another) by the city government survived for at least a few years. The
other founders chose parish churches. The brothers John and Walter
Daniel, both merchants and former mayors, asked in their joint will of
1418 for a chantry to be founded for them in St Stephen's parish church
where they wanted to be buried; but there is no evidence that it was
established. Robert Thorpe, a wealthy alderman, acquired a licence in
1497 to found a chantry in the parish church of St Michael of Coslany in
which he later asked to be buried; it existed when he wrote his will in
1501 and survived until at least 1535. Robert Jannys, a grocer and former
mayor, left money in his will of 1530 for a chantry to be founded in the
parish church of his birth-place, Aylsham in Norfolk. The priest was also
to keep a free grammar school there. He was to be appointed by the
executors of the will until the last one died and thereafter by the vicar, the
"bailie churchwardens" and four "substantial men" of the town.[277]
However, the foundation does not appear to have been realised, perhaps
because it was overtaken by the Reformation.

ii. The Requests: Funerals

Although few inhabitants of any town could afford a perpetual chantry,
every Christian dying within the Church had a right to a Christian
burial.[278] Almost all the people from late medieval Norwich whose wills
survive asked to be buried in a church or cemetery.[279] Nobody explicitly
rejected in his will burial in a sacred place, though this is not surprising in
view of the Church's supervision of wills. The closest people came to
expressing the Lollard view that it was as good to be buried in a field as in
a church or cemetery[280] was the request made by a few testators, mostly
clerics and mostly in the fifteenth century, to be buried "wherever it
pleases God" or "wherever I happen to die." [281]

[276] N.C.R., Case 17b, Liber Albus, fol. 53r-v.
[277] See pp. 249-250.
[278] *Corpus iuris canonici*, Decretales Gregorii ix, 5.3.42; *Councils*, ed. Powicke, 1: 116.
[279] For the places chosen, see pp. 11-14.
[280] Thomson, *Later Lollards*, p. 247; *Heresy Trials*, ed. Tanner, pp. 108 and 112.
[281] E.g., N.C.C., Reg. Hyrnyng, fols. 10r (Berford), 51r (Mundes), 51r (Appleyard) and
101r (Letlee).

Doubtless the bequest left by almost every testator to the parish church or religious house in which, or in whose cemetery, he wished to be buried was partly intended as payment for his funeral. In addition, a fair number of testators left bequests specifically for their funeral expenses or, more frequently, asked for them to be paid for out of the residues of their estates. Some provided for elaborate funerals. A butcher called Thomas Snellyng, for example, wanted a Dirge to be said for him the evening before his burial and left fourpence to each priest, twopence to each clerk and a halfpenny to each child who attended. Bread, cheese and drink were to be provided afterwards. There was to be a hearse with eighteen poor men holding lights, each of whom was to be rewarded with a penny and a dinner; all his neighbours and fellow-parishioners, both rich and poor, were to be invited to a "repast" on the day of his burial; and every other poor man, woman and child coming along after his funeral Mass was to be offered a halfpenny worth of bread.[282] However, the number of testators requesting elaborate and costly funerals was small, surprisingly so in view of the amount of money spent on Masses and prayers.

Mr McFarlane thought injunctions against funeral pomp were a characteristic of Lollard wills.[283] Several testators from Norwich issued such injunctions, though none of them is known to have been suspected of heresy. Doctor Edmund Stubbes, rector of St Michael of Coslany from 1505 until his death in 1514,[284] wanted his "miserable" body to be buried "poorly and without pomp," and no more than thirteen shillings and fourpence spent on his burial.[285] Bishop Lyhert asked in 1472 that his funeral expenses be "not superfluous or excessive, but rather sufficiently moderate as to provide refreshment for the weak and needy rather than solace for the rich." [286] Bishop Wakeryng had expressed similar thoughts in 1425: "I want the vigils of the dead to be performed in the ordinary way immediately after my death, without elaborate ceremonies and processions, which solace the living, according to the blessed Augustine, rather than help the dead";[287] and Catherine Felbrigge declared in 1460,

---

[282] N.C.C., Reg. Ryxe, fols. 383v-384r (Snellyng).

[283] McFarlane, *Lancastrian Kings*, p. 210. See also below, p. 234.

[284] Emden, *BRUC*, p. 563 (Edmund Stubbes).

[285] "Miserum," "pauperime et sine pompa" (PROB/11/17 [Reg. Fetiplace, 1511-1514], fol. 31 [Stubb]).

[286] "Non sint superflui vel excessivi, sed adeo moderati quod non sint divitum aut habundancium solacia, sed pocius egentibus et debilibus recreacio et refeccio" (PROB/11/6 [Reg. Wattys, 1471-1480], fol. 7 [Lyhert]).

[287] "Volo quod vigilie mortuorum communi modo immediate post mortem meam fiant, cessantibus pomposis exequiis et arraiatibus, qui pocius sunt, secundum beatum

"I do not want, indeed I expressly forbid, my executors to lay on large banquets or other useless provisions, rather they are to provide for my burial rites in a discreet and fitting manner as will better please God and help my soul." [288]

iii. The Requests: Other Masses and Prayers for the Dead [289]

Funerals were meant to help the souls of the deceased as soon after death as possible; perpetual chantries were meant to help them with a regular flow of intercession into the indefinite future. Christians also sought for their souls immediate or enduring intercession, or both, by a variety of other arrangements.

The arrangement most favoured by the testators from Norwich, and the one upon which much the largest amount of money was spent, was the employment of a priest to "celebrate" or to "sing and pray" for the testator's soul for a specified period of time or – the phrase normally used before about 1425 but rarely thereafter – to "say an annual of Masses" (annuale Missarum). They normally left £5 6s. 8d. (eight marks) for a priest to "celebrate" or "sing and pray" for a year but normally rather less, frequently between five marks and £4, for an annual of Masses. The difference may represent an increase in the wages of chantry priests in the early fifteenth century rather than a difference in duties. But possibly "celebrating" or "singing and praying" for a limited period of time, which may be called a temporary chantry, [290] involved the recitation of the Office of the Dead to which, according to Miss Wood-Legh, [291] most priests of perpetual chantries were bound, in addition to a daily Mass, which may have been all that was required of a priest saying an annual of Masses.

Between a third and two-fifths of the testators left bequests for temporary chantries or annuals of Masses. Using a sample that included a much larger proportion of very wealthy testators, [292] Dr Thomson found the corresponding figure for late medieval London was about two-fifths. He founds the peak decades were in the early fifteenth century when the

---

Augustinum, solacia vivorum quam subsidia mortuorum" (Register of Chichele, ed. Jacob, 2: 312).

[288] "Nolo, sed expresse prohibeo, ne executores mei faciant magna convivia seu vanas expensas ad mundanam gloriam; sed ordinent discrete et honeste pro meis funeralibus modo meliori quo valeant magis Deo placere et anime mee prodesse" (N.C.C., Reg. Brosyard, fol. 185r [Felbrigge]).

[289] Throughout the remainder of this section, see Appendix 11 (pp. 220-221). The figures are based on the sample of wills used in chapter 3 (see pp. 114-116 and 225).

[290] The phrase does not appear in the records; it is my description.

[291] Wood-Legh, Perpetual Chantries, pp. 296-297.

[292] See p. 113.

figure was about forty-five per cent. In Norwich they were later, immediately before Luther's break with Rome, when the figures were fifty-five per cent of the clergy and forty-four per cent of the laity. There followed a slight decline among the lay testators, which was accentuated by a drop in the average number of years of service requested, and a more marked decline among clerical testators. Reformers' criticisms of chantries may have made their value and future appear doubtful. The decline, however, does not appear to have been as sharp in Norwich as in London where the figure in Dr Thomson's sample was down to one in five by 1529-1530.[293]

One to four years were the most popular amounts of service. But a fair number of testators, especially among the laity, wanted five or more years and, on the other hand, periods of less than a year were frequently requested by the laity after about 1517. Usually the years of service were to be taken consecutively by one or more priests. A few testators, however, wanted them to be taken by several priests concurrently. Thomas de Bumpsted, for example, wanted annuals of Masses to be said by twenty priests as soon after his death as possible,[294] and John Shouldham wanted twelve annuals of Masses to be said for his soul in the year after he died.[295]

Surprisingly few of the testators who asked for temporary chantries or annuals of Masses were more explicit about the services and prayers that they desired than simply to instruct the priests to "celebrate" or "sing and pray" or "say Masses" for their souls and those of various other people. Robert Belton, who made his will in 1502, was one of the few who were more specific. He wanted a Dominican friar to "sing" the following for him and his friend for seven years: Mass in the morning, and in the afternoon Vespers and Compline of the day and Vespers and Compline of the Dead.[296] A few priests were instructed to go to Rome as part of their employment. Nicholas Lathe, a parchmenter who made his will in 1499, instructed his executors to find a priest to "sing and pray" for a year for his and his wife's souls and for those of their friends and of all Christians, during which time he was to go to the "Court of Rome." There he was to "go the Stations" for Nicholas and his friends and to sing five Masses for him during Lent at the indulgenced altar of Scala Caeli: one Mass in

[293] John A. Thomson, "Piety and Charity in Late Medieval London," *Journal of Ecclesiastical History* 16 (1965) 191.

[294] N.C.C., Reg. Harsyk, fol. 54r (Bumpsted).

[295] Ibid., fol. 294v (Shouldham).

[296] PROB/11/13 (Reg. Blamyr, 1501-1503), fol. 8 (Belton).

worship of the Holy Trinity, another in worship of our Lord's resurrection, a third in worship of our Lady's assumption into heaven, a fourth in worship of all the saints and a Requiem Mass.[297] Robert Gardener, an alderman who made his will in 1508, wanted his priest to spend a quarter of his year's service in Rome where he was to buy a bull – if it could be purchased for less than £5 – which granted 300 days of pardon to every well disposed person who prayed at his grave for his and his two wives' souls.[298]

Temporary chantries and annuals of Masses provided a regular flow of Masses over a given period of time. Many testators were less concerned with regularity, some simply asking for a certain number of Masses – sometimes specified as Requiem Masses – to be said for their souls, others asking them to be said on a particular day, such as the day of their burial or of their anniversary. Often the number requested was fairly small. In the will made in 1504 by a mason called John Wrane, for example, the only request for Masses or prayers was for six Masses to be said for his soul and the souls of all Christians on the day of his burial.[299] Thirty Masses, usually called a Trental and for which ten shillings was normally offered, was a popular number. A few testators asked for many more. Bishop Wakeryng wanted a thousand Masses to be said for him on the day he died, if at all possible![300] William Setman, the former mayor who made his will in 1429 and had founded a perpetual chantry in 1412,[301] came well at the top of the list. He asked in his will for four thousand Masses to be said for his soul immediately after his death.[302] This was an exceptional number for even the greatest in the kingdom: of all the persons from the province of Canterbury whose wills were registered in the first volume of Archbishop Chichele's register, only one[303] asked for more Masses to be said immediately after death.

Various votive and indulgenced Masses were in some demand, especially after about 1440, though they never approached in popularity ordinary and Requiem Masses. The most popular were Trentals of St Gregory which were thirty Masses said on thirty consecutive days after the example of the thirty Masses allegedly said on the saint's instructions

---

[297] Ibid., fol. 12 (Lathe).
[298] N.C.C., Reg. Spyltymber, fol. 94r (Gardener).
[299] A.N.C., Reg. Cook (1503-1538), fol. 26r (Wrane).
[300] *Register of Chichele*, ed. Jacob, 2: 312.
[301] See pp. 97 and 214.
[302] See p. 244.
[303] Joan Beauchamp, lady of Abergavenny, who asked for five thousand Masses (*Register of Chichele*, ed. Jacob, 2: 535 and 811).

to free the monk Justus from Purgatory,[304] and Masses (of the Name) of Jesus. All the bequests for the latter came after 1450. They provide further evidence of the popularity of the feast of the Name of Jesus during the time it was gaining official approval.[305] Most of them took the form of bequests to chantries of the Mass (of the Name) of Jesus (maintained by confraternities) in the city.[306] There was some demand after 1490 for the Mass of the Five Wounds of Jesus, a votive Mass which began to appear in English missals in the fifteenth and early sixteenth centuries.[307] Bequests for Masses at the altar of Scala Caeli in Rome have been mentioned.[308] There were also a few bequests for Masses to be said at altars in England which had been granted the same indulgence as the altar in Rome:[309] one in 1517 for Masses at the altar of Scala Caeli at Westminster;[310] and half a dozen, beginning in 1517[311] or possibly 1464,[312] for Masses at the altar of Scala Caeli in the Augustinian friary in Norwich. The other votive Masses requested are listed in Appendix 11.[313]

Masses, funeral services and the Divine Office belonged to the official liturgy of the Church and were, for the most part, celebrated by priests. A considerable number of testators left bequests to the laity to attend these services or for people to say for them prayers that did not form part of, or were only on the fringe of, the official liturgy of the Church. The most common were bequests for people simply "to pray" for their souls. Popular, too, were those left to the poor on condition that they attended services for their souls. For example, William Kynges, a wealthy barker who made his will in 1484, left a tenement to his parish church so that the wardens (*economi*) of the parish might be able, among other things, to distributed food and drink worth 1s. 4d. to poor people and beggars attending a Requiem Mass, and Matins and Vespers of the Dead, which were to be said for him in the parish church once a year for ever.[314] The

---

[304] St Gregory I, Pope, *Dialogorum libri quatuor*, 4.55, Patrologia Latina, 77, ed. Jacques P. Migne (Paris 1849), cols. 420-421. Testators who simply asked for thirty, or a Trental of, Masses may well have had the same example in mind.

[305] Pfaff, *New Feasts*, pp. 62-83.

[306] See pp. 94, 216 and 219.

[307] Pfaff, *New Feasts*, pp. 84-86.

[308] See pp. 87 and 101-102.

[309] Blomefield, *Norfolk* (1805-1810), 4: 90; John Foxe, *Acts and Monuments*, Book 8, section on Boston Pardons, ed. Josiah Pratt (London 1877), 5: 365.

[310] A.N.C., Reg. Cook (1503-1538), fol. 48v (Norman).

[311] Ibid., fol. 50r (Norwich).

[312] D. and C., Reg. 1461-1559, fol. 8r (Wedyrfeld).

[313] See p. 221.

[314] PROB/11/10 (Reg. Vox, 1493-1496), fol. 5 (Kynges).

attendance of the poor at Thomas Snellyng's funeral has been mentioned.[315] A few testators demanded prayers during attendance at the services. Bishop Goldwell, for example, wanted fourpence to be given every week for three years to each of twenty poor men who were to go to the Cathedral every Sunday during the three years and pray for his soul beside his tomb throughout the high Mass. The same arrangement was to continue indefinitely thereafter, except that each man was to be paid only a penny a week.[316] Robert Belton wanted sevenpence to be given every week for seven years to each of three poor men who were to pray in the following manner for his and his wife's souls and for those of his friends and all Christians in St Andrew's parish church every day during the seven years. They were to say the rosary[317] in the morning, and Vespers and Matins of the Dead and Commendation in the afternoon, if they were "learned"; if they were not learned, they were to say only the rosary.[318] They were also to attend – presumably in part-fulfilment of these requirements – Mass in the morning, and in the afternoon Vespers and Compline of the day together with Vespers and Matins of the Dead, all of which were to be sung by a Dominican friar in St Andrew's parish church![319]

iv. The Mentality behind the Requests

The requests for Masses and prayers for the dead suggest a considerable level of belief in several doctrines that were crucial to late medieval Christianity but were also attacked by many reformers: Purgatory and the possibility of Christians alleviating the pains of souls suffering there; and the value of various services officially approved by the Church, chiefly the Mass. Wills must, of course, be used with caution in trying to measure belief in such doctrines. It is true that a considerable number of the testators, especially before 1440, left no bequests for Masses or prayers, though almost all of them requested a Christian burial and that the residue of their estates be "disposed for their souls." In a few cases the absence or paucity of such bequests is conspicuous.[320] But much more striking is the number of testators leaving bequests for Masses and prayers that were worth too much to be merely conventional gestures. A third of the lay testators – two-fifths after 1489 – left for this purpose at least £5, which is

---

[315] See p. 99.
[316] PROB/11/11 (Reg. Horne, 1496-1500), fol. 35 (Goldwelle).
[317] MS reads "oure Lady sawter."
[318] MS reads "oure Lady sawter."
[319] PROB/11/13 (Reg. Blamyr, 1501-1503), fol. 8 (Belton).
[320] See p. 136.

thought to have been about the average annual wage of a building labourer in southern England in the fifteenth and early sixteenth centuries.[321] Excluding from consideration bequests to members of their families, testators left more money for Masses and prayers than for any other purpose. That perpetual chantries were a characteristic of late medieval Christianity is well known. The evidence from Norwich is further evidence of this, and shows that perpetual chantries continued to be founded until shortly before their final dissolution. What is especially interesting about the evidence from Norwich is that it reveals a remarkable demand for Masses and prayers for the dead among those ranks of the middle class who could not afford to found perpetual chantries.

The council of Canterbury province held at Lambeth in 1281 pointed, somewhat confusedly, to the theological problems involved in multiplying Masses: "Although the canon[322] says that nothing less is received when a Mass is said for several people collectively than if one Mass were to be said for each of them, nevertheless it is speaking about Masses said with an anxious heart: after all, far be it from any Catholic to think that one Mass devoutly celebrated for a thousand persons would benefit them as much as if a thousand Masses were sung for them with similar devotion; for although the sacrifice – namely Christ – is of infinite merit, nevertheless in the sacrament or sacrifice it is not effected in its full immensity, since otherwise it would never be necessary to say more than one Mass for each deceased person." [323] Nobody from Norwich explicitly faced up in his will to this problem, of why many Masses should be said for a soul when a single Mass was thought to be of infinite value. But the fact that those requesting Masses almost invariably asked for more than one clearly implies that they thought the merit gained would be proportional to the number said. A Mass was regarded very much as a unit of merit which could be assigned to dead persons at will. There generally seems to have been a fairly direct correlation between the wealth of a testator and the number of Masses requested.

The testators in question were not wholly selfish in their desire for Masses and prayers. As in other parts of the country[324] many of them stated that they wanted them to be said for their relatives and friends, and for "all the faithful departed," as well as for themselves. Many, too,

---

[321] Brown, "Building Wages," ed. Carus-Wilson, 2: 177.
[322] I.e., *Corpus iuris canonici*, Decretum Gratiani, 3.5.24.
[323] *Councils*, ed. Powicke, 2: 896.
[324] Rosenthal, *Purchase of Paradise*, pp. 15-28.

wanted them to be said "for those to whom they were bound." [325] A few
were more specific in this respect. Walter Daniel, for example, wanted
three annuals of Masses to be said for the souls of all the faithful departed,
and especially for those of any carpenters and tradesmen whom he had
cheated, knowingly or unknowingly, in the course of business;[326] and
John Pilly wanted two annuals of Masses to be said for the souls of all the
people with whom he had traded, to atone for his faults and sins against
them ![327]

Considerable concern was shown over timing. It suggests that life after
death, at least in Purgatory, was regarded as still being in some sense
subject to time. Most testators wanted a combination of a large number of
Masses and prayers immediately after death together with smaller
numbers continuing at regular intervals for a long time. But the former
was usually preferred when a choice was made between the two. Some
citizens even tried to anticipate death. A priest called Thomas Love, for
example, asked in his will for the first ten Masses of a Trental to be said
for him while he lay "in extremis";[328] and, as mentioned,[329] several
citizens founded perpetual chantries for their souls which began to
function before they died.

Much less concern was generally shown over the kind of services to be
celebrated than over their quantity and timing. A few testators devised
elaborate programmes or asked for special kinds of Masses and prayers,
but the overwhelming majority stuck to a few well-tried forms, chiefly
ordinary and Requiem Masses.

v. Social and Economic Effects

The most important social and economic effects of the demand for
Masses and prayers for the dead were the employment of priests to say
them, the endowments received by various religious institutions, and the
diversion of wealth away from relatives and friends who might otherwise
have been the beneficiaries. There is no direct evidence from Norwich
about how the citizens felt on the last matter.

The sums of money left to found perpetual chantries varied considerably. Sir Thomas Kerdeston hoped the Augustinian friars would found
three of them for £200.[330] Per chantry this was the smallest sum known to

---

[325] "Omnibus pro quibus teneor" was the usual phrase.
[326] N.C.C., Reg. Hyrnyng, fol. 149r-v (Daniel).
[327] N.C.C., Reg. Harsyk, fol. 197v (Pilly).
[328] N.C.C., Reg. Spurlinge, fol. 14v (Love).
[329] See pp. 95-98.
[330] N.C.C., Reg. Wylbey, fol. 137r (Kerdeston).

have been left for a foundation in late medieval Norwich. At the top of the scale Bishop Lyhert left 400 marks for a chantry which was to be managed by the Cathedral Priory,[331] and the executors of Bishop Goldwell's will were licensed to give endowments to the value of £35 6s. 8d. a year to St Giles's Hospital for the foundation of three chantries.[332] The amount normally given to found one perpetual chantry was at least £100 or property worth between £8 and £10 a year. For the College of St Mary in the Fields, and probably for St Giles's Hospital, the advantage of receiving the endowment was balanced by the expense of hiring a priest who was not already a member of the college or hospital to celebrate the chantry services and often of providing him with accommodation.[333] But the founders who entrusted their chantries to the Cathedral Priory, or to other houses of religious orders, usually expected the services to be celebrated by members of the houses and so the expense of hiring extra priests was avoided. The Cathedral Priory appears, however, to have been the institution in the city that was most remiss in maintaining the chantries entrusted to its care. Negligence in maintaining them was the subject of several complaints made at visitations of the priory in 1492 and 1514[334] and, as mentioned,[335] the priory probably united two chantries into one on two occasions. Two likely reasons for the negligence are that the livelihood of a monk, unlike that of most chantry priests, was more or less guaranteed even if he failed to celebrate the chantry services for which he was responsible; and that monks, being in theory unable to acquire private possessions, were much less certain than most chantry priests of being paid for the services they performed. The records of the visitation of 1492 certainly suggest that there may have been a causal connection between failure to pay monks for celebrating chantry services and failure to celebrate the services.[336] The College of St Mary in the Fields, on the other hand, appears to have been especially diligent in maintaining its chantries, perhaps partly because the city government acted as guarantor of many of them.[337]

As for temporary chantries and annuals of Masses, the large majority of them were entrusted to the secular clergy. Thus between 1490 and 1517,

[331] *Cal. Close R., 1485-1500*, p. 245.
[332] N.C.R., Case 3i, Private Deeds, Box 7, "Chapel Field College."
[333] *Visitations*, ed. Jessopp, p. 12; see pp. 213-219.
[334] *Visitations*, ed. Jessopp, pp. 73-74 and 78.
[335] See pp. 94 and 96.
[336] *Visitations*, ed. Jessopp, pp. 73-74 and 77-78.
[337] See pp. 95-97.

when the demand for temporary chantries and annuals of Masses appears
to have reached a peak, only about 60 of the approximately 444 years of
such services requested (by the sample of 288[338] testators) were entrusted
to religious orders. In the case of almost all the approximately 384 years of
service remaining, the testators either said they wanted the celebrants to
be secular priests or implied the same by stating that the services were to
be celebrated in parish churches. The celebration of 384 years of such
services within twenty-eight years (i.e., 1490 to 1517) would have given
full-time employment to between thirteen and fourteen priests. The 288
testators constituted just under half the citizens who made wills that
survive, and perhaps somewhat more than five per cent of all the citizens
who died as adults, during the 28 years.[339] How many years of service
were requested by all the citizens – including those requested outside wills
or in wills that no longer survive – is difficult to estimate partly because
the testators came disproportionately from the upper ranks of urban
society[340] and therefore, no doubt, asked for more years of service than
was the average among all the citizens, and partly because there is almost
no evidence about how many years of service were requested outside
wills. However, the known requests of the testators indicate that
celebrating temporary chantry services or annuals of Masses was a regular
form of employment for many secular priests in the city, not just an
occasional wind-fall.

As has been mentioned,[341] there was a change in Norwich about 1425
from annuals of Masses to "celebrating" or "singing and praying," and a
priest was normally offered eight marks to do the latter for a year, but
rather less to say an annual of Masses. That the normal fee remained at
eight marks from about 1425 until the 1520s reflects the stability of wages
and prices in England during these hundred years[342] and suggests that
during this period, unlike the years immediately after the Black Death,[343]
the supply of priests matched the demand for Masses. A fair number of
testators offered slightly more than eight marks after 1520. But since the
demand for Masses appears to have declined about the same time,[344]

[338] I.e., 62 clerics and 226 lay persons (see p. 220).
[339] See p. 115, n. 15, and pp. 224-225.
[340] See pp. 115-116.
[341] See p. 100.
[342] Ernest H. Phelps Brown and Sheila V. Hopkins, "Seven Centuries of the Prices of
Consumables, Compared with Builders' Wages," in *Essays in Economic History*, ed.
Eleanora M. Carus-Wilson (London 1954-1962), 2: 188 and 194.
[343] Bertha H. Putnam, "Maximum Wage Laws for Priests after the Black Death, 1348-
1381," *American Historical Review* 21 (1915-1916) 13-14.
[344] See p. 101.

without there being evidence of any dramatic drop in the number of priests,[345] the increase probably reflects the beginning of the sixteenth-century price rise.

Eight marks was one mark more than the sum prescribed by Archbishop Sudbury and his suffragans, when they re-issued the constitution "Effrenata" in its third and final form between 1378 and 1379, as the maximum annual wage of a priest celebrating chantry services on a temporary basis.[346] It was slightly more than what is thought to have been the average annual wage of a building labourer in southern England in the fifteenth and early sixteenth centuries.[347] In view of how light the duties were – daily Mass and possibly the recitation of the Office of the Dead[348] – it was a remarkably generous wage and one that would have given the priests time to lead lives of considerable independence or to supplement their wages with other earnings. It helps to explain why many of the unbeneficed priests in the city appear to have been fairly well off towards the end of their lives.[349] By offering such attractive employment, the donors helped both to create and to support the unbeneficed clerical proletariat.

Besides stating that the celebrant was to be a secular priest, many testators added moral and other qualifications. Those most frequently mentioned were suitability for the task, honesty and a good reputation. Alexander Penny, for example, wanted a secular priest who was "suitable, discreet and well governed." [350] Such requirements probably express the wish that deserving priests find employment rather than the belief that the value of a Mass comes "ex opere operantis" not "ex opere operato." Bishop Lyhert wanted a priest who was learned in the Bible,[351] and one of the qualifications laid down by a citizen in 1503 suggests that priests were coming from afar, perhaps even from abroad, to find work in Norwich and shows hostility to such foreign labour: he wanted an "honest young priest, a secular man newly made priest, of wisdom and reason and no outlandish man." [352]

---

[345] See pp. 18-23.

[346] Putnam, "Maximum Wage Laws," pp. 22 and 25-27; Wood-Legh, *Perpetual Chantries*, p. 191.

[347] Brown, "Building Wages," ed. Carus-Wilson, 2: 177.

[348] See p. 100.

[349] See pp. 50-51.

[350] N.C.C., Reg. Aleyn, fol. 89r (Penny).

[351] PROB/11/6 (Reg. Wattys, 1471-1480), fol. 7 (Lyhert).

[352] MS reads "and noon owtlondissh man" (PROB/11/14 [Reg. Holgrave, 1504-1506], fol. 1 [Smyth]).

Some testators hoped to combine the advantage of having Masses and prayers said for their souls with giving employment to their clerical relatives, sometimes even as part-time domestic servants. A brewer called Thomas Glanville, for example, wanted a year's chantry services for his and his wife's souls to be celebrated by his son who was a friar at the Franciscan friary in Norwich;[353] and Richard Ferrour, a former mayor, left to a nephew of his who was a priest £64 on two conditions, first that he did not obtain a benefice and second that he "sang" for his and various others' souls for twelve years and "waited" upon his (Ferrour's) wife and went to "board" with her or some other "honest" person in the parish during the twelve years.[354]

Several testators wanted their chantry priests to combine religious duties with study at a university, and they sometimes offered these chantry-scholarships to their sons or other relatives.[355] But only a small minority of the foundations of temporary or perpetual chantries included educational projects. This agrees with what Miss Wood-Legh found regarding perpetual chantries in the country as a whole.[356] Dr Hughes's claim that chantry priests "generally" had the obligation of keeping a grammar school[357] is untrue of late medieval Norwich: Robert Jannys was the only citizen known to have tried to impose such an obligation on a chantry priest.[358]

Finally, bequests to the poor to say prayers or to attend religious services must have had some effect as a form of poor relief. But it appears to have been a fairly limited one. Few of the known bequests for such purposes can have amounted to more than small and occasional wind-falls for the poor. Bequests on the scale of Sir John Wodehous's,[359] Bishop Goldwell's[360] or Robert Belton's[361] were very exceptional.

E. A NOTE ON THE RELIGIOUS EDUCATION OF THE LAITY

The growth of a devout and educated laity in the late Middle Ages resulted partly from men and women seeking to lead religious lives without

[353] N.C.C., Reg. Ryxe, fol. 400v (Glanville).
[354] PROB/11/13 (Reg. Blamyr, 1501-1503), fol. 7 (Ferrour).
[355] E.g., N.C.C., Reg. Jekkys, fol. 183r-v (Goose).
[356] Wood-Legh, *Perpetual Chantries*, p. 269.
[357] Hughes, *Reformation in England*, 2: 151.
[358] See p. 98.
[359] See pp. 97 and 214-215.
[360] See p. 104.
[361] See p. 104.

becoming priests or entering religious orders and partly from the growing literacy of the laity. It resulted, too, from initiatives in the Church from above, especially the decrees of the Lateran Council of 1215 and constitutions of English bishops in the thirteenth century which sought, both directly and through a better educated clergy, to improve the religious life of the laity. Thus much of our knowledge of the religious education of the laity in late medieval Norwich depends on what has already been said about the education of the clergy[362] and about various means by which the laity were instructed in their religion: the liturgy, especially the Mass,[363] advice that the clergy gave to the laity in the sacrament of Penance and at other times,[364] preaching,[365] mystery plays,[366] and so on.

Books mentioned in the wills of the laity form another important source of information.[367] They appear in just under four per cent of the wills in question. Most of them were standard liturgical books, chiefly Missals, Breviaries, Primers and Psalters. Their appearance is evidence that at least some of the laity took an active and interested part in the two most important acts of worship in the official liturgy of the Church – the Mass and the Divine Office. John de Cove, an advocate at the Norwich Consistory Court, owned the compilation of canons called *Sext* as well as "Hostienc'" [368] which was presumably a work by the thirteenth-century Italian canonist, Henry of Segusio, who was commonly called "Hostiensis." John Eastgate, another advocate at the Consistory Court, owned "John Acton" [369] which was presumably a work by the early fourteenth-century English canonist called John Acton (or Ayton). William Cannered, a butcher who wrote his will in 1542, was the only lay person known to have owned a (complete?) Bible.[370] Sir Robert Norwich, who was said to be living with the prior of the Cathedral Priory when he made his will in 1442, left a book of the meditations of Sts Anselm and Bernard and others, a "calendar," an unnamed work of

[362] See pp. 28-42.
[363] See pp. 8-10.
[364] See pp. 10 and 14-15.
[365] See pp. 10-11.
[366] See pp. 71-72.
[367] See Appendix 6 (pp. 193-197). It is not always clear whether the testator owned the book or rather wanted it to be bought and given to the beneficiary. No book is mentioned in the only surviving inventory of the goods of a lay person (D. and C., Reg. 1461-1559, fol. 31r-v [Wausse]).
[368] N.C.C., Reg. Heydon, fol. 33v (Cove).
[369] N.C.C., Reg. Jekkys, fol. 64r (Eastgate).
[370] N.C.C., Reg. Cooke, fol. 195r (Cannered).

Hoccleve (the English poet), an unnamed book "made" by the duke of
York's household and "a small book of verses about the kings of
England." [371] A widow called Catherine Kerr left "the book of St
Katherine" in 1497. [372] Isabel Liston, another widow, left to her daughter
in 1491 "my English book of Saint Margaret's life" and an "English book
called *Partonope*" [373] which was presumably one of the English versions
of the twelfth-century French romance, *Partenopeus de Blois*. The most
interesting collection was left by a third widow, Margaret Purdans, who
made her will in 1481. She left an "English psalter" to a priest and her
"small psalter" to her son. To the Franciscan nuns of Bruisyard in Suffolk
she left "Le Doctrine of the Herte" which was presumably a translation of
De doctrina cordis, the treatise addressed to a woman on how to lead a
devout life which was usually ascribed to Bishop Grosseteste of Lincoln.
She left her "English book of Saint Bridget" to the Benedictine nuns of
Thetford; and to a certain Alice Barly she left "a book called Hylton"
which was presumably a work by Walter Hilton, the fourteenth-century
English mystic. [374] Her books suggest that she was a kind of bourgeois
equivalent of the devout aristocratic laywoman, Duchess Cicely of York,
and would seem to place her squarely in the line of devout and literate lay
persons to which Dr Pantin has drawn attention. [375] The duchess recited
the breviary daily and had read to her, among other books, works of
Hilton and the *Revelations* of St Bridget. [376] Margery Kempe also read, or
had read to her, works of Hilton and of St Bridget. [377] It is interesting that
these works of Hilton, St Bridget and St Catherine (probably St Catherine
of Siena), which were the only works by or about late medieval mystics
known to have been privately owned by clerics or by lay people from late
medieval Norwich, were owned by lay women.

[371] N.C.C., Reg. Doke, fol. 5r (Norwich).
[372] N.C.C., Reg. Multon, fol. 90v (Kerr).
[373] N.C.C., Reg. Wolman, fol. 171v (Liston).
[374] N.C.C., Reg. A. Caston, fols. 163v-164r (Purdans).
[375] William A. Pantin, "Instructions for a Devout and Literate Layman," in *Medieval
Learning and Literature: Essays presented to Richard William Hunt*, ed. Jonathan G.
Alexander and Margaret T. Gibson (Oxford 1976), pp. 398-422.
[376] William A. Pantin, *The English Church in the Fourteenth Century* (Cambridge
1955), p. 254.
[377] Margery Kempe, *The Book*, 1: 17, ed. Meech, p. 39.

3

Testamentary Bequests

A. Introduction [1]

Norwich is one of a very few English towns for which sufficiently large numbers of wills survive to permit significant statements about trends in bequests to the Church during the late Middle Ages. The wills of at least 15,000 Londoners written before 1530 survive.[2] Dr Thomson has discussed the religious and charitable bequests in them, mainly using a sample of wills proved in the Prerogative Court of Canterbury between 1400 and 1530. Comparisons will be made with his conclusions but it must be remembered that his sample contained a much larger proportion of very wealthy people than the testators examined in this book.[3] There are extant wills of at least 3,000 citizens of York written between the late

---

[1] Throughout this chapter see Appendix 12 (pp. 222-223). Testators from late medieval Norwich, as in the rest of the country, did not draw a clear distinction between will (dealing with real estate) and testament (dealing with personal or movable property). In Norwich "testament" was the term normally used until the last quarter of the fifteenth century, but the testaments frequently dealt with real estate. "Testament and last will" was the term normally used thereafter, but the testament and last will was almost invariably a single unit which did not distinguish where the testament ended from where the will began. In this book "will," not "testament," is always used as the noun and "testament-ary" as the adjective, and "will" includes both copies of wills transcribed into registers and original wills.

[2] For most of the wills see: *Calendar of Wills Proved and Enrolled in the Court of Hustings, London, A.D. 1258 - A.D. 1688*, ed. Reginald R. Sharpe (London 1889-1890), 1: xxvi and 1-701, and 2: 1-635; *Index to Testamentary Records in the Commissary Court of London*, ed. Marc Fitch, Index Library, 82 and 86 (London 1969 and 1974); *Index of Wills Proved in the Prerogative Court of Canterbury, 1383-1558*, ed. John C. Smith, Index Library, 9 and 11 (London 1893 and 1895), 2: 646-656. For other wills, see Anthony J. Camp, *Wills and their Whereabouts*, 4th ed. (London 1974), pp. 82-83 and 86-91.

[3] Thomson, "Piety and Charity," pp. 178-195, and "Clergy and Laity," chapter 3. The samples of wills used by him in the two works vary slightly. Comparisons in this chapter are with the figures given in the first work.

fourteenth and early sixteenth centuries[4] and of about 1,500 citizens of Canterbury written before 1530, though most of the latter were written after 1480.[5] No comprehensive analyses of the religious and charitable bequests in the wills from Canterbury and York have been made. For other towns substantially fewer wills survive.[6]

Wills from Norwich survive in large numbers from 1370, the date of the earliest surviving will proved in the Norwich Consistory Court. Between 1370 and 1532 altogether 1,804 inhabitants of the city[7] made wills that survive.[8] All the wills have been examined for the purposes of this chapter, but the statistics are based on the wills of a sample comprising 615 of the 1,515 lay men and women and on those of all the 289 clerics.[9]

All the clerics were members of the secular clergy. The absence of wills of the regular clergy is to be expected since its members were not permitted to own anything as individuals and since rules of religious orders, as well as the council of Canterbury province held at Oxford in 1222,[10] forbade them to make wills. The number of secular priests in Norwich seems to have fluctuated between about 85 and 120 between 1370 and 1532.[11] The priests whose wills survive therefore constitute a large proportion of all the secular priests of the city. Their wills provide a picture of the testamentary wishes of the secular clergy that is exceptionally full for a late medieval city. The testators comprised 5

---

[4] For most of the wills see: *Index of Wills in the York Registry, 1389-1514*, ed. Francis Collins, Yorkshire Archaeological and Topographical Association, Record Series, 6 (no place, 1889), pp. 1-192. For other wills, see Camp, *Wills*, pp. 155-157 and 171-172.

[5] For most of the wills see: *Index of Wills*, ed. Smith, 2: 636; *Calendar of Wills and Administrations now Preserved in the Probate Registry at Canterbury, 1396-1558 and 1640-1650*, ed. Henry R. Plomer, Kent Archaeological Society, Records Branch, 6 (London 1920), pp. 1-535. For other wills, see Camp, *Wills*, pp. 54-55.

[6] See Camp, *Wills*, pp. 1-176.

[7] The following criteria, sometimes in combination, have been used to decide who should be considered inhabitants of the city: first, if the testator was described as a citizen of Norwich, as "of Norwich" or as the wife of such a person; second, if the testator held a benefice or ecclesiastical position in Norwich, provided it was not merely one among many others held outside the city; third, if the house in which the testator lived or his only known messuage or the bulk of his known property lay in the city; fourth, in the absence of the preceding criteria and paying attention to the place in which he wished to be buried, if the will strongly suggests that the bulk of the testator's interests lay in Norwich and that he therefore most probably lived in the city.

[8] See Appendix 13, section A (pp. 224-225).

[9] See Appendix 13, section B (p. 225). Whether a testator was a cleric can almost invariably be deduced from the will or from external evidence.

[10] *Councils*, ed. Powicke, 1: 124.

[11] See pp. 18-23.

bishops of Norwich, 62 clerics with parochial and 21 with non-parochial benefices, 197 unbeneficed clerics (most of whom were probably stipendiary priests attached to parish churches or colleges of secular priests), 1 cleric in minor orders[12] and 3 parish clerks.[13] Their wealth and backgrounds have been discussed.[14]

As for the lay testators, men exceeded women by slightly more than three to one. They represented only a small proportion of the laity living in the city.[15] Moreover they came disproportionately from the upper ranks of urban society. The evidence as to where, more precisely, they stood in the social spectrum is somewhat conflicting. On the one hand the large majority of the wills were proved in the Prerogative Court of Canterbury or in the Norwich Consistory Court, for whose probates testators were supposed to possess substantial goods in more than one diocese and in more than one archdeaconry respectively, while only a small proportion of the wills were proved in the court of the archdeacon of Norwich or by the dean of Norwich, who appear to have been legally responsible for proving the wills of lesser people.[16] On the other hand the observance of these rules of probate was probably never exact[17] and can hardly be reconciled with the fact that in the will-registers the notes of probate of about a fifth of the wills in question, including many proved in the Norwich Consistory Court, were accompanied by the marginal note "dimissus est in forma pauperis" or its equivalent. (According to the law of Canterbury Province, the note indicates that the objects mentioned in the inventory of the deceased's goods were probably worth less than thirty shillings.)[18] On balance the evidence suggests that more testators came from lower down the social scale than might be expected but the majority, and far more than was proportional with the actual mixture of social classes in the city, came from the upper ranks of urban society.

[12] John Excestre (see p. 50).

[13] N.C.C., Reg. Ryxe, fol. 454r (Stalon), and Reg. Gylys, fols. 79r (Bowen) and 172v (Gilbert).

[14] See pp. 23-55.

[15] The 1,515 lay persons who made wills that survive represent something like one in fifty of the lay inhabitants of the city who reached adulthood in the late fourteenth and early fifteenth centuries, rising to about one in ten by the late fifteenth and early sixteenth centuries (see p. xvi, n. 4, for the city's population).

[16] Burnham, "Episcopal Administration," pp. 181-183; Irene J. Churchill, *Canterbury Administration* (London 1933), 1: 200 and 380, and 2: 77-78; Camp, *Wills*, pp. xxv and xxx; see Appendix 13 (pp. 224-225). The only will known to have been proved by the dean of Norwich during the period in question was N.C.R., Case 16c, Assembly Minute Books, 1 (1492-1510), fols. 135v-136r (Spycer).

[17] Camp, *Wills*, p. xxvii.

[18] William Lyndwood, *Provinciale* (Oxford 1679), pp. 181-182.

Certainly the top of Norwich society was well represented. The sample includes the wills of 29 of the 66 men who were mayors of the city between 1404, when the office was created, and 1532 and who had died by the latter year. Twenty-six others were described as aldermen of Norwich, a dozen as knights, gentlemen or "armigeri." The occupations of 200 men were mentioned. They formed a wide spectrum of some 60 crafts and trades, but one which reflects Norwich's position as a centre of the cloth trade. There were 21 worsted-weavers and 9 other types of weavers, 16 tailors and 9 mercers; 10 were described as merchants, 8 as carpenters and 7 as cordwainers. Two were described as labourers,[19] but few other menial or unskilled occupations were mentioned. All but a handful of the women were widows. The scarcity of women making wills while their husbands were alive reflects the victory of English common law over the attempts of canon law to preserve the testamentary rights of women during their marriages.[20] In so far as they were described, the widows' former husbands formed a spectrum of society similar to that formed by the (lay) men whose wills survive.

Most of the testators were close to death when they made their wills: less than a year elapsed between the will being written and probate being given in over four-fifths of the cases in which both were dated. The imminence of death concentrates the mind, and doubtless it concentrated the minds of many medieval Christians on the future of their souls. Moreover wealth can be disposed of at rather less personal cost in a will than at other times because the transference is not made until after death. No doubt, therefore, the wills of medieval Christians reflect a more religious outlook than many of them possessed earlier in their lives. On the other hand a person is, in many ways, most authentic when facing death: in some ways a will sums up a person's attitude to life.

Several factors, however, limited the testator's freedom to dispose of his or her goods. Henry Swinburne, the earliest national authority on the subject, wrote at the end of the sixteenth century that in many parts of the country custom required that, after a man's debts and funeral expenses had been paid, a third of his personal goods must pass to his wife if she survived him, another third to any surviving children and only the last third, sometimes called "Death's Part," could be disposed of as he

[19] N.C.C., Reg. Haywarde, fol. 77v (Cowper); A.N.C., Reg. Cook (1503-1538), fol. 42v (Crosse).

[20] Michael M. Sheehan, "The Influence of Canon Law on the Property Rights of Married Women in England," *Mediaeval Studies* 25 (1963) 119-120.

wished.[21] This had been the common law in England until at least the early thirteenth century.[22] There are suggestions in a few wills that the custom had some influence in late medieval Norwich,[23] but no clear reference to it has been found in the city's records,[24] and Dr Houlbrooke has found no evidence that the mid-sixteenth-century judges of the Norwich Consistory Court upheld possible customary limitations on the testator's freedom of decision in favour of his family, and believes they were very careful not to allow wills to be impugned on other grounds without good proofs.[25] In Norwich, as in the rest of the country, wills followed conventional patterns to a considerable extent. Precisely who wrote the wills is obscure but it seems certain that much of the phraseology, and some of the bequests, were suggested to testators by the parish priests[26] or other people who helped in the making of wills.

Despite these restrictions, testators enjoyed considerable freedom to give to some branches of the Church rather than to others, for some religious or charitable purposes rather than for others. The variety of wills shows that this freedom was exercised.[27] Wills are invaluable evidence of the way in which many Christians chose in these matters, and therefore of their attitudes towards Christianity. They are specially important for the Middle Ages because there survive for the period so few private letters, diaries or other records that describe directly and in first-person terms the attitudes of Christians – particularly of large numbers below the topmost rungs of society – towards their religion.

Bequest for Masses and prayers,[28] for pilgrimages,[29] for the preaching of sermons[30] and for scholarships[31] have already been mentioned. Bequests to the following will now be discussed: votive lights; religious houses; parish churches and the parish clergy; hermits, anchorites and communities resembling beguinages; craft guilds and pious confraternities; hospitals, prisoners and charitable works; and civic projects. Together they cover almost all the bequests in the wills in question apart from those

---

[21] Henry Swinburne, *A Briefe Treatise of Testaments and Last Willes* (London 1590), pp. 104-106.

[22] Camp, *Wills*, p. xi.

[23] N.C.C., Reg. Harsyk, fol. 54r (Bumpsted), and Reg. Hyrnyng, fol. 32v (Daniel).

[24] *Records of Norwich*, ed. Hudson, 1: 236, n. 1.

[25] Houlbrooke, "Church Courts" (1970), p. 215.

[26] Houlbrooke, *Church Courts* (1979), p. 101.

[27] See Appendix 14 (pp. 226-252).

[28] See pp. 91-110.

[29] See pp. 85-87.

[30] See pp. 11 and 94.

[31] See pp. 31 and 33.

left to relatives, friends and servants. The bequests will be examined from the point of view of their value to the beneficiaries, but primarily as indications of the beneficiaries' popularity with the citizens. This chapter thus covers from another angle most of the institutions and activities discussed in the two previous chapters, namely from that of the attitude towards them of people who were not, for the most part, directly involved in them.

B. Analysis of the Bequests

i. *Bequests to Votive Lights*

The saints and the mysteries of Christ to which most of the lights were dedicated have been discussed.[32] In addition, a few testators left bequests for lights to burn near their corpses or during services for their souls.

Some bequests were of considerable value. Robert Belton, for example, left £2 10s. 0d. in 1502 to "find" a light which was to burn continuously for a year before the Sacrament in St Andrew's parish church, where he wanted to be buried;[33] Robert Kerr, a chaplain who made his will in 1444, left half an acre of land to keep St Mary's light, in Shipdham parish church, burning for ever;[34] and Thomas Bokenham, a former mayor who made his will in 1492, left all his tenements in a street in St Stephen's parish to the church-wardens and parishioners "unto the use" of a lamp which was to burn over his grave in the church, day and night for ever.[35] These bequests, however, were exceptional. Few lights were left more than 3s. 4d. by a single testator; most were left a shilling or a few pennies. But frequently, especially after 1490, a testator left bequests to several lights. Margery Dogett, for example, gave to eleven lights.[36]

Almost all the lights were in parish churches, not in the churches of religious houses. The bequests, as well as offerings to the lights from people not making their wills, must have formed an important source of income for the parish churches. The proportion of testators leaving such bequests rose steadily during the period, with almost half the laity leaving them between 1518 and 1532. This is interesting since devotion to the saints was attacked by many reformers, and votive lights might be considered one of its more superstitious forms.

---

[32] See p. 84.

[33] PROB/11/13 (Reg. Blamyr, 1501-1502), fol. 8 (Belton).

[34] N.C.C., Reg. Wylbey, fol. 6v (Kerr).

[35] PROB/11/9 (Reg. Dogett, 1491-1493), fol. 17 (Bokenham).

[36] See p. 230.

ii. Bequests to Religious Houses

The two most significant points about the bequests to religious houses are first, the large number of both clergy and laity who left bequests to such houses throughout the period in question, which is generally regarded as a time of internal decline and loss of public support for religious orders, and second the fact that far more of the clerical testators, all of whom belonged to the secular clergy, left bequests to houses of religious orders than to colleges of their fellow secular priests.

The Four Friaries. Each of the four friaries in Norwich received bequests from between 44 and 47 per cent of both lay and clerical testators between 1370 and 1532. Bequests to friaries were a common feature of late medieval wills but they appear to have been unusually numerous in Norwich: only 36 per cent of the much wealthier group of testators from London examined by Dr Thomson left a bequest to a friary,[37] and in late medieval Oxford rather fewer than this appear to have given to the Franciscans.[38] In York the proportion giving to one or more of the city's friaries was one in three between 1501 and 1538;[39] in London the proportion appears to have risen somewhat as the Reformation approached.[40] In Norwich, however, it remained fairly constant until about 1517 when it began to drop significantly. The large number of bequests from clerical testators is a significant indication of generally good relations in the city between the friars and the secular clergy.

In most cases testators who gave to one of the city's friaries gave, usually equal sums, to all four of them. Preferences for a particular friary, which were often for the one in which the testator wanted to be buried, were very evenly divided among them. The amount usually left to one was between 3s. 4d. and £1, though a fair number of testators left several pounds. This regular stream of moderately valuable bequests must have been an important source of income for them, especially if they had few endowments. It is a local illustration of the mendicants' dependence on townspeople, and connections with them, throughout late medieval Christendom.

Most testators left their bequests to the friaries without further specification. A few left them to individual friars, sometimes different sums being given according to their status. A chaplain called William

---

[37] Thomson, "Piety and Charity," p. 189.
[38] Little, *Grey Friars*, pp. 101-102.
[39] Palliser, *Reformation in York*, p. 2.
[40] Thomson, "Piety and Charity," pp. 179 and 189-190.

Lockwood, for example, who asked to be buried in the choir of the Dominican church, left the following sums to members of the friary: 1s. 8d. to the prior and each doctor of theology, 1s. to each priest, 6d. to each deacon, 4d. to each subdeacon and 2d. to each novice.[41] A few testators mentioned particular purposes. Edmund Wright, for example, left a sheep to each friary for a "pittance"![42] Some made their bequests conditional upon the friars performing religious services for their souls. Sometimes chantry services were requested,[43] but more commonly the friars were asked to say a Requiem Mass and part of the Office of the Dead, services specially suited to being sung in choir.[44] The most valuable bequest from a citizen came from Margaret Wetherby, widow of the former mayor, Thomas Wetherby. She asked to be buried alongside her husband in the church of the Augustinian friary and left 100 marks to the friars to enable them to build a new library, on condition that they said various Masses for her and her husband's souls and wrote their names into the glass windows of the library as well as in all the books "for future memory." [45] They also received large bequests from county families. Sir Thomas Kerdeston of Claxton, for example, left £200 to the Augustinians to found three perpetual chantries;[46] the country gentry appear to have been responsible for much of the building of the Dominicans' magnificent new church in the fifteenth century;[47] and Sir Thomas Erpingham gave to the Augustinians' church in 1419 what must have been a very remarkable new east window, containing his coat of arms and the names and arms of all those "lords, barons, bannerets and knights who had died without issue male in Norfolk and Suffolk since the coronation of Edward III." [48]

The Cathedral Priory. One difference between bequests to the Cathedral Priory and those to the friaries is that the majority of the former were left to the church rather than to the priory, whereas the latter were almost invariably left to the friaries or individual friars rather than to their churches. The distinction may seem insignificant since bequests to the Cathedral church went to the priory. But the wills give the impression that it was primarily the church – often referred to as "my mother

---

[41] N.C.C., Reg. Jekkys, fol. 231r (Lockwood alias Clynelond).
[42] N.C.C., Reg. Ryxe, fol. 175v (Wright).
[43] See pp. 107-108.
[44] E.g., N.C.C., Reg. Palgrave, fol. 66v (Burgh).
[45] N.C.C., Reg. Brosyard, fols. 83v-84r (Wetherby).
[46] See pp. 106 and 216.
[47] Helen Sutermeister, The Norwich Blackfriars (Norwich 1977), p. 4.
[48] Kenneth B. MacFarlane, The Nobility of Later Medieval England (Oxford 1973), pp. 145-146.

church" – rather than the monks that the testators wished to support. Most bequests ranged between 3s. 4d. and £1, though a fair number after 1490 were smaller sums, sometimes only a few pennies. Large bequests came from bishops of Norwich and county magnates, chiefly to found chantries,[49] but large bequests from the laity of the city, like John de Berney's,[50] were rare. Over the whole period 1370 to 1532 bequests were fewer than to any of the friaries, but they increased considerably during the period, unlike bequests to the friaries. Much of the increase is accounted for by small bequests, many of which may have been little more than conventional gestures. Nevertheless the increase is one of the few significant changes in the pattern of testamentary bequests during the period, and may reflect the better relations which appear to have existed between the citizens and the priory after about 1450.[51]

The Secular Colleges. The four colleges of secular priests in the city were left far fewer bequests than the friaries. That the Carnary College and the college of chantry priests in the Bishop's Palace[52] were left few bequests is to be expected since they were small colleges outside the mainstream of life and notice. That St Giles's Hospital and the College of St Mary in the Fields were left fewer than half as many bequests as any of the friaries is perhaps surprising for several reasons. For they were considerably larger and more important than the other two colleges, their members might hope to attract benefactions from their fellow secular priests, St Giles's Hospital might hope to attract benefactions not only as a college but also as a hospital, and the church and cemetery of the College of St Mary in the Fields were much more popular with the secular clergy as places of burial than were those of the friaries.[53] Testators, however, may have been reluctant to give to them because they possessed endowed incomes and because many masters of the hospital and prebendaries of the college were wealthy pluralists and, in some cases, rarely resident.[54]

Most bequests to St Giles's Hospital were worth between 3s. 4d. and £1. The most valuable bequest came from John Smyth, master of the hospital, chiefly to found a perpetual chantry and anniversary services for his soul.[55] From "The Hospital of St Mary and St Giles," founded in the

[49] See pp. 94-96 and 107.
[50] See pp. 12-13.
[51] See pp. 152-154.
[52] Dissolved in 1449 (see p. 22).
[53] See p. 189.
[54] See pp. 42-45 and 49.
[55] See pp. 95 and 218; N.C.C., Reg. Typpes, fols. 17v-18v (Smyth).

mid thirteenth century "for aged priests and poor scholars of Norwich, receiving daily thirteen poor men and sick persons, with a master, brethren and minister," [56] the hospital had become by the late Middle Ages primarily a college of secular priests with stipendiary priests not on the foundation attached to it. But it remained a hospital for old and sick men; it was also a kind of choir school or seminary;[57] and St Helen's parish church had been incorporated into it. Some bequests reflect its rich variety of functions. Those left by Isabel de Brook in 1382, for example, showed support for its work as an alms-house as well as for the parish church. She left 1s. 8d. to be divided among the bed-ridden poor, 1s. to be divided among the three sisters who cared for them and 3s. for the upkeep of the chancel of the church.[58] Those left in 1521 by John Varies, a priest who was probably a member of its clerical staff, showed support for the priests and its work as some kind of a school as well as appreciation of the domestic staff: he left 10s. to "my master," half a mark to each priest-fellow and 5s. to each stipendiary priest, on condition that each of them said five Masses of the Five Wounds of Jesus for him, and sums ranging from 1s. to 2d. to the clerk, the porter, each "child of the chapel," the butler, the cook, the brewer and his wife, and the brewer's man.[59]

The College of St Mary in the Fields, like the Carnary College and the college of chantry priests in the Bishop's Palace, included neither an alms-house nor a parish church though boys, and clerics who were not priests, were attached to it.[60] Although few, bequests to the college were generally rather valuable: at least £1 was given by about half of both clergy and laity leaving a bequest to it.

Carrow Nunnery. Bequests to the Benedictine nunnery of Carrow in the suburbs of Norwich, which was the only nunnery in or near the city, were also much fewer than bequests to the friaries. This is somewhat surprising since the nunnery must have been well known to the citizens through their various contacts with it.[61] The nunnery's disputes with the city government,[62] and the facts that benefactors could not hope for Masses from nuns and that it was another religious house known to have an endowed income, may help to explain the dearth. Even so, the figures

[56] *Cal. Papal L., 1189-1304*, p. 312.
[57] See p. 33.
[58] N.C.C., Reg. Heydon, fol. 196v (Brook).
[59] N.C.C., Reg. Alblaster, fol. 107r (Varies).
[60] See p. 33.
[61] See pp. 27 and 67.
[62] See pp. 155-156.

of eighteen per cent of the clergy and sixteen per cent of the laity giving to the nunnery compare favourably with Dr Thomson's sample of Londoners, of whom only eleven per cent left something to a nunnery.[63] Most bequests were worth between 3s. 4d. and £1 with only a few worth more. Sometimes they were left to the nunnery but more frequently to individual nuns, occasionally quite large annuities being left to friends or relatives who were nuns there. The growth of private incomes among religious is generally regarded as part of the decline in discipline in religious orders during the late Middle Ages[64] and bequests to individual nuns at Carrow, as well as to individual friars,[65] suggest that the abuse existed in Norwich.

The different kinds of bequests are illustrated by those of Agnes Thorpe: she left £1 for the "repair" of the nunnery, half a mark each year to a nun who was a goddaughter of hers as long as she lived, and £1 to be equally divided among the nuns provided they "kept" Matins and Vespers of the Dead and a Requiem Mass for her and her friends' souls "as they keep for their other benefactors.[66]

Houses outside Norwich. Thirteen per cent of the laity and seventeen per cent of the clergy gave to religious houses outside Norwich. The donors represent one way in which Christians in Norwich took an interest in the wider Church.

Almost all the bequests to religious houses of women were left to the other ten nunneries (besides Carrow) in the diocese, sometimes bequests being left to all of them by a single testator.[67] The only beneficiaries outside the diocese were the Benedictine priories at Cambridge,[68] Swafham Bulbeck in Cambridgeshire[69] and Stratford-at-Bow in Middlesex,[70] the Franciscan convent at Denney in Cambridgeshire,[71] the Cistercian priory at Gokewell in Lincolnshire,[72] and the nuns and sisters at

[63] Thomson, "Piety and Charity," p. 189.
[64] Knowles, *Religious Orders*, 2: 240-244; Eileen E. Power, *Medieval English Nunneries* (Cambridge 1922), p. 331.
[65] See pp. 119-120.
[66] PROB/11/13 (Reg. Blamyr, 1501-1503), fol. 26 (Thorpe).
[67] E.g., Ab.C., Reg. Arundel 2 (1396-1414), fol. 165v (Totington); N.C.C., Reg. Harsyk, fol. 67r (Appleyard); see p. 242.
[68] See p. 242.
[69] See p. 242.
[70] N.C.C., Reg. Aleyn, fol. 24v (Cheese).
[71] N.C.C., Reg. Hyrnyng, fol. 95v (Blickling), and Reg. Spyltymber, fol. 214r (Corpusty); see p. 242.
[72] N.C.C., Reg. Johnson, fol. 141v (Hewettson).

Lincoln-without-the-Gates[73] who were probably the women looking after St Sepulchre Hospital.

As for houses of men, bequests were left to some forty houses inside the diocese and about the same number outside it. Prominent among the latter were colleges and halls at Oxford and Cambridge, the benefactor usually being a priest known to have studied there earlier in his life. The most popular was Gonville Hall at Cambridge, which had enjoyed close connections with Norwich from the time of William Bateman (ca. 1298-1355), who was joint founder of the hall and was the son of a bailiff of Norwich and became its bishop;[74] seven testators gave to it. Sometimes other connections can be discerned: for example, Roger Medilton, rector of St Peter Mancroft, left £40 in 1375 to Gloucester Abbey which had presented him to his valuable living fourteen years earlier;[75] and John Shouldham left £5 in 1402 to his son who was a monk at Walden Abbey in Essex.[76]

Three of the half-dozen houses of men outside the diocese to which more than one testator left a bequest were the London Charterhouse with bequests from five testators, and Sheen Charterhouse in Surrey and the Brigettine Abbey of Syon in Middlesex with bequests from two (probably) each. One testator left a bequest to Mountgrace Charterhouse in Yorkshire. The bequests suggest support for monasteries which were recent foundations and whose monks led, or were thought to lead, austere lives. Dr Thomson also found support for such monasteries among Londoners.[77] The donors form an interesting cross-section of Norwich society. The first was William Ashwell, a merchant and former mayor, who left half a mark in 1458 to Mountgrace Charterhouse and the same amount to the London Charterhouse.[78] Dr Richard Poringland, formerly vicar of St Stephen's,[79] left one mark in 1471 to each of the London Charterhouse, Sheen Charterhouse and Syon Abbey, claiming to be a confrater of each place;[80] and Dr Geoffrey Chaumpneis, vicar of St Stephen's, left 2s. in 1472 to the prior of the London Charterhouse, 1s. to

---

[73] N.C.C., Reg. Multon, fol. 143r (West).

[74] *D.N.B.*, 3: 395-397 (William Bateman); John A. Venn, *Caius College* (London 1901), pp. 14-32.

[75] N.C.C., Reg. Heydon, fol. 54v (Medilton); REG/2, Book 5, fol. 54v.

[76] N.C.C., Reg. Harsyk, fol. 294r-v (Shouldham).

[77] Thomson, "Piety and Charity," pp. 189-190.

[78] PROB/11/4 (Reg. Stokton, 1454-1458), fol. 12 (Ashwell).

[79] See p. 47.

[80] N.C.C., Reg. Gelour, fol. 92r (Poringland).

each monk and various books to the house as well as 1s. to "my father the prior of Syon, commonly called Sheen," and 4d. to each monk there.[81] The bequests of the two vicars are perhaps further evidence of their following in the steps of their predecessor, Richard Caistor, as unusual men of radical views.[82] William Hemming, an unbeneficed priest, left his missal to Syon Abbey in 1486 so that the monks might pray for him and his parents;[83] and John Cowper, a tailor, left 3s. 4d. to the London Charterhouse in 1503, asking the monks to pray for him.[84] Finally Agnes Thorpe, the widow of a wealthy alderman, left £1 in 1503 to the prior and monks of the London Charterhouse, asking them to "keep" Matins and Vespers of the Dead and a Requiem Mass for her and her two husbands' souls, £1 for the upkeep of the house and half a mark to one of the monks, and she said that she had letters of confraternity with the house which she wanted to be delivered to the monks.[85] The popularity of the Carthusians is one reason why it is surprising that a Charterhouse was never founded in East Anglia.

The Hospice of St Thomas in Rome, which provided accommodation for English pilgrims there, was the only house outside England to which bequests were left. Three priests[86] and two lay men[87] gave to it. The hospice had its own collector in England,[88] and one testator directed his bequest to be paid to him.[89] There was also a bequest of half a mark in 1428 "for the defence of the fortress of Saint Peter," [90] perhaps the Castel Sant' Angelo in Rome; and one of £10 in 1521 for the building of the "holy church of Rome," [91] presumably the new St Peter's church.

---

[81] See p. 235. Evidently there is a confusion as to whether Sheen Charterhouse or Syon Abbey is intended. Probably the former is meant since the bequest immediately follows those to the London Charterhouse, and since "my father the prior" probably refers to the head of the house, and while the head of the Sheen Charterhouse was a prior, Syon had an abbot.

[82] See pp. 41, 47-48 and 231-236.

[83] N.C.C., Reg. A. Caston, fol. 294v (Hemming).

[84] A.N.C., Reg. Cook (1501-1538), fol. 27v (Cowper).

[85] PROB/11/13 (Reg. Blamyr, 1501-1503), fol. 26 (Thorpe); PROB/11/12 (Reg. Moone, 1500-1501), fol. 19 (Thorpe).

[86] N.C.C., Reg. Doke, fol. 235v (Couteshale), Reg. Spyltymber, fol. 126r (Sharpe), and Reg. Ryxe, fol. 305v (Waller).

[87] PROB/11/10 (Reg. Vox, 1493-1496), fol. 3 (Smyth); N.C.C., Reg. Ryxe, fol. 195r (Carter).

[88] Francis A. Gasquet, *A History of the Venerable English College, Rome* (London 1920), pp. 40-41.

[89] N.C.C., Reg. Ryxe, fol. 305v (Waller).

[90] "Ad defensionem castri Sancti Petri" (N.C.C., Reg. Surflete, fol. 26r [Sistede]).

[91] PROB/11/20 (Reg. Maynwaring, 1520-1522), fol. 8 (Hare).

iii. *Bequests to Parish Churches and the Parish Clergy*

It is often difficult to distinguish bequests to parish churches from those to the parish clergy. Bequests to the former, moreover, may well have ended up in the pockets of the latter. The parish clergy, including priests attached to parish churches as stipendiaries, were left many bequests on condition that they said Masses and prayers.[92] They also received bequests to act as executors and supervisors of wills, between a quarter and a third of the laity and about three-quarters of the clergy choosing at least one member of the secular clergy to act in such a capacity;[93] and they were rewarded in the same way as their lay counterparts, with bequests usually worth between 3s. 4d. and £1. Bequests to the parish clergy that were without conditions were left by few of the laity but by a rather higher proportion of the clergy. Dr Geoffrey Chaumpneis, for example, left a number of bequests to the clergy of the two parishes of which he had been vicar, St Stephen's in Norwich and Cromer in north Norfolk.[94] He left his best surplice and all his wax in the chancel of St Stephen's to his successor as vicar, 1s. and a book called "Rosarium"[95] to the then vicar of Cromer and forgave him any debts, and 4d. to every priest in the two parishes.[96] Bequests to the parish clergy from their fellow secular priests, and the frequent choice of each other as executors and supervisors of their wills, are further aspects of clerical society in the city.

Even when bequests to the clergy are excluded, more testators gave to parish churches than to anything else. Only bequests for Masses and prayers averaged per testator more in value. Eighty-five per cent of the clergy and ninety-five per cent of the laity gave to at least one parish church, the lower figure for the clergy perhaps being due to priests who were members of secular colleges feeling themselves to be outside the parish system. The parish church was not an institution that was much attacked by reformers, and it is noticeable that in Norwich the decline in some types of religious bequests after about 1517[97] was not paralleled by any significant decline in bequests to parish churches. Their popularity may be explained partly by their importance in the lives of the citizens, and partly by the feeling of parishioners that their parish churches belonged to them and were their responsibility more than religious houses

---

[92] See pp. 92-110.
[93] See p. 14.
[94] Emden, *BRUC*, p. 130 (Geoffrey Champeneys).
[95] See p. 41.
[96] See pp. 235-236.
[97] See pp. 101 and 119.

or hospitals were. Many testators gave to more than one church but they almost invariably preferred their own. William Burstymer, for example, left 4s. 4d. to his own church in Norwich and 1s. to the parish church at Gateshead where he had been born;[98] William Mayne, parish chaplain of St James's, left bequests of equal value to his own church and to the church of the parish in which he had been born, and lesser sums to the church in which he had sung his first Mass and to three others.[99] Robert Toppes, a former mayor, was one of half a dozen testators who left a bequest to every parish church in the city. He left 20 marks to St Peter Mancroft, which was almost certainly his own church, 3s. 4d. to every other parish church in the city, and sums ranging from 3s. 4d. to £2 to seventeen others in East Anglia.[100]

The bequests were mainly of two types – to the high altar, and for the upkeep of the church. Most testators left both types of bequests to the same church. The distinction probably represents a fashion in phrasing wills more than a difference of substance. Bequests "to the high altar" became, as has been mentioned,[101] bequests "to the high altar for unpaid tithes" after about 1490; and bequests couched in both phrases were usually worth between 1s. and 3s. 4d., rarely more than £1. Bequests for the upkeep of churches too, were often expressed in set phrases such as "for the repair of" or "to the fabric of," phrases that were standard throughout late medieval English wills. These were usually worth rather more than bequests to the high altar, and quite frequently large sums were involved. An alderman called Robert Browne, for example, left £20 in 1530 for the repair of St Stephen's;[102] and William Setman, a former mayor, left 40 marks in 1429 for the repair of St Peter Mancroft.[103]

Many bequests for the upkeep of churches were more specific. Sometimes this was the case with small sums; Margaret Wright, for example, left 1s. towards making the rood-loft of one church, and 1s. towards repairing the bells of another, as well as a bequest to the high altar of her own church.[104] But usually bequests of this kind involved fairly large amounts of money, to meet the cost of buying service-books and other liturgical items. A mercer called John Copping, for example, left

[98] A.N.C., Reg. Cook (1503-1538), fol. 28r (Burstymer).
[99] N.C.C., Reg. Haywarde, fol. 72r-v (Mayne).
[100] N.C.C., Reg. Jekkys, fols. 97r-98r (Toppe).
[101] See p. 5.
[102] PROB/11/24 (Reg. Thower, 1531-1533), fol. 3 (Browne).
[103] See p. 242.
[104] D. and C., Reg. 1461-1559, fol. 30r (Wryght).

to St Andrew's in 1430 the money needed to buy a missal costing up to 20 marks and a vestment costing up to £20;[105] John Terry, a former mayor, left 40 marks to St John's Maddermarket in 1524 to buy a silver and gilt cross;[106] and John Gilbert, another former mayor, left 100 marks to St Andrew's in 1466 to buy a vestment or an ornament.[107] Liturgical items could have the added advantage of serving as a memorial of the donor. Thus Thomas Daywell, parish chaplain of St Martin at the Palace Gates, left to his church in 1505 a new lectern and a cloth for it "with an image of Saint Martin on one side and upon the other side Mary Magdalen, myself kneeling to the one image and Robert Shynbone to the other." [108] Many of the clergy and a few of the laity left their personal belongings: William Bruyn, a priest, wanted his *Legenda aurea* to be kept in the choir of one church, and his "book of the Doubt of the Legend both Temporal and Sanctorum" in the chancel of another, for the benefit of anybody wishing to read them;[109] William Swetman, rector of All Saints of Berstreet, wanted his breviary to be kept chained in the chancel of his church;[110] Robert Baxter, a former mayor, left his gold thurible to St Giles's;[111] Alice Carre left to St Stephen's her best coral beads to beautify the images of various saints on their feast-days, and her small coral beads to be "daily about the image of St Anne";[112] and John Basse wanted his best tippet to be decorated at his cost with buttons and tassels and given to St Martin of Coslany "to cover the Sacrament on dead days and interment days." [113]

Bequests for the upkeep of churches included a fair number of large bequests for particular building projects. They were concentrated upon relatively few churches: St Andrew's, Holy Cross, St Edmund's, St George at Tombland, St Gregory's, St Laurence's, St Martin at the Palace Gates, St Michael of Coslany, St Peter Mancroft and St Stephen's. They help to explain the extensive rebuilding of the city's churches in the late Middle Ages.[114] Bartholomew Appleyard, for example, left £20 in 1386 to

---

[105] PROB/11/3 (Reg. Luffenham, 1423-1449), fol. 15 (Copping).
[106] See p. 245.
[107] N.C.C., Reg. Jekkys, fol. 47v (Gilbert).
[108] N.C.C., Reg. Ryxe, fol. 193v (Daywell); see p. 188.
[109] N.C.C., Reg. A. Caston, fol. 106v (Bruyn).
[110] N.C.C., Reg. Popy, fol. 549r (Swetman).
[111] N.C.C., Reg. Surflete, fol. 88r (Baxter).
[112] N.C.C., Reg. Groundesburgh, fol. 8r (Carre).
[113] N.C.C., Reg. Ryxe, fol. 340v (Basse).
[114] See p. 4.

lead the roof of his parish church, St Andrew's;[115] and John Moore, rector of St Edmund's from 1467 until his death in 1507,[116] wanted the roof of the chancel of his church to be "leaded up" at his cost.[117] Richard Browne, a former mayor, left 40 marks in 1461 "to the making of" the steeple of Holy Cross "for to be remembered and my brother Sygrim and all my good friends." [118] Robert Pert left £20 to the "economi" of St Peter Mancroft in 1445 so that they might build a new gable at the east end of the church.[119] This was in the middle of the period during which the church was completely rebuilt.[120] It is interesting that he entrusted the money to lay parishioners, not to the clergy. John Swan, an unbeneficed priest, provided in 1467 for a bell which was to harmonise with the four others in the belfry of St Stephen's;[121] John Savage, rector of St Clement at Fye Bridge, left two marks in 1448 for a window in the chancel of his church which was to represent the story of St John the Baptist;[122] and John Reynolds, a grocer, offered the parishioners of St Andrew's 10 marks in 1499 for a window, if they built a new church.[123] It is interesting that Reynolds expected the initiative for building the church to come from the parishioners and that he, like Robert Pert, entrusted the money to them, not to the clergy. William Haywarde, who made his will in 1506, also made his bequest conditional upon contributions by others: he was willing to pay for the glazing of the east window and a side window in St Peter Parmentergate provided the chancel was built within four years.[124]

In short, the wills of both the laity and the clergy give an impression of considerable enthusiasm for the parish churches of the city: to rebuild and adorn them, and to provide them with the liturgical items needed for celebrating services. This enthusiasm indicates their continuing vitality in the late Middle Ages, despite the arrival of houses of religious orders and colleges of secular priests and of new religious movements with a special appeal to the laity.

---

[115] N.C.C., Reg. Harsyk, fol. 67r (Appleyard).

[116] REG/6, Book 11, fol. 162r; REG/8, Book 13, second series of folios, fol. 86r.

[117] N.C.C., Reg. Ryxe, fol. 469v (Moore).

[118] PROB/11/4 (Reg. Stokton, 1454-1458), fol. 23 (Browne).

[119] N.C.C., Reg. Wylbey, fol. 58r (Pert).

[120] "Report of the Summer Meeting of the Institute at Norwich, 1949," *Archaeological Journal* 106 (1949) 95.

[121] N.C.C., Reg. Jekkys, fol. 71v (Swan).

[122] N.C.C., Reg. Aleyn, fol. 12r (Savage).

[123] Ab.C., Reg. Morton 2 (1486-1500), fol. 44r (Reynold).

[124] PROB/11/15 (Reg. Adean, 1506-1508), fol. 7 (Hayward).

iv. *Bequests to Hermits, Anchorites and*
Communities resembling Beguinages

Norwich was exceptional among late medieval English towns in the number of its hermits and anchorites and in having two or three communities of women resembling beguinages.[125] The city appears to have been exceptional, too, in that about one in five testators left bequests to them. Bequests to recluses from Londoners and from the English nobility, for instance, appear to have been much rarer.[126] That the clergy of Norwich were as keen as the laity in supporting them is interesting inasmuch as they might be thought to represent in part a reaction against the life-styles of priests and nuns.

All but seventeen of the bequests were left to hermits or anchorites rather than to the communities resembling beguinages. By far the largest was the £40 left to Robert Ferneys, hermit of Newbridge, to make a pilgrimage to Rome and Jerusalem.[127] Before about 1470 the hermits and anchorites to whom bequests were left were normally named individually in the wills, usually between sixpence and half a mark, occasionally as much as £1 being given to each. After about 1470 they were normally left "to each anchor and anchoress in Norwich," and usually between 4d. and 1s. 8d. was given to each. The change marked the development whereby bequests to recluses, from being occasional and seemingly dependent upon the express wishes of a particular testator, became almost customary in at least the longer wills. Moreover it followed by about half a century the development whereby recluses themselves from being rare and exceptional figures, had become established pieces in the religious scenery of the city.

Most bequests were without conditions. A few of those left to anchors or hermits who were priests were conditional upon Masses being said for the donors' souls,[128] and a few were left to the recluses' servants.[129] Agnes Thorpe provided for spiritual services: she left 2 marks in 1503 for a priest to "sing before" the anchoress attached to St Julian's parish church.[130] Presumably he was to sing Mass in the parish church, with the anchoress attending through a squint connecting her anchorage to the church.

---

[125] See pp. 57-59 and 64-65.

[126] See Rosenthal, *Purchase of Paradise*, and Thomson, "Piety and Charity," where such bequests are not mentioned.

[127] See p. 62.

[128] E.g., N.C.C., Reg. Jekkys, fols. 39v (Furbisshor) and 91v (Machon).

[129] E.g., N.C.C., Reg. Aleyn, fol. 108r (Colman), and Reg. Gelour, fol. 19v (Poringland).

[130] PROB/11/13 (Reg. Blamyr, 1501-1503), fol. 26 (Thorpe).

If testamentary bequests to hermits and anchorites are a guide to the money given to them at other times, they explain how even poor people could have become recluses and lived off the alms of the faithful. Paradoxically the most ambitious attempt to provide them with some kind of regular income came shortly before they disappeared: Robert Jannys, a former mayor who made his will in 1530, wanted each anchorite in the city to have 13d. of his money every three months for twenty years.[131]

Bequests to communities resembling beguinages never attained the popularity of those to anchorites and hermits. It would be interesting to know whether lack of financial support was a cause of their disappearance.[132] The seventeen bequests left to them ranged from 4d. to 10s. Seven donors were clerics: John Riche, rector of St Michael of Coslany;[133] John Dyra, rector of St John's Maddermarket;[134] four unbeneficed priests;[135] and John Excestre, the bishop's registrar.[136] The other donors included four former mayors[137] and two of their wives.[138]

v. Bequests to Craft Guilds and Pious Confraternities

Craft guilds and pious confraternities were the only beneficiaries of a religious or charitable nature, apart from the College of St Mary in the Fields, to which the clergy and the laity gave in noticeably differing proportions.

The clergy's support for Corpus Christi confraternity explains the difference. Between 1440 and 1489 a quarter of them gave to this confraternity for priests,[139] a half between 1490 and 1532. Some of them left bequests without conditions, never exceeding £1 and usually ranging between 3s. 4d. and half a mark. More commonly they left sums ranging between 2d. and 8d. to every member of the confraternity who attended various services for their souls – Exequies, a Requiem Mass and sometimes Matins of the Dead – which they expected the confraternity to arrange. The gatherings attracted by these rewards must have been a further feature of clerical society in the city.

---

[131] See p. 251.

[132] See pp. 65-66.

[133] N.C.C., Reg. Hyrnyng, fol. 151v (Riche).

[134] N.C.C., Reg. Aleyn, fol. 61r (Dyra).

[135] N.C.C., Reg. Doke, fol. 88r (Parlet), Reg. Aleyn, fol. 59r (Veautre), and Reg. Brosyard, fols. 102r (Goodsweyn) and 160r (Child).

[136] N.C.C., Reg. Wylbey, fol. 107r (Excestre); see p. 50.

[137] N.C.C., Reg. Surflete, fol. 86r (Baxter), and Reg. Jekkys, fol. 48r (Gilbert); PROB/11/4 (Reg. Stokton, 1454-1462), fol. 23 (Browne); see p. 242.

[138] N.C.C., Reg. Cobald, fol. 68r (Brown), and Reg. Jekkys, fol. 49v (Gilbert).

[139] See pp. 75-76.

Bequests to the confraternities of the Mass of Jesus in St Peter Mancroft parish church, and of the Mass of Jesus in the Cathedral, were probably intended for their chantries;[140] and a few bequests to the confraternity of Our Lady in St Stephen's parish church were left to its chantry priest[141] or for the performance of religious services by the confraternity.[142] Apart from these bequests and those to Corpus Christi confraternity just mentioned, testators rarely specified whether their bequests were to be spent on the confraternities' religious activities or rather on their charitable or civic activities. Almost all of them were left to confraternities rather than to guilds,[143] and they were usually worth between one and ten shillings. The largest bequest in cash came from an alderman called Henry Salter who left £10 in 1530 to the confraternity of Our Lady in St Stephen's parish church to help to pay the wages of its chantry priest for ten years;[144] the only bequest of real estate came from Robert Browne, another alderman, who left an "enclose" in the city, including a barn, to the same confraternity in the same year so that it might keep an annual obit for his soul.[145]

Corpus Christi confraternity received by far the most bequests, even though none of the laity gave to it. Other popular confraternities were St George's, Our Lady's in St Stephen's parish church and St Anne's in St Peter Mancroft parish church. As mentioned, a fair number of testators gave to more than one confraternity, and some gave to confraternities outside the city.[146]

It is rather surprising that only fifteen per cent of the laity gave to guilds or confraternities. They were the only religious bodies apart from parishes to which most lay people could belong, and they were largely controlled by the laity. Lack of support for them is another indication that new movements did not replace the old institutions as the mainstay of the local Church.

vi. Bequests to Hospitals, Prisoners and Charitable Works

Testators could hope for the double advantage of helping people in need and benefiting their own souls by leaving bequests for works of mercy; charitable bequests had religious dimensions.

[140] See p. 94.

[141] See p. 94.

[142] E.g., PROB/11/24 (Reg. Thower, 1531-1533), fols. 3 (Browne) and 4 (Salter); and N.C.C., Reg. Palgrave, fol. 81v (Bower).

[143] See p. 67, n. 70.

[144] PROB/11/24 (Reg. Thower, 1531-1533), fol. 4 (Salter).

[145] Ibid., fol. 3 (Browne).

[146] See p. 75.

Bequests to St Giles's Hospital have been discussed.[147] It appears to have been primarily a college of secular priests, only secondarily a hospital, in the late Middle Ages. Of the other nine hospitals known to have existed in the city and its suburbs in the late Middle Ages, three received very few bequests: Magdalen Hospital, Hildebrond's Hospital (sometimes called St Mary's Hospital or Ivy Hall) and some alms-houses connected with the Daniel family. The first two appear to have been small institutions, and this helps to explain the lack of bequests. The alms-houses were the only hospital founded between 1370 and the Reformation, but their existence appears to have been brief. The brothers John and Walter Daniel, both of whom had been mayors of Norwich, provided in their joint will of 1418 for the future maintenance of the alms-houses which, the will said, had recently been built in St Stephen's and St Catherine's parishes. Their bequest suggests that they had been responsible for having them built,[148] but with the possible exception of a bequest in another will of Walter Daniel, made in 1424,[149] no further bequest to them is known and it is unlikely that they survived for long.[150] Perhaps the abundance of existing hospitals rendered them superfluous.

There were five sick-houses just outside five of the city's gates: those outside St Giles Gate, St Augustine's Gate, St Stephen's or Needham Gate, St Benedict's or Westwick Gate, and Magdalen or Fyebridge Gate. Each of them was probably no larger than Hildebrond's or Magdalen Hospital, yet almost two in five testators left bequests to them. This was probably in part because they were well known collectively, testators usually leaving bequests to each house or to each inmate of each house. By the late Middle Ages they were probably alms-houses for old and sick men (they were sometimes called sick-houses) and no longer leper-houses (which they had been founded as and which they continued to be usually called). Bequests were always modest sums, usually between 6d. and 1s. 8d. to each house or between one and four pennies to each inmate of each house.

There was also a steady flow of bequests to St Paul's Hospital, some-times called Norman's Hospital. It was the largest hospital in the city with the possible exception of St Giles's. Like the latter its church also acted as a parish church, and a few bequests were left to it. But during the period in question it was primarily a hospice for women, numbering twenty-four in the mid fifteenth century and a dozen in the early sixteenth century,

---

147 See pp. 121-122.
148 N.C.C., Reg. Hyrnyng, fol. 32v (Daniel).
149 Ibid., fol. 148v (Daniel).
150 For the only evidence of their survival, see Blomefield, *Norfolk* (1805-1810), 4: 164.

divided roughly equally into "whole sisters" and "half sisters."[151] It also took in men who were called brothers until the late fourteenth or early fifteenth century,[152] and it was maintaining a subsidiary alms-house for poor people in the second half of the fifteenth century.[153] The large majority of bequests were left to the sisters, usually between a penny and a shilling to each. Since the citizens of Norwich appear to have been reluctant to give to religious institutions with endowed incomes, or whose members seemed to live comfortably or could not say Masses for their benefactors,[154] it is perhaps surprising that almost a third of the testators left bequests to the sisters. For, Masses could not be hoped for from them; the hospital had a fairly substantial income from endowments;[155] it was supposed to pay the sisters a weekly allowance (8d. a week for each "whole sister" and 3d. a week for each "half sister" in 1433/44);[156] and women apparently had to be fairly well off to become sisters, at least in the late fifteenth century, since one of the complaints at the visitation of the hospital in 1492 was that nobody could become a sister without paying an entrance fee of at least ten marks.[157]

The proportion of testators leaving bequests to one or more hospitals appears to have been much higher in Norwich than in London, where it was less than a fifth in Dr Thomson's sample.[158] On the other hand Norwich compares unfavourably with London in bequests to prisoners. Over a quarter of Dr Thomson's sample gave to them[159] whereas the proportion in Norwich was sixteen per cent of the laity and eleven per cent of the clergy. All the bequests were left to prisoners in the Guild Hall or in the Castle, which accommodated prisoners from the city of Norwich and the county of Norfolk respectively. (There were also gaols in the city belonging to the bishop of Norwich and the prior of the Cathedral Priory,[160] but prisoners were probably held in them only occasionally and so it is hardly surprising that bequests were not left to them.) Walter Daniel, the wealthy merchant and former mayor whose scruples about his

[151] D. and C. Mun., Obedientiary Rolls, nos. 1399-1404; *Visitations*, ed. Jessopp, pp. 15 and 273.
[152] N.C.C., Reg. Harsyk, fol. 67r (Appleyard); Blomefield, *Norfolk* (1805-1810), 4: 432.
[153] D. and C., Reg. 1461-1559, fols. 7r (Martyn) and 15r (Narborgh).
[154] See pp. 121-122.
[155] Saunders, *Obedientiary Rolls*, p. 147.
[156] D. and C. Mun., Obedientiary Rolls, no. 1399; *Visitations*, ed. Jessopp, p. 14.
[157] *Visitations*, ed. Jessopp, p. 14.
[158] Thomson, "Piety and Charity," p. 187.
[159] Ibid., p. 185.
[160] *Cal. Pat. R., 1441-1446*, p. 233; *Heresy Trials*, ed. Tanner, pp. 200 and 213.

own business dealings have been mentioned,[161] left £10 in 1424 to be spent on releasing poor people imprisoned for debt in the two places, by paying up to £1 of each person's debts;[162] and Thomas Aldriche, another former mayor, left £4 for the same purpose in 1529.[163] But these were exceptionally large bequests. Usually between 6d. and 3s. 4d., normally in cash but occasionally the value in food and drink, was left collectively to the prisoners in each gaol, or between one and three pennies to each prisoner.

The wills contained a wide variety of other charitable bequests. The most popular form was for a testator to leave the residue of his estate, or part of it, to be disposed "for his soul" in alms to the poor, or in works of mercy and charity, or in some similar way. Some testators left money to poor people with a view to their praying, or attending services, for their souls.[164] Others simply instructed their executors to distribute sums of money to the poor and needy, often on the day of their burial or their anniversary. Many bequests of the last kind were large sums, quite often £10 or more. William Setman, for example, the former mayor who made his will in 1429, left £20 to be distributed immediately after his death to the poor and needy of Norwich and the surrounding towns, 40 marks to be distributed immediately after his death to the poor and needy of a dozen other towns in East Anglia, and £40 to be distributed to the poor, the blind, the deaf and the infirm of Norwich at the rate of 3d. per person per week for three years after his death.[165] A century later Robert Jannys, another former mayor, wanted a penny to be given to each of eighty poor persons every Friday for twenty years, a bequest that would have cost £346 13s. 4d.; and he left £20 for the marriages of "maidens," presumably as dowries for poor brides, to be distributed at the rate of £1 per bride.[166]

Professor Jordan argued that charitable bequests in the wills of Englishmen increased during the century after 1540, and that the increase was due to the Reformation.[167] Be that as it may, the above evidence shows that charitable bequests were a prominent and regular feature of wills in Norwich long before the beginning of the Reformation – indeed from as early as wills survive in large numbers, namely from the late

[161] See p. 106.
[162] N.C.C., Reg. Hyrnyng, fol. 149v (Daniel).
[163] PROB/11/23 (Reg. Jankyn, 1523-1530), fol. 9 (Aldriche).
[164] See pp. 99 and 103-104.
[165] See p. 243.
[166] See pp. 249 and 251.
[167] William K. Jordan, *Philanthropy in England, 1480-1660* (London 1959), pp. 151-153 and 368.

fourteenth century. On the other hand, testators from Norwich who left significantly more money in charitable bequests than in bequests of a directly religious nature were very rare in the late Middle Ages, whereas they no longer were by the second half of the sixteenth century. Thus, to take some of the more prominent examples, William Setman, Robert Jannys and the Daniel brothers may have given much to charity,[168] but they also founded, or tried to found, perpetual chantries;[169] and William Setman wanted 4,000 Masses to be said for his soul immediately after his death.[170] The most notable exceptions were Richard Caistor, vicar of St Stephen's from 1402 until his death in 1420, and John Terry, a wealthy merchant and mayor in 1523, who made his will in 1524 and had died by January 1525. Richard Caistor's brief will contained no bequests for Masses or prayers. Apart from a legacy of £10 for the purchase of two antiphonaries for his church, he wanted his wealth to be given to the poor on the grounds that "the goods of the Church, according to Canon Law, belong to the poor." His will is discussed later in the context of his life and cult.[171]

John Terry left considerably more money in charitable bequests than any other citizen, including the bishops of Norwich. In many ways he was the closest equivalent in Norwich to Francesco di Marco Datini, the merchant of Prato in Italy who made his final will in 1410. Both men left some bequests to churches and religious houses and for Masses, as well as bequests to members of their families. But the bulk of their fortunes was left to charity. Terry left 8d. to each "whole sister" and 1s. to each "half sister" of St Paul's Hospital, 6d. to each of the five sick-houses outside the gates of the city, and £866 13s. 4d. to the following. Two hundred pounds was to be lent free of interest to "such indigent and needful persons as merchants, craftsmen or other occupiers or artificers, being citizens of the said city of Norwich," at the rate of up to £40 per person and for periods of up to three years; the management of the scheme was entrusted to the three executors of his will who were a notary and two laymen, and after their deaths to the mayors of Norwich and two Justices of the Peace of the city. Two hundred pounds was to be disposed by his executors "in deeds of charity and pity" for his and his friends' souls; four hundred marks was to be spent, presumably by his executors, "in deeds of charity" on the day of his burial and on the first ten anniversaries of his death; and £200 was

[168] See pp. 133, 135 and 241.
[169] See pp. 97-98.
[170] See p. 102.
[171] See pp. 231-233.

to be spent by his executors on buying property in Norwich, the income from which was to be used to discharge the poor of the city from paying royal taxes. In addition he wanted the money coming from the sale, after his wife's death, of an unspecified number of houses, tenements and land to be "done in deeds of charity." It is noticeable that whereas Datini founded a hospital, Terry avoided charitable institutions, neither founding one nor giving more than token sums to those that existed. He may have felt that money so given would be swallowed up in administration or by their staff, without much ever reaching the poor. It is noticeable, too, that Terry entrusted his bequests to laymen and a notary, not to priests or religious bodies. In this respect he agreed with Datini, who stipulated that his hospital was in no way to be controlled by the Church or by an ecclesiastic.[172]

vii. Bequests for Civic Projects

Bequests for civic projects – chiefly the repair of streets, walls, gates, bridges and rivers, chiefly those in Norwich – were rare throughout the period in question, though there was a small increase in their number around 1500. They appear to have been considerably rarer than in late medieval London, where twelve per cent of Dr Thomson's sample left bequests for the repair of roads alone,[173] but not noticeably rarer than in the country as a whole between the late fifteenth and mid seventeenth centuries.[174] Most of them were large sums, normally more than £1 and frequently £10 or more, almost all of them coming from the wealthiest testators. An alderman called John Jowell, for example, left £20 in 1500 "to the use of the commonalty of the city of Norwich, to be expended upon the walls and the river at the will of master mayor of the said city and his brethren";[175] and Thomas Aldriche, a former mayor, left up to £40 in 1529 to "some common cost as paving of streets or repairing of walls." [176] In no case did a testator's bequests for civic projects approach in value his bequests of a charitable or of a religious nature.

Many of the testators whose wills survive belonged to the ruling class of the city. Between the mid fourteenth and early sixteenth centuries the city government greatly increased its power and the range of its activities, and triumphed over the most formidable branch of the Church in the city,

---

[172] Iris Origo, *The Merchant of Prato* (London 1957), pp. 336-338; see below, pp. 245-247.

[173] Thomson, "Piety and Charity," pp. 179 and 187-188.

[174] Jordan, *Philanthropy in England*, pp. 368 and 372.

[175] PROB/11/12 (Reg. Moone, 1500-1501), fol. 2 (Jowell).

[176] PROB/11/23 (Reg. Jankyn, 1523-1530), fol. 9 (Aldriche).

the Cathedral Priory.[177] It is therefore perhaps surprising that these developments were not paralleled by a more marked switch away from bequests to the Church towards bequests to the city.

C. Conclusion

The most striking points about the wills in question, from a religious point of view, are the sheer number of bequests of a religious nature and the amount of money so bequeathed. Wills, of their nature, provide evidence of piety, not of irreligion or anti-clericalism. They highlight one side of the coin. But comparing the wills of the citizens written in the 1530s and 1540s with those written before the Reformation reveals how radically bequests could change within a short time, and how much more concerned with the visible Church were those of the earlier period. One after another, during the latter two decades, there disappear from the wills bequests to houses of religious orders and colleges of secular priests, bequest for Masses, to votive lights, to hermits and anchorites, to craft guilds and pious confraternities, indeed most bequests of a directly religious nature.

It is difficult to say whether the wills from Norwich were exceptional for the late Middle Ages. Comparing them with English wills which have been printed,[178] and with Dr Rosenthal's conclusions about the wills of the English nobility,[179] suggests that, with two exceptions, Norwich did not differ significantly from the rest of the country regarding the types of religious bequests. That is to say, the same kinds of people and institutions received bequests, and for the same purposes; the exceptions were bequests to hermits and anchorites, and to communities resembling beguinages. As to their number, it is noticeable that the citizens of Norwich kept pace with Dr Thomson's much wealthier group from London, which is the only English city with which comparisons of statistical significance are at present possible, and in several respects surpassed them. Thus in the late fifteenth and early sixteenth centuries more testators from Norwich than from London were leaving bequests for temporary chantries and annuals of Masses, and throughout the fifteenth and early sixteenth centuries more of them gave to friars, to nuns and, almost certainly, to hermits and anchorites. My guess is that wills from

[177] See pp. 143 and 152-154.
[178] See Heath, *Parish Clergy*, pp. 218-219.
[179] Rosenthal, *Purchase of Paradise*, passim.

Norwich were significantly more religious than those from most other English towns.

An interesting point is the extent of support for aspects of the late medieval Church which were often attacked by reformers. Belief in Purgatory and in the value of multiplying Masses, as expressed by bequests for Masses and prayers for the dead, have been discussed;[180] belief in Purgatory was also expressed by testators who left charitable bequests "for their souls"; devotion to the saints and belief in the power of their intercession were expressed by bequests to votive lights; and houses of religious orders, especially friaries, were well supported.

The wills give the general impression that the local Church was solidly founded in the support of the people. They do little to explain why so much of the edifice was destroyed so quickly, and apparently with so little opposition, or why the city had become a Puritan stronghold by the reign of Elizabeth.[181] Compared with the previous decades, the years between 1518 and 1532 saw small but significant drops in bequests for chantry services and to most religious houses; no doubt the outbreak of the Reformation on the Continent, as well as events in England, made many testators insecure about their value and future. Perhaps it was a continuing sense of insecurity more than virulent opposition to the old order that explains the disappearance of so many types of religious bequests in the 1530s and 1540s, in anticipation of the various Dissolutions.

There were several significant changes in the pattern of bequests between 1370 and 1532, besides the declines in bequests for chantry services and to religious houses after about 1517. Bequests to votive lights, especially from the laity, grew considerably throughout the period; the increase in the number of hermits and anchorites was followed by an increase in bequests to them; and bequests to the Cathedral church and priory grew throughout the fifteenth century, as did those from the clergy to confraternities. In general religious and charitable bequests were rather fewer before about 1440 than after, reflecting the fact that wills were altogether briefer in the earlier period. They reached a peak at the turn of the fifteenth and sixteenth centuries and declined slightly after the beginning of the Reformation on the Continent. But much more striking than the changes is the consistency throughout the period of both the proportion of testators giving to a particular beneficiary and the average

---

[180] See pp. 104-106.

[181] Patrick Collinson, *The Elizabethan Puritan Movement* (London 1967), pp. 127, 186-187 and 213.

amount of money so bequeathed. The same consistency has been noted in the wills of the English nobility.[182] The similarity between the bequests of the clergy and those of the laity is also noticeable. All the clergy were secular clerics; anchorites and hermits represented, in part, a reaction against the clerical life. It is therefore particularly significant that the clerical testators were as keen as the laity in giving to the regular clergy as well as to hermits and anchorites. There were two important differences. First, more of the clergy than of the laity gave to confraternities; this is largely explained by bequests from the former to the clerical confraternity of Corpus Christi. Second, more of the clergy gave to the College of St Mary in the Fields, and this may be explained by the fact that they were supporting a college of their fellow secular priests.

The support given to the various branches of the Church reflects fairly accurately their importance in the religious life of the city. Parish churches and houses of religious orders were especially well supported, and there were lesser flows of bequests to confraternities and to hermits and anchorites. The difference reflects the fact that the latter were important but never replaced the old institutions as the mainstay of the local Church, and that these older institutions appear to have retained considerable vitality and appeal.

[182] Rosenthal, *Purchase of Paradise* (London 1972), p. 112.

4

Conflicts

A. The Conflict between the Citizens and the Cathedral Priory

Although Norwich was the seat of a bishopric, its most formidable religious institution from the point of view of the citizens was the Benedictine Cathedral Priory. The disputes between the citizens and the priory formed the most glaring conflict in the Church in late medieval Norwich.

The citizens' assault on the priory in 1272 was one of the most violent attacks on a religious institution in medieval England. The assault, recorded by many of the national chroniclers, appears to have escalated from a scuffle between townsmen and servants or tenants of the priory at a quintain held on Tombland, an area just outside the precincts of the priory. Further acts of provocation were committed by both sides though chiefly, it seems, by the priory. Finally a crowd from the city, including three of the four bailiffs and other prominent citizens, attacked the priory, burnt some of its buildings and part of the Cathedral and killed at least thirteen people, though no monk is known to have perished. The reprisals were equally savage. The bishop of Norwich and later the pope excommunicated the citizens involved in the attack and laid Norwich under an interdict; the liberties of the city were seized by the king; the city was condemned to pay £2,000 towards repairing the damage done to the Cathedral; and about thirty citizens are known to have been hanged in punishment. The clash was the climax of several earlier incidents, and the tension remained.[1] It is against this background that the conflict after 1370 must be seen.

---

[1] Walter Rye, "The Riot between the Monks and Citizens of Norwich in 1272," *Norfolk Antiquarian Miscellany* 2 (1883) 17-89; *Records of Norwich*, ed. Hudson, 1: xiv-xv; Campbell, *Norwich*, p. 12.

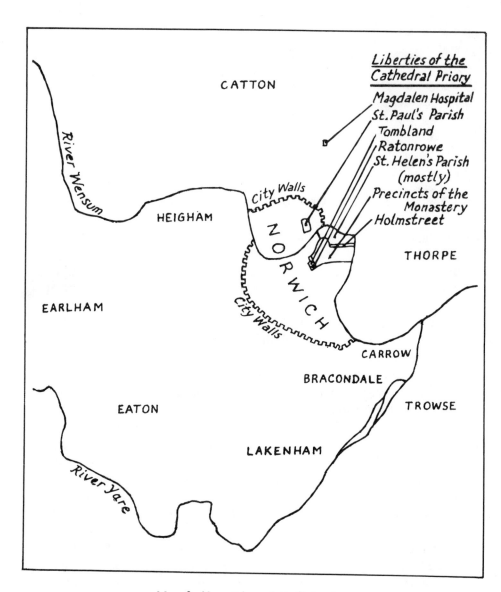

Map 2: Norwich and its Suburbs

The general context of the conflict, which had its parallel in many other towns in medieval England,[2] was the growing power and ambitions of the city government on the one hand and the formidable position of the priory in the economic, political and religious life of the city on the other hand. The priory appointed the parish priests of close to half the parishes in the city.[3] It must have been the largest employer in the city, probably employing in the late Middle Ages at least a hundred and fifty lay men and women within the monastery alone.[4] It was by far the most extensive owner of land and property in the city and its suburbs.[5] Indeed the city was almost wholly surrounded by lands of religious houses and ecclesiastics, chiefly those of the Cathedral Priory but also those of Carrow Nunnery in the southern tip of the city and in Carrow, those of the bishop of Norwich in Thorpe and those of the Abbey of St Benet of Hulme in Heigham.[6] That the large majority of the monks probably came from outside Norwich[7] may well have made the citizens hostile to the priory for the additional reason that it appeared an alien body. On the other hand the dramatic growth in the power and ambitions of the city government in the fourteenth and early fifteenth centuries,[8] which was marked by the creation of the county of "the city of Norwich" with its mayor and by the building of the Guild Hall, brought it into conflict with several parties: with Yarmouth, for example, in the fourteenth century when the city government successfully contested Yarmouth's claim to exact tolls on goods travelling to and from Norwich as they passed through the mouth of the river Yare;[9] and with the Crown, also in the fourteenth century, over how much of the area within the Castle fee was to be exempt from the city's jurisdiction.[10] The Cathedral Priory was therefore only one among several bodies with which the city government clashed.

[2] William Savage, *The Making of our Towns* (London 1952), pp. 97-101.
[3] See column 3 of Appendix 1 (pp. 173-178).
[4] Saunders, *Obedientiary Rolls*, pp. 162-163.
[5] Ibid., map facing p. 1; Norwich, Norfolk Record Office, Colman MS 115, fol. 4r-v.
[6] Blomefield, *Norfolk* (1805-1810), 4: 503-505, and 7: 258-261; Rye, *Carrow Abbey*, pp. xxxi and xxxiv; Saunders, *Obedientiary Rolls*, map facing p. 1; Barbara Dowell, "The Foundations of Norwich Cathedral," *Transactions of the Royal Historical Society*, 5th ser., 7 (1957) 13-14; *VCH Norfolk*, 2: 351-352; Campbell, *Norwich*, pp. 8-9.
[7] See p. 25.
[8] *Records of Norwich*, ed. Hudson, 1: lii-lxxiv, and 2: xxxiv-xl; Campbell, *Norwich*, p. 15.
[9] *Records of Norwich*, ed. Hudson, 1: xli; Campbell, *Norwich*, p. 14.
[10] *Records of Norwich*, ed. Hudson, 1: xlii and 23-27; Campbell, *Norwich*, pp. 12 and 15.

Disputes between citizens and the priory arising from the latter's position as patron of many parish churches in the city have been discussed.[11] Separate from these disputes, though possibly exacerbated by them, was the prolonged conflict between the citizens and the priory over their respective temporal jurisdictions and certain economic benefits flowing from them. The crux of the problem was that the exempt liberties of the priory within the city as well as the jurisdiction of the city government in the suburbs, much of which were grazing lands of the priory, had been defined in incompatible terms by royal charters granted to both parties. On the one hand charters granted to the citizens had given them jurisdiction within the city and its suburbs without explicitly exempting the priory's lands from it.[12] In particular the Crown granted to the citizens in the charter of 1404, which made the city a county and gave it a mayor, "that the said city and all the land within the city and its liberty, together with the suburbs and their hamlets and surrounds, and all the land around the city within the liberty of our said city of Norwich ... are to be separate from the said county (i.e., Norfolk) ... and that the said city of Norwich and suburbs (etc.) shall henceforth form a county of its own and shall be called for ever the county of the city of Norwich." [13] On the other hand the priory rightly claimed that the late eleventh and early twelfth-century charters, giving it lands and liberties in Norwich and its suburbs,[14] antedated the charters granted to the citizens and had not been revoked by them. The Crown was still confirming the priory's liberties in the fifteenth century.[15] Moreover, none of the charters granting jurisdiction to the citizens in the suburbs of Norwich, including the charter of 1404, defined precisely the boundaries of the suburbs or stated that they included the priory's grazing lands. The citizens never seriously tried to abolish the priory's franchises altogether. In practice the disputes centred on three points. First, whether the following areas lay within the priory's exempt liberties: Tombland, Ratonrowe and Holmstreet, which were small pieces of land lying just outside the precincts of the priory; St Paul's parish, sometimes called Normansland or Spiteland, which was a separate enclave in the northern ward of the city and included St Paul's

[11] See pp. 6-7.

[12] *Records of Norwich*, ed. Hudson, 1: 11-43.

[13] *Evidences relating to the Town Close Estate, Norwich*, ed. anon. (Norwich 1887), p. 32.

[14] William Dugdale, *Monasticon anglicanum* (London 1817-1830), 4: 13-18; *The First Register of Norwich Cathedral Priory*, ed. Herbert W. Saunders, Norfolk Record Society, 11 (no place, 1939), pp. 25-63; *Charters*, ed. Dodwell, pp. 1-40 and 52-56.

[15] E.g., *Cal. Pat. R., 1436-1441*, pp. 552-553.

Hospital; and Magdalen Hospital, situated in the northern suburbs of the city. Second, the priory's rights in holding an annual fair over Pentecost, on Tombland, from which the priory, not the city government, received the tolls and at which the priory held its own court. Third, the extent of the rights of the priory and of the citizens over grazing lands in Eaton and Lakenham, suburbs to the southwest of the city.[16] In practice neither side denied to the other all rights of grazing in these lands, at least after 1205.[17] The issue appears to have been a combination of where the boundaries between their respective areas lay and the number of sheep that each party was permitted to graze.

These unresolved issues, on top of the more general rivalry, provided endless opportunities for friction between the priory and the citizens, especially the city government. Scarcely a decade passed between 1370 and the Reformation during which a clash between the two sides, frequently of a bizarre nature, is not recorded in the city's own records or in the Patent Rolls. In 1373, for example, a quarrel developed over the capture of a woman in St Paul's parish church which lay within the area claimed by each side to be subject to its jurisdiction. The bailiffs of the city had arrested the woman, but some monks from the priory together with a group of men had seized her and carried her off, to the fury of the city government.[18] In 1380 and 1441 the city government threatened to disenfranchise any citizen impleading anybody in the prior's court during the priory's annual fair or at other times.[19] In February 1436, according to a jury of fifteen people, the prior and a servant of his had forcibly entered a house of Robert Chapeleyn, the mayor, and had cut down and carried off twenty of his willow trees![20] In 1486 the mayor and aldermen, with the consent of the Common Assembly, had fixed two posts at one end of Holmstreet to assert their claim that Tombland, Ratonrowe and Holmstreet were subject to the city's jurisdiction and not exempt liberties of the priory; tenants of the priory had pulled the posts up, and a long suit followed when the municipality indicted the tenants for riot.[21] And in

---

[16] *Records of Norwich*, ed. Hudson, 1: lxxix-lxxxii, and 2: cxxxvii-cxl; *Cal. Pat. R., 1436-1441*, pp. 552-553; Campbell, *Norwich*, pp. 12-13.

[17] *Evidences*, p. 4.

[18] N.C.R., Case 8d, Rolls of the City Assembly, Roll 46-47 Edward III.

[19] *Records of Norwich*, ed. Hudson, 2: 84; N.C.R., Case 16d, Proceedings of the Municipal Assembly, Book 1 (1434-1491), fol. 14v/17v.

[20] N.C.R., Case 8a, Presentments of Assault 1439-1441, m. 4.

[21] Blomefield, *Norfolk* (1805-1810), 3: 175, is the only known evidence for the details of the dispute, though an entry in the proceedings of the Common Assembly (N.C.R., Case 16d, Proceedings of the Municipal Assembly, Book 1 [1434-1491], fol. 128r/133r) suggests that an incident had occurred.

1506 the prior and three monks with a band of some two dozen men fought with one of the sheriffs and the keeper of the city's gaol to rescue a certain William Herries, possibly a servant or tenant of the priory, whom the keeper and sheriff had arrested.[22]

The most serious clash after 1370 occurred in 1443. That it occurred then and not in 1381 or 1450, just as the most violent clash of all had occurred in 1272 and not during the preceding baronial wars, illustrates how local and comparatively unconnected with national events the conflict was.[23] For several reasons relations between the priory and the municipality were more than usually strained in the 1430s and early 1440s. The citizens resented as too generous to the priory an agreement reached with the city government in 1429. Two of its terms, in particular, appear to have rankled with the citizens: an annual rent of four shillings to be paid to the priory by the city, and recognition of the priory's liberties in the suburbs, possibly because this seemed to deny the citizen's rights of pasture there.[24] The Crown, moreover, had prejudiced peace between the two parties by fining the mayor and various citizens for much earlier breaches of its own rights and those of the priory in the suburbs, and by upholding against the city government the more extreme claims of the priory to jurisdiction in parts of the city and its suburbs.[25] John Heverlond, prior from 1436 until his death in 1453,[26] appears to have been an aggressive man; his clash with the bishop of Norwich will be discussed later.[27] As well as his alleged attack on Robert Chapeleyn's property in 1436, juries stated that he and a band of men in 1440 had beaten and insulted the sheriffs' sergeant and rescued a man arrested by the sergeant for debt, and that in 1441 he and Thomas Wetherby had instigated over forty men to beat and imprison the mayor, the two sheriffs and various other citizens![28]

The priory allied itself with a variety of parties with grievances against the city government. The alliance was the main reason why matters came to a head in 1443. Besides, as just mentioned, fining the mayor and various citizens and supporting the priory against the city government, the

[22] *Records of Norwich*, ed. Hudson, 2: 368-369.

[23] Norwich was of course a centre of disturbance in the Peasants' Revolt in 1381 but I cannot find any evidence that the priory was attacked.

[24] N.C.R., Case 17b, Liber Albus, fols. 45v-47v. For the dissatisfaction of the citizens with the two terms, see also below, p. 150.

[25] *Records of Norwich*, ed. Hudson, 1: lxxxi-lxxxii and 320-324; *Cal. Pat. R., 1436-1441*, pp. 552-553.

[26] Saunders, *Obedientiary Rolls*, p. 190.

[27] See pp. 160-161.

[28] N.C.R., Case 8a, Presentments of Assault 1439-1441, mm. 1 and 3.

Crown was angered by the request made by the citizens in 1440 that £100 lent by the city to the king be repaid, and by their refusal of a further loan in the following year.[29] Thomas Wetherby, allegedly the prior's ally by 1441, was a very wealthy man and had been mayor in 1427 and 1432. He tried unsuccessfully to get his nominees elected to the office in 1433 and 1437 and led a minority faction in the city oligarchy into increasingly bitter opposition to the majority. Wetherby and the prior collected the support of many East Anglian magnates, several of whom are known to have had old scores to settle with the city and who included the earl of Suffolk and the duke of Norfolk, and also the support of Bishop Brown of Norwich, notwithstanding the prior's clash with the bishop over other matters.[30] The alliance was joined by the abbots of two monasteries in Norfolk, the Benedictine abbey of St Benet of Hulme and the Premonstratensian abbey of Wendling. The abbots were probably persuaded by Wetherby to join in so that they might prosecute their grievances against the city more effectively.[31] The grievance of the abbot of St Benet's concerned some new mills which the city had built sometime before 1431 on the northern stretch of the river Wensum within the city walls. They were evidently very important to the bakers of Norwich.[32] The abbot claimed that these new mills obstructed the flow of water from his own mills in Heigham, the northwestern suburb of the city, threatened his lands there with flooding and prevented his boats from passing freely up and down the river. As the citizens pointed out, the abbot's complaints were tenuous since the new mills were further down-stream from the abbot's property than the city's old ones, and so were less likely to affect it.[33] Perhaps the true reason for the abbot's hostility was that business was being taken away from his mills by the city's new ones. The abbot of Wendling's complaint was that the city had defaulted in paying rent which it owed him for the lease of some property in St Clement of Conisford parish which included the advowson of the parish church and a quay on the river Wensum, and in 1438 he had seized the property in retaliation.[34]

---

[29] *Records of Norwich*, ed. Hudson, 1: lxxxvii and 283.

[30] Robin L. Storey, *The End of the House of Lancaster* (London 1966), pp. 217-221; *Records of Norwich*, ed. Hudson, 1: xcii and 344-347; see pp. 160-161.

[31] *Records of Norwich*, ed. Hudson, 1: lxxxvii and 348.

[32] Ibid., 1: 350 and 352; "Chronological Memoranda touching the City of Norwich," ed. Goddard Johnson, *Norfolk Archaeology* 1 (1847) 141.

[33] *Records of Norwich*, ed. Hudson, 1: 350 and 354.

[34] N.C.R., Case 16d, Proceedings of the Municipal Assembly, Book 1 (1434-1491), fol. 9/12; *Cal. Close R., 1441-1447*, p. 99.

The abbots' grievances, together with Prior Heverlond's claim that the city government had violated various rights of the priory in its liberties and during its Whitsun fair, were first heard by a commission of Oyer and Terminer at Thetford in July 1441.[35] The disputes – and some obscure complaints of the bishop of Norwich against the citizens, possibly connected with his rights in the liberties of the Cathedral Priory – were then submitted by both sides to the arbitration of the earl of Suffolk.[36] The earl made his award sometime in 1442.[37] The whole of it is not known but it evidently went in favour of the ecclesiastics. Part of it ordered the citizens to destroy their new mills and give bonds of £100, £50 and £50 to the abbot of St Benet's, to Prior Heverlond and to Bishop Brown respectively, presumably as pledges that they would carry out the award.[38]

The city government refused to accept the award, despite considerable pressure from their opponents to do so.[39] Their refusal finally broke out into one of the most remarkable anti-clerical disturbances in fifteenth-century England, "Gladman's Insurrection." There are two rather different accounts of it. Defending the conduct of the citizens about five years after the event, the city government claimed there had not been a riot but only a "disport (sic) as is and ever has been the custom in any city or borough through all this realm on Fastyngong (sic) Tuesday" in which a certain John Gladman rode through the city on a horse, crowned as King of Christmas, with representations of the season carried before and after him.[40] The second account is the report of a presentment made by a jury of twelve men from Norfolk before an inquisiton held at Thetford on 28 February 1443.[41] This was barely a month after the event. The jury appears to have been packed with Wetherby's supporters,[42] and the account may exaggerate the disturbance and the extent to which it was premeditated. But it seems nearer the truth than the city government's version for several reasons besides the fact that the latter was much later in time than the jury's presentment. The disturbance certainly occurred around 25 January, as the report of the presentment says,[43] and the city

---

[35] *Records of Norwich*, ed. Hudson, 1: lxxxvii-lxxxviii, 325-327 and 349.

[36] Jacob, "Two Documents," p. 432; *Cal. Pat. R., 1436-1441*, pp. 552-553; *Records of Norwich*, ed. Hudson, 1: 349.

[37] *Records of Norwich*, ed. Hudson, 1: lxxxix.

[38] Ibid., 1: 349-350 and 352.

[39] Ibid., 1: 350-351.

[40] Ibid., 1: xc and 345.

[41] Ibid., 1: 340 and 351-352.

[42] Storey, *House of Lancaster*, p. 225.

[43] *Records of Norwich*, ed. Hudson, 1: xc, 340 and 350-351.

government offered no explanation why a "disport" such as was customary on Shrove Tuesday took place more than a month earlier.[44] Furthermore, though it only covers the build-up to the disturbance, the account written in 1482 into the city's official chronicle, the Liber Albus, correlates much better with the report than with the city government's version. The Liber Albus says that Wetherby and the "council" of the abbot of St Benet of Hulme, in their efforts to get the bond of £100 sealed for the abbot with the common seal of the city, persuaded the mayor on 25 January to call an assembly; but the "commons" of the city came to the assembly in great numbers and removed the common seal in order to prevent the bond being sealed.[45] The jury reportedly gave the following description of what then took place.

> William Hempsted[46] of the city of Norwich, merchant of the same, and the commonalty of the city, on Tuesday 22nd January 1443, in the said city, planned to make a common insurrection and disturbance of all the liege subjects of the lord king in the said city and surrounding country. They believed that by this insurrection and disturbance they would be sufficiently powerful, in the said city and surrounding country, as to be able to force Thomas, bishop of Norwich, John, abbot of St Benedict of Hulme, and John, prior of the church of the Holy Trinity[47] in Norwich, by threats of burning, killing and plundering, to surrender various actions of theirs which they possessed against the said mayor and commonalty and many others of the same city. They believed too that, because the city formed a county of its own, separated from the county of Norfolk by letters patent of King Henry IV,[48] and because of their strength and the large number of people who would gather round them, the king would neither dare nor be able to punish them by his law for the aforesaid transgressions. Accordingly they then and there arranged for John Gladman of the said city, merchant, to ride in the city on a horse, like a crowned king, with a sceptre and sword carried before him by three unknown men; and Robert Suger of Norwich, souter, Robert Hennyng of the same, hosteler, Richard Dallyng, cutler, and twenty-four other persons to likewise ride on horseback, before the said John Gladman, with a crown upon their arms and carrying bows and arrows, as if they were valets of the crown of the lord king; and a hundred other unknown persons, some on horseback and some on foot, to follow the same John Gladman, carrying bows and arrows and swords.

[44] Shrove Tuesday fell on 5 March in 1443.
[45] *Records of Norwich*, ed. Hudson, 1: 350-351.
[46] Then mayor.
[47] I.e., the Cathedral, which was dedicated to the Trinity.
[48] See p. 144.

They went around urging people in the city to come together and to make an insurrection and riots there. On 25 January 1443 they were able, thanks to the lack of good government there, to ring and have rung in turn various bells in the city. Thereupon the mayor and commonalty, with many other unknown persons from the said city to the number of three thousand, having been summoned by the said ringing of bells, were able, thanks to the lack of good government in the city, to come together in bands and to make a violent insurrection throughout the entire city; that is to say, they were armed with swords, bows and arrows, hauberks and coats of armour, and with other weapons collected for a warlike purpose. They were able to cross over to the priory of the Cathedral Church of the Holy Trinity of Norwich, in the county of Norfolk. There they shouted, "Let us burn the priory, and kill the prior and monks," and immediately dug under the gates of the priory so as to enter in, brought wood to burn the priory and placed cannons – that is to say guns – pointing towards the priory.

From that day until four o'clock in the afternoon on the following day they broke the peace by attacking the priory in order to burn it, and plotted to kill the prior and monks. They continued their insurrection until Richard Walsham and John Wychyngham, fellow monks of the prior, due to these threats and assaults, surrendered to them a certain evidence belonging to the prior which was sealed with the city's common seal. In this evidence it was stated, among other things, that Robert Baxter, formerly mayor of the city, John Sypater and William Iselham, former sheriffs, and the commonalty of the city granted by the said document to William Worsted, who was the present prior's predecessor, and to his successors for ever an annual rent of four shillings, which was to be paid in Norwich by the mayor and sheriffs and their successors, each year on the feast of Saint Michael for ever; and also that neither the then mayor and commonalty nor their successors would ever hold any court dealing with persons or real estate, whether arising from a suit or from a writ of the king, or any court of the sheriff dealing with any lands, tenements or rents, whether it concerned a contract or any actual, possible or future matter, in the meadows called Conisford Meadows or the fields, heath lands, meadows and pasture lands in Bracondale, Eaton, Lakenham and Earlham.[49] Thus they forcibly removed the aforesaid evidences belonging to the prior which had been kept in the priory.

They kept the city with closed gates and in a state of arms, like a city at war with the lord king, from Monday 28 January to Monday 4 February 1443. They kept John, duke of Norfolk, outside the city for a whole week from Tuesday 29 January 1443 and John Veer, earl of Oxford, and other

---

[49] The two clauses formed part of the agreement reached in 1429 (see p. 146).

ministers of the lord king from Monday 26 to Wednesday 28 September 1442[50] – whom the lord king had appointed, by his letters patent of commission, to deal with the insurrection and riots, to arrest, to restore peace in the city and to restore good government to it – and they would not allow the said duke and earl to enter the city during this time.[51]

As in 1272 both the Church and the Crown struck back. Archbishop Chichele excommunicated the citizens involved, though Bishop Brown claimed to have tried to defer execution of the sentence and refused to lay the city under an interdict.[52] William Hempsted, the mayor, was imprisoned in the Fleet in London "per consilium regis" from 13 February to 26 March 1443 and was fined £50.[53] During the mayor's imprisonment Wetherby and his faction appear to have controlled the city and carried out the earl of Suffolk's award. According to the Liber Albus they wrecked the city's new mills to such an extent that they were useless for many years, and Wetherby sealed the three bonds of £100, £50 and £50 with the common seal of the city and gave them to the abbot of St Benet of Hulme, to Prior Heverlond and to Bishop Brown.[54] Finally, in March 1443 a commission appointed to inquire into the disturbance declared the city's liberties forfeit, imposed a collective fine of £2,000 on the city and fined individual rioters sums totalling £1,504 17s. 4d. The liberties of the city were not restored until November 1447, by which time the collective fine, reduced to 1,000 marks, had been paid.[55]

Gladman's Insurrection resembled the disturbance of 1272 inasmuch as both were revolts of townsmen directed against the temporalities of the Church and both resulted in assaults on the Cathedral Priory. It began as dangerously as the disturbance of 1272, but nobody is known to have been killed during it or in punishment, whereas many died in 1272. Maybe the monks in 1443 showed more prudence than valour. None of the secular clergy is known to have been involved in 1443 whereas some

[50] These dates are clearly wrong. The manuscript reads "a die Lune proximo post festum Sancti Mathei Apostoli anno supradicto usque diem Mercurii tunc proximum sequentem." "Mathei" (Matthew) may be a scribal error for "Mathie" (Matthias), which would make the dates 25 to 27 February 1443, but even these dates can scarcely be correct since the statement allegedly formed part of a presentment made at Thetford on 28 February 1443 (see p. 148).

[51] N.C.R., Case 17b, Book of Pleas, fols. 17v-18r (new fols. 40v-41r). The translation of the passage in *Records of Norwich*, ed. Hudson, 1: 340-341, is much abbreviated and not always accurate.

[52] Jacob, "Two Documents," pp. 428-429 and 432.

[53] *Records of Norwich*, ed. Hudson, 1: 351 and 355.

[54] Ibid., 1: 352.

[55] Storey, *House of Lancaster*, p. 224.

were in 1272; nor are the friars known to have taken part, though the complaint made by the prior of the Cathedral Priory in about 1360, that the friars had preached in the Cathedral "against ... the liberty of the Church," [56] may possibly refer to encouragement given to the citizens at an earlier date.

As mentioned, the citizens and the priory continued to quarrel after 1443.[57] But the conflict was never as fierce as it had been in the early 1440s, and the priory never again enjoyed such an ascendancy over the city. John Heverlond died in 1453; his successors as prior, at least until Robert Catton (1504-1530),[58] appear to have been less aggressive men. Thomas Wetherby died in 1444 or 1445.[59] After his death at least one prominent citizen who fell out with the city government – a former sheriff called Robert Curteys[60] – allied himself with the priory against the municipality. But no citizen after Wetherby produced such a deep split within the city government or united various parties against it so successfully. Less tangible, but perhaps of more importance, was the central government's change of attitude. Until the 1440s the Crown always seems, in the last resort, to have supported the priory against the citizens. Later it was less willing to rescue the priory. The change began in Edward IV's reign. It may have been in return for support given by citizens of Norwich to the Yorkist cause on several occasions.[61] It was confirmed by Cardinal Wolsey's determination that the priory, as well as the citizens, should compromise so that a lasting settlement to the conflict might be reached.

The municipality's quarrels with the Cathedral Priory and with the abbeys of St Benet of Hulme and Wendling were resolved largely in the city's favour between 1450 and 1530. In a sense, therefore, the municipality had obtained most of what it wanted from the three monasteries before they were dissolved. In 1459 the city government repurchased from the abbot of Wendling the quay and some property in St Clement of Conisford parish and the advowson of the parish church, apparently for 100 marks.[62] Sometime after 1447 the citizens repaired

---

[56] See p. 11.

[57] See pp. 145-146.

[58] Saunders, *Obedientiary Rolls*, p. 190.

[59] N.C.C., Reg. Wylbey, fols. 30v and 32r (Wetherby).

[60] Blomefield, *Norfolk* (1805-1810), 3: 175; N.C.R., Case 16d, Proceedings of the Municipal Assembly, Book 1 (1434-1491), fol. 128r/133r.

[61] Storey, *House of Lancaster*, p. 225.

[62] N.C.R., Case 16d, Proceedings of the Municipal Assembly, Book 1 (1434-1491), fols. 30v/33v and 38v/41v.

their mills; and in 1481 the judges of the Common Pleas and of the King's Bench ruled that the abbot of St Benet's plea – that the city owed him £100 to which Wetherby had bound it in 1443 – was invalid because, as the city urged in its defence, the mayor had been in prison, thanks partly to the collusion of the then abbot, when the bond had been sealed. On losing the suit the abbot dropped his complaint that the repairing of the city's mills caused his mills and lands in Heigham to flood.[63]

One of the citizens' grievances against the Cathedral Priory was partly removed in 1482 when Edward IV granted them the right to hold two fairs each year, though they do not appear to have prospered and the priory continued to hold its annual fair over Pentecost.[64] In the early 1490s the central government began to put pressure on the priory and the citizens to reach a lasting settlement to all the matters in dispute.[65] The efforts failed, apparently because both parties refused to compromise over their claims to jurisdiction within the precincts of the priory and, probably more importantly, the three areas just outside the precincts – Tombland, Raton-rowe and Holmstreet.[66] The efforts were renewed by Cardinal Wolsey in 1517.[67] After long and costly negotiations[68] agreement was reached in 1524. The city government very reluctantly[69] made the greater concessions over grazing rights in the suburbs. The priory gave the city eighty acres of land in Eaton and Lakenham, subsequently called the Town Close, for which it was to receive twenty marks a year from the city. In return the city surrendered its claims to grazing rights elsewhere in the two suburbs. The other concessions came from the priory: it surrendered to the city its right to hold a fair over Pentecost and the profits and jurisdiction stemming from it, and its claims to jurisdiction in Tombland, Ratonrowe and Holmstreet and in all its other liberties within the "county of Norwich" except within the precincts of the priory.[70] The

[63] Ibid., fols. 74v/77v, 100v/104v, 103r/107r, 107v/111v, 110v/114v and 114r/118r; *Records of Norwich*, ed. Hudson, 1: 353-354; *VCH Norfolk*, 2: 334 and 336.

[64] *Records of Norwich*, ed. Hudson, 2: cxxxvi.

[65] N.C.R., Case 18a, Chamberlains' Accounts, Book 2 (1470-1490), fols. 223v-226r; N.C.R., Case 16d, Proceedings of the Municipal Assembly, Book 1 (1434-1491), fol. 137v/142v, and Book 2 (1491-1553), fols. 4v/23v, 5r/24r and 9v/28v.

[66] N.C.R., Case 16d, Proceedings of the Municipal Assembly, Book 1 (1434-1491), fol. 137v/142v, and Book 2 (1491-1553), fol. 9v/28v.

[67] N.C.R., Case 16c, Assembly Minute Book 2 (1510-1550), fols. 46v-47r; and see *Letters and Papers, Foreign and Domestic, of the Reign of Henry VIII*, ed. John S. Brewer, James Gairdner and Robert H. Brodie (London 1862-1910), 4 (1524-1530): 2562.

[68] N.C.R., Case 16c, Assembly Minute Book 2 (1510-1550), fols. 46v-101v passim.

[69] Ibid., fols. 98v-99r.

[70] *Evidences*, pp. 52-61.

agreement was ratified by two royal charters in 1524 and 1525.[71] It appears to have ended the conflict until the Dissolution, though the boundaries of the city's jurisdiction in the suburbs were not finally settled to its satisfaction until the royal charter of 1556.[72]

Hudson and Tingey have provided the best account of the conflict. They argued that it was concerned largely, if not exclusively, with the profits of jurisdiction and was in no sense religious.[73] It is true that the conflict concerned the priory's temporalities; but the temporalities of the Church were considered a religious matter, at least by their defenders. The priory, like any religious house, was closely identified with the Church on earth. Bishop Brown indicated the religious dimension of the conflict when he said of the citizens who had assaulted the priory in 1443 that they "have offended God, ... done violation to the liberty and freedom of the Church ... [and] made rebellion against the church of Norwich which is their mother church." [74]

Dr Jones thought the conflicts between the citizens and the Benedictine abbey in Chester, which were similar to those in Norwich, fostered among the middle classes "that anti-clerical spirit which was to culminate in the Protestant revolution." [75] Mrs Green drew the same conclusion from disputes between townsmen and churchmen throughout late medieval England.[76] To some extent their conclusion is valid for Norwich. The assaults on the priory in 1272 and 1443, as well as many lesser incidents, were expressions of anti-clericalism and not simply attacks on an economic corporation. On the other hand, the citizens obtained much of what they wanted from the priory as well as from the abbeys of Wendling and St Benet of Hulme during the ninety years before they were dissolved. In a sense, therefore, the Dissolution was unnecessary rather than an inevitable culmination. The increase in testamentary bequests from the laity to the Cathedral church and priory in the late fifteenth and early sixteenth centuries[77] is a further indication that better relations prevailed on the eve of the Reformation.

[71] Ibid., pp. 62-64; *Records of Norwich*, ed. Hudson, 1: 43-44.

[72] *Records of Norwich*, ed. Hudson, 1: cxii; Campbell, *Norwich*, p. 13.

[73] *Records of Norwich*, ed. Hudson, 1: lxxxvi-xc and cix-cxi, and 2: cxxxvi-cxxxix.

[74] Jacob, "Two Documents," p. 432.

[75] Douglas Jones, *The Church in Chester, 1300-1540*, Chetham Society, 3rd ser., 7 (Manchester 1957), p. 39.

[76] Alice S. Green, *Town Life in the Fifteenth Century* (London 1894), 1: 382-383.

[77] See pp. 121 and 222.

B. OTHER CONFLICTS

i. Conflicts involving the Laity

Carrow Nunnery. The Benedictine nunnery of Carrow in the suburbs of Norwich was involved in disputes with the city government which not only resembled those of the Cathedral Priory, albeit on a smaller scale, but were also resolved in favour of the municipality shortly before the Dissolution. The nunnery was founded in about 1146,[78] and the disputes went back at least to the thirteenth century. In 1290, to settle the outstanding issues and in return for various concessions and confirmation by the municipality of various of its rights, including holding an annual three-day fair, the nunnery agreed to surrender to the city government its view of frank-pledge of its tenants in an area in Norwich called Little Neugate, and its right to receive a toll on all corn sold in the city during the fair.[79] Matters may have come to a head again during the Peasants' Revolt. According to Mr Powell, who did not quote his source, on 18 June 1381 "the rioters, under Adam Smith and Henry Stanford, both of Wroxham,[80] advanced on Carrow Priory, close by Norwich, and by threats of violence obtained various deeds and court rolls from Margaret de Euges, the prioress, which they afterwards burnt in Norwich, in the presence of [Geoffrey] Lister and John de Trunch." [81] The two parties were again quarrelling in the 1430s, though the issues are obscure.[82] The Crown declared in 1443, as part of a wider judgment, that the nunnery was in Norfolk and did not form part of Norwich.[83] So the point at issue may have been whether the nunnery and its adjacent lands were subject to the city government's jurisdiction.[84] By 1488 the conflict centred on the nunnery's grazing lands, called Butterhills, which lay within the southern tip of the city.[85] The city government seized the lands in 1495 or 1496 and

[78] Knowles, *Religious Houses*, pp. 254 and 262.

[79] *Records of Norwich*, ed. Hudson, 2: cxxxv and 254-258; Campbell, *Norwich*, p. 13.

[80] North-east Norfolk.

[81] Edgar Powell, *The Rising in East Anglia in 1381* (Cambridge 1896), p. 32.

[82] N.C.R., Case 16d, Proceedings of the Municipal Assembly, Book 1 (1434-1491), fol. 4v/7v.

[83] *Records of Norwich*, ed. Hudson, 1: 328.

[84] See also ibid., 1: 267. But earlier in the fifteenth century the prioress of Carrow had claimed, in order to avoid two lawsuits, that her nunnery lay within Norwich and not within Norfolk (ibid., 1: 319-320).

[85] N.C.R., Case 16d, Proceedings of the Municipal Assembly, Book 1 (1434-1491), fol. 132v/137v.

kept hold of them, paying an annual rent of about ten shillings.[86] A settlement was not reached until 1523, which was only a year before the settlement with the Cathedral Priory.[87] It too was largely a victory for the municipality. The nunnery surrendered Butterhills to the city in return for an unspecified sum of money and an annual rent of ten shillings.[88] The prioress styled herself in the agreement "prioress of the house of nuns or priory of the Blessed Mary of Carrow in the county of the city of Norwich."[89] So if the question of whether the nunnery lay within Norwich or within Norfolk had been an issue between the two parties, the prioress was yielding on this point as well.

The city's disputes with the nunnery appear to have proceeded independently of those with the Cathedral Priory, despite their similarities. Moreover they appear to have been largely confined to the city government, and to have provoked the hostility of the mass of citizens much less than those with the priory did. The smaller scale of the conflict reflects the less serious nature of the points at issue and the fact that the nunnery was smaller, less powerful and further distant from the city than the priory.

The Friaries and the College of St Mary in the Fields. Unlike the Cathedral Priory or Carrow Nunnery, the four friaries and the College of St Mary in the Fields were noticeably free from disputes with the city government during the period in question.

The college had a large site, but on what had previously been open ground,[90] and it never acquired extensive rights in the city of which the citizens could be jealous. This was partly because the city government was already fairly well established when the college was founded in the mid thirteenth century. Indeed, the college enjoyed close ties with the municipality. Thus William Appleyard, John Alderford and William Setman, all prominent oligarchs, entrusted their chantries to the college;[91] the confraternities of the Bachelery and of the Annunciation of St Mary, which were closely connected with the city government, were attached to the college;[92] the city government often met in the college before the Guild

---

[86] Rye, *Carrow Abbey*, p. xxxiv.
[87] See pp. 153-154.
[88] *Evidences*, pp. 51-52.
[89] Ibid., p. 51.
[90] Campbell, *Norwich*, p. 11.
[91] See pp. 97 and 213-214.
[92] See pp. 77-78.

Hall was built;[93] and it chose the college in 1456 for its annual obit service for benefactors of the community.[94]

The friaries in Norwich, like friaries throughout England, had acquired many pieces of property to enlarge their sites in the thirteenth and early fourteenth centuries.[95] The acquisitions of the Dominican friary had brought it into conflict with the citizens as well as with the Crown in the early fourteenth century,[96] but no complaints against the four friaries are known to have been made at the inquisition which was held in the city in 1352, as one of a series of inquisitions held throughout the country, to investigate property acquired by friars.[97] Local records as well as the Patent and Close Rolls mention few pieces of property acquired by the four friaries after 1368,[98] which was the year in which the Augustinians incorporated St Michael of Conisford parish church into their site.[99] The friaries appear to have rounded off their sites by the mid fourteenth century, and to have concentrated thereafter on erecting new buildings on them.[100] Neither the citizens nor the central government appear to have objected to the latter pursuit.

The Carmelite friary, like the College of St Mary in the Fields, enjoyed a special relationship with the city government. Thus the commonalty agreed in 1488, apparently at the invitation of the Carmelites,[101] to become the second founder of the friary in succession to Philip Cowgate, the merchant who had originally founded it in the thirteenth century, the mayor becoming "the principal founder;" [102] acting on this the mayor and commonalty, eleven years later, exempted the Carmelites from all tolls in the city.[103]

---

[93] E.g., N.C.R., Case 8d, Rolls of the City Assembly, Rolls 39-42 and 47 Edward III and 8 Richard II.

[94] *Records of Norwich*, ed. Hudson, 2: 92.

[95] Campbell, *Norwich*, p. 11; N.C.R., Cases 3g-4b, Private Deeds, Box 1, "Friars Preachers in St Andrew," Box 5, "Friars Preachers in St Clement," Box 10, "St John Maddermarket," Box 11, "St Mary Unbrent," and Box 12, "St Peter Hungate."

[96] *Cal. Close R., 1330-1333*, pp. 430 and 433-434.

[97] Andrew G. Little, "A Royal Inquiry into Property Held by the Mendicant Friars in England in 1349 and 1350," in *Historical Essays in Honour of James Tait*, ed. John G. Edwards, Vivian H. Galbraith and Ernest F. Jacob (Manchester 1933), pp. 186-187.

[98] I.e., *Cal. Pat. R., 1377-1381*, p. 496; *Cal. Close R., 1385-1389*, p. 279; *Cal. Pat. R., 1429-1436*, p. 119.

[99] *Inventory*, ed. Watkin, 1: 24; Blomefield, *Norfolk* (1805-1810), 4: 84-85.

[100] Campbell, *Norwich*, pp. 11 and 17.

[101] N.C.R., Case 4a, Private Deeds, Box 10, "St James."

[102] N.C.R., Case 16d, Proceedings of the Municipal Assembly, Book 1 (1434-1491), fol. 132r/137r.

[103] N.C.R., Case 16c, Assembly Minute Book 1 (1492-1510), fol. 73v.

Others. Something has been said about friction between the citizens and their parish clergy over paying tithes, attending Mass in their parish churches and receiving the Eucharist from, and confessing to, their parish priests.[104] There is evidence of only isolated instances of conflict over these matters, except perhaps over absenteeism from Mass. Indeed, widespread and deep hostility among the citizens towards the clergy seems to have confined itself to hostility towards the monks of the Cathedral Priory. There is little to suggest that it extended to a more general anti-clericalism embracing the friars and the secular clergy. Testamentary bequests left by the laity to friars and to parish churches,[105] as well as the number of sons of citizens who became priests or joined religious orders,[106] are more positive evidence against the existence of widespread anti-clericalism in the city.

ii. *Conflicts within the Clerical Body*

The Cathedral Priory, the Friars and the Parish Clergy. Besides their conflicts with the laity, the clergy are known to have quarrelled among themselves over several issues. In these disputes, too, it is noticeable how frequently the Cathedral Priory was one of the parties. Those involving the rights and emoluments of the parish clergy, in many of which the priory was involved as patron of a parish church, and those between the priory and the friars over preaching in the Cathedral, have been discussed.[107]

In addition, the rectors and parish chaplains of the city quarrelled with the sacrist of the Cathedral Priory in the late fourteenth century over a procession they made into the Cathedral on the first Sunday after Trinity. The only known record of the dispute is the settlement imposed by Bishop Dispenser in 1390.[108] The dispute was said to have been going on for some years, but the settlement does not make clear the points at issue. The bishop ordered all the rectors and parish chaplains to participate in the annual procession and emphasised the need for order and quiet. Possibly a once great procession had become a shambles with many clergy absenting themselves. There was also disagreement among a group of the clergy about who should read a Collect and whether the procession should begin at St Michael at Plea parish church, but it is not clear whether they were

---

[104] See pp. 5-10.
[105] See pp. 119-120, 126-129 and 222-223.
[106] See pp. 25-26.
[107] See pp. 6-7 and 11-15.
[108] REG/3, Book 6, fol. 204v.

vying with each other to read the prayer and to have the procession start from their own parish church, or whether they wanted to avoid the responsibilities.

The opposition over the procession was the only semblance of collective opposition to the priory known to have come from the secular clergy of the city during the period in question. As patron of many parish churches in Norwich, the priory exercised much control over the parishes; yet many regarded the parish as the preserve of the secular clergy. It is therefore surprising that the secular clergy of the city did not offer the priory a greater degree of collective opposition. Perhaps the priory's extensive ecclesiastical patronage in the city rendered them subservient rather than openly hostile.

The Cathedral Priory and Carrow Nunnery. The Cathedral Priory clashed with Carrow Nunnery on several occasions in the fourteenth and early fifteenth centuries over their respective jurisdictions in various areas of the city and its suburbs and over the economic profits flowing therefrom. Thus the priory and the nunnery received tithes from the inhabitants of the suburban parishes of Bracondale and Carrow respectively, and in the fourteenth century they were quarrelling over the boundary common to the two parishes and consequently over who should receive the tithes of various inhabitants.[109] Another dispute over their rights in the suburbs had arisen by 1416. In that year the prior and another monk were brought to court by the prioress for seizing some of the nunnery's cattle grazing in Carrow, and driving them off to the priory's neighbouring lands in Lakenham. At the same time both parties were disputing their rights of leet and view of frank-pledge in areas in the southern tip of the city and in the suburb of Trowse. A settlement to the latter dispute was reached in 1418 when agreement was reached on the boundaries dividing their respective jurisdictions.[110] There is no evidence of conflict later.

The Cathedral Priory and the Bishops of Norwich. The Cathedral Priory's most serious conflict, apart from its disputes with the citizens, was with various bishops of Norwich. In many ways the prior eclipsed the bishop in importance in his own episcopal city, and the bishop needed the consent of the prior and chapter for important diocesan acts.[111] The

---

[109] D. and C. Mun., Box "Disputes and Agreements, v Carrow, v Carmelites," nos. 1582, 1584, 1590, 2418 and 4801-4803.

[110] Ibid., nos. 1583 and 1595; *Records of Norwich*, ed. Hudson, 1: lxxx and 319.

[111] Burnham, "Episcopal Administration," pp. 80-81 and 187.

inevitable rivalry produced plenty of scope for conflict. The disputes centred around two issues: the bishop's rights in the government of the priory and its property and secondly the "reverencialia" due to him.

The first issue was contested chiefly during the later years of the episcopate of Henry Dispenser (1370-1396). The bishop's rights in several matters were disputed: the admission of novices, the profession and punishment of monks, their promotion to and removal from offices; the disposal of corrodies and of the priory's properties; visitations of the priory, and of the Carnary College and St Paul's Hospital, which belonged to the priory; and payments to the priory, by the bishop, of various tithes and dues.[112] Dispenser's aggressiveness seems to have been the main cause of the dispute[113] and of its escalation. In the course of an enormous amount of litigation the case was brought before the Crown, the archbishop of Canterbury and the pope.[114] A settlement was not reached until 1411, by which time Alexander Totington, who had been prior during the quarrel, had succeeded Dispenser as bishop. It was reached through the arbitration of Archbishop Arundel and while it saved the appearances for the bishop it went in favour of the priory on most points of substance.[115] One of the points – the bishop's rights in removing monks from offices – reappeared briefly during the episcopate of Walter Lyhert (1446-1472). Thus in 1467 Pope Pius II appointed a commission of three abbots to adjudicate the claim made by John Molet, the prior, that Bishop Lyhert had openly threatened to remove him from office without reasonable cause.[116] Molet was not, however, removed from office and no more is heard of the matter.

The "reverencialia" due to the bishop from the monks became an issue during the episcopate of Thomas Brown (1436-1445). The bishop complained that the monks, especially Prior John Heverlond, were not paying him various marks of respect due to him on account of his superior status when he was celebrating the liturgy in the Cathedral or visiting the priory or on various other occasions. Prior Heverlond yielded to the bishop's demands in 1441. But Bishop Brown appealed to the archbishop of Canterbury and the pope two years later on the grounds that the prior had broken the agreement by failing to minister the crucifix

---

[112] Carter, *Studies*, p. 40; *Cal. Papal L., 1362-1404*, p. 525; *Cal. Papal L., 1396-1404*, pp. 586-587.

[113] Carter, *Studies*, pp. 37-39; see also REG/3, Book 6, fols. 89r-v and 90v.

[114] Carter, *Studies*, p. 37; *Cal. Papal L., 1362-1404*, pp. 518 and 525; *Cal. Papal L., 1396-1404*, pp. 11-12, 273-274, 318-319, 526-527 and 586-587.

[115] Carter, *Studies*, pp. 49-57.

[116] *Cal. Papal L., 1458-1471*, p. 560.

or the osculatory to him when he entered the Cathedral. The settlement reached in 1444 was a compromise on the issue that had been the immediate cause of the bishop's appeal: the crucifix or osculatory was to be ministered by the prior only if the bishop had been away fom the Cathedral for at least two months. Otherwise it was a victory for the bishop. The priory agreed that the prior, if present, should minister the following to the bishop in a reverent manner: the crucifix after the Confiteor, the gospel-book after the Gospel had been read, the osculatory and the pax when the bishop celebrated Mass in the Cathedral, and the crucifix and the pax when he heard Mass in the Cathedral or elsewhere. The priory also agreed that the prior should walk slightly behind the bishop, not level with him, and should hold the hem of his cloak during processions in the Cathedral. Finally, the priory agreed to ring the bells of the Cathedral in the same way as those of the parish churches of the city were rung when the bishop entered the Cathedral after an absence of two months, and to pay him various marks of respect when he entered the Cathedral to begin his septennial visitations of the priory.[117] Bishop Brown died the next year, but the "reverencialia" were still an issue when Bishop Goldwell visited the priory in 1492. He annulled all the statutes made by the senior monks and an unnamed former prior[118] whereby marks of respect that should, he thought, be reserved for the bishop were to be paid to the prior; ordered under pain of excommunication the leaves containing the offending statutes to be destroyed without delay; and forbade the present and future masters of novices to teach their charges the offending customs![119]

The disputes were typical of struggles throughout medieval Christendom between bishops and their cathedral chapters. They raised important questions about the power of bishops over religious houses in general and their cathedral chapters in particular. Even the disputed "reverencialia" were taken seriously by both sides, however petty they may appear.[120] But they were primarily personal clashes. Thus it is noticeable that the most bitter clashes appear to have been caused largely by two men known to have been aggressive in other spheres: Bishop Dispenser whose warlike qualities need no elaboration, and Prior Heverlond whose activities

---

[117] REG/5, Book 10, fols. 101r, 102r-v, 108r and 110r-111r. See also, Ernest F. Jacob, "Thomas Brouns, Bishop of Norwich, 1436-1445," in *Essays in British History Presented to Sir Keith Feiling*, ed. Hugh Trevor-Roper (London and New York, 1964), pp. 77-78.

[118] John Heverlond?

[119] *Visitations*, ed. Jessopp, p. 5.

[120] For similar disputes in other English dioceses, see Alfred H. Sweet, "The Apostolic See and the Heads of English Religious Houses," *Speculum* 28 (1953) 476-481.

against the citizens have been mentioned.[121] Paradoxically, though the two men and possibly Bishop Lyhert appear to have been the chief aggressors, Bishop Dispenser posthumously and Bishop Lyhert and Prior Heverlond during their lives lost the phases of the conflict in which they were involved. Mr Burnham argued that, outside fairly short periods of conflict, relations between the bishops and the priory were on the whole good;[122] and that many of the bishops entrusted their chantries to the priory[123] is an indication that good relations were the norm. The disputes were probably common knowledge among the citizens, especially those between Bishop Brown and Prior Heverlond involving public services in the Cathedral. No doubt the sight of the two most prominent pillars of the local Church quarrelling was a disedifying spectacle, and one that contributed towards the laity's scepticism of ecclesiastical authority. But the quarrels were probably not sufficiently serious or unusual for the effect to have been great.

iii. Conclusion

The Church in Norwich does not appear to have been in a state of prolonged crisis between the late fourteenth and early sixteenth centuries. During the period conflicts within the local Church were sufficiently numerous and varied to affect most of its members, but they concerned peripheral matters or were insufficiently sustained to threaten the existence of any branch of the Church, let alone the local Church as such. By far the most serious was the dispute between the Cathedral Priory and the citizens, and the priory was involved in most of the other known quarrels. Yet the disputes concerned the borders of the priory's authority; they never threatened its existence, except perhaps momentarily in 1443. Most of the tensions had their origins in the early or high Middle Ages. In general the period in question, especially after 1450, saw the gradual solution of many quarrels, not the growth of conflict that inevitably culminated in the Reformation.

C. Heresy

Norwich appears to have been remarkably free of heresy in the late Middle Ages. Only a handful of citizens are known to have been heretics,

---

[121] See pp. 146-152.
[122] Burnham, "Episcopal Administration," p. 187.
[123] See pp. 94-95.

and nothing suggests that the city had a continuous tradition of Lollardy such as London had.

The prior of the Cathedral Priory had accused the friars of the city in about 1360 of expressing views "against the norm of sound doctrine and the liberty of the Church." [124] It is doubtful, however, whether the offending views were heretical. They may have been connected with the Fitzralph controversy,[125] in which the friars remained more or less within the bounds of orthodoxy. No connections between the city and early Lollardy are known apart from Bale's largely unsubstantiated claim that Richard Caistor, vicar of St Stephen's, was a Wycliffite.[126] Nobody from Norwich is known to have taken part in Oldcastle's rising in 1414.[127]

The earliest cases of citizens known to have been heretics, after Oldcastle's rising, come from records of trials of suspected Lollards conducted by Bishop Alnwick between 1428 and 1431. Two citizens were convicted of heresy, though their beliefs were not specified: the wife of a certain John Weston and Thomas Wade, a tailor from the parish of St Mary of Coslany.[128] A few other suggestions were made at the trials that some citizens were influenced by Lollard views.[129] The next known case was not until the early sixteenth century: according to Foxe, a priest from Norwich called Thomas was degraded from the priesthood and burnt in the village of Eckeles[130] in about 1510,[131] presumably for heresy. Bishop Nykke thought that heresy was spreading in his diocese immediately before the end of the period in question. He complained, in a letter written in 1530, of the influx of "erroneous books in English" and thought that merchants and people living near the sea were particularly infected by them.[132] He may well have had his episcopal city in mind. But the nearest to concrete cases up to 1532, of heretics closely connected with Nor-

---

[124] See p. 11.

[125] Pantin, *English Church*, p. 177.

[126] See p. 232.

[127] Kenneth B. McFarlane, *John Wycliffe and the Beginnings of English Nonconformity* (London 1952), pp. 172-173.

[128] *Heresy Trials*, ed. Tanner, pp. 35-38 and 195.

[129] Ibid., pp. 43-50 and 60.

[130] Probably Eccles in south Norfolk (see next footnote).

[131] Foxe, *Acts and Monuments*, Book 6, section on Thomas Chase of Amersham, ed. Pratt, 4: 773. Thomas Ayers, priest of Norwich, was burnt at Eccles in 1510, according to Blomefield, *Norfolk* (1805-1810), 3: 193; and a priest from Eccles was burnt at Norwich for his views on the Sacrament during the pontificate of Leo x, according to Bale, *Scriptorum catalogus*, p. 648. Possibly one and the same man is being referred to.

[132] London, British Museum, MS Cotton, Cleopatra E. V., fol. 389r-v (old fol. 360r-v).

wich,[133] were Thomas Bilney and one of his followers; and it is doubtful whether Bilney was more than an orthodox radical or whether his connections with Norwich were close. Blomefield said he was a native of Norfolk, probably of Norwich or East Bilney,[134] but there is no evidence to support the claim. Foxe thought that he had preached in Norfolk before his arrest by Bishop Tunstall of London in 1527.[135] He was in Norwich when he was arrested for the last time in 1531, and Sir Thomas More said that he had "infected various people of the city (i.e., Norwich) before." [136] His only identifiable disciple in the city was an anchoress attached to the Dominican friary, presumably Katherine Manne.[137] He gave her Tyndale's translation of the New Testament and Tyndale's *Obedience of a Christian Man*; but he said, to calm her conscience, that he had never taught her anything heretical.[138] After his arrest by Bishop Nykke's officers in 1531, Bilney was degraded from the priesthood and handed over to the secular authorities for execution as a lapsed heretic. He was burnt just outside one of the city gates. Beforehand he appears to have retracted some opinions, though it was hotly disputed whether he had made a full recantation.[139]

Heresy's apparent lack of impact on late medieval Norwich is remarkable. As a provincial capital Norwich might be expected to have been a centre of Lollardy in the way that London, Bristol, Coventry and some other cities were.[140] Moreover the development of new religious movements in the city,[141] the increase in the number of its clergy with university degrees,[142] and its geographical and trading links with the Low Countries and the Rhineland, then the most fertile areas for religious movements north of the Alps, show that late medieval Norwich was no conservative backwater in its religion. It is remarkable, too, because the

---

[133] See Ralph Houlbrooke, "Persecution of Heresy and Protestantism in the Diocese of Norwich under Henry VIII," *Norfolk Archaeology* 35 (1970-1973) 314 and 322-323.

[134] Blomefield, *Norfolk* (1805-1810), 3: 199, and 9: 461.

[135] Foxe, *Acts and Monuments*, Book 8, section on Thomas Bilney, ed. Pratt, 4: 620-621.

[136] Ibid., Book 8, section on Thomas Bilney, ed. Pratt, 4: 642; Thomas More, *The Confutation of Tyndale's Answer*, Preface, ed. Louis A. Schuster and others, in *The Complete Works of St Thomas More*, 8 (New Haven 1973), p. 23.

[137] See p. 199.

[138] Foxe, *Acts and Monuments*, Book 8, section on Thomas Bilney, ed. Pratt, 4: 642, and (after p. 778) "Documents relating to Thomas Bilney, Martyr," section III.

[139] Ibid., Book 8, section on Thomas Bilney, ed. Pratt, 4: 643, 652 and (after p. 778) "Documents relating to Thomas Bilney, Martyr," section IV.

[140] Thomson, *Later Lollards*, pp. 20-47, 100-116 and 139-171.

[141] See pp. 57-112.

[142] See pp. 28-32.

city had become a Puritan stronghold by the reign of Elizabeth[143] and remained one.

The apparent absence of heresy can scarcely be explained by lack of vigilance in detecting it on the part of the bishops of Norwich. Bishops Dispenser (1370-1406), Wakeryng (1415-1425), Alnwick (1426-1436), Brown (1436-1445) and Nykke (1501-1535) were all noted for their opposition to heresy.[144] The strongest evidence that the city was truly, not just apparently, little affected by heresy comes from the records of the trials conducted by Bishop Alnwick between 1428 and 1431 which have just been mentioned. In showing that Lollardy was then widespread in East Anglia, they reveal its lack of impact in Norwich as all the more remarkable. The city, moreover, might be expected to have yielded an unusually large number of suspects since it was the site of most of the trials[145] and since the bishop of Norwich might be expected to have been specially vigilant in his own city. However, only two of the approximately fifty men and women from the diocese who were convicted and whose home towns or villages are known came from Norwich, and there are only a few other indications that heresy had penetrated the city. This compares with several towns and villages in the diocese that each produced half a dozen of those condemned.[146]

Thomas Wade, the tailor of Norwich convicted in 1428, was sentenced to floggings in the Cathedral, in his parish church and in the market-place of Norwich.[147] The wife of John Weston of Norwich was sentenced to do "solemn penance" in the Cathedral in 1431.[148] Many people from other parts of the diocese convicted at these trials between 1428 and 1431 were sentenced to be flogged or to do "solemn penance" in the city.[149] William White, Hugh Pye and John (or William) Waddon were burnt as heretics in the city in 1428.[150] Thomas Bilney, and three or four men without

[143] Collinson, *Puritan Movement*, pp. 127, 141, 186-187 and 213.

[144] For Bishop Dispenser see Thomas Walsingham, *Historia Anglicana*, ed. Henry T. Riley, Rolls Series (London 1863-1864), 2: 188-189; for Bishop Wakeryng see Foxe, *Acts and Monuments*, Book 6, sections on John Florence and Richard Belward and others, ed. Pratt, 3: 584-586 and 848; for Bishop Alnwick see *Heresy Trials*, ed. Tanner, pp. 8-9 and passim; for Bishop Brown see Jacob, "Thomas Brouns," p. 66; and for Bishop Nykke see *D.N.B.*, 41: 74 (Richard Nix or Nykke), and Houlbrooke, "Persecution of Heresy," pp. 309-313.

[145] *Heresy Trials*, ed. Tanner, pp. 8-9.

[146] Ibid., pp. 8, 22 and 27; Thomson, *Later Lollards*, p. 120.

[147] *Heresy Trials*, ed. Tanner, pp. 35-38.

[148] Ibid., p. 195.

[149] Ibid., p. 23.

[150] Ibid., p. 8.

known connections with Norwich, were burnt in the city for heresy during the first third of the sixteenth century.[151] The sight of the punishments, and the known vigilance of the bishops of Norwich, may have deterred the citizens from indulging in heresy. But the findings of this book suggest that an important reason for the lack of interest in Lollardy was that the religion provided by the local Church was sufficiently rich and varied, and sufficiently tolerant towards what might be called the left wing of orthodoxy, as to cater for the tastes of most citizens.

[151] Blomefield, *Norfolk* (1805-1810), 3: 182; Foxe, *Acts and Monuments*, Book 6, section on Thomas Chase of Amersham, ed. Pratt, 4: 126 and 773; Bale, *Scriptorum catalogus*; pp. 644 and 648; Houlbrooke, "Persecution of Heresy," pp. 322-323; see pp. 163-164.

Conclusion

The evidence on which this study is based is uneven. In places it is unusually full, especially the number of wills. But there are the gaps in it that are to be expected from the Middle Ages. In particular, there is no autobiographical material that gives a comprehensive view of what it was like to be a Christian in the city. Even the *Revelations of Divine Love* of Julian of Norwich, which perhaps comes closest to it, records special experiences. It would be fascinating to know more directly and more fully what Richard Caistor or Margaret Purdans or John Terry thought about the Church in Norwich, or to have an equivalent of *The Book of Margery Kempe* discussing religion in the city. General conclusions must therefore be treated with caution because they are not based on comprehensive evidence. Moreover the book presents a fair amount of varied and complex evidence, and to some extent the reader must draw his or her own conclusions.

However, one important conclusion emerges fairly clearly. It is something of a paradox: that the older and more clerical aspects of the Church in Norwich, which had blossomed in the early and high Middle Ages, continued to flourish in the late Middle Ages; but simultaneously there developed new religious movements which were largely products of late medieval Christendom and largely directed towards the laity. The result was a religion of considerable richness and variety, a kind of High Church, almost Baroque, Christianity. The local church appears to have been very much a going concern. This conflicts with the generally held view that the Church was in an advanced state of decay towards the end of the Middle Ages.

The continuing vitality of the older and more clerical institutions and ideals manifested itself in several ways. The parishes, which dated back for the most part to the eleventh or early twelfth centuries,[1] seem to have remained in the late Middle Ages the branch of the Church that touched most citizens most closely.[2] Support for them was shown by the huge

---

[1] See p. 3.
[2] See pp. 1-18.

programme of rebuilding parish churches,[3] by the number and value of testamentary bequests to them,[4] by the number of citizens who asked to be buried in the church or cemetery of their parish,[5] and by the fact that the churches appear to have been well staffed and well equipped.[6] The only serious indications to the contrary were absenteeism from Mass on Sundays and feastdays,[7] and a certain lack of interest on the part of the laity in running the parishes.[8] Support for the priesthood and life in a religious order was shown by the remarkably high proportion of testators' sons who were priests or members of religious orders,[9] and by the number of testators leaving bequests to religious houses.[10] The rise in the number of beneficed clergy who were university graduates suggests a better educated clergy.[11] As for the number of priests and religious in the city, the populations of the four friaries are not known with any accuracy;[12] the number of monks at the Cathedral Priory declined after 1460;[13] but the secular clergy appears to have grown considerably between the late fourteenth and early sixteenth centuries,[14] though this was matched by an increase in the total population of the city.[15] At all events the evidence does not suggest that in Norwich the "old order" of the Church was in a state of marked decline in the late Middle Ages. Nor does it suggest a radical rejection of the institutional Church.

New movements in the late medieval Church were represented in Norwich by hermits, anchorites and groups resembling beguinages; by craft guilds with their guild-days, processions and mystery plays; by pious confraternities; by pilgrimages and other devotions to the saints; by improvements in the religious education of the laity; and by the multiplication of Masses and prayers for the dead. Hermits, anchorites and groups resembling beguinages flourished in a way that was exceptional for any city in England. Thus Julian of Norwich, the anchoress, mystic and author of the *Revelations of Divine Love*, was

---

[3] See pp. 4 and 128-129.
[4] See pp. 126-129 and 223.
[5] See pp. 12-13 and 17.
[6] See pp. 4-5 and 8-9.
[7] See pp. 9-10.
[8] See p. 16.
[9] See pp. 25-26.
[10] See pp. 119-125 and 222-223.
[11] See pp. 28-30.
[12] See pp. 19-20 and 23.
[13] See pp. 19 and 23.
[14] See pp. 18-19 and 21-23.
[15] See p. xvi, n. 4, and p. 21.

remarkable by any standards; more hermits and anchorites appear to have been living in Norwich in the fifteenth and early sixteenth centuries than in any other town in England;[16] testamentary bequests to them appear to have been exceptionally numerous;[17] and Norwich was the only town in England known to have had groups of women closely resembling Continental beguinages.[18] The findings concerning the hermits and anchorites and groups resembling beguinages are among the most important in the book.

A second conclusion is that tension within the Church in Norwich appears to have diminished, not increased, during the late fifteenth and early sixteenth centuries. This is another reason why Norwich does not support the general thesis that the Church was disintegrating in the late Middle Ages. The dispute between the citizens and the Cathedral Priory, which was the most serious conflict within the Church in Norwich, was settled in 1524 largely in favour of the citizens.[19] Moreover the citizens settled their disputes with Carrow Nunnery and the abbeys of Wendling and St Benet of Hulme almost entirely in their favour between 1450 and 1523.[20] The settlements removed important reasons why the citizens might have welcomed the dissolution of religious houses. There is little evidence of other conflicts between the laity and the clergy,[21] even over tithes.[22] Disputes among the secular and regular clergy, the nuns of Carrow and the bishops of Norwich also appear to have been fewer and less intense after about 1450 than before.[23] Testamentary bequests from the laity to both the secular and the regular clergy,[24] as well as bequests from the secular clergy to religious houses[25] and to lay men and women living as hermits or anchorites,[26] are further indications that relations between the clergy and the laity were, for the most part, harmonious. Finally, Lollardy's apparent lack of impact in the city[27] suggests that the local Church was not rent by doctrinal controversy.

[16] See pp. 58-59.
[17] See pp. 130 and 223.
[18] See pp. 64-66 and 202-203.
[19] See pp. 153-154.
[20] See pp. 152-153 and 155-156.
[21] See p. 158.
[22] See pp. 5-7.
[23] See pp. 158-162.
[24] See pp. 119-126 and 222-223.
[25] See pp. 119-125 and 222-223.
[26] See pp. 130 and 223.
[27] See pp. 162-166.

The resolution of the citizens' disputes with various religious houses, the generally good relations that appear to have existed between the laity and the clergy, and Lollardy's lack of impact in the city, make the Reformation in Norwich puzzling. Looking at the city in isolation from the rest of the country, there are few indications in the late Middle Ages that the Reformation was imminent. The Church appears remarkably healthy until the second decade of the sixteenth century. Thus religious bequests in wills did not decline before 1517,[28] and the apparent harmony between the old order and new movements suggests that the Church was satisfying the religious aspirations of most citizens. On the other hand the Reformation appears to have met little resistance in the city, and it had become a Puritan stronghold by the reign of Elizabeth. Some portents appeared during the fifteen years after the beginning of the Reformation on the Continent: there was a decline in testamentary bequests for chantry services[29] as well as in offerings to the high altar of the Cathedral,[30] and the number of monks at the Cathedral Priory dropped rapidly in the early 1530s.[31] But the evidence for the fifteen years does not indicate a mounting crisis leading to violent changes. It suggests, rather, a creeping insecurity about the value and future of the old religion which created a vacuum in the religious life of the city. The vacuum was filled from outside, by the Reformation coming from elsewhere in England and from the Continent. To some extent, however, the Reformation must be seen as a development from within the late medieval Church rather than as a reaction against it, as E. G. Léonard has insisted.[32] Thus the Reformation was possible in Norwich in 1530, and not in 1370, partly because improvements in religious education meant that there were by 1530 many more citizens capable of understanding the issues at stake in the Reformation than there had been in 1370. To some extent educational improvements and the increasingly important part played by the laity in some aspects of the life of the Church, shown by their role in craft guilds and pious confraternities and by lay people living as hermits or anchorites or in communities resembling beguinages, issued naturally in the Puritanism of Elizabethan Norwich.[33]

---

[28] See pp. 101, 139 and 220-223.

[29] See pp. 101 and 220-221.

[30] See p. 88; but see pp. 120-121 and 222.

[31] Saunders, *Obedientiary Rolls*, p. 161.

[32] Émile G. Léonard, *Histoire générale du Protestantisme* (Paris 1961-1964), 1: 10.

[33] For the Reformation in Norwich up to 1559, see Elaine M. Sheppard, "The Reformation and the Citizens of Norwich," *Norfolk Archaeology* 38 (1981-) 44-58, which unfortunately appeared too late for her interesting findings to be taken into consideration.

Finally, how Christian was late medieval Norwich? Probably everybody in the city considered himself a Christian. The Jews had been expelled in 1290,[34] and even the few citizens convicted of heresy no doubt regarded themselves as Christians. The question is rather theological and cultural: how far had Christianity in late medieval Norwich become so reduced to a merely cultural phenomenon that it had ceased to be Christianity? The question is impossibly vague but important to ask, I think, because the religion of medieval Europe is too readily assumed to have been almost wholly Christian in inspiration or even to be normative for what Christianity should be today. One general observation must suffice. The growth of new movements in the late Middle Ages alongside the enduring vitality of the old institutions suggests both development and continuity. Religion in late medieval Norwich appears neither as a complete break with the religion of the early and high Middle Ages nor as a fossilized ritualism. It seems to have been in contact with the aspirations of the citizens while remaining a stimulating, at best an elevating, force – as Christianity should be. This conclusion is easier to accept if the Reformation in Norwich is seen as a development from within the late medieval Church as much as a reaction against it. Otherwise it is difficult to explain why the religion of a city that appears to have been in a healthy state was jettisoned within two generations.

[34] Vivian D. Lipman, *The Jews of Medieval Norwich* (London 1967), p. 184.

Appendix 1

The Parish Churches of Norwich
and their Chapels of Ease, 1370-1532

Abbreviations:

(A)	Augustinian Canons	P.Chapl.	Parish Chaplain
(B)	Benedictine	Py.	Priory
(BC)	Benedictine, Cluniac	Stip.	Stipendiary Priest
(P)	Premonstratensian Canons		

Parish Church or Chapel[1]	Status[2]	Patron[2]	Staff in 1492[3]	Value in 1368[4]	Value in 1535[5]
Northern Ward					
St. Augustine	Rectory	Norwich Cathedral Py. (B)	Rector	13s. 4d.	£6.17.10
St. Martin of Coslany	"	" " " "	P.Chapl. & Stip.	13s. 4d.	£2.13.4
St. Botulph	"	Various citizens of Norwich; 1456- Horsham St Faith Py., Norfolk (B)	Rector	13s. 4d.	£2.7.8

[1] The parish churches are listed in the same order as they appear in the record of the visitation of Norwich deanery in 1492 (see pp. 179-188), except that parish churches not appearing in the record have been inserted in appropriate places. Chapels (of ease) are marked with an asterisk and belonged, with the partial exception of the chapel in the Castle, to the preceding parish.

[2] Columns 2 and 3 are based on the following, except where other references are given:

— REG/2, Book 4, to REG/10, Book 16. The institutions to parochial benefices mentioned in these episcopal registers are fairly accurately indexed, according to parishes, in REG/30, pp. 1-53.
— D. and C. Mun., Box "Papal and Archiepiscopal," no. 2388 (Churches belonging to Norwich Cathedral Priory, 1411).
— Norwich, Norfolk Record Office, Colman MS 115 (Taxation of the Religious within Norfolk, 1428), fols. 2v and 14v.
— *Valor ecclesiasticus*, ed. Caley, 3: 284, 289, 293-294 and 369.
— Campbell, *Norwich*, Appendix II (pp. 23-24).

The dates of change of status, or of patrons, refer to the earliest known dates of the changes, not necessarily to the actual dates.

[3] See pp. 179-188.

[4] *Inventory*, ed. Watkin, 1: 1-27.

[5] *Valor ecclesiasticus*, ed. Caley, 3: 284, 289, 293-294, 369 and 493.

Parish Church or Chapel	Status	Patron	Staff in 1492	Value in 1368	Value in 1535
St Mary of Coslany	Rectory	Coxford Py., Norfolk (A)	P.Chapl. & Stip.	£3.13.4	£6.13.4
St Michael of Coslany	,,	1353- Thomas Hobbe of Acle; 1387- John Frythe, vicar of St Stephen's, Norwich; 1395- various citizens of Norwich; 1427- Sir Thomas Erpingham and others; 1442- Gonville Hall, Cambridge[6]	Rector & 4 Stip.	£4.13.4	£13.6.11
St George of Colegate	,,	Norwich Cathedral Py. (B)	P.Chapl. & Stip.	13s. 4d.	£3.6.8
*St Margaret of Newbridge	Chapel[7]			13s. 4d.	
St Olave of Colegate	Rectory; probably Chapel in St George of Colegate parish by 1492[8]	,, ,, ,, ,,		13s. 4d.	
St Clement at Fye Bridge	Rectory	Mendham Py., Suffolk (BC)	Rector	£4.13.4	£8
St Edmund	,,	Clere family of Ormesby, Norfolk	Rector & Stip.	£1	£4.6.6
St James	,,	Norwich Cathedral Py. (B)	P.Chapl.	£1.6.8	£3
St Saviour	,,	,, ,, ,, ,,	P.Chapl.[9]	13s. 4d.	
All Saints at Fye Bridge	,,	,, ,, ,, ,,	P.Chapl.	£1.6.8	
St Margaret at Fye Bridge	Rectory; probably Chapel in All Saints at Fye Bridge parish sometime after 1453[10]	,, ,, ,, ,,		13s. 4d.	
St Mary Unbrent	Rectory	College of St Mary in the Fields, Norwich	Rector[11]	£1	£3.9.0

[6] John A. Venn and others, *Biographical History of Gonville and Caius College* (Cambridge 1897-), 3: 317.

[7] Blomefield, *Norfolk* (1805-1810), 4: 474; *Inventory*, ed. Watkin, 1: xiv.

[8] Ab.C., Reg. Morton 2 (1486-1500), fol. 29r (Wigge); Blomefield, *Norfolk* (1805-1810), 4: 475; see below, p. 181, where St Olave's is not mentioned as a parish church; *Inventory*, ed. Watkin, 1: xv and 9.

[9] He was the same person as the rector of St Mary Unbrent (see p. 181).

[10] REG/6, Book 11, fol. 29v; Blomefield, *Norfolk* (1805-1810), 4: 439; see below, p. 181, where St Margaret's is not mentioned as a parish church; Campbell, *Norwich*, p. 24.

[11] He was the same person as the parish chaplain of St Saviour's (see p. 181).

Parish Church or Chapel	Status	Patron	Staff in 1492	Value in 1368	Value in 1535
Wimer Ward					
Sts Simon and Jude	United (together with Crostwick, Norfolk)	Bishop of Norwich	Rector[12] & P.Chapl. & Stip.	£2	£3.10.0
St Swithin	Rectory		Rector[12] & P.Chapl. & Stip.	£1	£6.3.5
St George at Tombland	Rectory	College of St Mary in the Fields, Norwich	P.Chapl.	£3.6.8	£1.12.0
St Peter Hungate	"	College of St Mary in the Fields, Norwich; 1458-[13] or 1469- Paston family of Paston, Norfolk	Rector & P.Chapl.	£1.10.0	£3.1.4
St Michael at Plea	"	Various lay lords and knights and their wives (Blomefield thought the advowson belonged to the lords of Horsford and of Sprowston, both in Norfolk, alternately[14]	Rector & 2 Stip.	£1	£6.10.3
St Andrew	"	College of St Mary in the Fields, Norwich	3 Stip.	£5	£11
Holy Cross or St Crowche	"	Norwich Cathedral Py. (B)	P.Chapl.	£1.10.0	
St John's Maddermarket	"	Newton Longville Py., Bucks. (Alien BC); 1386- King (having seized Py.'s property); 1441- New College, Oxford[15]	Rector	£3.6.8	£7.17.0
St Gregory	"	Norwich Cathedral Py. (B)	P.Chapl. & 4 Stip.	£3.6.8	£4
St Laurence	"	Abbot of Bury St Edmund's (B)	Rector & 2 Stip.	£3.6.8	£4.14.0
St Margaret of Westwick	"	Various laymen, many of whom were lords of the manor of Yoxford in Suffolk	Rector & 2 Stip.	£2	£5.4.11
(St Swithin: see above, after Sts Simon and Jude)					
St Benedict	"	Buckenham Py., Norfolk (A)	P.Chapl. & Stip.	£5	
Mancroft Ward					
St Giles	Rectory	Norwich Cathedral Py. (B)	P.Chapl. & Stip.	£3.6.8	5s.

[12] The rector of Sts Simon and Jude was the same person as the rector of St Swithin's (see pp. 181 and 184).
[13] *Paston Letters*, ed. Gairdner, 4: 230, n. 1.
[14] Blomefield, *Norfolk* (1805-1810), 4: 327.
[15] *Cal. Pat. R., 1436-1441*, p. 558; REG/6, Book 11, fol. 26r.

Parish Church or Chapel	Status	Patron	Staff in 1492	Value in 1368	Value in 1535
St Peter Mancroft	"	Gloucester Abbey (B); 1384- College of St Mary in the Fields, Norwich[16]	P.Chapl. & 2 Chantry Chaplains & 9 Stip.	£16.13.4	£16.18.11
St Stephen	Vicarage	Norwich Cathedral Py. (B)	Vicar & 4 Stip.	£6.13.4	£11.13.7

Conisford Ward

Parish Church or Chapel	Status	Patron	Staff in 1492	Value in 1368	Value in 1535
St John of Timberhill	Rectory	Norwich Cathedral Py. (B)	P.Chapl. & 3 Stip.	£2.13.4	£1
All Saints of Berstreet	"	Carrow Nunnery, near Norwich (B)	Rector	£2	£3.14.8
St Catherine or St Winewaloy	Rectory, or (Free) Chapel in All Saints of Berstreet parish[17]	Carrow Nunnery, near Norwich (B)		6s. 8d.	16s. 4d.
St John and the Holy Sepulchre	Rectory	Norwich Cathedral Py. (B)	P.Chapl.	£3.6.8	£1
St Bartholomew	"	Wymondham Py., Norfolk (B)[18]	P.Chapl.	£2.13.4	£2.13.7
St Peter Southgate	"	Abbey of St Benet of Hulme, Norfolk (B)	Rector & Stip.	£2	£2.17.3
St Etheldreda	"	Norwich Cathedral Py. (B)	P.Chapl.	£2	
St Edward } St Julian } St Clement of Conisford	United Rectory Rectory	United Rectory 1483- ? 1492 and 1522-	Carrow Nunnery, near Norwich (B); ? Wendling Abbey, Norfolk (P);[19] 1398- various citizens of Norwich, probably on behalf of the City Government;[20] 1414- City Government of Norwich; ? 1438- ? 1459 Wendling Abbey, Norfolk (P);[21] 1459- City Government of Norwich[22]	P.Chapl. & 2 Stip.	£2 £2 Patron: (when united) Carrow Nunnery and the City Government of Norwich	£3.10.6

[16] *Cal. Pat. R., 1381-1385*, p. 406 (where the college is incorrectly said to be in London).

[17] REG/5, Book 10, fol. 22v; REG/8, Book 13, fols. 29r and 93r; Campbell, *Norwich*, pp. 16 and 23-24; *Inventory*, ed. Watkin, 1: 20; see below, p. 186, where St Catherine's is not mentioned as a parish church.

[18] Blomefield, *Norfolk* (1805-1810), 4: 136.

[19] N.C.R., Case 17b, Liber Albus, fols. 9v-10r.

[20] Ibid., fols. 9v-10r.

[21] N.C.R., Case 16d, Proceedings of the Municipal Assembly, Book 1 (1434-1491), fols. 9r/12r, 30v/33v and 38v/41v.

[22] Ibid., fols. 30v/33v and 38v/41v.

Parish Church or Chapel	Status	Patron	Staff in 1492	Value in 1368	Value in 1535
*St Anne	Chapel (demolished some time after 1389)[23]				
St Peter Parmentergate	Rectory	Norwich Cathedral Py. (B)	P.Chapl. & Stip.	£2	£3.6.8
St Vedast	"	" " " "	P.Chapl.	£1.13.4	
St Cuthbert (Church demolished ca. 1530)[24]	United Rectory[25]	" " " "	P.Chapl.	£1.10.0	
St Mary the Less				£1.10.0	
St Michael of Berstreet / St Martin in the Bailey	United Rectory[26]	Horsham St Faith Py., Norfolk (B)	P.Chapl.	£3	

Castle Fee

*Chapel in the Castle	Free Chapel[27]	King			

Liberties of the Cathedral Priory

St Martin at the Palace Gates	Rectory	Norwich Cathedral Py. (B)	P.Chapl.	8s.	£1
St Matthew	Rectory (last rector died in 1377 or 1378, church later demolished)[28]	Archdeacon of Norwich Status: United Parish from 1349 or ca. 1377 onwards[29]			
St Paul	Rectory (also church of St Paul's Hospital)	Norwich Cathedral Py. (B)	P.Chapl. & Stip.	£1.13.4	£1.6.8

[23] William Hudson, *History of the Parish of St Peter Permountergate, Part 1* (Norwich, 1889), pp. 51-52; N.C.C., Reg. Harsyk, fol. 141v (Birkeley).

[24] Kent, "Church of St Cuthbert," p. 95.

[25] Ibid., pp. 94-95; *Charters*, ed. Dodwell, p. 132; *Inventory*, ed. Watkin, 1: 26; see below, p. 187.

[26] *Inventory*, ed. Watkin, 1: 22-23; see below, p. 188.

[27] *Inventory*, ed. Watkin, 1: 23; Campbell, *Norwich*, p. 24; Blomefield, *Norfolk* (1805-1810), 4: 122 and 125.

[28] Blomefield, *Norfolk* (1805-1810), 4: 375; N.C.C., Reg. Heydon, fol. 141v (Limpenhowe).

[29] *Inventory*, ed. Watkin, 1: 26-27; Blomefield, *Norfolk* (1805-1810), 4: 375; N.C.C., Reg. Heydon, fol. 141v (Limpenhowe).

Parish Church or Chapel	Status	Patron	Staff in 1492	Value in 1368	Value in 1535
St Helen	Rectory (also church of St Giles's Hospital)	Norwich Cathedral Py. (B)			
St Mary in the Marsh	Rectory	,, ,, ,, ,,	Rector[30]		£5.0.8
*St Ethelbert	Chapel[31]				

[30] See p. 18, n. 116.
[31] Blomefield, *Norfolk* (1805-1810), 4: 54; *Charters*, ed. Dodwell, p. 132.

Appendix 2

Bishop Goldwell's Visitation of Norwich in 1492

Transcript of Oxford, Bodleian Library,
MS Tanner 100, fols. 40r-42v.[1]

Visitacio ordinaria generalis reverendi in Christo patris et domini Jacobi, Dei et Apostolice Sedis gratia episcopi Norwicensis, in ecclesia parochiali Sancti Petri in Norwico pro civitate et decanatu Norwic' personaliter per eum exercita, sequitur sub hac verborum serie. In nomine Domini, Amen. Die lune, videlicet octavo die mensis Octobris anno Domini millesimo CCCC nonagesimo secundo, prefatus reverendus pater, ad dictam ecclesiam, visitaciones suas huiusmodi exercendi causa, ad portam occidentalem eiusdem ecclesie accedens, ibidem a singulis capellanis eiusdem ecclesie solenni cum processione receptus fuit. Et deinde, responsorio "Summe Trinitati" a cantore incepto, vexilloque sancte crucis in aiere erecto, campanis pulsantibus, organis eciam psallentibus, usque summum altare venit. Ubi, precibus in immortali Deo devote porrectis, aliisque ceremoniis in ea parte peractis, suaque episcopali benediccione astantibus solenniter impensa,[2] verboque Dei per Magistrum Henricum Falk, dicti reverendi patris commissarium generalem, publice proposito, ad statim comparuit personaliter quidam Magister Johannes Wyteratt, officialem se pretendens domini archidiaconi Norwici. Et quasdam litteras certificatorias sigillo officii sui sigillatas, una cum quadam scedula eisdem annexa, in qua singula nomina et cognomina citatorum sunt inserta, que apud registrum predicti reverendi patris remanent, realiter exhibuit. Quibus quidem litteris certificatoriis ad tunc et ibidem publice perlectis, et omnibus ac singulis citatis huiusmodi preconizatis, nomina tam comparencium quam non comparencium inferius sequuntur.

Ecclesia Sancti Augustini

Dominus Nicholaus Fale, rector, pre ordinario et examinatus.[3]

---

[1] The visitation covered all, and only, the parishes within the city.
[2] "vel" deleted in MS.
[3] See next footnote.

Ecclesia Sancti Martini in Coslany

Prior et conventus Norwic', proprietarii ibidem, comparuerunt per Magistrum
    Fuller, procuratorem.
Dominus Thomas Plowman, capellanus parochialis, pre ordinario et examinatus.
Dominus Edwardus Hoole, stipendarius, pre ordinario et examinatus.

Willelmus Brown
Robertus Fox   } Inquisitores recesserunt sub nova monicione.

Ecclesia Sancti Botulphi

Dominus Johannes Julyan, rector ibidem, comparuit pre ordinario et examina-
    tus.[4]

Ricardus Hervy   } Inquisitores nihil dicunt sed recesserunt sub nova
Robertus Swaffham   } monicione.

Ecclesia Sancte Marie de Coslany

Prior et conventus de Cokkesford, proprietarii ibidem, comparuerunt per
    Magistrum Fuller.
Dominus Robertus Malyn, capellanus parochialis, comparuit pre ordinario et
    examinatus.
Dominus Willelmus Knyght, stipendarius ibidem, comparuit pre ordinario et
    examinatus.

Johannes Brewyn   } Inquisitores ibidem comparuerunt et examinati dicunt
Robertus Derne   } quod Thomas Cak, nuper de parochia Sancti Martini ad
                    Portas Palacii, adheret suspiciose Marione Deynes, nuper
                    de parochia; Henricus Spark absentat se [ab] ecclesia
                    tempore divinorum; Robertus Brewyn, alias Pulham,
                    absentat se ab ecclesia tempore divinorum; Margareta,
                    uxor Roberti Brewyn, alias Pulham, notatur quod est
                    communis litigatrix cum vicinis suis; et eadem Margareta
                    servat continue publicam tabernam tempore divinorum.

[fol. 40v] *Ecclesia Sancti Michaelis in Coslany*

Magister Thomas Drantall, rector ibidem, comparuit pre ordinario.

Dominus Alanus Holcham		examinatus
Magister Johannes Dykeman	Stipendarii ibidem	examinatus
Dominus Ricardus Grene	comparuerunt pre ordinario	examinatus
Dominus Ricardus Ferror		non examinatus

Ricardus Lemman   } Inquisitores ibidem comparuerunt et habent prox' sub
Johannes Skott   } nova monicione.

----

[4] This seems the most likely expansion of "comparuit p[r]. o. et ex[t]," which is what
appears, in whole or in part, here and throughout the document; the "et ex[t]" was always
added later.

Ecclesia Sancti Georgii de Colgate

Prior et conventus Norwici, proprietarii ibidem, comparuerunt per Magistrum Willelmum Fuller.

Dominus Johannes Corpusty, capellanus parochialis ibidem, comparuit pre ordinario et examinatus.

Dominus Georgius Conyngham, stipendarius ibidem, comparuit pre ordinario et examinatus.

Johannes Smyth } Inquisitores ibidem comparuerunt et habent prox' sub
Willelmus Budde } nova monicione.

Ecclesia Sancti Clementis ad Pontem

Magister Thomas Bevyse, rector ibidem, comparuit pre ordinario et examinatus.

Prior de Mendham pro porcione in eadem non comparuit.

Prior de Stoke pro porcione ibidem non comparuit.

Robertus Gylmyn } Inquisitores ibidem comparuerunt et habent prox' sub
Robertus Pye } nova monicione.

Ecclesia Sancti Edmundi

Dominus Johannes Moor, rector ibidem, comparuit pre ordinario et examinatus.

Dominus Henricus Munford, stipendarius, comparuit pre ordinario et examinatus.

Robertus Sywhat comparuit et habet prox' sub nova monicione.

Ecclesia Sancti Jacobi

Dominus Thomas Cartun, capellanus parochialis, comparuit pre ordinario.

Johannes Myleham } Inquisitores comparuerunt. Examinati dicunt quod Ricar-
Nicholaus Burman } dus Senior iniuste detinet et non solvit decimas parsonales curato, et habent prox' sub nova monicione.

Ecclesia Sancti Salvatoris

Dominus Johannes Owdolff, capellanus parochialis, comparuit pre ordinario.

Willelmus Stevens, inquisitor, non comparuit.

Ecclesia Omnium Sanctorum in Fybryggate

Frater Ricardus Rene, capellanus parochialis ibidem, comparuit pre ordinario.

Edmundus Barnard } Inquisitores comparuerunt et habent prox' sub nova
Walterus Plomer } monicione.

Ecclesia Sancte Marie Combuste

Dominus Johannes Owdolff, rector ibidem, comparuit pre ordinario.

Johannes Andrews, inquisitor, non comparuit.

Ecclesia Sanctorum Simonis et Jude

Dominus Walterus Goos, rector ibidem, comparuit pre ordinario et examinatus.

Dominus Willelmus Burnham, capellanus parochialis ibidem, comparuit pre ordinario.

Dominus Thomas Kele, stipendarius ibidem, comparuit pre ordinario et examinatus.

Willelmus Patynmaker }
Galfridus Crome   } Inquisitores non comparuerunt.

[fol. 41r] *Ecclesia Sancti Georgii ad Portas Palacii*

Decanus et capitulum[5] Capelle Beate Marie de Campis in Norwico, proprietarii ibidem, non comparuerunt.

Dominus Galfridus Newman, capellanus parochialis ibidem, comparuit pre ordinario et examinatus.

Johannes Bowche   } Inquisitores[6] comparuerunt et habent prox' sub nova
Willelmus Samson   } monicione.

Ecclesia Sancti Petri de Hungate

Magister Robertus Thompson, rector ibidem, comparuit pre ordinario.
Frater Thomas Somerton, capellanus parochialis, non comparuit.

Ecclesia Sancti Michaelis ad Placita

Magister Edmundus Rightwis, rector ibidem.
Dominus Thomas Cornewayle } Stipendarii ibidem comparuerunt
Dominus Robertus Lenys   } pre ordinario.   et examinatus
Johannes Havyr   } Inquisitores[7] comparuerunt et habent prox' sub nova
Johannes Aylward   } monicione.

Ecclesia Sancti Andree

Decanus et capitulum[8] Capelle de Campis, proprietarii ibidem.
Dominus Jacobus Wardolk[9] | non examinatus
Dominus Willelmus Qwyntyn | Stipendarii comparuerunt   non examinatus
Dominus Robertus Est | pre ordinario   et examinatus
Robertus Crowche   } Inquisitores ibidem comparuerunt et habent prox' sub
Ricardus Pertryk   } nova monicione.

Ecclesia Sancte Crucis

Dominus Robertus Playford, capellanus parochialis, comparuit pre ordinario et examinatus.

---

[5] MS reads "capituli."
[6] "non" deleted in MS.
[7] "non" deleted in MS.
[8] MS reads "capituli."
[9] Possibly "Wardolf."

Willelmus Wulcy } Inquisitores non comparuerunt.
Willelmus Mador'

Ecclesia Sancti Johannis de Madermarkett

Magister Johannes Awdeley, rector ibidem, comparuit pre ordinario et examinatus.

Prior de Longa Villa pro porcione in eadem non comparuit.

Ricardus Coton } Inquisitores comparuerunt. Examinati dicunt quod Johannes
Johannes Basse Andrws absentat se ab ecclesia sua parochiali diebus festivis atque Dominicis, et idem Johannes notatur quod divertit se a societate uxoris sue, et non adheret sibi prout tenetur, sed dimittit uxorem suam in mancione sua ibidem, et ipse conduxit aliam domum in parochia Sancti Petri de Mancroft, et ibidem pernoctat pro maiore parte.

Ecclesia Sancti Gregorii

Magister Robertus Balle, capellanus parochialis, comparuit pre ordinario et examinatus.

Magister Thomas Halle		et examinatus
Dominus Thomas Gryme	Stipendarii ibidem	et examinatus
Dominus Willelmus Foster	comparuerunt pre ordinario.	
Dominus Thomas Toly		

Johannes Reed

. } Inquisitores non comparuerunt.
.
.

[fol. 41v] Ecclesia Sancti Laurencii

Magister Thomas Nevyle, rector ibidem, comparuit pre ordinario et examinatus.

Abbas Sancti Edmundi de Bury pro porcione in eadem non comparuit.

Dominus Johannes Haydon } Stipendarii ibidem et examinatus
Dominus Willelmus Murkyn comparuerunt pre ordinario.

Johannes Maydysse } Inquisitores comparuerunt et habent prox' sub nova moni-
Johannes Kyng cione.

Ecclesia Sancte Margarete de Westwyk

Dominus Johannes Barker, rector ibidem, comparuit pre ordinario.

Dominus Willelmus Canon } Stipendarii ibidem et examinatus
Dominus Alexander Johnson comparuerunt pre ordinario. et examinatus

Robertus Curle } Inquisitores ibidem comparuerunt et habent prox' sub
Robertus Lushere nova monicione.

Ecclesia Sancti Swythuni

Dominus Walterus Goos, rector ibidem, non[10] comparuit.

Dominus Willelmus Cabyll, stipendarius ibidem, comparuit pre ordinario et
    examinatus.

Dominus Willelmus Goor, capellanus parochialis ibidem, comparuit pre ordina-
    rio et examinatus.

Henricus Stawn   } Inquisitores comparuerunt et habent prox' sub nova moni-
Thomas Avelyn   } cione.

Ecclesia Sancti Benedicti

Prior et conventus de Bokenham, proprietarii ibidem, non comparuerunt.

Dominus Willelmus Norwich, capellanus parochialis, comparuit pre ordinario et
    examinatus.

Dominus Johannes Smyth, stipendarius ibidem, comparuit pre ordinario et
    examinatus.

Willelmus Fox   } Inquisitores comparuerunt et habent prox' sub nova moni-
Johannes Kyng   } cione.

Ecclesia Sancti Egidii

Dominus Ricardus Lyster, capellanus parochialis ibidem, comparuit pre ordinario
    et examinatus.

Dominus Johannes Luston, stipendarius ibidem, comparuit pre ordinario.

Thomas Glannvyle   } Inquisitores ibidem comparuerunt et habent
Johannes Carter, senior   } prox' sub nova monicione.

Ecclesia Sancti Petri de Mancroft

Abbas Gloucestr' pro porcione in eadem non comparuit.

Dominus Robertus Beverle, capellanus parochialis, comparuit pre ordinario et
    examinatus.

Dominus Willelmus Billern   } capellani cantar' com-
Dominus Robertus Cutteler   } paruerunt pre ordinario.   et examinatus
Magister Thomas Warne   ⎤
Dominus Davyd Cardyn | et examinatus
Dominus Johannes Palmer | et examinatus
Dominus Willelmus Purdy | Stipendarii ibidem   et examinatus
Dominus Philippus Johnson   } comparuerunt   et examinatus
Dominus Robertus Purdy | pre ordinario.
Dominus Johannes Deraunt | et examinatus
Dominus Johannes Hogon | et examinatus
Dominus Thomas Curson   ⎦

---

[10] "non" has been inserted above the line in MS.

Thomas Philipps
Johannes Sotheryngton
Henricus Jakson
Robertus Belle

Inquisitores comparuerunt. Examinati[11] dicunt quod Johanna   ,[12] manens in tenur' Alicie Balles, notatur quod est communis meretrix cum diversis personis; item quod Katarina Grey notatur quod tenet publicam tabernam tempore divinorum; item quod Willelmus Bloker absentat se ab ecclesia sua parochiali diebus Dominicis et festivis tempore divinorum; item quod Willelmus Qwiney absentat se ab ecclesia sua parochiali tempore divinorum; item quod Thomas Newhaw absentat se ab ecclesia sua parochiali tempore divinorum diebus Dominicis atque festivis; item quod Nicholaus Wattys notatur quod fovet lenocinium; item quod Anna Abbat notatur super crimine adulterii cum quodam Massenger; item quod Robertus Balles, cowper, notatur quod fovet lenocinium, et quod sustentat publicam tabernam tempore divinorum; item quod Helena, manens in tenur' prioris Norwic', notatur super crimine adulterii cum diversis.

[fol. 42r] *Ecclesia Sancti Stephani*

Magister Robertus Calton, vicarius ibidem, comparuit pre ordinario.

Infirmarius ecclesie Cathedralis Norwici pro pencione in eadem non comparuit.

Dominus Robertus Buschell
Dominus Nicholaus Bervyle
Dominus Willelmus Barowe
Dominus Thomas Gleymesford

Stipendarii ibidem comparuerunt pre ordinario.

Johannes Brown
Thomas Smert
Robertus Brown
Johannes Gyrdeler

Inquisitores comparuerunt. Examinati dicunt quod Johanna Qwyk est communis meretrix cum diversis hominibus; item quod Margareta Crow notatur quod est communis lenona, et sustentat domum lenocinii; item quod Adrianus Spectaclemaker notatur super crimine adulterii cum dicta Margareta Crow; item quod Johannes Herner absentat se ab ecclesia sua parochiali tempore divinorum diebus Dominicis et festivis.

Ecclesia Sancti Johannis de Berstrete

Dominus Willelmus Arnold, canonicus,[13] capellanus parochialis, comparuit pre ordinario.

---

[11] "et" follows "Examinati" in MS.
[12] Blank space follows "Johanna" in MS.
[13] Possibly "canonicus" is an adjective qualifying "capellanus parochialis," not a noun.

Dominus Stephanus Chaunbr
Dominus Laurencius Aleyn } Stipendarii ibidem comparuerunt pre ordinario.
Dominus Johannes Mareys

} Inquisitores non comparuerunt.

Ecclesia Omnium Sanctorum de Berstrete

Dominus Willelmus Swetman, rector ibidem comparuit pre ordinario.

Willelmus Norfolk } Inquisitores comparuerunt. Examinati dicunt quod uxor
Johannes Lovett Ricardi Palys servat malam normam cum diversis familiaribus proximorum, qui ibi sedent et bibunt tempore divinorum. Et habent prox' sub nova monicione.

Ecclesia Sancti Sepulcri

Dominus Ricardus Tompson, capellanus parochialis, comparuit pre ordinario.

Edwardus Norman } Inquisitores comparuerunt et habent prox' sub nova
Willelmus Milner monicione.

Ecclesia Sancti Bartholomei

Dominus Thomas Pekke, capellanus parochialis ibidem, comparuit pre ordinario.

Robertus Kempe } Inquisitores[14] comparuerunt et habent prox' sub nova
Johannes Melford monicione.

Ecclesia Sancti Petri de Southgate

Dominus Willelmus Swan, rector ibidem, comparuit pre ordinario.
Dominus Nicholaus Clerk, stipendarius ibidem, comparuit pre ordinario.
Abbas Sancti Benedicti de Hulmo pro pencione in eadem non comparuit.
Thomas Barton
Georgius Watton } Inquisitores non comparuerunt.

Ecclesia Sancte Etheldrede

Frater Willelmus Davy, capellanus parochialis ibidem, non comparuit.

Robertus Umfrey } Inquisitores[15] comparuerunt. Examinati dicunt quod Ha-
Robertus Osburn wisia Kyrkehows notatur quod fovet lenocinium in domo sua in tantum quod quedam mulier, vocata Elizabeth Lylburn, ibidem bina vice peperit, et proles erant mortui ante sepultur' quia non erant baptizati.

---

[14] "Comparuerunt et," before "Inquisitores," deleted in MS.
[15] "Inquisitores," before "Inquisitores," deleted in MS.

[fol. 42v] *Ecclesia Sanctorum Edwardi et Juliani*

Dominus Thomas Lyng, stipendarius ibidem, comparuit pre ordinario.

Dominus Thomas Antyngham, capellanus parochialis, comparuit pre ordinario.

Magister Thomas Bowde
Dominus Johannes Porter } Stipendarii ibidem non comparuerunt.

Thomas Smyt
Johannes Adred } Inquisitores ibidem comparuerunt. Examinati dicunt quod quidam Willelmus Drake notatur quod custodit quamdam mulierem ibidem[16] pregnatam, et nescitur per quem.

Ecclesia Sancti Clementis in Conesford

Johannes Spylman
Walterus Wellys } Inquisitores comparuerunt et habent prox' sub nova monicione.

Ecclesia Sancti Petri Permantergate

Dominus Willelmus Nele, capellanus parochialis, comparuit pre ordinario.

Dominus Edmundus Southwell, stipendarius ibidem, comparuit pre ordinario.

Johannes Knott
Willelmus Caster } Inquisitores comparuerunt. Examinati dicunt quod Johanna Clerk absentat se ab ecclesia sua parochiali diebus Dominicis et festivis tempore divinorum; item quod Matilda Godewyn notatur quod fovet lenocinium inter diversis; item quod eadem Matilda notatur super crimine adulterii cum Thoma Gyrdyng, alias Thoma Cook; item quod[17]   Vyncent et uxor sua absantant eos ab ecclesia sua parochiali tempore divinorum diebus Dominicis et festivis; item quod Frater Johannes Caster notatur super crimine incontinencie cum Isabella Chapman, junior.

Ecclesia Sancti Vedasti

Dompnus Johannes Castelacr', capellanus parochialis, non comparuit.

Stephanus Godewyn
David Johnson } Inquisitores comparuerunt et habent prox' sub nova monicione.

Ecclesia Sancti Cuthberti et Marie Parve

Dominus Galfridus Cottyng, capellanus parochialis, comparuit pre ordinario.

Johannes Hyrdeler
Johannes Baddyng } Inquisitores comparuerunt. Examinati dicunt quod Agnes Saunder fovet lenocinium inter presbiteros, mulieres, fratres, canonicos et ex omni genere; item quod Katarina May notatur super crimine adulterii cum quodam Tylere.

---

[16] "pregnantem" deleted in MS.
[17] Blank space follows "quod" in MS.

Ecclesia Sanctorum Michaelis et Martini

Prior et conventus[18] de Horsham Sancte Fidis, proprietarii ibidem, non comparuerunt.

Frater Thomas Balbroke, capellanus parochialis, comparuit pre ordinario.

} Inquisitores non comparuerunt.

Ecclesia Sancti Martini ad Portas Palacii

Dominus Thomas Daywell, capellanus parochialis, non comparuit.

Robertus Gyles } Inquisitores comparuerunt et habent prox' sub nova
      Aylward } monicione.

Ecclesia Sancti Pauli

Dominus Ricardus Castr', capellanus parochialis,[19] comparuit pre ordinario et examinatus.

Dominus Johannes Gyremonde, stipendarius, comparuit pre ordinario et examinatus.

Inquisit' non comparu't.

Ecclesia Sancte Helene

Robertus Dervy, inquisitor, non comparuit.

Ecclesia Sancte Marie in Marisco

Magister Johannes Styward comparuit per Magistrum Fuller.

Inquisit' non comparu't.

---

[18] "ibidem" deleted in MS.
[19] "non comparuit" deleted in MS.

Appendix 3

Testamentary Requests for Burial in Churches and Cemeteries of Religious Houses

Period	Laity					Clergy				
	1370-1439	1440-1489	1490-1517	1518-1532	Total	1370-1439	1440-1489	1490-1517	1518-1532	Total
Number of persons whose wills have been examined[1]	167	525	546	277	1515	96	104	62	27	289
Dominican Friary in Norwich[2]	2	16	22	5	45	1	2	–	–	3
Franciscan Friary in Norwich	5	19	14	1	39	1	1	–	–	2
Carmelite Friary in Norwich	3	9	5	3	20	1	1	–	–	2
Augustinian Friary in Norwich	4	12	9	3	28	1	–	2	1	4
Total in Norwich friaries as percentage of all testators	8%	11%	9%	4%	9%	4%	4%	3%	4%	4%
Cathedral Priory in Norwich	1	4	1	–	6	6	4	3	1	14
College of St Mary in the Fields in Norwich (St Giles's Hospital in Norwich)[3]	2	6	1	–	9	4	9	9	1	23
Carnary College in Norwich	–	1	–	–	1	–	–	–	2	2
Carrow Nunnery in the suburbs of Norwich	1	1	1	–	3	–	–	–	–	–
Houses of religious orders and colleges of secular priests outside Norwich	2	–	–	–	2	1	–	1	–	2
Total	20	68	53	12	153	15	17	15	5	52
Total as percentage of all testators	12%	13%	10%	4%	10%	16%	16%	24%	19%	18%

[1] I.e., all the inhabitants of the city whose wills survive – see Appendix 13, section A (pp. 224-225).

[2] The figures after the religious house indicate the numbers of persons who asked in their wills to be buried in its church or cemetery.

[3] St Giles's Hospital, which was also a college of secular priests, has been ignored because its church was also the parish church of St Helen's parish.

Appendix 4

Testamentary Bequests for People to Study

Period	Laity				Clergy			
	1370-1439	1440-1489	1490-1517	1518-1532	1370-1439	1440-1489	1490-1517	1518-1532
Number of persons whose wills have been examined[1]	167	525	546	277	96	104	62	27
Number of persons who left bequests in their wills for people to study	–	17	33	8	–	5	7	–

[1] I.e., all the inhabitants of the city whose wills survive – see Appendix 13, section A (pp. 224-225).

Appendix 5

Writers from Norwich

This appendix lists writers from Norwich who were included in Bale's *Catalogus*[1] and who flourished between the late fourteenth and the early sixteenth centuries.

Abbreviations:
fl. *floruit* † died

	Date[2]	Reference to *Catalogus*
Monks of the Benedictine Cathedral Priory		
Thomas Brinton (later bishop of Rochester)	† 1389[3]	2: 80
Adam Easton (later Cardinal)	*fl.* late 14th c.	1: 516-7
Casterton	*fl.* late 14th c.	1: 495
Richard Folsham	*fl.* early 15th c.	2: 59
John Stowe	*fl.* mid 15th c.	2: 61
Robert Veyse	?	2: 88
Friars of the Carmelite Friary		
William de Sancta Fide	† 1372	1: 478
Robert de Sancta Fide	*fl.* late 14th c.	2: 156
Thomas Colby	*fl.* 1400	1: 534-5
Walter Dysse	† 1405	1: 527-8
Adam Helmyngton	*fl.* early 15th c.	2: 62
Robert Rose	† 1420	1: 555
John Torpe/Thorpe	† 1440	1: 579
Henry Wichingham	† 1448	1: 585-6
John Kenynghale	† 1451	1: 592-3
Peter de Sancta Fide	† 1452	1: 593
Thomas Scrope *alias* Bradley (later an anchor[4] and bishop of Dromore)	† 1492	1: 629-30
Thomas Wichingham	?	2: 155

[1] John Bale, *Scriptorum illustrium maioris Brytannie catalogus* (Basle 1557).
[2] The dates are those given by Bale except where other references have been provided.
[3] Emden, *BRUO*, 1: 269 (Thomas de Brinton).
[4] See pp. 59 and 198.

	Date	Reference to *Catalogus*
Friars of the Franciscan Friary		
John Wichingham	*fl.* 1362	2: 53
? Simon de Tunstede	† 1369	1: 473-4
Reginald Langham	*fl.* 1410	1: 539-40
Robert Colman	*fl.* 1428	1: 563
Robert Finyngham	alive ca. 1440	1: 597
Friars of the Augustinian Friary		
Richard Chefer	*fl.* early 15th c.	1: 532
John Sloley	† 1477	1: 612-3
John Tonneys	*fl.* late 15th c. † 1514[5]	1: 630
John Langham	?	2: 87-8
Friars of the Dominican Friary		
John Somerton	*fl.* 1469[6]	2: 91
Others		
Richard Caistor (vicar of St Stephen's)	† 1420	1: 556
? John Seguarde (poet)	*fl.* early 15th c.	1: 553-4

[5] Emden, *BRUC*, p. 591 (John Toneys).
[6] Ibid., p. 541 (John Somerton).

Appendix 6

Books Mentioned in Wills and Inventories

Period	Laity					Clergy				
	1370-1439	1440-1489	1490-1517	1518-1532	1533-1549	1370-1439	1440-1489	1490-1517	1518-1532	1533-1549
Number of persons whose wills, and the inventories of whose goods, have been examined[1]	167	525	546	277	190	96	104	62	27	24
A. Number of persons in whose wills, or in the inventories of whose goods, one or more books were mentioned	9	29	17	5	5	30	40	22	8	4
B. Number of persons in whose wills, or in the inventories of whose goods, the following books were mentioned[2]										
1. *Liturgical Books*										
Antiphonary / Antiphonarium	1	2	3			3	3	3		
Breviary / Coucher / Breviarium / Portiforium / Portos	1	5	2			12	9	6	1	1
Dirige Book							2	1		
Glosa Sequenciarum						1				
Grail / Graduale		2	3			1	3	3		
De Invitator' de Venite						1				
Jurnall Book						1				
Kalendar		1								
Letania secundum Ordinale						1				

[1] For the periods between 1370 and 1532 all the surviving wills of the inhabitants of the city have been examined – see Appendix 13, section A (pp. 224-225). For the period 1533 to 1549 all the surviving wills of the inhabitants that were proved in the Norwich Consistory Court have been examined. For the only two inventories, see p. 35 and p. 111, n. 367.

[2] The titles of books mentioned in several wills have been standardised; the titles of books mentioned in only one will have been left as in the original. In some cases, chiefly with liturgical works, it it impossible to know whether the testator was bequeathing his own book or whether he wanted the book to be bought by his executors and given to the beneficiary. For documentary references to the books, see footnotes on pp. 36-41 and 111-112.

Period	Laity					Clergy				
	1370-1439	1440-1489	1490-1517	1518-1532	1533-1549	1370-1439	1440-1489	1490-1517	1518-1532	1533-1549
Manual / Manuale		2				4	1	1	1	
Martyrology / Martilogium						1		1		
Missal / Mass Book / Missale	3	4	4	1		10	8	1	3	
Qwayers with the New Service of the Visitation of Our Lady and of the Transfiguracion of Our Lord God and of the Blessed Name of Jhu'								1		
Ordinale		1								
Liber cum Placebo et Dirige et Devocionibus							1			
Prick-Song Book				1	1		1	1	1	
Primer / Primarium	1	12	1	1		1	6			
Processional / Processionarium	1	2	3	1		6	8	3	1	
Psalter / Psalterium	6	8	3	1	1	7	4	1	1	2
Pye							1			
Rationale Divinorum						1			1	
Salve Book								1		
Song Book							1			
Temporale							1			
Troperium						2				
Ympnarium						1				
2. *Legal Works*										
Abbas super Decretalibus								1		
iiii bokys of Abbott									1	
John Acton		1								
Casus Longi Bernardi									1	
Henricus Bohyc								1		
Clementines						1			1	
Decrees									2	
Decretals						1		1	2	
Hostienc'	1									
Institutes								1	1	
Lynwod									1	
Modus Legendi									1	
Repertorium utriusque (i.e., of Sext and of Clementines)						1				
Sext	1					1			2	
iiiª pars Speculi									1	
Vocabularius Iuris									1	
W. de Speculat'									1	
3. *Scriptural Works and Commentaries*										
Acton super Epistolas et Evangelia							1			

Period	Laity					Clergy				
	1370-1439	1440-1489	1490-1517	1518-1532	1533-1549	1370-1439	1440-1489	1490-1517	1518-1532	1533-1549
Bible / Biblia					1	1	1		2	1
Evangelia	1									
Glossa Communis super Psalterium						1	1			
Gorhain							1			
Gorhain super Psalterium							1			
The Story of Saynt Gregory in Explanacione Cantaci Canticorum								1		
Communis Glosa super Quinque Libros Sapienciales et Hugo de Vienna in margine							1			
Moralia Lire						1				
Newe Testament Glosed with Lyra the Doctor										1
Lira super Novum Testamentum							1			
Lira super Psalterium							1			
Magister Historiarum						1				
Philippus de Monte Calereo: Postilla super libros Genesis, Isaye, Danyell et Tren'							1			
Liber de Sacra Scriptura							1			
Liber vocatus a Vangeler							1			
4. *Other Religious Books*										
Albertus Magnus									1	
Books of Alexander of Halye										1
Summa Angelica								1		
Confessiones Sancti Augustini							1			
Diversi libri Augustini								1		
Sermones Prioris Bartholomei						1				
Liber de Meditacionibus Bernardi, Anselmi et ceterorum		1								
Sermones Boneaventure de Sanctis							1			
Liber Anglicanus Sancte Brigitte		1								
Dieta Salutis						1		1		
Le Doctrine of the Herte		1								
Boke of the Dowt' of the Legend both Temporall and Sanctorum							1			
Opuscula Sancti Eusebii							1			
Fasciculus Morum							1			
Fasciculus Temporum								1		
Quaternum de Fide Catholica							1			
Flores Doctorum								1		
Formula Noviciorum							1			

Period	Laity					Clergy				
	1370-1439	1440-1489	1490-1517	1518-1532	1533-1549	1370-1439	1440-1489	1490-1517	1518-1532	1533-1549
Sermones Magistri Fysher									1	
Dialog' Sancti Gregorii							1			
Hugo de Claustro Anime							1			
Liber vocatus Hylton		1								
Ye book of St Kateryn			1							
Legend / Legenda / Legendarium						1	5			
Legenda Aurea / Legenda Auri						2	2	1	1	
Legenda Sanctorum / Sanctorum						2	3	1		
Englysshe boke of Seynt Margaret' Lyfe			1							
Oculus Moralis						1				
Credo Pacisiens' [3]							1			
Liber vocatus Pars Oculi							1			
Liber Preceptor'									1	
Pupilla Oculi / Pupilla						2	1	2	1	
Liber vocatus Quat' Novissimarum								1		
Qui Bene Presunt							1			
Repyngton							2			
Tractatus qui dicitur Scintillarum							1			
Sermones Discipuli									1	
Sermones Dormii									1	
Sermones Parati									1	
Sermones Sanctorum						1				
Liber incipiens Suma Justicie Christi Fidelium						1				
Suma Predicancium						1				
Sermones Vincencii									1	
Vite Patrum							1			
Quaternum sermonum meorum (i.e., of John Wakeryng, bishop of Norwich 1415-1425)						1				
5. *Other (and Unidentifiable) Books*										
De Abstinencia						1				
A book of rethorike called Alanus de Planctu								1		
Beve de Hampton							1			
Liber Boicii						1				
Liber vocatus Catholicon							1			
Cato						1				

[3] *Sic* in ms, but see p. 40.

Period	Laity					Clergy				
	1370-1439	1440-1489	1490-1517	1518-1532	1533-1549	1370-1439	1440-1489	1490-1517	1518-1532	1533-1549
Colleccio Virtutum							1			
Cronica							1			
Distinctionarium								1		
Donatus						1				
Liber papireus factus de hospicio ducis Eboraci' cum ceteris contentis in eodem		1								
Libri mei prapticorum[4] ex labore meo (i.e., John Excestre[5]) facti et perquisiti							1			
Liber de Graciis								1		
Le grene book		1								
Hocclef		1								
Lac Parvulorum						1				
Ortus Vocabulorum									1	
Englysshe boke called Partonope			1							
Franciscus Petrartha de Remediis Utriusque Fortune							1			
Liber vocatus a Qualit'									1	
Quaternum papireum de Regibus Anglie versificatum		1								
Rosarium in papiro									1	
Tractatus Versificand'									1	
De Vicio Lingue								1		

[4] *Sic* in MS.
[5] See p. 50.

Appendix 7

Hermits, Anchorites and Communities Resembling Beguinages in Norwich, 1370-1549

A. HERMITS AND ANCHORITES[1]

1. *Attached to Religious Houses*

Carmelite Friary
 – anchor of or at   ca. 1425 or 1441 – 1522[2]
    – "Frater" Thomas Scrope, *alias*
       Bradley (priest)   ca. 1425 or 1441 – ca. 1446[3]
    – "Frater" John Castelacre (priest)   1460-1469[4]
    – "Frater" Thomas Barton   1479[5]
    – Benper   1491[6]
    – Buknham (priest)   1519[7]
 – "Domina" Emma, daughter of Sir
    Miles Stapleton, anchoress of   1421-1422[8]

Dominican Friary

 – anchoress at   1472 – ca. 1548[9]

---

[1] For the use of the words hermit, anchorite, anchor and anchoress, see p. 57, n. 1. Dates refer to the earliest and last known dates of the person's existence as an anchor or anchoress or hermit.

[2] Bale, *Scriptorum catalogus*, pp. 629-630; *Cal. Papal L., 1431-1447*, p. 241; N.C.C., Reg. Alblaster, fol. 132v (Reed).

[3] Bale, *Scriptorum catalogus*, pp. 629-630; *Cal. Papal L., 1431-1447*, p. 241; N.C.C., Reg. Doke, fol. 5r (Norwich), and Reg. Wylbey, fol. 79r (Ball). Scrope must have stopped leading the life of an anchor by 1450, in which year he was consecrated bishop of Dromore in Ireland and started to act as a suffragan bishop in the diocese of Norwich (*Handbook of Chronology*, ed. Powicke, p. 317), and it was probably before his consecration that he was sent as a papal legate to Rhodes (*D.N.B.*, 51: 148 [Thomas Scrope]).

[4] N.C.C., Reg. Jekkys, fols. 91v (Machon) and 206r (Molicourt).

[5] N.C.C., Reg. A. Caston, fol. 201v (Gladen).

[6] N.C.R., Case 8f, Account Rolls of the Guild of St George, 1491/2.

[7] N.C.C., Reg. Groundesburgh, fol. 24r (Foster).

[8] Bale, *Scriptorum catalogus*, p. 565; *Monumenta carmelitana*, ed. Zimmerman, p. 408; Oxford, Bodleian Library, MS Bodley 73, fol. 51v. The statements of Blomefield (*Norfolk* (1805-1810), 4: 21) and of Miss Clay (*Hermits*, pp. 77 and 235), that she died in 1442, appear to be the result of misreading MS Bodley 73, fol. 51v.

[9] N.C.C., Reg. Gelour, fol. 69v (Joye), and Reg. A. Caston, fol. 294v (Hemming); Clay, *Hermits*, p. 185.

– "Domina" Katherine Foster	1472-1486[10]
– Katherine Manne	1530 – ca. 1548[11]
– anchor of	1514[12]

Franciscan Friary

– anchor of or at	1511-1537[13]
– "Magister" Hugh Kestren	1520[14]

College of St Mary in the Fields

– "an ankyr whech was a monke of a fer cuntre & dwellyd in þe Chapel of þe Felde"	1415[15]
– Richard, hermit of Norwich, dwelling at	1455[16]

Carrow Nunnery (in the suburbs of Norwich)

– "Dominus" Roger, recluse at	1404[17]
– anchoress of or at	1427 – ca. 1546[18]
– "Domina" Julian Lampett	1428-1478[19]
– "Mistress" Kydman	ca. 1546[20]
– "each anchor or anchoress in"	1499[21]

2. Attached to Parishes or to Parish Churches

St Edward's

– anchorite of	1420-1493[22]
– Robert (priest)	1465-1478[23]

[10] N.C.C., Reg. Gelour, fol. 69v (Joye), and Reg. A. Caston, fols. 163v (Purdans) and 294v (Hemming).

[11] See p. 251; she was referred to as "late recluse in the house of the late Blak Freres" in 1548 (Clay, Hermits, pp. 184-185).

[12] N.C.C., Reg. Spurlinge, fol. 103v (Godfrey).

[13] A.N.C., Reg. Cook (1503-1538), fol. 37v (Chaunt); N.C.C., Reg. Underwoode, fol. 62v (Essod).

[14] Norwich Depositions, ed. Stone, no. 216.

[15] Margery Kempe, The Book, 1: 43, ed. Meech, p. 103. Meech and Allen assigned Margery's meeting with the anchor to 1415 (ibid., ed. Meech, p. xlix). Margery said that "be-for-tyme" he had much loved her (ibid., 1: 43, ed. Meech, p. 103), which may suggest that he had been in the area for some time. He may have been the same person as the anchor called Sir Thomas who, according to Taylor (who did not quote his source), was living in an anchorage near the Chapel in the Fields in Norwich in about 1410 (Richard C. Taylor, Index monasticus [London, 1821], p. 65).

[16] N.C.C., Reg. Brosyard, fol. 1r (Brosyard). He may have been the same person as Richard, hermit in the parish of St Giles (see p. 200), or as Richard Ferneys, hermit of Newbridge (see p. 202), who asked to be buried in the church of the College of St Mary in the Fields (see p. 233), or both.

[17] Ab. C., Reg. Arundel 1 (1396-1414), fol. 540v (Emund).

[18] N.C.C., Reg. Hyrnyng, fol. 151v (Riche), and Reg. Wymer, fol. 77r (Waterman).

[19] Register of Chichele, ed. Jacob, 2: 380; N.C.C., Reg. Gelour, fol. 195r (Hales).

[20] She was referred to in 1546 as "somtime ancras of Carowe" (N.C.C., Reg. Wymer, fol. 77r [Waterman]).

[21] PROB/11/13 (Reg. Blamyr, 1501-1503), fol. 12 (Lathe).

[22] N.C.C., Reg. Hyrnyng, fol. 95v (Blickling), and Reg. Aubry, fol. 132v (Gibson).

[23] N.C.C., Reg. Cobald, fols. 68r (Brown) and 90r (Nythe), and Reg. Gelour, fols. 195r (Hales) and 186v (Frances).

– anchoress of	1485-1531[24]
– anchor of	1537[25]

St Etheldreda's

– anchoress of	1472-1518[26]

St Giles's

– Richard, hermit in the parish of, recently dwelling at St. Giles Gate (in the city walls)	1429[27]

St Julian's

– anchoress of or at	1394 – ca. 1546[28]
– "Dame" Julian (author of *Revelations of Divine Love*)	1394 – 1416 or 1429[29]
– "Domina" Agnes or Anneys	1445 or 1449 – 1475[30]
– "Domina" Elizabeth Scott	1481-1511[31]
– "Domina" Agnes Edryge	1524[32]

[24] N.C.C., Reg. Multon, fol. 110v (Fack), and Reg. Haywarde, fol. 63v (Benham).

[25] N.C.C., Reg. Underwoode, fol. 62v (Essod).

[26] N.C.C., Reg. Gelour, fol. 4v (Norwich), and Reg. Gylys, fol. 164r (Worlich).

[27] See pp. 242 and 244. For other places to which he may have been attached as an anchor or hermit, see p. 199, n. 16.

[28] N.C.C., Reg. Harsyk, fol. 194v (Reed), and Reg. Wymer, fols. 64v (Swayn) and 76r (Waterman).

[29] Julian said that her mystical experiences occured in 1373 (Julian, *Revelations*, Long Text, chapter 2, ed. Colledge, p. 285), but there is no evidence that she was an anchoress at the time. The first known reference to her as an anchoress is contained in a will written in 1394 (N.C.C., Reg. Harsyk, fol. 194v [Reed]). The only conclusive evidence that her anchorage was attached to the parish church of St Julian in Norwich is contained in the will of Thomas Emund, who left a bequest in 1404 "Juliane anachorite apud ecclesiam St Juliane in Norwico" (Ab. C, Reg. Arundel 1 [1396-1414], fol. 540v [Emund]). Probably in 1413, Margery Kempe visited an anchoress in Norwich called "Dame Ielyan" (Margery Kempe, *The Book*, 1: 18, ed. Meech, pp. xlix and 42), and the author of the preface to the short text of the *Revelations* said that Julian was living as a recluse in Norwich in 1413 (Julian, *Revelations*, Short Text, chapter 1, ed. Colledge, p. 201). She was evidently still alive and still an anchoress in 1416 (*Register of Chichele*, ed. Jacob, 2: 95), and she was probably alive in 1429 since testamentary bequests to an unnamed anchoress of St Julian's church continued until that date (N.C.C., Reg. Surflete, fol. 86r [Baxter]). No references to an anchoress of St Julian's are known between 1430 and 1438 inclusive. Juliana, anchoress of Conisford (see p. 201), who was referred to in a will written in 1443 (N.C.C., Reg. Doke, fol. 233r [Blomvyle]), and who was probably the same person as the recluse of St Julian's church referred to in a will written in 1439 (N.C.C., Reg. Doke, fol. 99r [Holme]), was probably a different person since Julian, author of the *Revelations*, was born in 1342 or 1343 (Julian, *Revelations*, Long Text, 2 and 3, ed. Colledge, pp. 285 and 289) and so would have been about a hundred years old by 1443. Blomefield's statement that Julian, author of the *Revelations*, was alive in 1443 was almost certainly the result of misreading MCCCCXIII as MCCCCXLII and of identifying her with the above-mentioned Juliana, anchoress of Conisford (Blomefield, *Norfolk* [1805-1810], 4: 81; Julian, *Revelations*, Short Text, chapter 1, ed. Colledge, p. 201).

[30] N.C.C., Reg. Wylbey, fol. 26r (Tuke), Reg. Aleyn, fols. 24v (Cheese) and 130r (Blickling), and Reg. Gelour, fol. 183r (Spendlove).

[31] N.C.C., Reg. A. Caston, fol. 164v (Purdans); A.N.C., Reg. Cook (1503-1538), fol. 37v (Chaunt).

[32] N.C.C., Reg. Palgrave, fol. 216r (Catelyn).

— priest-anchor of	1472[33]	
St Peter's[34]		
— recluse in the parish of St Peter	1472[35]	same person ?
— anchorite of St Peter in Hungate	1493[36]	
St Stephen's		
— Thomas Basset, hermit of the parish of	ca. 1435[37]	

3. Others

Berstreet Gate	
— Thomas, hermit at	1446 or 1455 – 1459 or 1464[38]
Bishopsgate	
— hermit of	?1400/1-?1435/6[39]
Conisford[40]	
— anchoress of	1429-1511[41]
— "Dompna" Johanna	1429[42]
— Juliana	1443[43]
— two anchoresses in	1468-1511[44]
— anchor or hermit of	1455-1479[45]
— John, hermit of	1455[46]

[33] N.C.C., Reg. Gelour, fol. 69v (Joye).

[34] There were four parish churches in Norwich dedicated to St Peter, one of them being called St Peter Hungate.

[35] See p. 235.

[36] N.C.C., Reg. Aubrey, fol. 132v (Gibson).

[37] His undated will was proved in 1435 (N.C.C., Reg. Surflete, fol. 169r-v [Basset]).

[38] N.C.C., Reg. Wylbey, fol. 78v (Ball), and Reg. Brosyard, fols. 1r (Brosyard) and 156r (Allen); see p. 233.

[39] D. and C. Mun., Obedientiary Rolls, nos. 999, 1012 and 1014.

[40] Conisford Great Ward was divided into the small wards of South Conisford, North Conisford and Berstreet. Anchorites are known to have been attached to three of the parishes in Conisford Great Ward: St Julian's, St Edward's and St Etheldreda's, all three of which were in South Conisford Small Ward. At least some of the anchors and anchoresses of Conisford probably belonged to the anchorages in these three parishes, and were probably identical with some of the unnamed anchorites that have been listed under the three parishes.

[41] See p. 242; A.N.C., Reg. Cook (1503-1538), fol. 37v (Chaunt).

[42] See p. 242. Blomefield, *Norfolk* (1805-1810), 4: 70, said that she was anchoress of St Edward's parish church.

[43] N.C.C., Reg. Doke, fol. 233r (Blomvyle). She probably succeeded Julian, author of *Revelations of Divine Love*, as anchoress of St Julian's parish church (see p. 200, n. 29).

[44] N.C.C., Reg. Jekkys, fol. 115r (Fyce); A.N.C., Reg. Cook (1503-1538), fol. 37v (Chaunt).

[45] N.C.C., Reg. Brosyard, fol. 1r (Brosyard), and Reg. A. Caston, fol. 36v (Buckingham).

[46] N.C.C., Reg. Brosyard, fol. 1r (Brosyard).

Newbridge

– hermit of	1428-1464[47]
– Richard Ferneys	1429 – before 1465[48]
– John Martin	1429[49]
– John	1464[50] same person ?

St Stephen's (or Needham) Gate

– Robert Godard, hermit of	1483[51]

Attachments (if any) unknown

– John Felton, hermit	1457-1475[52]
– John Levot, hermit	?1503 – 1509 or 1510[53]
– Robert Farnell, hermit	1514[54]

4. *Hermits possibly, but not certainly, living in Norwich*

– Alice	late 14th or early 15th century[55]
– Peter	1479[56]
– Thomas	1509[57]
– "Master" William Clyffe (priest)	1516[58]

B. COMMUNITIES RESEMBLING BEGUINAGES

– Sisters, dedicated to chastity, living in a tenement of John Pellet (or Pyllet) in St Swithin's parish	1427 or 1430 – 1444[59]

[47] N.C.C., Reg. Surflete, fol. 26r (Sistede); see p. 233.

[48] N.C.C., Reg. Surflete, fol. 86v (Baxter); he described himself in the will which he made in 1464 as "heremita quondam de Newbrygg" (see p. 233). For other places to which he may have been attached as a hermit, see p. 199, n. 16.

[49] N.C.C., Reg. Surflete, fol. 86v (Baxter).

[50] See p. 233.

[51] N.C.R., Case 16d, Proceedings of the Municipal Assembly, Book 1 (1434-1491), fol. 122r.

[52] N.C.C., Reg. Brosyard, fol. 58v (Brasier), and Reg. Gelour, fol. 183r (Spendlove).

[53] N.C.C., Reg. Popy, fol. 548v (Swetman), and Reg. Spyltymber, fol. 224r (Levot).

[54] Hay, "Pilgrims," p. 142.

[55] There is a reference to "calix ex dono Alicie Hermyte" given to St Giles's parish church in Norwich some time after 1367 (*Inventory*, ed. Watkin, 1: 18). "Hermyte" is probably a description of her style of life, though it could be her surname. There is no clear evidence that she lived in Norwich. She may have once been a servant of Julian, author of the *Revelations*, while the latter was living as an anchoress at St Julian's parish church between 1394 and 1416 or 1429 (*Inventory*, ed. Watkin, 2: 161; Julian, *Revelations*, ed. Colledge, pp. 33-34).

[56] N.C.C., Reg. Aubry, fol. 21r (Everard).

[57] PROB/11/16 (Reg. Bennett, 1508-1511), fol. 28 (Haydon).

[58] William Clyffe, priest and hermit, witnessed a will written in Norwich in 1516 (see p. 231); and in a will made by a man from Norwich in the same year a bequest to "Maister Clyff, heremite," immediately followed a bequest to "every ankir and ankresse within Norwich" (N.C.C., Reg. Briggs, fol. 19v [Elsy]). He is not mentioned in Emden, *BRUO* and *BRUC*, and he cannot have been the Master William Clyffe who was instituted rector of North Lynn in 1505 since the latter had died by 1509 (REG/8, Book 13, second series of folios, fols. 55r and 91v).

[59] N.C.C., Reg. Hyrnyng, fol. 151v (Riche), Reg. Surflete, fol. 55r (Christian), and

- Three sisters (two after 1456), dedicated to chastity, living in a tenement
  in St Laurence's parish which had re-
  cently belonged to John Asger   1442-1472[60]
- (Sisters living under a religious vow
  in a house at the northwest corner of
  St Peter Hungate churchyard)[61]   ?

Reg. Wylbey, fol. 31r (Wetherby); PROB/11/3 (Reg. Luffenham, 1423-1449), fol. 15 (Copping).

[60] N.C.C., Reg. Doke, fol. 177v (Braklee), Reg. Aleyn, fols. 112v-113r (Estwegt), Reg. Brosyard, fol. 61r (Estwegt), and Reg. Gelour, fol. 69v (Joye).

[61] The statements of Blomefield, *Norfolk* (1805-1810), 4: 333-334, and of Taylor, *Index monasticus*, p. 65, who do not quote their sources, are the only evidence that these sisters existed.

Appendix 8

Craft Guilds and Pious Confraternities

This appendix tabulates our information about craft guilds and pious confraternities in late medieval Norwich.[1] The following legend explains the abbreviations.

A = made a return in 1389 to the Guild Ordinance of 1 November 1388, claiming in the return to do one or more of the following:

    1 = to have an annual "guild-day" or "day of the confraternity" on which religious services were held,

    2 = to maintain a votive light,

    3 = to provide religious services for a member when he or she died,

    4 = to provide alms for poor members.[2]

B = processed with a banner behind the Body of Christ, on the feast of Corpus Christi, to the College of St Mary in the Fields in Norwich probably ca. 1489, possibly ca. 1449.[3]

C = performed one of the following "pageantes" ca. 1530:

    1 = "Creacion of the World,"

    2 = "Helle Carte,"

    3 = "Paradyse,"

    4 = "Abell and Cayme,"

    5 = "Noyse Shipp,"

    6 = "Abraham and Isaak,"

    7 = "Moises and Aron with the Children of Israell and Pharo with his Knyghtes,"

    8 = "Conflicte of David and Golias,"

    9 = "The Birth of Crist with Sheperdes and iii Kynges of Colen,"

    10 = "The Baptysme of Criste,"

    11 = "The Resureccion,"

    12 = "The Holy Gost." [4]

D = had a guild-day (usually a Sunday) in 1543 assigned to it by the city government. The activities were, for the most part, to be held in the Common Hall (formerly the church of the Dominican Friary). The wardens of the craft were to offer lights to burn before the Sacrament in St John's Chapel there; a guild-Mass was to be said there and attended by the members of the craft (except that the pewterers, braziers, plumbers, bellfounders, glaziers, stainers and some other unnamed crafts, who all together comprised St

---

[1] For the use of the terms craft guild and pious confraternity, see p. 67, n. 70.

[2] The returns are printed in one or more of the following: *English Guilds*, ed. Smith, pp. 14-44; "Norfolk Guilds," ed. John L'Estrange and Walter Rye, *Norfolk Archaeology* 7 (1872) 105-121; "Hitherto Unpublished Certificates," ed. Tingey, pp. 288-305. A table correlating the returns is to be found on p. 287 of the last article. For the Guild Ordinance, see *Cal. Close R., 1385-1389*, p. 624.

[3] *Records of Norwich*, ed. Hudson, 2: 230. The date of the procession is discussed in *Non-Cycle Plays*, ed. Davis, p. xxx.

[4] *Non-Cycle Plays*, ed. Davis, pp. xxix-xxx.

Luke's guild, were to have their Mass in the Cathedral, the worsted-weavers' Mass was also to be in the Cathedral and the tanners were to have theirs in St Swithin's parish church); a feast was to be eaten there; and on the following or another day the members of the craft were to attend a Mass for the living and dead members of the craft in the same St John's Chapel.[5]

A. CRAFT GUILDS

Craft	A	B	C	D	Guild dedicated to[6]	Guild's religious activities performed in[7]
artificers and operators	A1,2,?4				St Michael	St Michael's Chapel (in the suburbs of Norwich)
bag-makers			C10			
bakers		B	C5			
barbers	A1,2	B	C10		God, St Mary and St John the Baptist	Carnary College
barkers		B			Our Lady (in 1504)[8]	
basket-makers				D		
bed-weavers		B				
bellfounders				D		
bowers		B		D		
braziers		B	C9	D		
brewers		B	C5			
broiderers			C6	D		
butchers		B	C11	D		
calenderers			C9	D		
candlemakers	A2				St Mary	Carmelite Friary
cappers			C10			
cardmakers			C10			
carpenters	A1,2,3,4	B	C2	D	Holy Trinity	Cathedral
carriers			C2	D		
claymen				D		
cobblers[9]				D		
collar-makers			C2	D		
cooks			C5			
coopers			C5			
cordwaners			C7	D		
coverlet-weavers /makers			C4	D		
curriers		B	C7	D		

[5] *Records of Norwich*, ed. Hudson, 2: liv, 296-299 and 310-311.
[6] Except where other references have been given, information about the dedications is derived from the returns made by the guilds in 1389 (see p. 204, n. 2).
[7] Except where other references have been given, information about the places in which the religious activities were performed is derived from the returns made by the guilds in 1389 (see p. 204, n. 2). For places of religious activities in 1543, see above, pp. 204-205, explanation of "D."
[8] N.C.C., Reg. Popy, fol. 188v (Stalon).
[9] A guild of cobblers existed in 1292/3 (*Leet Jurisdiction*, ed. Hudson, p. 42).

Craft	A	B	C	D	Guild dedicated to	Guild's religious activities performed in
dornick-weavers				D		
drapers		B	C1	D		
dyers		B	C9	D		
fishers/fresh-water-fishers		B		D		St Peter Southgate parish church (in 1479)[10]
fishmongers		B	C11	D		St Peter Mancroft parish church (in 1470)[11]
fletchers		B		D		
fullers[12]		B	C4	D		
girdlers			C10	D		
glaziers			C2	D		
glovers			C10	D		
gold-beaters			C9			
goldsmiths		B	C9	D		
gravers			C2	D		
grocers		B	C3			
haberdashers			C1			
hardwaremen			C10	D		
hatters			C10			
hosiers				D		
innkeepers			C5			
joiners				D		
keelmen				D		
lime-burners			C4	D		
linen-weavers				D		
masons		B	C4	D		
mercers		B	C1	D		? College of St Mary in the Fields (in 1526)[13]
millers			C5			
minstrels				D	Our Lady (in 1504)[14]	
parchmenters/parchment-makers			C2	D		
parish clerks				D		
patyn-makers		B				
peltiers	A1,2,3,4				Holy Trinity, St Mary, St William of Norwich and All Saints	Cathedral
pewterers		B	C9	D		
physicians			C10			
pinners			C10			
plumbers				D		

[10] N.C.C., Reg. Aubry, fol. 34v (Hood).
[11] N.C.C., Reg. Jekkys, fol. 174r (Petiston).
[12] A guild of fullers existed in 1292/3 (*Leet Jurisdiction*, ed. Hudson, p. 43).
[13] PROB/11/12 (Reg. Perche, 1525-1528), fol. 11 (Fuller).
[14] N.C.C., Reg. Spyltymber, fol. 58r (Barwyke).

Craft	A	B	C	D	Guild dedicated to	Guild's religious activities performed in
point-makers			C10			
pursers			C10			
raffmen		B	C3			
reders		B	C6	D		
redesellers				D		
saddlers[15]	} A1,2,3 {		C9	D	St Mary and All Saints	Carrow Nunnery (in the suburbs of Norwich)
spuriers						
sawers				D		
scriveners			C2	D		
sextons				D		
shearmen		B	C4	D		
shoemakers		B			St Augustine[16]	Augustinian Friary (in 1492)[17]
sieve-makers				D		
skeppers			C10			
skinners		B	C10	D		
smiths		B	C8	D		
(spurriers: see above, after saddlers)						
stainers			C2	D		
surgeons			C10			
tailors	A1,2,3,4	B	C6	D	Ascension of Christ and the Blessed Virgin Mary	College of St Mary in the Fields
tanners[18]			C7	D	Our Lady (in 1522)[19]	St Swithin's parish church (in 1522)[20]
thatchers				D		
thickwoollen-weavers			C4			
tilers			C6	D		
turners				D		
vintners			C5			
waits				D		
watermen			C11			
wax-chandlers		B	C10			
wheelwrights			C2	D		
wire-drawers			C10			
wool-chapmen				D		
woollen-weavers		B		D		
worsted-weavers		B	C12	D	Holy Ghost (in 1505)[21]	

---

[15] A guild of saddlers existed in 1292/3 (*Leet Jurisdiction*, ed. Hudson, p. 43).

[16] N.C.C., Reg. Wolman, fol. 195v (Southwell).

[17] Ibid.

[18] A guild of tanners existed between 1287/8 and 1290/1 (*Leet Jurisdiction*, ed. Hudson, pp. 13 and 39).

[19] N.C.C., Reg. Alblaster, fol. 164r (Fuller).

[20] Ibid.

[21] N.C.C., Reg. Ryxe, fol. 271v (Richeman).

B. Pious Confraternities and Dates of Their Known Existence Down to 1532

1. *Attached to the Cathedral or to Religious Houses*

Name	Attached to:	A	Dates
Holy Trinity	Cathedral	A1,2,3,4	1364-1389 and 1516-1527[22]
Holy Trinity and St Mary	"	A1,2,3,4	1366-1389[23]
St George's	"	A1,2,3,4	1385 – after 1532[24]
Of the Mass of Jesus	"		?1466 or 1468 – ?1525[25]
St Christopher's	Augustinian Friary	A1,2,3,4	1384-1389[26]
Holy Cross	" "		1492-1506[27]
St Margaret's	" "		?1509-1530[28]
St Barbara's	Carmelite Friary		1502-1522[29]
St Gation's	" "		1530[30]
Our Lady's	Dominican Friary	A1,2	1360-1389[31]
Holy Roode	" "		1527[32]
St Barbara's	Franciscan Friary		1497-1521[33]
Our Lady's	" "		ca. 1498[34]
St John the Evangelist's	" "		1503-1522[35]
Corpus Christi / The Priests'	College of St Mary in the Fields	A1,2,3,?4	1278 – after 1532[36]
Annunciation of St Mary, called the Great Guild	College of St Mary in the Fields	A1,2,3,4	said in 1389 to have been founded in time out of mind – 1402[37]
The Bachelery	College of St Mary in the Fields		1414-1443[38]
Of Carrow } same?	{ Carrow Nunnery		1429/30[39]
St James's }	{ (in the suburbs of Norwich)		1493[40]

---

[22] *English Guilds*, ed. Smith, pp. 25-26; N.C.C., Reg. Briggs, fols. 19v-20r (Elsy); D. and C., Reg. 1461-1559, fol. 55v (Markes).

[23] "Hitherto Unpublished Certificates," ed. Tingey, pp. 302-304.

[24] *English Guilds*, ed. Smith, pp. 17-18; *Records of St George*, ed. Grace, p. 134.

[25] D. and C. Mun., Obedientiary Rolls, no. 299; N.C.C., Reg. Jekkys, fol. 115r (Fyce), and Reg. Haywarde, fols. 156v-157r (Wether).

[26] *English Guilds*, ed. Smith, pp. 22-24.

[27] N.C.C., Reg. Wolman, fol. 195v (Southwell); PROB/11/15 (Reg. Adean, 1506-1508), fol. 7 (Hayward).

[28] A.N.C., Reg. Cook (1503-1538), fols. 34r (Payne) and 64r (Thirkill).

[29] N.C.C., Reg. Popy, fol. 247r (Radcliffe *alias* Curteys), and Reg. Alblaster, fol. 179r (King).

[30] A.N.C., Reg. Cook (1503-1538), fol. 64r (Thirkill).

[31] *English Guilds*, ed. Smith, p. 14.

[32] N.C.C., Reg. Palgrave, fol. 17v (Boleyn).

[33] N.C.C., Reg. Multon, fol. 55r (Peterson), and Reg. Alblaster, fol. 150v (Marchant).

[34] N.C.C., Reg. Multon, fol. 91v (Barnard).

[35] N.C.C., Reg. Popy, fol. 508v (Styward), and Reg. Alblaster, fol. 148v (Boys).

[36] "Hitherto Unpublished Certificates," ed. Tingey, pp. 300-302; N.C.C., Reg. Wymer, fol. 6r (Pennyman).

[37] "Hitherto Unpublished Certificates," ed. Tingey, pp. 288-300; N.C.C., Reg. Harsyk, fol. 294r (Shouldham).

[38] *Records of Norwich*, ed. Hudson, 1: 72 and 341-342.

[39] N.C.R., Case 8e, Account Rolls of the Guild of St George, 1429/30.

[40] N.C.C., Reg. Norman, fol. 34v (Cock).

2. *Attached to Parishes*

Name	Parish to which it was Attached	A	Dates
Our Lady's	? Holy Cross		1528[41]
Our Lady's	St Andrew's		1514-1527[42]
Of the Poor Men of St Augustine's Parish	St Augustine's	A1,2,3,4	1380-1389[43]
St Bartholomew's } same? {	St Bartholomew's	A1,2,3	1365-1389[44]
Of the Parish Church of St Bartholomew's	" "		1384[45]
St Botulph's	St Botulph's	A1,2,3,4	1384-1389[46]
Our Lady's	St Giles's		1463-1466[47]
St James's	St James's	A,?1,3,4	1389, 1528[48]
Of the Parish Church of the Holy Sepulchre	St John and the Holy Sepulchre		1384[49]
Our Lady's	St John of Timberhill		1442-1482[50]
St Margaret's	St Margaret at Fye Bridge		1521[51]
St Anne's	St Martin at the Palace Gates		1505-?1506[52]
St Anne's	St Martin in the Bailey		1373[53]
St Thomas the Martyr's	St Martin of Coslany		1522[54]
Of the Parish of St Mary in the Marsh	St Mary in the Marsh		1508[55]
Of the Parish of St Mary of Coslany	St Mary of Coslany		1436/37[56]
Of the Parish of St Mary the Less	St Mary the Less		1442[57]
St Austin's	? St Michael of Berstreet		1501[58]
Of the Mass (of the Name) of Jesus	St Peter Mancroft		1458 – after 1532[59]

[41] N.C.C., Reg. Palgrave, fol. 34r (Browse).
[42] N.C.C., Reg. Coppinger, fol. 112v (Todde), and Reg. Haywarde, fol. 0r (Holley).
[43] *English Guilds*, ed. Smith, pp. 40-41.
[44] "Hitherto Unpublished Certificates," ed. Tingey, pp. 304-305.
[45] N.C.C., Reg. Harsyk, fol. 115r (Buckingham).
[46] *English Guilds*, ed. Smith, pp. 15-16.
[47] N.C.C., Reg. Brosyard, fol. 315r (Multon), and Reg. Cobald, fol. 89r (Cannwold).
[48] "Norfolk Guilds," ed. L'Estrange, pp. 111-112; N.C.C., Reg. Haywarde, fol. 116v (Westgate).
[49] N.C.C., Reg. Harsyk, fol. 115r (Buckingham).
[50] N.C.C., Reg. Doke, fol. 206v (Mowt), and Reg. A. Caston, fol. 123v (Rusburgh).
[51] N.C.C., Reg. Alblaster, fol. 116v (Webster). By this date the (former) parish of St Margaret at Fye Bridge probably formed part of All Saints at Fye Bridge parish (see p. 174).
[52] N.C.C., Reg. Ryxe, fols. 194r (Daywell) and 449r (Blomfield).
[53] N.C.C., Reg. Heydon, fol. 24v (Ladde).
[54] N.C.C., Reg. Alblaster, fol. 216v (Richeman).
[55] N.C.C., Reg. Spyltymber, fol. 66r (Weston).
[56] N.C.R., Case 8e, Account Rolls of the Guild of St George, 1436/7.
[57] N.C.C., Reg. Doke, fol. 206v (Mowt).
[58] N.C.C., Reg. Popy, fol. 365v (Taylor).
[59] N.C.C., Reg. Brosyard, fol. 192r (At Fen), and Reg. Underwoode, fol. 56r (At Mere).

Name	Parish to which it was Attached	A	Dates
St Peter's	St Peter Mancroft		1474[60]
St Anne's	" " "		1479-1529[61]
Of the Parish of St Peter Southgate	St Peter Southgate		1506[62]
St Catherine's	Sts Simon and Jude	A1,2,3,4	1307-1389[63]
Our Lady's	St Stephen's		1440 – after 1532[64]
Our Lady's	St Swithin's		1505 – after 1532[65]

3. *Others*

Name	Dates
St Augustine's (possibly the same as the confraternity of the Poor Men of St Augustine's parish, or as St Austin's confraternity attached to the parish of St Michael of Berstreet)	1525[66]
St Eligius's / St Leoy's	1470-1528[67]
St Luke's (in ca. 1543 was a guild composed of pewterers, braziers, plumbers, bellfounders, glaziers, stainers and "other occupations")[69]	1429 – after 1532[68]
St Olave's	1490-1516[70]
St William's (possibly attached to the Dominican Friary in 1521)[72]	ca. 1397-1436, 1521[71]

[60] PROB/11/6 (Reg. Wattys, 1471-1480), fol. 19 (Shareman).
[61] N.C.C., Reg. Aubry, fol. 32r (Kempe), and Reg. Haywarde, fol. 149r (Petifer).
[62] N.C.C., Reg. Ryxe, fol. 444v (Swanton).
[63] *English Guilds*, ed. Smith, pp. 19-20.
[64] N.C.C., Reg. Doke, fol. 153v (Burgony), and Reg. Underwoode, fol. 19r (Loveday).
[65] N.C.C., Reg. Ryxe, fol. 262r (Whitlake), and Reg. Mingaye, fol. 79r (Walter).
[66] N.C.C., Reg. Groundesburgh, fol. 111r (Baddyng).
[67] N.C.C., Reg. Gilberd, fol. 36v (Swan), and Reg. Godsalve, fol. 47r (Larke).
[68] N.C.R., Case 8e, Account Rolls of the Guild of St George, 1429/30; D. and C. Mun., Obedientiary Rolls, no. 334.
[69] *Records of Norwich*, ed. Hudson, 2: 311.
[70] N.C.C., Reg. Wolman, fol. 151r (Radbode *alias* Bewflowr), and Reg. Briggs, fol. 20r (Elsy).
[71] N.C.R., Case 17b, Domesday Book, fols. 36r and 43v; N.C.C., Reg. Surflete, fol. 200v (Baningham), and Reg. Alblaster, fol. 116v (Webster).
[72] N.C.C., Reg. Alblaster, fol. 116v (Webster).

Appendix 9

Christian Names of Testators from Norwich, 1370-1532

MEN:[1]

John, 439; William, 218; Thomas, 190; Robert, 168; Richard, 74; Henry, 43; Nicholas, 39; Edmund, 38; Geoffrey, 18; Peter, 17; Roger, 16; Walter, 13; Adam, 12; Simon, 11; Ralph, 10; Edward, 9; Andrew, Hugh, Reginald/Reynold, 8; Alexander, James, Stephen, 7; Christopher, 6; Clement, Gerard, 4; Alan, Christian, George, Gregory, Philip, 3; Austin, Bartholomew, Charles, David, Semeine, 2; Adrian, Ambrose, Brian, Ellis, Florence, Goodwyn, Laurence, Leonard, Martin, Michael, Moresse, Newell, Samson, 1.

WOMEN:

Margaret, 71; Alice, 50; Agnes, 49; Johanna/Joan, 48; Elizabeth/Isabel, 34; Catherine, 28; Cecilia/Cecily, 19; Margery, 14; Matilda/Maud, 11; Sybil, 7; Helen, 6; Anna/Anne, Beatrice, Emma, Marion, 5; Petronilla/Parnel, 4; Rose, 3; Amy, Annabell, Annora, Avice, Colette, Etheldreda/Audrey, 2; Anastas, Christine, Clare, Dionise, Eleanor, Emily, Evelyn, Frances, Hawicia, Helwys, Hevyn, Jowet, Juliana, Mabel, Millicent, Olyve, 1.

[1] The figures refer to the number of testators bearing a particular name. The total number of testators is 1,412 men and 392 women (total 1,804, see p. 224). Spelling has been modernised except with names borne by only one testator.

Appendix 10

Foundations of Perpetual Chantries

The following is a list of the foundations of perpetual chantries requiring more or less daily services of a priest, which were made or attempted in Norwich or by the inhabitants of the city outside it, between 1370 and 1547.

1373:   licence to found a chantry for the soul of Thomas Percy, bishop of Norwich 1356-1369, obtained by three executors of his will; a monk of the Cathedral Priory daily to celebrate divine service for his soul; the chantry was not mentioned in his will, and it is unclear whether it was ever established.[1]

ca. 1375:   founded by Dionisia, widow of Sir Peter de Tye, and her son, Robert; the Cathedral Priory to find two "capellani scolares"[2] to "celebrare" for the souls of John de Hoo and Dionysia,[3] his wife, their son and all the faithful departed; still being performed, probably by only one priest, in 1535/6.[4]

1376:   founded by the peltiers' guild; the guild claiming in 1389 that one of the purposes of the guild's foundation in 1376 was "ad ... sustentacionis duorum capellanorum Deo ibidem (i.e., in the Cathedral) serviencium relevamen."[5]

ca. 1387:   founded by St George's confraternity; a chaplain to "divina celebrare" daily in the Cathedral; from 1417 onwards the chaplain was to do the same for the good estate of King Henry v and of the brothers and sisters of the confraternity, while they were alive, and for their souls when they were dead, and for the souls of the king's ancestors and of all the faithful departed; still being performed in 1547.[6]

---

[1] *Cal. Pat. R., 1370-1374*, pp. 373-374; Ab.C, Reg. Whittlesey (1368-1374), fols. 105v-106r (Percy).

[2] *Sic* in MS, possibly a scribal error for "seculares."

[3] Probably the same woman, John de Hoo probably being a previous husband.

[4] N.C.C., Reg. Heydon, fol. 94r-v (Tye); D. and C. Mun., Obedientiary Rolls, no. 1134.

[5] *English Guilds*, ed. Smith, pp. 1 and 29.

[6] *Records of St George*, ed. Grace, pp. 28-29, 142 and 156-157.

1388: a secular priest to become a member of the College of St Mary in the Fields and to "divina celebrare" daily for the souls of William Appleyard, later mayor of Norwich, and Bartholomew, his deceased father,[7] their ancestors and descendants and all the faithful departed;[8] still being performed in 1492.[9]

1389 or earlier: founded by the confraternity of the Annunciation of St Mary; two chaplains, elected by the brothers of the confraternity, to attend daily the Divine Office in the College of St Mary in the Fields and to "divina celebrare" and pray for the good estate of the king and the duke of Lancaster, for the souls of their ancestors, for the living and dead brothers and sisters of the confraternity, and for the souls of all the faithful departed; a similar chantry service to be performed by a Carmelite priest in the Carmelite Friary.[10]

1391: Ralph Churchman, cleric and citizen of Norwich, provided in his will for a chaplain to "divina celebrare" for ever, in the church of the College of St Mary in the Fields, for his soul and the souls of Alice Renter and of the people to whom he was bound;[11] unclear whether the chantry was established.

1406: founded by John Alderford, who was a prominent citizen of Norwich,[12] and his wife; further endowed in 1422 by the same John Alderford and by Simon Felbridge, knight, Roger Prat, formerly master of St Giles's Hospital, and Walter Daniel, mayor; a secular priest was to become a member of the College of St Mary in the Fields and to say Mass and "alia divina officia" withing the college for ever for the souls of Robert Kenton and William Rees and their wives and parents, and for the good estate of John Alderford and his wife, Roger Prat, Walter Daniel, Simon Felbridge and William Paston, and for their souls when they died; he was also to perform various annual obit services for the Kentons and Reeses;[13] still being performed – as William Rees's chantry – in 1492.[14]

1410: licence obtained to found a chantry for John Derlyngton, formerly master of St Giles's Hospital[15] and archdeacon of Norwich; a chaplain was to celebrate divine service in the hospital for his soul and the souls of his parents, brothers and sisters;[16] unclear whether the chantry was established.

---

[7] N.C.C., Reg. Harsyk, fol. 67r (Appleyard).
[8] N.C.R., Case 3i, Private Deeds, Box 7, "Chapel Field College."
[9] *Visitations*, ed. Jessopp, p. 12.
[10] "Hitherto Unpublished Certificates," ed. Tingey, pp. 293-295.
[11] N.C.C., Reg. Harsyk, fol. 158r (Churchman).
[12] Blomefield, *Norfolk* (1805-1810), 3: 126, 136, 163 and 165, and 4: 454.
[13] N.C.R., Case 3i, Private Deeds, Box 7 "Chapel Field College."
[14] *Visitations*, ed. Jessopp, p. 12.
[15] Emden, *BRUC*, p. 185 (John Derlyngton).
[16] *Cal. Pat. R., 1408-1413*, p. 187.

1412:   Alexander Tottington, bishop of Norwich 1406-1413, provided in his
            will for each professed monk of the Cathedral Priory to take it in turn,
            a week at a time, to "celebrare" daily in the Cathedral at six o'clock in
            the morning in the chapel of St Mary the Virgin, in which he wanted
            to be buried, for his soul and the souls of his father and mother, his
            "parochiani," Henry Dispenser (his predecessor as bishop) and all the
            faithful departed; after Mass the priest was to say at the bishop's tomb
            the "De Profundis" and the prayers "Deus qui inter apostolicos
            sacerdotes famulos tuos H'bertum et Alexandrum etc." and "Inclina
            etc. pro fidelibus defunctis"; once a week he was to say a Requiem
            Mass for the above-mentioned souls;[17] unclear whether the chantry
            was established.

1412:   founded by William Setman, mercer and later mayor; a secular priest,
            without the cure of souls, was to become a member of the College of
            St Mary in the Fields and to say the Divine Office in the college, and
            Mass in the college and in St Peter Mancroft parish church on
            alternate weeks, for the good estate of him and his wife, and for their
            souls when they died; still being performed in 1492.[18]

1418:   John Daniel and his brother, Walter, merchants and former mayors,
            provided in their joint will for a priest to "celebrare" for ever in St
            Stephen's parish church, in which they wished to be buried,[19] for their
            souls and the souls of their wives, various relatives, the people to
            whom they were bound and all the faithful departed; for the first forty
            years a light was to burn during each Mass at the elevation of the
            Host; the first chantry priest was to say the "De Profundis" for the
            above-mentioned souls at John Daniel's tomb after each Mass;[20]
            unclear whether the chantry was established.

1421:   licence to found a chantry obtained at the request of Sir John
            Wodehous, one of the chamberlains of the Exchequer; a chaplain,
            without any other benefice or stipend, was to say daily in the chapel of
            the Carnary College, Matins, Mass, the other Hours and the seven
            Penitential Psalms with a litany, all before nine o'clock in the morning,
            and after nine o'clock in the morning Vespers and Matins of the Dead
            and Lauds and Commendation, for the good estate of King Henry v,
            Queen Catherine and Sir John Wodehous, and for their souls after
            their deaths, and for the souls of their ancestors; every Friday the
            priest was to distribute a penny to each of five poor persons in honour
            of the five wounds of Our Lord Jesus Christ, and every other day he

---

[17] Ab. C., Reg. Arundel 2 (1396-1414), fols. 165v-166r (Totington).
[18] *Cal. Pat. R., 1408-1413*, p. 268; N.C.R., Case 3i, Private Deeds, Box 7, "Chapel
Field College"; *Visitations*, ed. Jessopp, p. 12; see below p. 243.
[19] N.C.C., Reg. Hyrnyng, fols. 32r (Daniel) and 148v (Daniel).
[20] Ibid., fol. 32v (Daniel).

was to distribute a penny to each of three poor persons in honour of the Holy and Undivided Trinity, and these poor people were to attend the priest's Mass and to say fifteen "orisons" and fifteen "salutations"[21] for the above-mentioned persons and souls; on the feast of St Blaise the priest, together with the principal and fellows of the Carnary College, were to say Vespers and Matins of the Dead and Lauds, and a Requiem Mass the following morning, for Henry v's grandfather, John duke of Lancaster; the same services were to be performed for Henry iv over the feast of St Cuthbert, for the parents and benefactors of Sir John Wodehous over the first Sunday of Lent, and for the souls of Henry v, Queen Catherine and Sir John Wodehous over the anniversaries of their deaths;[22] unclear whether the chantry was established.

1425:   founded by John Wakeryng, bishop of Norwich 1415-1425; a monk or a secular priest was to "celebrare" for his soul for ever in the Cathedral;[23] still being performed in 1496/7[24] and – probably as a united chantry with Sir Thomas Erpingham's (see next chantry) – in 1535/6.[25]

before 1429:   founded by Sir Thomas Erpingham; a monk was to sing Mass daily for him and his family for ever at Holy Cross altar in the Cathedral and to keep his anniversary;[26] still being performed in 1496/7[27] and – probably as a united chantry with Bishop Wakeryng's (see previous chantry) – in 1535/6.[28]

1444:   Justice William Paston, according to his wife Agnes, provided for there to be paid "dayly for ever to the monke that for that day singeth the Mass of the Holy Goste in Our Lady chapell in Norwiche (Cathedral), where he purposed to leye his body, every day iiii d. to sing and pray for his sowle and myn (Agnes's) and all the sowles that he and I have hade any goode of or be beholdyn to pray for";[29] the Mass was said for their souls daily only for a short time.[30]

1445:   Thomas Brown, bishop of Norwich 1436-1445, provided in his will for a monk to say Mass daily for ever, for his and his parents' souls, at seven o'clock in the morning in front of his tomb in the Cathedral; the

---

[21] Presumably "Our Fathers" and "Hail Marys."
[22] *Cal. Pat. R., 1416-1422*, pp. 376-377.
[23] *Register of Chichele*, ed. Jacob, 2: 312.
[24] D. and C. Mun., Obedientiary Rolls, no. 1105a.
[25] Ibid., no. 1134.
[26] Blomefield, *Norfolk* (1805-1810), 4: 39.
[27] D. and C. Mun., Obedientiary Rolls, no. 1105a.
[28] Ibid., no. 1134.
[29] *Paston Letters*, ed. Davis, 1: liii and 44-45.
[30] Ibid., 1: 46, and 2: 609-611.

monk was also to say an annual Requiem Mass for his soul on the day of his death;[31] unclear whether the chantry was established.

1446:   Sir Thomas Kerdeston of Claxton[32] provided in his will for three friars of the Augustinian Friary to "celebrare" for ever for his, his two wives' and his ancestors' souls;[33] unclear whether the chantries were established.

by 1458: founded by the confraternity of the Mass (of the Name) of Jesus attached to St Peter Mancroft parish church: a chantry service of the Mass (of the Name) of Jesus; still being performed in the 1540s; unclear whether the Mass was said daily.[34]

1460:   founded by John Wygenhale, archdeacon of Sudbury and formerly dean of the College of St Mary in the Fields; a secular priest, without the cure of souls, was to become a member of the college and to say Mass and the Divine Office for his good estate, and for his soul when he died, and for the souls of his parents, all his friends and benefactors and all the faithful departed; still being performed in 1492.[35]

by 1466 or 1468:   founded by the confraternity of the Mass of Jesus in the Cathedral; a chantry service of the Mass of Jesus; doubtful whether the Mass was ever said daily, and by 1525 was being said only once a week.[36]

1471:   Walter Lyhert, bishop of Norwich 1446-1472, provided in his will for a secular or regular priest, learned in Scripture, to celebrate daily service in the Cathedral for ever, at the altar to the north of his tomb, for his soul and the souls of his parents, a relative called John Lyhert, a servant of his called Richard Hedge and his predecessors as bishops of Norwich, especially Thomas Brown; each week he was to say the Exequies of the Dead and a Requiem Mass for the above-mentioned souls, and was to preach to the people of the diocese each year during Advent and Lent;[37] unclear whether the chantry was established.

1472:   founded by the executors of Richard Brown and Ralph Segrym, former mayors; a secular priest, without a benefice or the cure of souls or other stipendiary services, was to be appointed by the master and fellows of St Giles's Hospital to say for ever Vespers and Matins on Sundays and feastdays, and Mass every day, in St Barbara's Chapel in

---

[31] Jacob, "Two Documents," p. 437.
[32] Blomefield, *Norfolk* (1805-1810), 10: 114.
[33] N.C.C., Reg. Wylbey, fol. 137r (Kerdeston).
[34] N.C.C., Reg. Brosyard, fol. 192r (At Fen); *Cal. Pat. R., 1548-1549*, p. 215.
[35] N.C.R., Case 3i, Private Deeds, Box 7, "Chapel Field College"; Emden, *BRUC*, p. 655 (John Wygenhale *alias* Saresson); *Visitations*, ed. Jessopp, p. 12.
[36] D. and C. Mun., Obedientiary Rolls, no. 299; N.C.C., Reg. Jekkys, fol. 115r (Fyce), and Reg. Haywarde, fol. 157r (Wether).
[37] PROB/11/6 (Reg. Wattys, 1471-1480), fol. 7 (Lyhert).

the Guild Hall, for the relief and comfort of those imprisoned there, for the good estate of the mayor and community of Norwich and for the souls of Richard Brown, Ralph Segrym, their wives, John Wilby, who had formerly been an alderman and at whose expense the chapel had been built, and his wife and all the benefactors of the said chapel;[38] still being performed in 1478/9.[39]

between 1475 and about 1505: founded by James Goldwell, bishop of Norwich 1472-1499, and his brother, Nicholas, who at various times was archdeacon of Norwich and dean of the College of St Mary in the Fields as well as an executor of his brother's will; a chaplain was to pray at Holy Trinity altar in the parish church of Great Chart in Kent, which was their home town, for the good estate of King Edward IV, Queen Elizabeth, their children, the bishop and his parents, and for their souls after their deaths; in 1505 Nicholas Goldwell added himself, King Henry VII, the king's parents and children, and their souls after their deaths, to those who were to be prayed for; still being performed until some time between 1534 and 1546.[40]

1478: founded by Elizabeth Clere, widow of Sir Robert Clere of Ormesby; the monks of the Cathedral Priory were to take it in turn for ever, a week at a time, to say Mass daily at St George's altar in the Cathedral; the monk or his cleric was to announce the following in English before the Confiteor, "alle men that will praye and seye a Pater Noster and an Ave Maria devoutely for the soules of Robert Clere and Elizabeth and for alle Crysten soules in tyme of this Messe folowyng shall have   dayes[41] of pardon"; the monk was to say in his Mass the Collect "Deus qui Caritatis Dona etc." while Elizabeth, her son and various other people were alive, and after their deaths the Collect "Inclina, Domine, aurem tuam ad preces nostras quibus misericordiam tuam supplices deprecavimus ut animam famuli tui Roberti et animam famule tue Elizabeth hic quiescentis etc."; after Mass he was to say the "De Profundis" and the prayer "Fidelium Deus Omnium Conditor" at Elizabeth's tomb.[42]

1479: founded by Sir Edmund Bokenham of Snetterton; an honest priest of good conversation was to "sing and pray" for his, his wife's and all his friends' souls in the church of the College of St Mary in the Fields; he

[38] N.C.R., Case 17b, Liber Albus, fol. 53r.
[39] N.C.R., Case 24a, Great Hospital Account Rolls, "General" 1478/9.
[40] *Kent Chantries*, ed. Arthur Hussey, Kent Archaeological Society, Records Branch, 12 (Ashford 1936), pp. 98-99; Emden, *BRUO*, 2: 783 (James Goldwell) and 786 (Nicholas Goldwell).
[41] Blank space precedes "dayes" in MS.
[42] D. and C. Mun., Box "Chantries", no. 1835 (Indenture between Elizabeth Clere ...).

was also to attend divine service in the choir of the college and to obey the college's rules;[43] still being performed in 1492.[44]

1483:   Mass of St Mary in St Stephen's parish church;[45] still being said, at least every Saturday, in 1543;[46] probably the same as the chantry of St Mary's confraternity attached to St Stephen's parish church, which was being performed at least from 1524[47] – possibly from 1465[48] – until at least 1540.[49]

1489:   John Smyth, master of St Giles's Hospital and rector of Yaxham and of Coltishall, provided in his will for the master and fellows of the hospital to find a priest to "celebrare" for his soul and the souls of his parents, Master Peter Shelton, various relatives, his benefactors, various other people and all the faithful departed for eighty years or, if a licence for alienation in mortmain could be obtained, for ever;[50] unclear whether the chantry was established.

1497:   founded by Robert Thorpe, alderman; a perpetual chantry of one priest in St Michael of Coslany parish church, in which he wanted to be buried, for the good estate and souls of the king, Sir Reynold Bray, at whose request the licence to found the chantry was granted, Robert Thorpe, his three wives, his brother, his son and all the faithful departed; still being performed until some time between 1535 and 1548.[51]

1502:   founded by the executors of James Goldwell, bishop of Norwich 1472-1499; the fellows of All Souls College, Oxford, were to take it in turn for ever, a month at a time, to celebrate service daily for the souls of the bishop and of his brother, Nicholas, both of whom had been fellows of the college; still being performed in 1535.[52]

1503:   founded by the executors of James Goldwell, bishop of Norwich 1472-1499; St Giles's Hospital was to find three secular or regular priests who were to "divina celebrare" for ever for the souls of the bishop, his parents and all the faithful departed; the hospital sub-

[43] N.C.C., Reg. A. Caston, fol. 38r (Buckingham).
[44] *Visitations*, ed. Jessopp, p. 12.
[45] N.C.C., Reg. A. Caston, fol. 147r (Grime).
[46] N.C.C., Reg. Mingaye, fol. 277r (Godsalve).
[47] N.C.C., Reg. Groundesburgh, fol. 7v (Carre).
[48] N.C.C., Reg. Jekkys, fol. 24r (Kerbrook).
[49] N.C.C., Reg. Attmere, fol. 390v (Grene); *Valor ecclesiasticus*, ed. Caley, 3: 294.
[50] N.C.C., Reg. Typpes, fol. 17v (Smyth).
[51] *Cal. Pat. R., 1494-1509*, p. 84; *Cal. Pat. R., 1547-1548*, pp. 272-273; PROB/11/12 (Reg. Moone, 1500-1501), fol. 19 (Thorpe); *Valor ecclesiasticus*, ed. Caley, 3: 294.
[52] Anthony Wood, *The History and Antiquities of the Colleges and Halls in the University of Oxford*, chapter on All Souls, ed. John Gutch (Oxford 1786), p. 262; Emden, *BRUO*, 2: 783 (James Goldwell) and 786 (Nicholas Goldwell); *Valor ecclesiasticus*, ed. Caley, 2: 235.

contracted one of the three chantries out to the College of St Mary in the Fields and another to the Cathedral Priory, the latter surviving until at least 1535.[53]

by 1516: Sir James Hobart of Hales Hall near Loddon, an attorney of King Henry vii, provided in his will for a perpetual chantry of one priest within the Augustinian friary;[54] unclear whether the chantry was established.

1521: Mass of Jesus, probably in St Stephen's parish church;[55] doubtful whether the Mass was said daily.

1524: see under 1483.

1530: Robert Jannys, grocer and former mayor, provided in his will for a priest to "sing" for him and his friends in the parish church of Aylsham in Norfolk, where he had been born, and to keep a free grammar school in the town; he was to exhort his pupils to say the "De Profundis" daily for the souls of Robert and his friends;[56] unclear whether the chantry was established.

1531: Mass of Jesus in St Gregory's parish church;[57] still being said in 1537;[58] doubtful whether the Mass was said daily.

1531: Mass of St John in St Peter Mancroft parish church;[59] doubtful whether the Mass was said daily.

1543: the City Government ordered the craft guilds to support financially a priest "singing" in St John's Chapel in the Common Hall (formerly the church of the Dominican friary) for the king, the queen, the prince, the King's Council, the living and dead members of the guilds, and the prosperity and welfare of Norwich.[60]

---

[53] N.C.R., Case 24b, "Writings relating to St Giles Hospital," no. 66, Parcel "Licence for Executors of Bishop Goldwell"; N.C.R., Case 3i, Private Deeds, Box 7, "Chapel Field College"; *Valor ecclesiasticus*, ed. Caley, 3: 285.

[54] PROB/11/19 (Reg. Ayloffe, 1517-1520), fol. 33 (Hobart); *D.N.B.*, 27: 31 (James Hobart).

[55] N.C.C., Reg. Alblaster, fol. 69r (Catelyn).

[56] See pp. 240 and 249.

[57] N.C.C., Reg. Alpe, fol. 69r (Barker).

[58] N.C.C., Reg. Godsalve, fol. 242r (Cory).

[59] N.C.C., Reg. Palgrave, fol. 119r (Brown).

[60] *Records of Norwich*, ed. Hudson, 2: 310.

Appendix 11

Testamentary Bequests for Masses, Prayers and Religious Services

Period	Laity					Clergy				
	1370-1439	1440-1489	1490-1517	1518-1532	total	1370-1439	1440-1489	1490-1517	1518-1532	total
Number of persons whose wills have been examined[1]	133	118	226	138	615	96	104	62	27	289
A. Percentage of testators who left one or more bequests in their wills for Masses, prayers or religious services:[2]	47	54	73	68	62	35	71	89	81	64
B. Approximate amounts of money[3] left by testators in their wills for Masses, prayers and religious services :										
% of testators who left £100 or more for such purposes	3	1	3	2	2	3	3	2		2
% leaving £50 – £99 19s. 11d.	4	5	3	1	3		1	2	7	1
% leaving £20 – £49 19s. 11d.	5	8	9	5	7	1	7	5	7	4
% leaving £10 – £19 19s. 11d.	6	8	9	7	8	3	15	21		11
% leaving £5 – £9 19s. 11d.	8	11	19	12	13	6	20	25	11	16
% leaving £1 – £4 19s. 11d.	14	9	7	15	11	6	5	16	15	9
% leaving 1d. – 19s. 11d.	7	13	23	25	18	17	20	18	41	20
C. Percentage of testators who left one or more bequests in their wills for perpetual										

[1] See p. xi for the abbreviations used.

[2] The wills are dated from when they were written, not from when they were proved, unless only the date of probate survives.

[3] When no sum of money was mentioned it has been assumed that the normal offering/fee for the particular religious service was being left. When a sum of money was left to each of an unspecified number of persons to celebrate a particular service, a multiplier at the lower end of the likely range has been adopted.

Period	Laity					Clergy				
	1370-1439	1440-1489	1490-1517	1518-1532	total	1370-1439	1440-1489	1490-1517	1518-1532	total
or temporary chantries or for annuals of Masses:[4]	24	34	44	38	36	18	47	55	30	37
% who left bequests for perpetual chantries	2		1/2	1	1	2	3			2
% who left bequests for between 10 years (of such services) and less than an infinite number of years	5	4	3	3	4	1			4	1
% leaving for 5 – less than 10 years	5	5	8	3	6		3	2	7	2
% leaving for 2 – less than 5 years	9	9	12	7	10	5	20	26	4	15
% leaving for 1 – less than 2 years	5	13	18	12	13	9	21	23	11	17
% leaving for 1/4 – less than 1 year		3	2	12	4			5	4	1
D. Number of testators (not expressed as a percentage) who left bequests in their wills for the following votive and indulgenced Masses :										
Mass of the Holy Trinity	1	1	1		3	1	1	1		3
Mass of Jesus/ Mass of the Name of Jesus		5	32	20	57		8	8	3	19
Mass of the Five Wounds of Jesus			6	10	16				3	3
Mass of the Holy Cross							1			1
Mass of Our Lord's Resurrection			1		1					
Mass of the Holy Spirit	1			1	2		1			1
Mass of the Angels							1			1
Mass of St Mary	1	1	2	1	5		1	1		2
Mass of the Assumption of St Mary			1		1					
Mass of St Peter the Apostle							1			1
Mass of St John the Evangelist							1			1
Mass of St Benedict		1			1					
Mass of St William		1			1					
Mass of All Saints	1	1	1		3			1		1
Trental of St Gregory[5]	5	7	15	12	39		3	2	3	8
Mass at an altar of Scala Caeli[6]		1	4	4	9				1	1

[4] For the meaning of the terms see pp. 92 and 100.
[5] See pp. 102-103.
[6] See p. 103.

Appendix 12

Analysis of Testamentary Bequests

Period	Laity					Clergy				
	1370-1439	1440-1489	1490-1517	1518-1532	total	1370-1439	1440-1489	1490-1517	1518-1532	total
Number of persons whose wills have been examined[1]	133	118	226	138	615	96	104	62	27	289
Percentage of testators who left one or more bequests in their wills to or for the following:[2]										
Masses, prayers and religious services	47	54	73	68	62	35	71	89	81	64
Votive lights	8	13	35	48	28	5	11	18	33	12
Religious houses										
In Norwich and its suburbs										
Dominican Friary	51	43	48	41	46	36	48	53	33	44
Franciscan Friary	52	46	47	39	46	36	49	52	33	44
Carmelite Friary	52	47	49	40	47	43	48	52	33	46
Augustinian Friary	53	42	50	42	47	43	45	55	44	46
Cathedral Church and Priory	14	23	46	49	35	17	38	61	52	37
College of St Mary in the Fields	9	6	5	4	6	14	21	32	15	21
St Giles's Hospital	35	14	11	5	15	22	23	23	22	22
Carnary College	2		1/2	1	1	4	1	3	11	3

[1] See Appendix 13, section B (p. 225).

[2] Bequests falling under two categories (e.g., a bequest to a friary so that the friars might pray for the testator's soul) have normally been included under both categories, except that bequests to votive lights have not been included under the institutions that owned them. The figures exclude from consideration bequests (of unspecified sums of money) that were to be paid out of the residues of testator's estates, chiefly general requests for prayers or for "works of charity to be done," since bequests of this kind were probably little more than conventional phrases with which the scribe concluded the will.

Period	Laity					Clergy				
	1370-1439	1440-1489	1490-1517	1518-1532	total	1370-1439	1440-1489	1490-1517	1518-1532	total
College of chantry priests in the Bishop's Palace	1					1	1			1
Carrow Nunnery	11	19	17	14	16	4	21	35	21	4
Elsewhere	18	14	14	7	13	13	17	26	15	17
Parish churches	94	92	97	95	95	78	89	89	89	85
Hermits, anchorites and communities resembling beguinages	8	18	21	25	18	5	32	27	19	21
Craft guilds and pious confraternities	6	11	22	14	15	7	31	61	56	32
Works of charity (St Giles's Hospital in Norwich: see above, under "Religious houses")										
St Paul's Hospital in Norwich	36	34	32	22	31	24	40	53	22	36
Hildebrond's Hospital in Norwich	1	1		1						
Daniel's Alms-Houses in Norwich	2									
Five sick-houses at the gates of Norwich[3]	43	41	39	30	38	31	40	50	33	39
Magdalen Hospital in the suburbs of Norwich	3	7	4		3		3	3	4	2
Prisoners in the Guild Hall or in the Castle of Norwich[4]	8	14	22	18	16	1	10	27	19	11
Other works of charity	19	23	20	18	20	23	34	35	44	31
Civic projects	1	3	8	3	5	1		3		1

[3] The figures are based on the numbers of testators who gave to at least one of the five sick-houses, but almost all who gave to one gave to all five.

[4] The figures are based on the numbers of testators who gave to the prisoners in at least one of the two prisons, but almost all who gave to those in one gave to those in both.

Appendix 13

Documentary Sources of the Wills of Inhabitants of Norwich, 1370-1532

A. Documentary sources of all the surviving wills of inhabitants of Norwich which were written and proved between 1370 and 1532:

Source[1]	Period[2]	Laity					Clergy				
		1370-1439	1440-1489	1490-1517	1518-1532	total	1370-1439	1440-1489	1490-1517	1518-1532	total
	Total number of wills[3]	167	525	546	277	1515	96	104	62	27	289
PROB/11[4]		3	15	46	13	77		1	6	1	8
Ab.C.[5]		11	9	4		24	3	2	1		6
Canterbury, Cathedral Archives and Library, Registers of the Dean and Chapter[6]									1		1
N.C.C.[7]		135	486	390	219	1230	91	101	52	21	265
REG[8]		1				1	2				2
A.N.C.[9]			1	81	37	119					
D. and C., Reg. 1444-1455, Reg. 1461-1559 and Reg. 1500-1530[10]			9	22	8	39			2	5	7

[1] See p. ix for the abbreviations used.

[2] The wills are dated from when they were written, not from when they were proved, unless only the date of probate survives.

[3] With one partial exception, which was provided by the Daniel brothers, each will was made by one testator: John Daniel made a "testamentum" to which the joint "ultima voluntas" of him and his brother, Walter, was appended (N.C.C., Reg. Hyrnyng, fols. 32r-33r), but Walter Daniel later made a "testamentum et ultima voluntas" of his own (ibid., fols. 148r-150r). A few wills were copied into more than one of the records indicated, but the figures given in the chart allow for only one of the copies. Therefore the numbers of wills in the chart equal the numbers of testators.

[4] Indexed in *Index of Wills*, ed. Smith.

[5] Indexed in "Calendar of Lambeth Wills," ed. John C. Smith, *Genealogist*, new ser., 34 (1917-1918) 53-64, 149-160 and 219-234, and 35 (1918-1919) 45-51 and 102-126.

[6] I.e., the will of Robert Calton (or Catton) in Register F, fol. 154r. For a few other wills of inhabitants of Norwich copied into these registers – wills that were also copied into others of the records mentioned – see *Sede Vacante Wills*, ed. Charles E. Woodruff, Kent Archaeological Society, Records Branch, 3 (Canterbury 1914), p. 54.

[7] Indexed in *Index of Wills*, ed. Farrow, pp. 1-412.

[8] Indexed in ibid., pp. 413-423.

[9] A manuscript index of the wills is kept in the Norfolk Record Office, Norwich.

[10] A manuscript index of the wills is kept in the Norfolk Record Office, Norwich.

Source	Period	Laity					Clergy				
		1370-1439	1440-1489	1490-1517	1518-1532	total	1370-1439	1440-1489	1490-1517	1518-1532	total
D. and C. Mun., Box "Acta et Comperta"[11]		17				17					
N.C.R., Cases 1c-1d, Court Rolls 19 (1461-1483) and 20 (1483-1508)[12]			4	2		6					
N.C.R., Case 3g, Private Deeds, Box 1, "Friars Preachers in St Andrew"[13]			1			1					
N.C.R., Case 16c, Assembly Minute Book 1 (1492-1510)[14]				1		1					

B. Documentary sources of the sample of 904 wills used in Chapter 3 and elsewhere:

Source	Period	Laity					Clergy				
		1370-1439	1440-1489	1490-1517	1518-1532	total	1370-1439	1440-1489	1490-1517	1518-1532	total
	Number of wills	133	118	226	138	615	96	104	62	27	289

As under Section A for the clergy.
As under Section A for the laity, except that:

- wills recorded in the last three sources (N.C.R., Cases 1c-1d, Court Rolls 19 [1461-1483] and 20 [1483-1508] ; N.C.R., Case 3g, Private Deeds, Box 1, "Friars Preachers in St Andrew"; N.C.R., Case 16c, Assembly Minute Book 1 [1492-1510]) have not been included,
- of the wills proved in the Norwich Consistory Court (= N.C.C.), only the following have been included:
  - all the wills in registers Heydon (1370-1383), Harsyk (1384-1408), Hyrnyng (1416-1426) and Surflete (1426-1436) for the period 1370-1439 (= 101 wills),
  - all the wills in register Jekkys (1464-1472) and in the second half of register Cobald (1465-1468) for the period 1440-1489 (= 84 wills),
  - all the wills in register Ryxe (1504-1507) for the period 1490-1517 (= 73 wills),
  - all the wills written and proved between 1526 and 1532 (= 80 wills).

[11] A manuscript index of the wills is kept in the Norfolk Record Office, Norwich.
[12] I.e., the wills of John Awbry, John Calowe, William Lyndys, John May, Thomas Moos and Elizabeth Styward. For these wills, for a few other complete wills of inhabitants of Norwich (which are also to be found in the will-registers of the Norwich Consistory Court), and for extracts (relating exclusively to tenements in Norwich) from many other wills of the citizens, see *Index of Wills*, ed. Farrow, pp. 413-423.
[13] I.e., no. 17 (Smyth). No. 18 (Ingham) is the same as N.C.C., Reg. Aleyn, fols. 107r-108r (Ingham).
[14] I.e., fols. 135v-136r (Spycer). Fols. 133r (Sharyngton) and 142r-v (Radbode alias Bewflour) are the same as N.C.C., Reg. Wolman, fols. 102r-v (Sharington) and 151r (Radbode alias Bewflowr).

Appendix 14

Transcripts of Twelve Wills and One Inventory

The wills of these five persons have been selected primarily to illustrate the typical features of short and medium-length wills. Most wills fell into these categories, and exceptional wills must be seen in this context.

The wills of John Honyng and Edward Ive illustrate the typical features of short wills in which only three or four bequests were left. Almost every will contained at least one bequest to a parish church, and the two wills illustrate the most common forms: one to the high altar, another for the upkeep of the church. Following such bequests in popularity were those left for the performance of religious services. Edward Ive wanted Masses and Dirges; John Honyng wanted his funeral expenses to be paid for out of the residue of his estate.

The wills of Guy de Burdeux, Adam Kerbrok and Margery Dogett indicate the kinds of pious and charitable bequests that were most popular with testators who could afford more than the bare minimum of legacies. Those to votive lights were represented – on an unusually large scale – in Margery Dogett's will. She also left 3s. 4d. to the Cathedral, and both she and Guy de Burdeux left 3s. 4d. to each of the four friaries, the latter giving the money in the hope that they might "celebrate" for his soul. All of them left something to the members of a religious house outside the city walls, Kerbrok and Dogett giving to the nuns of Carrow and de Burdeux to the Knights Hospitallers at Carbrooke. Bequests to recluses were represented by a shilling left to the recluse of Carrow, and fourpence left to each anchor and anchoress in the city; those to craft guilds and pious confraternities were represented by the various objects for saying Mass that Kerbrok left to a confraternity attached to his parish church and by his bequest to Corpus Christi confraternity. There were also bequests to people in St Giles's Hospital, St Paul's Hospital and the sick-houses at the gates of the city, as well as a variety of bequests to needy citizens who were not catered for by charitable institutions; and the bequests to "either howse in the Castell and Gilde Halle" were probably intended for the prisoners in the two buildings.

The five wills illustrate, too, how wills normally began and ended. After invoking God's name, almost all testators commended their souls. The phrases used by Honyng are typical of the period up to about 1490, when wills were normally written in Latin; the wills of Ive and Dogett follow the later custom of omitting St Mary's title of Virgin.[1] The extent to which the commendatory clauses were conventional is indicated by "etc." in de Burdeux's will. He was one of the very few testators who did not mention where they wanted to be buried; most, like the other four testators in question, asked to be buried in a parish church or its cemetery.[2] After dealing with individual bequests, almost every will contained a clause about the residue of the estate. Honyng's will included many of the usual features: with the residue of his goods his executors were to take care of his funeral, to pay his debts and to do other "opera pietatis" ("et caritatis" was often added) for his soul according as they thought would please God and profit his soul.

The wills indicate the extent to which the pious and charitable bequests of the clergy were similar to those of the laity.[3] They indicate, too, the extent to which wills had become standardized by the late fourteenth century and continued to follow the same conventional patterns – apart from the change from Latin to English – throughout the period in question.[4] At the same time they show that even the briefest wills could be subject to the personal wishes of the testator. Thus Honyng specifically mentioned that he wanted to be buried "ante crucifixum," and Ive's very short will contained a highly individualistic clause about the kind of religious services that he wanted to be performed. Somewhat longer wills, like those of de Burdeux, Kerbrok and Dogett, gave more scope for picking and choosing within a range of possible beneficiaries, and for varying the amounts of money given.

Most of the wills that survive were written when death was approaching.[5] Kerbrok's was one of the very few that were proved long after they had been made.[6] In his case the lapse of time was not the result of inefficiency on the part of his executors or of the court providing probate. A note stated that twenty years after he had written his will Kerbrok, now seriously ill, had confirmed that the will, which had been placed upon an altar in his room, was indeed his; the only changes concerned his executors, perhaps because his mother and Robert Hawes – the original executors – had died in the meantime.

Will of Guy de Burdeux[7]

In Dei nomine, Amen. Ego, Gwido de Burdeux, civis Norwic', in bona memoria condo testamentum meum apud Norwicum xvi die Aprilis anno

[1] See p. 83.
[2] See p. 98.
[3] See pp. 140 and 222-223.
[4] See pp. 117 and 139-140.
[5] See p. 116.
[6] N.C.C., Reg. Jekkys, fol. 24r-v (Kerbrook).
[7] N.C.C., Reg. Heydon, fol. 20r (Burdeux).

Domini millesimo CCC^mo lxxi in hunc modum. In primis commendo animam meam etc'. Item lego summo altari ecclesie Sancti Petri de Southgate in Conesford pro defectibus meis x s., et emendacioni eiusdem ecclesie xl d. Item lego cuilibet ordini fratrum mendicancium Norwic' ii s. ad celebrandum pro anima mea. Item lego pauperibus in hospitali Sancti Egidii Norwic' ii s. Item pauperibus hospitalis Sancti Pauli Norwic' ii s. Item lego ad distribuendum inter leprosos Norwic' xl d. Item lego fratribus domus Sancti Johannis de Kerbrok' xl d. Item lego Isabelle, uxori mee, heredibus et assignatis suis totum mesuagium meum cum edific' et sibi pertinentibus suis quod est in Norwico in parochia Sancti Petri de Suthgate predicta. Item lego xx s. ad expensas meas funerales faciendas. Residuum vero bonorum meorum mobilium et immobilium lego et do dicte Isabelle, uxori mee, ad inde faciendum et disponendum pro voluntate sua. Huius autem testamenti executores meos Jacobum Yne et[8] Rogerum Nichol, cives Norwic', ordino et constituo per presentes die et anno Domini supradictis.

Will of John Honyng[9]

In Dei nomine, Amen. Ego Johannes Honyng, capellanus de Norwico, in bona memoria mea condo testamentum meum apud Norwicum xxv^to die mensis Octobris anno Domini millesimo CCCC^mo xix^no [10] in hunc modum. In primis commendo animam meam Deo omnipotenti, Beate Marie Virgini et omnibus sanctis, et corpus meum ad sepelliendum in ecclesia Sancti Georgii ad Portas Sancte Trinitatis Norwici ante crucifixum. Et lego summo altari eiusdem ecclesie iii s. iiii d., et emendacioni eiusdem ecclesie vi s. viii d. Item lego summo altari ecclesie Cathedralis Sancte Trinitatis Norwicensis vi s. viii d. Residuum vero omnium bonorum do et lego in manus executorum meorum ad funeralia mea peragenda, debitaque solvenda ac ad cetera opera pietatis pro anima mea facienda prout melius viderint sibi Deo complacere et anime mee prodesse. Huius autem testamenti mei executores meos Dominum Johannem Thornegg, capellanum, et Ricardum Axme, sadeler, cive' Norwic', eligo et constituo per presentes. In cuius rei testimonium huic presenti testamento meo sigillum meum apposui. Dat' die, loco et anno Domini supradictis.

Will of Adam Kerbrok[11]

In Dei nomine, Amen. Vicesimo die mensis Julii anno Domini millesimo CCCC^mo quadragesimo quinto, ego, Adam Kerbrok, capellanus de parochia Sancti Stephani in Nowico, compos mentis et sane memorie existens, condo testamentum meum in hunc modum. In primis commendo animam meam Deo omnipotenti, Beate Marie et omnibus sanctis, et corpus meum ad sepeliendum infra cimiterium ecclesie Sancti Stephani predicte. Item lego emendacioni dicte

---

[8] "Nicholaum" deleted in MS.
[9] N.C.C., Reg. Hyrnyng, fol. 52v (Honing).
[10] "apud" deleted in MS.
[11] N.C.C., Reg. Jekkys, fol. 24r-v (Kerbrook).

ecclesie vi s. viii d. Item lego gilde Beate Marie in eadem ecclesia meum vestimentum rubeum et unam mappam de diaper ad serviendum altari Beate Marie in dicta ecclesia. Item lego dicte gilde unum corporale cum duobus coopertoriis, unum de purpyll velwete et aliud de purpill damaske. Item lego priorisse monialium de Carhowe xx d. Item lego cuilibet moniali[12] de Carhowe iiii d. Item lego recluse de Carhowe xii d. Item lego emendacioni ecclesie Sancti Andree in Norwico ii s. Item volo ut celebretur unum annuale in dicta ecclesia Sancti Andree pro anima mea et pro animabus parentum meorum. Item lego sacerdoti gilde Corporis Christi existenti in obsequiis meis iiii d. Item lego Thome Smyth de Bury Sancti Edmundi unum par precularum de jete. Item volo ut duo annualia celebrentur[13] in dicta ecclesia Sancti Stephani pro anima mea et animabus parentum meorum. Item lego filie Johannis Karr xii d. Item lego filiole mee, filie Gybsone, xii d. Item lego Johanni Brasyer, filio Ricardi Brayser, xii d. Item lego Alicie Colman ad portas de Nedham viii d. Item cuilibet leproso ad portas de Nedham i d. Item cuilibet mendico iacenti in lecto in parochia Sancti Stephani i d. Residuum vero omnium bonorum meorum non legatorum, post debita mea soluta et legata mea perimpleta, volo ut vendatur per manus executorum meorum, et pecuniam inde provenientem do et lego matri mee ad sustentacionem suam. Executores meos constituo matrem meam et Robertum Hawes.

Item prefatus Adam Kerbrok, xxvii° die mensis Aprilis anno Domini millesimo CCCC^mo lxvi^to in civitate Norwici gravi infirmitate detentus, suprascriptum testamentum pro suo testamento et ultima voluntate in camera sua super altare suum positum verbaliter affirmavit et declaravit. Ac Magistrum Galfridum Chaumpeneys, Ricardum Bumpsted, Thomam Kynggessey et Dominum Johannem Dowe, capellanum, ad exequendum testamentum predictum et administranda bona sua executores nominavit, elegit et constituit.

Will of Edward Ive[14]

In Dei nomine, Amen. I, Edward Ive, beynge of good and hooll memory the xi day of December in the yer of our Lord God mille CCCCCxiii make my last will. First I bequeth my sowle to God allmyghty, to our Lady Seynt Mary and to all the compeny in hevyn, and my body to be buryed in Seynt Clement' chircheyerd of Norwic'. To the wiche heigh autyer I bequeth viii d., to the reparacion of the same chirche xii d., and to have v Masses[15] att my buryall day of the v Wonds of our Lord Jhu', and so the space of iiii yeres a Dirige and a Masse of Requiem with v Masses de Quinque Vulneribus. The residue of all my goods I geve into the hands of myn executrice, whom I make Margarett, my wiff, and William Wright to be help to my wiff and to have for his labor xx d.

---

[12] MS reads "moniale."
[13] MS reads "celebrantur."
[14] A.N.C., Reg. Gloys (1509-1519), fol. 110v (Ive).
[15] "all" deleted in MS.

Will of Margery Dogett[16]

In the name of God, Amen. I, Margery[17] Dogett of Norwich, wedou, the xxiii day of February in the yer of Our Lord mille CCCCCxv in my good mynde at Norwiche aforseid make my testament in this wise. Firste I commende my sowle to allmyghty God, our Lady Seynt Mary and to all the holy compeny of hevyn, and my body for to be buryed att the chirche dore in Seynt Myghell' of Mustowe in Norwiche. To whos highe autyer I bequeth ii s., and to the reparacion of the same chirche iii s. iiii d., and my beste coverlyght to lye before ye highe autyer.

Item I bequeth to the sepultur light in the same chirche xii d. Item to the light of Seynt Myghell, to the perke light, to the light of Our Lady, the light of Seynt Anne, and to the light of Seynt Nicholas in the same chirche, to iche of them I bequeth vi d. Item to the[18] lampe afor the highe autyer, to the common light that brenneth over Myghellmess evyn and Myghelmes day, and to the light of Seynt Cristofir in the same chirche, to iche of them iiii d. Item to the Cathedral cherche of Norwiche iii s. iiii d. Item to the light of Jhesus Messe in the same chirche xii d. Item I bequeth to ye chirche of Bowthorpp xii d. Item to the chirche of Colney xii d. Item to the chirche of Seynt John of Bestrete xii d. Item to the chirche of Seynt Bartilmewe in Bestrete xii d. Item I bequeth to Seynt Julyans chirche my coverlight nexte the beste. Item I bequeth to the light of Our Lady in Seynt Stevyns parisshe xii d.

Item to the hole susters of Normans iiii d., and to the half susters vi d. Item I bequeth to eiche anker and ankeresse in Norwiche iiii d. Item to iche of the v howses of syke men by Norwiche gates iiii d. Item to every person beynge bedred withinne the parysshes of Seynt Myghell of Mustowe, Seynt Andrewes, Seynt Mary Litill and Seynt Petir of Hundegate, to yche of them ii d. Item to iche of the iiii orders of freres in Norwiche iii s. iiii d. Item to the nunnes of Carrowe xii d. Item I will that ther be disposed at my beryenge day xiii s. iiii d. to prests and clerks. Item I will ther be delte in brede to poore folk for my sowle to the value of xiii s. iiii d., and to every poor howse in Seynt Petirs and Seynt Vast' parysshes to have an halpeny. Item in wynter to poor folkes in woode xiii s. iiii d. Item to either howse in the Castell and Gilde Halle in Norwiche iiii d. Item I will that the poor paryssheners of Seynt Myghell of Mustowe have, iche[19] howse, iiii d. Item to iiii priests to bere my body to the chirche, to iche of them iiii d.

Item I bequeth to John Dogette, my sonne, iiii marcs, vi silvere spones, a masere, my gret brasse potte, my beste fetherbed, a donge, a fyne shete, ii trannsomes and all my brasse, laten and pewter in my howse. Item a chayer of esement. Item I bequeth to Agnes, his wiff, my beste gownne, my beste girdill and my beste bedes. Item I bequeth to yche of my susters an harneysed gyrdell of sylver. Item to Alice Hendrye of Taverham a grene gownne. Item to Margery

[16] A.N.C., Reg. Cook (1503-1538), fols. 46v-47r (Dogett).
[17] "Dok" deleted in MS.
[18] "laml" deleted in MS.
[19] "of" deleted in MS.

Appulton a tukkyng lace with silver aglettes. Item I will that Willdes wiff have my furred gowne. Item I wylle that Anne Lyston have my werser cloke. Item to Bretens wiff my beste kyrtill. Item to blynde Margaret my nexte beste kertill. Item to Medilgat' doughter my kertill that I were every day. Item I will that a certeyne be founde for my sowle by the spece of oon yer.

The residue of all my goods I commytte to the good disposicion of myn executors, whom I make and ordeyne John Dogett, my sone, and Ser William Breten, preste. And I bequeth to either of them for ther labor, vi s. viii d. Yoven the day, yer and place above seyd, theis berynge wittnes: Ser William Clyffe, preste, heremyte, and John Bett'.

B. RICHARD CAISTOR, VICAR OF ST STEPHEN'S, 1420

Richard (of) Caistor is said to have come from near Norwich, possibly the village of Caistor.[20] There is no evidence that he studied at a university. He was probably the Richard Caistor who had been tonsured by 1385 and was instituted to the vicarage of Sedgeford near Lynn in 1397. He was vicar of St Stephen's in Norwich from 1402 until his death in 1420. Bale and Pits said that he was the author of a book on the Ten Commandments, of another on (the meditations of) St Bernard, and of several homilies. The only extant work of his is the hymn "Jesu, lord, that madest me," which survives in numerous manuscripts, though eight of the twelve stanzas come from an earlier poem.[21]

He is of particular interest on account of his cult. Margery Kempe sought him out as a holy man and later went to pray at his grave;[22] nine years after his death Sir Thomas Colpepper, a Kentish knight, asked his son to make a pilgrimage to Norwich to offer "a le seint vicair[23] un coer quest en mon chapel door";[24] some twenty years later a certain John Falbeck, who probably came from Thorndon in Suffolk, left money in his will for a man to make a pilgrimage to St Stephen's church in Norwich;[25] John Leystofte, a later vicar of St Stephen's, began his will in 1462 by recommending his soul to Richard Caistor "sacre recordationis";[26] and in 1500 a mercer from Norwich called John Stalon left in his will a cloth of red tissue, which he had woven, to St Stephen's church to lie on "the good vekers grave."[27]

[20] Most of the documents relevant to his life and cult have been printed in, Dundas Harford, "Richard of Caister, and his Metrical Prayer," *Norfolk Archaeology* 17 (1908-1910) 221-224. Except where other references have been given, the following remarks are based on this article.
[21] *Religious Lyrics of the XVth Century*, ed. Carleton F. Brown (Oxford 1939), p. 313.
[22] Margery Kempe, *The Book*, 1: 17, 43 and 60, ed. Meech, pp. 38-40, 102 and 147.
[23] St Stephen's was the only vicarage in Norwich.
[24] *Register of Chichele*, ed. Jacob, 2: 385.
[25] N.C.C., Reg. Brosyard, fol. 124r (Falbeck).
[26] "Animam meam lego ... Deo ... beato Stephano sacre recordationis Ricardo de Castr' et omnibus sanctis" (N.C.C., Reg. Brosyard, fol. 272v [Leystofte]). Possibly, therefore, "sacre recordationis" qualifies St Stephen rather than Caistor.
[27] N.C.C., Reg. Wight, fol. 94r (Stalon).

Bale and Pits corroborate this. He was called "Bonus," they said, and was a devout and apostolic priest; a description with which Margery Kempe would surely have agreed.[28] Bale went further, saying that "Wiclevisticae doctrinae (potius Christianae) impense sed tacito favebat propter metum Papistarum, eorum in aliis expertus tyrannidem. Clericorum impudicos mores et exempla foedissima modesta correptione in concionibus deflebat, cum alias non posset curare." There is, however, no other direct evidence to suggest that he was a follower of Wycliffe. His will contains none of the features regarded by Mr McFarlane as characteristic of Lollard wills,[29] and he began it by recommending his soul to St Mary the Virgin and the saints. Even so, his will is very unusual, especially for a man who had been vicar of one of the most valuable livings in the city[30] for eighteen years. It is very brief: it contains no requests that Masses or prayers be said for his soul: and he wanted his wealth – apart from £10 that was to be spent on buying two antiphonaries for his church – to be given to the poor on the grounds that "bona Ecclesie secundum canones sunt bona pauperum."[31] The will certainly suggests a priest who sympathised with some of the views held by some Lollards. He appears, moreover, to have been one in a succession of radical vicars of St Stephen's.[32] He must be numbered among the small group of parish priests in late medieval England known to have enjoyed a reputation for sanctity both in life and long after death. John Felton, the early fifteenth century vicar of St Mary Magdalen's in Oxford, was another case in point. It is interesting that such a reputation should have stuck to a priest with views that were radical and possibly even marginally heretical.

Will of Richard Caistor[33]

In Dei nomine, Amen. Ego, Ricardus Castr', perpetuus vicarius ecclesie Sancti Stephani in Norwico, in bona memoria mea condo testamentum meum apud Norwicum vicesimo septimo die mensis Marcii anno Domini millesimo CCCC^{mo} vicesimo in hunc modum. In primis comendo animam meam Deo omnipotenti, Beate Marie Virgini et omnibus sanctis, et corpus meum ad sepiliendum in cancello Sancti Stephani supradicti. Item lego ad emenda duo antiphonaria ad serviendum Deo in dicta ecclesia in divinis x li. Item, ex quo bona Ecclesie secundum canones sunt bona pauperum, omnia cetera bona mea pro maiori parte lego pauperibus sic quod pauperes parrochie mee preferantur. Residuum vero omnium bonorum meorum do et lego in manus executorum meorum ut ipsi disponant et ordinent pro me prout melius viderint Deo complacere et anime mee prodesse. Huius autem testamenti mei executores meos Dominum Johannem

---

[28] Margery Kempe, *The Book*, 1: 17, 43 and 60, ed. Meech, pp. 38-40, 102 and 147.
[29] McFarlane, *Lancastrian Kings*, p. 210.
[30] See columns 1, 5 and 6 of Appendix 1 (pp. 173-178).
[31] He may have had in mind "quicquid habent clerici pauperum est" (*Corpus iuris canonici*, Decretum Gratiani, 2.16.1.68).
[32] See pp. 41, 47-48, 124-125 and 234-236.
[33] REG/4, Book 8, fol. 135r-v (Castre).

Barsham, rectorum Sancti Michaelis in Coslane, Dominum Henricum Brisslee, capellanum, et Dominum Johannem Riche, capellanum, eligo et constituo per presentes. In cuius rei testimonium huic presenti testamento meo sigillum meum apposui. Dat' die, loco et anno Domini supradictis.

C. RICHARD FERNEYS, "QUONDAM" HERMIT OF NEWBRIDGE, 1464

Richard Ferneys and his will have already been discussed.[34]

Will of Richard Ferneys[35]

In Dei nomine, Amen. Ego, Ricardus Ferneys, heremita quondam de Newbrygg, gravi langore correptus, sed Dei gratia sane memorie et compos mentis, anno Domini millesimo $CCCC^{mo}$ [36] lxiiii^{to} secundo die mensis Maii condo testamentum meum in hunc modum. In primo lego animam meam omnipotenti Deo, Beate Marie Virgini et omnibus sanctis, corpusque meum sepeliendum in ecclesia collegiata Beate Marie de Campis in Norwico. Ad cuius reparacionem lego vi s. viii d. Item decano eiusdem ii s., et singulis consociis eiusdem ibidem tempore obitus mei presentibus xii d. Item singulis aliis sacerdotibus ibidem tunc comorantibus xii d. Item cuilibet alteri clerico tunc ibidem ii d. Item singulis pueris tunc ibidem i d. Item cuilibet servienti tunc ibidem ii d. Item lego eidem ecclesie unum psalterium magnum pro choro ibidem cathenandum.

Item lego ecclesie Cathedrali Sancte Trinitatis Norwici ii s. Item fraternitati[37] Jhu' in ecclesia Sancti Petri de Mancroft ii s. Item fraternitati Beate Marie in ecclesia Sancti Stephani ii s. Item cuilibet sorori et dimidie de Normannis ii d. Item cuilibet pauperi et sorori de hospitali Sancti Egidii ii d. Item lego priorisse de Carrowe et conventui ibidem iii s. iiii d.

Item Domine Juliane Lampett, recluse ibidem, xii d. et i par lintheamentorum. Item Domine Margarete Purdaunce unum pannum deputatum cum ymagine Christi. Item[38] Alicie Kyngessey unam tabulam deputatum. Item Katerine Moryell unam patellam de laton et i parvam ollam eneam. Item Cristiane Veyl, sorori eius et custodi mee, i par lintheamentorum, i ollam eneam, unum cocliarium parvum et vi s. viii d. Item lego Johanni Sylver, puero meo, i par lodicum, i donge, i par lintheamentorum, unam cistam de Prusia et vi s. viii d. Item lego Johanni, heremite de Newbrygg, optimum epitogium meum, optimum capicium, unum scapularium. Item Johanni Felton, heremite in Norwico, vi d. Item Thome, heremite ibidem, iiii d. Item Basilie de parochia Sancti Gregorii i armilausam et vi d. Item Agneti Shotesham de Normann' aliam armilausam.

---

[34] See pp. 60-63 and 202.
[35] N.C.C., Reg. Jekkys, fols.15v-16r (Ferneys).
[36] "lxvii^{to} lxii^{do} die" deleted in MS.
[37] "Jol" deleted in MS.
[38] "Item" repeated in MS.

Residuum vero bonorum meorum et debitorum quorumcumque do et lego in manus Magistri Ricardi Porynglond, quem constituo et ordino executorem meum pro oneribus et expensis citra sepulturam meam faciendis, missisque celebrandis et in pios usus benefactorum meorum et aliorum pauperum, siquidem superfuerit, distribuendo prout anime mee viderit expedire. Cui pro labore suo lego iii s. iiii d. et unum psalterium glosatum ad terminum vite sue, ita quod postea remaneat collegio supradicto. In cuius rei testimonium sigillum meum presens est appensum. Dat' anno, loco et die supradictis.

D. Geoffrey Chaumpneis, Vicar of St Stephen's, 1472

Various points of interest in Chaumpneis's will have already been discussed.[39] Also of interest is the commendatory clause, which is the third sentence of the will. It is an interesting example from Norwich of a commendatory clause in which the unworthiness of the testator and the corruption of his body were emphasised.[40] Such emphases, according to Mr McFarlane, were two of the characteristic features of the wills of some known Lollards as well as of several prominent men who appear to have been of impeccable orthodoxy.[41] The clause complements the evidence from Norwich about injunctions against funeral pomp,[42] regarded by McFarlane as the third characteristic of Lollard wills.[43]

Will of Geoffrey Chaumpneis[44]

In Dei nomine, Amen. Anno Domini millesimo CCCC^{mo} lxxi Sancti Gregorii in obitu ego, Galfridus Chaumpneis, ecclesie Sancti Stephani Norwic' vicarius, hominis utriusque sospitate fruens veluti, spem gero divine pietatis in visceribus. In Norwico predicto, mea in prelibata parochia, meam voluntatem ultimam conficio in hunc modum. Primo Trinitati individue, sicuti creatrici sue, animam meam flebilem qualiter plasma[45] suum commendo, miseracionis in signum inibi perpetuo collocandam. Corpus item putridum, quia[46] cinis est et in cineres convertibile, terra feculente vermibus esca fiat. Unde si mea dicta in parochia vel saltem prope, dummodo quadraginta non excesserit milia, me emori contigerit illic in cimiterio vel in ecclesia, prout melius videatur executoribus, delego sepulturam.

---

[39] See pp. 41 and 124-126.

[40] For other examples from Norwich, see: N.C.C., Reg. Ryxe, fol. 305r (Waller); Canterbury, Cathedral Archives and Library, Registers of the Dean and Chapter, Register F, fol. 154r (Catton or Calton).

[41] McFarlane, *Lancastrian Kings*, p. 210.

[42] See pp. 99-100.

[43] McFarlane, *Lancastrian Kings*, p. 210.

[44] N.C.C., Reg. Jekkys, fols. 275v-276r (Champeneys).

[45] "in visceribus in Norwico predicto" deleted in ms.

[46] "sicut" deleted in ms.

Item successori meo, quicumque fuerit, optimum superpelicium et totam ceream meam in cancello remanentem. Volo insuper pro me et parentibus meis et pro quibus teneor, ut sic pro eis coram Deo satisfaciam, si in aliquo eis indebitatus fuero, habere duos presbiteros seculares qui in ecclesia Sancti Stephani prelibata celebrent et instanter exorent. Quod ut diligencius faciatur, do eorum cuilibet viii marcas vi s. viii d. Quod si Dominus Nicholaus Gyldensleve et Dominus Johannes Dowe exequi voluerint, ipsos pre eligo universis. Item lego summo altari ecclesie Sancte Trinitatis x s. Item do Dompno Johanni Chaumpneys, fratri meo, xl s. et preculas meas de gete et nigrum epitogium meum cum capicio; et domino priori xii d.; et cuilibet monacho infra monasterium vel in suis cellis sive in universitate alterutra manenti v d.

Item domino meo priori de Chartrehous prope London do ii s., et cuilibet confratri suo xii d. Et domui eiusdem de Chartrehous do Liram meam super Novum Testamentum in duobus voluminibus,[47] ut ipsis promiseram, et Liram super Psalterium et Communem Glosam super Psalterium. Item patri meo priori de Syon, vulgariter vocat' Shene,[48] xii d., et cuilibet confratri suo iiii d. Item vicario de Crowmer xii d. Et si quid mihi debuerit, remitto ei. Ac sibi et successoribus suis do Rosarium in papiro, et cuilibet presbitero eiusdem ville iiii d. Item Willelmo Coye ii s. Item filiolo meo, filio carnificis, xii d. Item Johanni Abbot, si vixerit, ii s. Item emendacioni ecclesie vi s. viii d. Item emerentur pere vi s. viii d., et in distributione pauperum xl s. Item Collegio de Gunvyle do ad reparacionem necessariorum capelle vel librarie, ut illis magis indigere videatur, xl s., et cuilibet socio xii d. Item librarie eorum do meum Repyngton si ipsum non habuerint, quem si habuerint do eidem librum vel libros quem vel quos [non] habuerint equalis valoris, scilicet vi marcarum. Do interea librarie communi universitatis librum notabilem, scilicet Communem Glosam super Quinque Libros Sapienciales et Hugonem de Vienna in margine. Quem librum si quis vendicet et sufficienter probet esse suum, universitatem requiro coram Deo ut ipsum sibi liberent. Item do Magistro Stephano et sorori mee si quid undique debuerint pro persona mea, et do illis xx s. Item Johanni Brasyer, nepoti meo, primarium meum. Item Katerine Conyn' xx s. vel valorem, et clamidem meum et le blew cusshon et cathedram. Item amice mee de Beccles iii s. iiii d. Item cuilibet de consanguineis meis iiii d. Item do cuilibet confratri gilde Corporis Christi ad exequias meas et ad missam venientem, si licite venire valeat, iiii d. Item Domine Juliane xii d., et domui de Carhowe ii s.

Item Domino Roberto, recluso, ii s., et recluso fratrum Carmelitarum xii d. Item recluse in Conesford ii s., et cuilibet domui fratrum mendicancium iii s. iiii d. Item in distribucione pauperum parochie mee xl s. Item cuilibet lazaro ad port' eiusdem parochie iiii d. Item cuilibet lazaro ad alias portas ii d. Item cuilibet sorori de Normannis et semisorori ii d., et Domine Katerine eiusdem domus xii d. Item recluse in parochia Sancti Petri xii d.

---

[47] MS reads "volun't."
[48] See p. 125, n. 81.

Item Domino Johanni Spendlose iii s., et Domino Willelmo[49] ii s. Item Ricardo Gronger viii d. vel valorem. Item Waltero, famulo nostro, ii s. Item Johanni Berlburd iii s. iiii d. Item volo quod quilibet sacerdos mee parochie ad obitum meum habeat iiii d.; item equaliter ad diem septimum vel octavum, cum pro me exequatur, cuilibet virilis etatis homini ii s.; et cuilibet eiusdem parochie puero in suppelicio i d. Item do Domino Thome Skenen' meam Legendam Auream; item libellum quem emi de Domino Willelmo Balle, Credo Pacisiens';[50] item quaternum quem dedit michi Dominus Willelmus; item satisfecit mihi pro portiforio meo. Item do sibi tractatum versificand'. Et unam de dong' meis eliget, et pilium meum cum quo equito. Item do Magistro Johanni Palm' vi s. viii d. Item Magistro Stephano et uxori eius, sorori mee, le fedyrbed quem iam occupo et optimum par lintheamentorum meorum, coopertorium blodium cum appenden-ciis eiusdem lecti et tocius camere. Volo ut rector ecclesie Sancti Michaelis de Coslen' habeat cronicam meam, si velit equaliter dare sicut quiscumque alius, et tunc do sibi iii s. iiii d. Item Margar' Bryxy do par precularum, quondam Domini Rogeri, et xii d. Item Domino Thome Pern' le paxbrede. Item Henrico Gronger viridam superlectilem meam et par lintheamentorum et par lodicum iuxta discrecionem executorum meorum. Item do successori meo et successoribus suis magnam patellam. Item do Capelle de Campis magnam ollam eneam. Item domui hospitalis Sancti Egidii vi s. viii d., et cuilibet sorori et pauperi eiusdem domus i d.

Huius voluntatis ultime executores constituo et ordino Magistrum Stephanum Brasyer et Thomam Kyngesey, ut si quid mihi debuerint illis remitto, item Dominum Johannem Dowe et supervisorem Magistrum Ricardum Porynglond, quorum cuilibet do pro labore suo xiii s. iiii d. Si quid comparere velint predictus supervisor et executores mei de bonis meis, volo ut emant sicut conscientia dictat ita quod rem quam unus emat pecuniam aliis de suis sociis persolvat. Item volo quod omnia bona mea habita et debita post discessum meum, et pecunie que ex tunc pervenient de vendicione eorum, reponant in custodia dicti supervisoris mei ad terminum vite sue quousque per consensum eius et executorum meorum fuerint, iuxta voluntatem meam, disponend'. Et si contigerit aliqua bona mea vel debita mea post eius discessum relinqui indisposita, tunc volo quod per communem consensum executorum meorum in aliquo loco tuto serventur et disponantur. Item si, quod absit, bona[51] mea et debita non sufficiant ad disposicionem et execucionem voluntatis mee[52] predicte, tunc diminucionem et moderacionem legatorum meorum predictorum committo consciencie et discre-cioni supervisoris et executorum meorum, non obstante quovis iurato eorum facto vel faciendo pro adimplecione voluntatis mee predicte.

---

[49] "Th" deleted in ms.
[50] See p. 40.
[51] "et" deleted in ms.
[52] "presentis" deleted in ms.

E. JOHN BAKER, RECTOR OF ST JOHN'S MADDERMARKET AND OF ALL SAINTS OF BERSTREET, 1518

John Baker, his will and the inventory of his goods have already been discussed.[53]

Will of John Baker and Inventory of his Goods[54]

In the name of God, Amen. I, John Baker, clerk, in good and hole mynde beinge at Pulham Mawdelen the last day of August in the yere of Owre Lord God Mille CCCCC xviii[th] make my testamentt and last will in this forme fo'owing. First I commend my soull to almyghtti God, Owr Lady Seint Mary and to all the seynts in hevyn; my bodi to be buried as shall please to purvay for it in sume holy sentuary. Item I bequeith to the high altar of our moder church in Norwich ii s. Item I bequeith to the fraternitie of the prest' gilde in Norwiche v s. Item I bequeith to ich prest being a brother of the said gilde present being at my Dirige and Mase for me to [be] done of the same bretherne v d. Item I will that myn executors do kepe a Dirige with Mase in the Chappell of the Feld for the soule of Richard Baxter, prest, whan thei have convenient leysor; and the same to be donne accordinge to the will of the same Richarde. Also all the other legatts expressed in the said will or testamentt of the said Richarde Baxter I will thei be fulfillede as it may reise and growe of the payments of the obligation in the wich Master Robert Bell stondith bownde to me. Item I bequeith to the reparacyon of the fonnte in the church of Alderford xx s., and that to be paid as may ryse and come of the paymentts of the obligacion in the which William Phillippis, baxster, stondith bounde. Item I bequeith to the church of Alhalows in Bestrett in Norwich xxxiii s. iiii d. for to bye a cope therwith, and to be paid as it may be born of my goods. Item I will ther be disposide after tenor and legatts of the will of Jaffray Carter iii li. as in the same mor playnly apperith, and that to be donn and fulfilled as it may be leved of my goods in processe of tym. Also I will that myn executors doo call to theme one Andrew Gyllis, sherman of Norwich, to serche and seik the books of his maister. Item I bequeith to[55] my father and to my mother xxxiii s. iiii d. to be delyveryd to them as they nede itt. Item I bequethe to iche of my systers vi s. viii d. The residew of my goods I committe in too the handys of myn executores, whome I orden and make Sir Robert Cirlyng, person of Brokdishe, and John Alen' of Norwiche, hoser. And I geve to the same Sir Robert Cirlyng my lynyd gowne; and alsoo to iche of my sayd executores for their labores x s. Theis wittnes: Sir Robert Edwarde, preist, my gostly father, William Wattys and Thomas Brown, dwellyng in Pulham.

The inventary of all the goods moveable of Sir John Baker, preist, to hym apperteynyng and belongyng in tyme of his dethe apprisid the viii day of the

---

[53] See pp. 35-37 and 48.
[54] N.C.C., Reg. Gylys, fols. 181r-183v (Baker).
[55] "ich of my" deleted in MS.

monythe of[56] Septembyr in the yere of our Lord God Mille CCCCC xviii by Thomas Cony and John Norma' of the parishe of Sainte Petirs of Mancroft in Norwiche:

In primis a violet goun furride with calabre	v li.
Item a russett gown furyd with foxe	xl s.
Item a violett goun fured with shanks	xxx s.
Item a russett gown fured with blake lambe	xvi s.
Item a worsted cote furred parte with white lambe	viii s.
Item a hood furred with white lambe	v s.
Item a tipett furred with blak cony	xvi d.
Item a singell tipett of puyke	iiii d.
Item a doblet of satten old	ii s.
Item a lute with[57]	
Item a remanentt of new canvas	xv d.
Item a carpet	xx d.
Item a old coverlet	vi d.
Item a coverynge of taptri worke	vi s. viii d.
Item a fetherbede with a bolster of teike	viii s.
Item a donnge	iii s.
Item a coverlett of	xvi d.
Item a bolster of canvas with floke	iiii d.
Item ii old blanketts	xvi d.
Item a donge	viii d.
Item a tawny gown[58]	xiii s. iiii d.
Item ii paire of hoses	xiiii d.
Item ii shirtts	ii s.
Item a pillow of canvas	vi d.
Item a bolster of lether	ii d.
Item a old fetherbed with a bolster	vi s.
Item[59] ii blanketts	ii s.
Item a peire of shets	ii s. iiii d.
Item a old blankett	iiii d.
Item a doblet of worsted	xii d.
Item a parlot of damaske	iiii d.
Item ii shetts	ii s. iiii d.
Item a towell	ii d.
Item ii pillows	xvi d.
Item an old coverlett blew	xii d.

[56] "Octobir" deleted in MS.
[57] "none of his" in left-hand margin of MS alongside "Item a lute with."
[58] "yeven" in left-hand margin of MS alongside "Item a tawny gown."
[59] "a" deleted in MS.

Item iiii chofyns with eglis	ii s. iiii d.
Item a pare sleppers	vi d.
Item viii stenyde clothis	iiii s.
Item a Sentt John hed in alleblaster	xii d.
Item a lectarne cofer	vi d.
Item ii li. of wexe	xii d.
Item a brois	i d.
Item a cover of a maser with a knopp of silver	vi d.
Item a towell of playn cloth	xii d.
Item a diapre tabil clothe	xii d.
Item a large shete	ii s. iiii d.
Item iii peyre of shetes	iiii s.
Item ii wypyng towell and ii white cortens	xvi d.
Item ii playn tabill clothes	ii s. iiii d.
Item a diapre towell	xx d.
Item v playn napkyns	vi d.
Item a pyllough with ii beres	viii d.
Item a cheist a counte	xi s.
Item iiii bokys of Abbott	x s.
Item the Sext, Decretalles and Decreis	xii s. iiii d.
Item ii di' portuas	ii s.
Item a boke callyd W. de Speculat'	iiii s.
Item a boke, iiiª pars Speculi	iii s. iiii d.
Item a Bybill and Institutes	iii s. iiii d.
Item a boke callyd Sermones Discipuli	xx d.
Item a boke, Ortus Vocabulorum	xii d.
Item a boke, Vocabularius Iuris	xii d.
Item Legenda Aurea	xvi d.
Item iiii small boks: Casus Longi Bernardi, Sermones Vincencii, Sermones Parati, Sermones Dormii	xl d.
Item xx other small boks	iiii s.
Item Liber Preceptor'	xii d.
Item a litill falt tabyll	iiii d.[60]
Item iiii turned chayres	xvi d.
Item a bok, Modus Legend'	iiii d.
Item Sermones Magistri Fysher	iiii d.
Item a bok, Lynwod	v s.
Item a bok, Albertus Magnus	iiii d.
Item a olde cofer	iiii d.
Item ii sydes for bedd'	xii d.
Item a old chayre with ii formes	viii d.

[60] "xii d." deleted in MS.

Item ii peyre of trostoles	iiii d.
Item a stole with a peyre of bellons	iiii d.
Item xxiii peces of pewter of xxxvi pounde wheight	ix s.
Item a tryvet with chaynes	iiii d.
Item a chafyng dishe	viii d.
Item a stons and a payle	iii d.
Item a panne with a sterte	iiii d.
Item a mowse snache with a fyrefork	ii d.
Item a lache panne	iiii d.
Item a spete, a rake, a peyre tonges	xii d.
Item a hangyng rake	iiii d.
Item a sadill	xvi d.
Item xii tronchers	i d.
Item a almery	iiii d.
Item a olde cofer	iii d.
Item a awndiron	iiii d.
Item iii brokyn irons	ii d.
Item iii old brasse and laton`	ix s.
Item a maser parsell gylt	xii s.
Item iii spones xv unces	xlv s.
Item a dobylett of velvett	
Item a typett of velvett	
Item a shorte ridyng gowne	
Item a ridying hoode of cha`belet	
Item a sarcinet tipett	
Item a sadyll and a brydill	

F. William Setman, Mercer and Former Mayor, 1429;
John Terry, Merchant and Former Mayor, 1524;
Robert Jannys, Grocer and Former Mayor, 1530

Some points of interest in the wills of the three men have already been mentioned.[61] They are interesting examples of the wills of very prominent citizens. All three of them were very wealthy men as well as important figures in the city government. William Setman, a mercer, was bailiff of Norwich in 1402, sheriff in 1413, three times burgess in Parliament and mayor in 1421.[62] John Terry, a merchant, was sheriff of the city in 1514 and mayor in 1523.[63] Robert Jannys, a grocer, was sheriff in 1509 and mayor in 1517 and 1524.[64] The wills of

---

[61] For Setman's will, see p. 102, p. 123, nn. 67-69 and 71, p. 127, p. 131, n. 137, and pp. 135-136; for Terrry's will, see pp. 128 and 136-137; for Jannys's will, see pp. 98, 131 and 135-136.

[62] Hardy, *Mayors of Norwich*, pp. 18-19.

[63] Ibid., p. 45.

[64] Ibid., p. 42. See also, Pound, "Social Structure," p. 51.

all three men are highly individualistic and illustrate the extent to which wills could depend upon the personal wishes of testators rather than upon conventions dictated by the scribes or other persons who wrote the wills. It is interesting to compare their bequests.

William Setman left a total of about £350 and rents from two houses. He left twenty-five marks to his executors, some £20 to £30 to relatives, ten marks each to two of his servants, and about £90 and the rents from two houses in charitable bequests. The remaining £200 or so he left in bequests of a directly religious nature: about £100 for Masses, prayers and religious services; about £80 to religious houses; about £35 to parish churches and the parochial clergy; and about £5 to anchorites and their servants, to hermits and to one of the communities of women resembling beguinages.[65]

John Terry left about £1,300 and an unspecified amount of jewels, household furnishings, houses, tenements and lands. He was exceptional in that he left the bulk of his huge fortune in charitable bequests, namely about £868 and the money coming from the sale after his wife's death of the houses, tenements and lands.[66] In addition, he left £30 to his executors, £200 for seven years to a servant of his and £20 to a boy; and to his wife he left £200, plate worth £40, all his jewels and "stuffe of housholde" and the houses, tenements and lands for the duration of her life. Bequests of a directly religious nature came to little more than a tenth of the £1,300: that is to say rather more than £100 for the saying of Masses and prayers, £8 to religious houses, about £30 to parish churches and about ten shillings to anchorites.

Robert Jannys left bequests in cash worth over £2,700, a few bequests in kind and his house. He said, with amazing vagueness, that he wanted £800 to be disposed for his soul and all Christian souls during twenty years, and a further £40 was to be disposed by his executors on the first anniversary of his death. He left forty marks and four gowns to his executors, and to his wife a thousand marks and the house in which she lived for the duration of her life. To various relatives he left £20; and to his brother, who was a priest, he left up to £120 so that he might celebrate chantry services for his soul. He left a further £45 and three gowns to servants of his and to various lay people, and £20 for repairing the city's streets and walls. His charitable bequests totalled about £400 exclusive of a bequest to the city of as much money as would buy land yielding £8 a year, which was to be spent "for to discharge tolles and custumes in the faires and all the gates of the cytie of Norwiche." His religious bequests came to almost £600: that is to say over £420 for the saying of Masses and prayers, including the bequest to his brother and £200 for the foundation of a combined perpetual chantry and

---

[65] The slight discrepancies, here and below, between individual sums and the total sums are accounted for by a few bequests − such as those left to friars in the hope that they would say Masses − that fall under more than one of the categories mentioned. What is said on p. 220, n. 3, applies here too.

[66] See pp. 136-137.

grammar school; about £160 to religious houses; about £65 and two copes to parish churches and the parochial clergy; and about £20 and a tenement to anchorites.

Will of William Setman[67]

In Dei nomine, Amen. Ego, Willelmus Setman, civis Norwici, compos mentis die Conversionis Sancti Pauli Anno Domini millesimo CCCC^{mo} xxviii° condo testamentum meum in hunc modum. In primis lego animam meam omnipotenti Deo Beateque Virgini Marie, matri eiusdem, et omnibus angelis eius gerarchiam curie celestis quovismodo occupantibus; et corpus meum sepeliendum in ecclesia Sancti Petri de[68] Mancroft civitatis Norwici coram altari vocato Brondys awter.

Item lego summo altari eiusdem ecclesie xl s., et emendacioni sive reparacioni eiusdem ecclesie xxvi li. xiii s. iiii d. Item lego cuilibet capellano in Collegio Beate Marie comoranti, et exequiis meis interessenti, ii s. Item lego capellano parochiali dicte ecclesie Sancti Petri sacramenta ecclesiastica mihi conferenti iii s. iiii d.; et cuilibet capellano in dicta ecclesia et exequiis meis interessenti xii d.; et clerico parochiali eiusdem ecclesie ii s.; ac sacriste eiusdem ecclesie xii d. Item lego emendacioni parochialis ecclesie Sancti Egidii xl s. Item lego emendacioni hospitalis Sancti Egidii in Norwico xiii li. vi s. viii d.; et cuilibet debili sive decrepito ibidem ii s.; item Matilde Upgate ibidem converse xx s.; item cuilibet converse ibidem et apud Normannes, cuiusque status fuerit, ii s.

Item lego Dompne Juliane, anachorite de Carrowe, xx s.; et cuilibet servienti eiusdem Juliane xl d.; et Dompne Johanne, anachorite de Consford, xx s.; et utrique famularum eiusdem iii s. iiii d. Item lego cuilibet domui quatuor ordinum fratrum mendicancium in Norwico lxvi s. viii d. Item lego cuilibet leprosorum ad quascumque portas civitatis Norwici xii d. Et cuilibet heremitarum in Norwico lego xii d. Item lego cuilibet sorori quasi converse in parochia Sancti Swithuni iii s. iiii d. Item lego Richardo, heremite in parochia Sancti Egidii, xl s.

Item lego[69] priori ecclesie Sancte Trinitatis Norwici x s. Et cuilibet ibidem gerenti habitum monachalem lego ii s. Item lego cuilibet monacho Sancte Fidis vi d., et cuilibet canonico de Bokenham ii s., et reparacioni eiusdem prioratus de Bokenham xl s. Item lego cuilibet monialium de Carrowe, Bosyerd, Flyxton, Bungeye, Thetford, Denneye, Marram, Scholdham, Crawows, Camppeseye, Cawnbregge, Swaffham in comitatu Cantabrigie et Redyngfeld in comitatu Suff' et Blakberwe ii s. Item lego ad sustentacionem Johannis, fratris mei, per manus executorum meorum disponend' vi li. xiii s. iiii d. Item lego cuilibet consanguineorum meorum in secundo gradu consanguinitatis a me distancium xx s. Item lego emendacioni librorum et aliorum ornamentorum in ecclesia de Skottowe magis necessariorum lxvi s. viii d. Item lego Johanni Cok, servienti meo, vi li.

---

[67] N.C.C., Reg. Surflete, fols. 124v-125v (Setman).
[68] "Mans" deleted in MS.
[69] "cuilibet monialium," with a line immediately above and another immediately below, follows "lego" in MS.

xiii s. iiii d. Item lego Emme, famule mee, vi li. xiii s. iiii d. Item lego Roberto Setman, filio Roberti Setman, vi li. xiii s. iiii d. Item lego Domine Alicie Blakeneye, moniali de Brosyerd, xx s.

Item lego cooperture cancelle ecclesie collegiate Beate Marie in Campis Norwici cum plumbo cooperiende xx li., condicione et forma subsequentibus: videlicet si decanus et canonici ibidem qui nunc sunt et qui in eventum erunt singuli per se in sua admissione corporale prestiterint iuramentum quod statim post mortem meam naturalem obitum meum in suo mortilegio, et nomen meum in libro dominicali in quo nomina defunctorum die Dominica recitantur,[70] cum effectu inserant et inscribant ipsumque obitum annuatim observent, et quod cantariam meam ibidem per me factam fideliter observabunt et facient observari futuris temporibus perpetuo duratur'.

Item volo quod statim post obitum meum distribuantur inter pauperes magis egentes in civitate Norwici et aliis villis circumadiacentibus xx li. Item volo quod inter pauperes et presertim claudos, cecos vel notabiliter debiles in civitate Norwici continue commorantes per tres annos continuos[71] proximos post obitum meum distribuantur xl li. sub hac forma, videlicet quod quelibet persona claudorum, cecorum sive debilium precedencium habeat septimanatim iii d. Item volo quod adstatim post obitum meum distribuantur inter pauperes magis egentes in villis de Skottowe, Lamesse, Cowteshale, Ryston, Slolee, Worstede, Swantone, Walsham, Skeyton, Totyngtone, Horstede, Holbesse Magna et Parva et Westwyk xxvi li. xiii s. iiii d.

Item volo quod septem celebrent sacerdotes per unum annum integrum in ecclesia Sancti Petri de Mancroft, si comode fieri poterit, alioquin successive quousque summa xl librarum de bonis meis plenarie persolvatur. Item volo quod prior de Scholdham, qualiscumque pro tempore fuerit, habeat de bonis meis post obitum meum xx li. sub ista condicione: videlicet quod si executoribus meis faciat securitatem sufficientem quod annuatim solvet seu solvi faciat Margarete et Margarete Page, monialibus sive conversis eiusdem domus, equaliter x s. quousque dicta summa xx li. plenarie fuerit persoluta, tunc presens legatum in suo robore permaneat vigore et effectu, alioquin in pios usus distribuatur[72] secundum discrecionem executorum meorum. Item volo quod Alicia Colman, leprosa, habeat de bonis meis per annum quamdiu vixerit vi s. viii d.

Item volo quod tractetur cum magistro de Ivy Halle, nuper vocat' le hospital in Conysford in Norwico, si magister qui pro tempore fuerit velit subire et cum effectu observare onus antiquum dicto hospitali impositum, quod tunc redditus ex antiquo proveniens de duabus domibus, quarum una situatur ad finem venelle que ducit ad ecclesiam Collegii Beate Marie ex parte boriali et alia domus nuper Johannis Spycer in Ou'nenport in Norwico, restituatur hospitali predicto.

---

[70] "et recitaverint" follows "recitantur" in MS.
[71] "prios" deleted in MS.
[72] "scdi'u" deleted in MS.

Item volo quod de bonis meis inveniatur unus cereus continue ardens die nocteque coram corpore Christi in cancella ecclesie Beati Petri de Mancroft predicta imperpetuum. Item volo quod statim post obitum meum celebrentur pro anima mea et animabus omnium quibus teneor iiii millia missarum.

Residuum vero bonorum meorum[73] mobilium legata mea predicta excedens, ac omnia terre et tenementa mea cum pertinenciis suis infra civitatem Norwici et extra ubicumque iacentia, lego executoribus meis ad vendendum et distribuendum simul[74] cum aliis bonis meis supra non legatis pauperibus: videlicet cecis, claudis, paraliticis, languentibus in lectis, decrepitis, leprosis, viduis, orphanis et aliis egenis maiorem necessitatem habentibus secundum discrecionem executorum meorum. Quos rogo et in quantum possum exortor in visceribus Jhu' Christi, ex consciencias coram summo judice onorando, quod omnia predicta fiant modo et forma supradicta secundum quod viderint magis Deo placere et anime mee ac animabus omnium benefactorum meorum et omnium fidelium defunctorum expedire.

Huius autem testamenti mei executores Magistrum Thomam Ryngstede, decanum collegii Beate Marie de Campis in Norwico, Dominum Rogerum Prat, magistrum hospitalis Sancti Egidii de Norwico, Dominum Edwardum Hu'tte, Dominum Johannem Bokebynder, clericos, ac Willelmum Zymme, civem Norwici, ordino et constituo per presentes. Volo eciam quod Ricardus, heremita nuper manens ad portas Sancti Egidii, sit intendens et adiutor executoribus meis, maxime in distribucione elemosinarum et in aliis agendis. Cuilibet executorum meorum administracionem huius testamenti mei accipienti lego pro labore suo v marcas. Item lego predicto Ricardo, heremite, pro labore suo secundum discrecionem executorum meorum. In cuius rei testimonium huic presenti testamento meo sigillum meum apposui. Dat' apud Norwicum die et anno supradictis.

Will of John Terry[75]

In Dei nomine, Amen. The xxx[ti] day of December in the yere of our Lord God a thousande fyve hundred and xxiiii, I, John Terry of Norwich, merchaunt, in my parfite and constant mynde, lawd and thanks be to almighty God, make this my present testament conteynyng my true and last will in the forme and condicion folowing. First I commende my soule to my savyor and maker, Lord God omnipotent, Jesu Criste, and his moder mylde Mary, Saint John Baptist, myn advowy, and to all the celestiall company of hevyn. My body to be cadaver, yf it fortune me to depart this wrecched worlde within Norwich, to be buried within the chapell of Saint John Baptist called Mathermerket in Norwich aforsaid, or ells where it shall pleas God to provide for the same.

---

[73] "mobl" deleted in MS.
[74] "cum aliis bonis meis" deleted in MS.
[75] PROB/11/12 (Reg. Bodfelde, 1523-1525), fol. 29 (Terry).

To whose high awter, for my tithes necligently forgotten and witholden, I bequeth xl s. Item I bequeth to the same churche of Saint John Baptist a crosse of silver and gilt to the summe and value of fourty marcs; and also towarde the makyng of a frame for an hersse to the sepulcre, for to sett tapers upon, whansoever the parish mynde and entende to endever themself to do make the same, xl s. Item I bequeth to ech house of the four orders of freres in Norwiche, that is to sey Prechours, Mynors, Augustynes and Carmelites, xl s. Item I bequeth to every parsone beyng anchor or anchores within Norwich xx d. Item I bequeth to every and singuler hoole suster beyng in the place of Normans viii d., and to every half suster of the same place xii d. Item I bequeth to every and singular house of lazers about the gates at Norwich vi d. Item I woll have a secular prest to synge and serve for me and my frends in the churche of Saint John Baptist aforsaid by the space and tyme of twenty yeres next and immediately after my deth. Item I bequeth to the reparacion of the church of Saint Petir in the market in Norwich x s. Item to the sustentacion of the masse of Jesu in the same church xx d.

Item I bequeth and will thre hundred marcs of my goods in corant money of Inglond be by my executours delivered unto suche indigent and nedefull persones as merchaunts, craftmen or other occupiers or artificers, citizenis being of the said citie of Norwich, as they in the tyme of their life thinke and mynde best in maner and fourme, use and condicion folowyng. That is to sey and to be understande, yf any yong man, merchaunt, artificer and craftisman beyng of the said citie of Norwiche, nede havyng and indigent beyng of comforte, helpe, releve or ayde of worldly substaunce as money and coyne at his nede and necessitie to be releved, socored and holpen, I woll he shal have of the said thre hundred marcs for his releve, mayntenannce and comforte suche summe or summes of money as shal be by my said executours their lyves or lyve during and after their decesse by maister mayor and two justices of peax of the said citie ever after perpetuall in tyme to come and for tyme beyng thought convenient, requisite and oportune to suche parsone or parsones to enjoye, exercise and occupie to their own propre and singuler use, commoditie and profite so as long tyme daies and yeres as the forsaid myn executors lyving, or maister mayer and ii justice of peace tyme after beyng, will assigne and limite; so it be not over and above the tyme, space and terme of thre yeres but he or they the said citezenis suche summe or summes of money of the said thre hundred marcs so having and occupying, those same summes by them so taken and receyved unto my said executours lyving, or after their deth maister mayor and two justice of peax than beyng, in good corant golde of Inglond shall repaye, deliver and content without delacion, collusion or delaye; provided alway that suche persones having and procuryng suche summes of money for his releve, helpe and comforte shall not have of the said thre hundred marcs over and above the sume of fourty pounds; and over that the same parson or parsones citizenis before the tyme of the havinge or receyving of the said summes of the said money with sufficient suertie in writing obligatory after the course and fourme of the king' lawe to be bounde unto my said executours their lyves enduring and after deceas to the mayor and two justice of peas of the said citie ever after in tyme comyng and than beyng as shal be thought able and sufficient for suche summes of money to be repaide and delivered agayn at suche day and dayes as by them above named shal be limited, ordred and assigned.

Item I woll that my servant, Robert Rugge, have delivered him after my deceas two hundred pounds in money or to the value in good wares, he therunto agreable and consenting, the same to enjoye and exercise and occupie to his propre advantage and profite by the terme and space of sevyn yeres next and immediatly folowing my deceas; first leying in unto the within named John Marsham [and] John Curat sufficient and goode suertie for the repayment of the same as shal be by the said John and John thought to the king' lawe according and requisite; and thies yeres complete and passed, finisshed and ended, the said Robert Rugge to redeliver and repaye the said two hundred pounds or like moche in good and corant money of Englonde unto the said John Marsham and John Curat, or to either of theym than lyving, within two yeres next and immediatly folowyng and ensuyng in maner and forme as afterward doth appere, that is to sey oon hundred pounde by yere unto the said two hundred pounds be paide; and than myn executours to dispoase the same in dedes of charitie and pitie for the helth of my soule and my frends soules as they shall thinke most pleasure to God and profite to my soule.

Item I woll that at my buriall day be expended in dedes of charitie oon hundred marcs at the leest; and so yerely at my memoriall day called yere day every and singuler yere during the tyme and space of ten yeres next and immediatly after my deth twenty pounds.

Item I bequeth to Letyce, my wife, thre hundred marcs of good corant and redy money immediatly after my decesse, to be delivered with fourty pounds worth of plate, suche as she shall think best and necessary for her, and all my juells, ryng, owches and cheynes and all apparell bilonging to hir body in any wise. Item I bequeth to the same Letice, my wife, all and singuler my stuffe of housholde, to occupie and enjoye to th use of this my will and testament; that is to sey she shall not at any tyme yeve nor bequeth suche stuffe of housholde as is to hir by me bequethed to any persone or persones but unto such as were to me tyme of my lyfe loving, frendfull and kynde; for yf she doo, I will her bequest be noo bequest but that stuffe by hir so bequethed and gevyn to be solde by myn executours or the executours of myn executours longest lyving. Item I woll my said wife, Letice, have, enjoye, occupie and exercise during tyme, space and terme of hir lyfe naturall all suche houses, tenements and lands free and bonde of myn in Norwich or without to hir propre use and profite; fynding and keping due, necessary and nedefull reparacions upon the same the tyme and terme above written. And after the decesse of my said wife out of this wrecched worlde, or in the meanetyme during hir lyfe, as it shal be thought moost expedient and requisite by myn executours, my said wif interest and title as is[76] above said during the terme and

---

[76] MS reads "it."

tyme above written alway reserved and excepted, the said houses, tenements and lands above specified I woll shal be solde and the money therof comyng doon in dedes of charite by my said executours or the executours of them longest lyving after their discrecion and wisdom.

Item I require, desire and exorte all my cofeoffees in the honor and in the wounds of our savyor, Jesu Crist, to yeve and deliver state and seasor laufull, as shal be thought by lerned counsell good and nedefull, to myn executours to th use of this my testament and last will at all tymes whan they or any of theym shal be therunto required and desired.

Item I bequeth to Ranf Sponer xx li. whan he come to th age of xviii yeres. And yf he dye or departe afore he come to that age, I woll the same xx li. be dispoased after the discrecions of myn executours or th executors of them lengest lyving.

Item I woll there be bought by myn executours as moch landes or rents in Saint Peters parishe in the market, or ells nygh unto the same, as may be possible obteyned and procured to the summe and value of thre hundred marcs at the lest. And that lands, tenements or rents so bought to be orderd and sett in fourme, in condicion yf the king' lawe woll therto permitte, for to bere, acquite and discharge the pour people of the said citie of Norwich of and upon the king' taxes and talages whansoever it be layde upon them within the said citie as farr as the rents, fermes and money receyved of the said lands and rents woll extende and surmount. And yf it cannot be brought aboute by councell lerned without the dannger of the king' lawes, than I woll the said lands, renters and tenements be solde by myn executours lyving, or by th executours of him myn executor lengest lyving, and the money therof comyng to be dispoased for my soule after their discrecions and wisdoms.

The residue of all my goodes not bequethed I will be ordred and rewled as it shall please myn executours, whom I ordeyn, constitute and make of this my present testament John Marsham of Norwiche, alderman, John Curat, notary, and Robert Rugg, my servant, or th executors of my said executors lengest lyving, to order and to rewle. To the which my said executours I bequeth thyrty pounds, that is to say to eche of them tenne pounds, and all their costs, charges and expenses of them and any of them doon and expended or to be doon and expended in any parte or in hool executing and fulfilling this my present testament and last will after their own good mynde and discrecion ever to be doon and expended; provided alwey and ever to be noted that if goods, detts and catalls that comyth to my said executours hands or shall come will not amount and extende to the summe or summes for to fully discharge and fulfill this my testament and last will in legates and bequests in every poynte and parte in the same, I will then my said executours defalcat and dymynishe the same my said legates and bequests after their discrecions and wisdoms, and to fulfil the residue after the quantitie after their receyts as will answere at the day of jugement.

Present at the making of this my testament and last will, and to the reding and repeting of the same therunto speciallye required, Richard Gryme of Norwich, inholder, and Robert Goye of the same, fishemonger.

Will of Robert Jannys[77]

In the name of God, Amen. The xx[ti] day of Apryll, the yere of owr Lorde mill` v[c] xxx[ty], I, Robert Jannys, cytyzen and alderman of Norwich, in my good and hole mynde, God be lauded, make my testament and last will in manir and forme following; and all other willes that I have made to be voyde and frustrat and of none effect, and this to be my last will and testament. First I bequeth my soule to allmighty God, my maker and creatour, and to our Blessid Lady Saint Marye, his blessid mother, and to all the blessid company of hevin; and my body to be buried in the chaunsell of Saint George in Norwiche aforesaid, before Saint George, my advoury aforesaid.

To the whiche high aulter for my tithes negligently forgottyn and not trewly content and paied I bequeth five pounds. Item I will and instantly require myn executors before all things that my bodye be buried, all necessaries had and don aboute the same, than that they trewly content and pay all my debts and recompense all wrongs, mysseprysonments [and] myssreconyngs by me doon, yf anny be provydid, before my legacies be fulfillid. I will restitucion be made to the uttermost. Also I bequeth to th onour of God and to the churche of Saint George a new redd coope of tyssew very lyke to the best cope. Also I bequeth to the said churche a newe white coope as good as the best white coope or better. Item I will have at my burying day vii solempe diriges, that is to say at Christ Churche and at the Chappell of the Feld, at th ospital of Sainte Gyle and at the iiii ordres of freres. Item I give unto the priour of Christe Churche iii s. iiii d., and to every monke being preest viii d., and to every novis iiii d. Item I give to the master of the Chappell of Feld, yf he be at dirige, xx d.; and to every preest viii d.; and to every clerke of the same place ii d. Item I give to the master of th ospital xx d., and to every preest viii d., and to every clerke and child ii d. And in every of the saide places the morning aftir masse of Requiem and allso to be offrid at every of the said masses, eche place vii d., by oon of myn executors or their assignes. Item I give to the iiii ordres of freres, every priour and doctour xii d., and to every preest iiii d., and to every novis ii d. And I will that every of the said ordres of freres sing a masse of Requiem as is aforesaid, and there to be offerid in every place vii d. Item I will have at my buriall C masses, and to every preest that saithe the said masses iiii d.

Item I give at my burying day to blynde, lame and sore with bedred within the cytie and at every gate abowte Norwich, to the susters of Normans, to every prysonier in the Castell and the Guyld Hall, to every oon of thes iiii d. Item I will that ther be delt at my burying day to every personne that will take allmes within their paroch i d. to pray for my soule and all Christen soules. Item I will there be given for me at my buryall day to xl poore men and women xl gownes lynyd and made. Item I will have every warking day next after my burying during xxx days a dirige over night and masse of Requiem the next day in the parisshe of Sainte

---

[77] PROB/11/24 (Reg. Thower, 1531-1533), fol. 1 (Jannys).

George aforesaid. That is to say I will have iiii secular preests and iiii freres, of eche place of religion oon. For the whiche I give to them iiii d.; and to the clerke and sexten for their labours, eche of them iiii d.; and to ii children i d. a pece. Item I will ther shal be given at my xxx day to every paroche within Norwiche a certeyne to poore creatures that hathe most nede and lest helpe, as it shal be thought nedefull by myn executours. Item I will have given at my xxx day xl gownes to poore men and women. Item I will that my executors shall give every weke to lxxx poore folke, men and women, i d. a pece of them every Fridaye during the space of xx^{ty} yeres.

Item I will have a dirige at the nonnes of Carow; and I will that the priores have xii d., and every nonne iiii d. and every suster iiii d., and every preest iiii d., and a masse of Requiem the next day. Item I will have a dirige and a masse at th abbey of Saint Faithes. And I will the prior have xii d., and every monke and preest iiii d., and every novis ii d. Item I give to the saide abbey of Saint Faithes v li. to pray for my soule, my frends and all Christen soules.

Item I give to eche of the places of the iiii ordres of freres within Norwiche to the reparacion of the said houses xii li. to be paid to them under this manier: that is to say, at my buryall day xl s. to eche place, and so forthe yerely xl s. a yere to eche of them tyll the sum aforesaid be fully content and paied; and they to pray for my soule and all Christen soules. Item I will that myn executours shall assigne at eche of the saide ordres of freres a good and wel disposed frere to syng yerely for me by the space of v yeres, and he to have for his stipend iiii marks to pray for me and my frends.

Item I will have an honest preest and a good quere man to syng and pray for me and my frends and them that I am bound to pray for in the church of Saint George by the space of xx yere, and he to have for his stipend ix marks. Item I will that my brother, Sir Thomas Jannis, have the service before expressid, that is to say to be song in Saynt Georg paroch, where I do dwell, for the terme before expressid, yf he live so long, so that he will resigne his benefice, or els not, and that doon I will he syng the terme expressid before.

Item I will have given and dispoasid at my twelve moneth day xl li. by the discretion of myn executors. Item I give bothe to the Castell and Gild Hall x s. a yere by the space of xx^{ti} yeres. Item I will that my executors shall dispose for my soule and all Christen soules every yere during xx yeres the sum of xl li.

Item I will that my executors shall purchase iii C marks worth of land, or as moche land as is worthe x li. by yere, for a preests service to sing for me and my frends in the churche of Aylesham, wher I was borne; and the forsaid preest to syng and kepe a free grammer scole within Aylesham foresaid; the saide preest to take no wages of no man nor scole hier of no scoller nor noon of his frends nor of non other man, but freely to give to the said scollers their learning; and the said master to exorte his scollers to say De Profundis for the soule of me, the said Robert Jannis, and my frends ones a daye; provided allwey that if the saide master take anny wagis or scole hier of anny scoller or any other man, that then the said scole master so provyd to restore the said partie or partes doble the valour of the som so takyn. Allso I will that the saide preest shal be at the nominacion and assignement of myn executours, and after the decease of the longest lyver of myn executours then I will that the said preest shal be at the nominacyon of the vicar of the towne, the bayly churchewardes and iiii of the substauncyall men of the towne of Aylesham aforesaid.

Item I will have in the paroche church of Sainte George, where as my bodye shal be buried, iiii quarters diriges, that is to say every quarter oon, and that they shal be lyke in every condicyon according as th other xxx diriges afore expressid, videlicet xxx. And I will have xii poore men at every quarter diriges, and I will that they shal have i d. a pece. Item I will have the next day after every of thes quarters diriges a masse of Requiem song for all thos personnes that wer present at dirige. Item I will that oon of the churche wardens shall offer for me and all Christen soules i d., and I will that he shall have for his labour iiii d. at eche of the quarters diriges before rehersid. Item I bequeth to the reparacions of the churche of Saint George iii s. iiii d. by yere during the space of xx yere. Item I give to the paroche preest of the said paroche for a certeyne iii s. iiii d. for xx yeres. Item to the clerk' wages of the said paroche iii s. iiii d. by yere by the space of xx^{ti} yere. Item to the light in the saide paroche churche iii s. iiii d. by the space of xx yeres. Item I give to every parisshe church within Norwich vi s. viii d. a pece. Item I give and bequeth to the churche of Saint Andrew in Norwiche towards the making of the high aulter tenne pounds. Item to the reparacions of Sainte Olaves chappell x s.

Item I will that my executours shall purchase as moche lands as shall amount to the yerely valewe of eyght pounds or better for the cytye of Norwiche for to discharge tolles and custumes in the faires and all the gates of the cytie of Norwiche aforesaid.

Item I will that Margarett, my wyfe, shall have my place that I dwell in, the whiche is callid the ii Rammes, for terme of her lyf, yf she kepe her sole unmaryed; and yf she, the said Margaret, be maryed, then I will that the said place be sold by myn executours imediatly after her mariage, and the mony of the payments therof to be dispoasid in almes and in deds of charitie for my soule, my wyfs soule and all my frends soules; provydid allwey that myn executours shall have free ingate and owtgate to and froo within the said place at all tymes for to accomplisshe and fulfill all suche things and busines concerning my testament withowt any contradiction, disturbaunce or lett of the said Margaret or anny other in her name. And yf the saied Margarete, my wyf, will not doe suffir[78] my executours to have free ingate and outgate to and fro at all tymes for reparacions of the saied place or otherwise, then I will the said Margaret, my wyf, shal be dispossessid of the said place by myn executours for ever. Item I give and bequeth to the said Margarete, my wyf, oon thowsand marks, that is to say in mony, plate, stuff of howshold and merchauntdises, as it shal be praysid by indifferent

---

[78] MS reads "suffic."

personnes, to be paied within oon yere next after my decease. Item I give and bequethe to the said Margaret, my wyf, all her morning clothes.

Item to the reparacions of the towne wales within the warde that I am allderman of x li. to be expendid by myn executours. Item I give to the paving of the streets within the said warde wher as most nede ys x li. to be dispendid by myn executours.

Item I give to Cycely Lege, my nece, v li; and a gowne clothe for her husband; and another for her. Item I give to John Tracye five pounds. Item to Robert Gray, sometyme my servant, v li. Item to Henry Bacon, my servant, three pounds. Item to Richard Goodwyn, my servant, xl s. Item to Alice Calle, my mayde, xl s. Item to Ele Smyth, my maide, xx s. Item I bequeth to Cycely Sebett, my mayde, xx s. Item to Robert Mundis xl s. Item to Robert Gates xl s. Item to Anthony Waren xl s. Item to Ranf Austen xl s. Item to John Hall, sherman, xl s. Item to Thomas Burley xl s. Item to Thomas Warde xl s. Item to Andrew Giles xx s. Item to Robert Day, sherman, xx s. Item to John Apariche v li. and a gowne clothe. Item I give to Thomas Basley xl s. and a gowne clothe. Item I give to John Petchet, loder, xl s. and a gowne clothe. Item I will that other of my custumers shal have, eche of them, a gowne cloth such as myn eexecutours shall appoynt.

Item I give to Katherynne Manne, the anchores at the Blacke Freires, for terme of her lyf a tenement in Sainte Georg' paroch that Robert Gat' dwellith in; and the said Katheryn to bere all reparacions, rents and charges of the said tenement by all the terme aforesaid; and after the decease of the said Katheryn I will the said tenement be sold by myn executours to the performaunce of this my last will.

Item I will that all my mese and tenements in Saynt Marys parisshe of Coslany, and all my meses and tenements in Saynt Georg' parrishe of Muspole, and my mese and tenements in Saynt[79] Martyns at th Oke, item I will that all thos my meases and tenements aforesaid, and all other elswhere within the cytye or countrye, be sold by myn executours to the performaunce of this my testament and last will. Item I requyre and charge all my cofeoffes that be enfeoffed in anny parcell of lands or tenements within the cytye or countrey that they delyver a sufficyaunt and laufull astate of and in all the sayde lands and tenements at all tymes or seasons when they shal be requyred by myn executours to th use of this my last will.

Item I bequeth to every ancre and ancres within Norwiche xiii d. a quarter the space of xx yeres. Item I bequeth to John Jannys of Aylesham, my brother, tenne pounds and a gowne clothe for hym and a gowne cloth for his wyf. Item to eche of his doughters xx s. Item I will that my apparrell, plate, stuff of houshold and my other wares and merchaundyses be sold by myn executours. Item I give to maydens mariages xx li., xx s. a pece. Item to every oon of my godchildren ii s. a pece. Item I bequethe to Sir Henry Faier, parisshe preest of Saint George, xvi li. to be payde viii marks by yere till the sum of xvi li. be full content and payed.

---

[79] MS reads "Faynt."

Item I will that yf anny of my executours do expend or geve anny money or be at anny mans coste and charges or losse of tyme for th execution of this my last will and testament, I graunt and will that they be alowid every penny of my good, rather more then lesse.

The residew of all my goods, lands and tenements not before bequetheid nor assignid I put them unto the disposicion of my executours, whome I ordeyne and make Nicolas Sywhat, Edmund Wood, Willyam Rogers and John Trase. And I give to eche of them for their labour x marks and a gowne, that my executours see my debts and legates fulfillid and paied to the most pleasur of God and proffyt of my sowle. Moreover I ordeyne and make of this my present testament and last will my surpervisour John Jannys, my brother. And I will that my executours shall accompt before my said supervisor every yere the weke after Easter, and that the said supervisor shal have knowlege of th accompte iiii weks before the day of th accompt, and that he shal be alowid his reasonable expenses by myn executours. By me, Robert Jannis. Hiis testibus: per me, Willelmum Buckingham, clericum; per me, Johannem Whiteacres, clericum; per me, Henricum Faire, confessorem et curatum predicti Roberti testatoris; per me, Dominum Willelmum Thompson.

Bibliography

A. Manuscript Sources

Canterbury, Cathedral Archives and Library, Registers of the Dean and Chapter, Register F (*Sede Vacante* wills).

London, British Museum, MS Cotton, Cleopatra E. V., fol. 389r-v / old fol. 360r-v (Letter of Bishop Nykke of Norwich).

London, Lambeth Palace Library, Registers of archbishops of Canterbury, Reg. Islip (1349-1366), Reg. Whittlesey (1368-1374), Reg. Arundel 1 and 2 (1396-1414), Reg. Stafford and Kempe (1443-1454) and Reg. Morton 2 (1486-1500).

London, Public Record Office, E.179/45/8 and 11 (Assessments of the clergy in Norwich diocese *temp.* Richard II).

    E.315/67 (Particulars for the sale of colleges and chantries *temp.* Henry VIII and Edward VI), fol. 647v.

    E.315/68 (Particulars for the sale of colleges and chantries *temp.* Henry VIII and Edward VI), fol. 325v.

    PROB/11 (Registered copies of wills proved in the Prerogative Court of Canterbury) /1 (Reg. Rous, 1384-1452) to /24 (Reg. Thower, 1531-1533).

Norwich, Norfolk Record Office, Colman MS 115 (Taxation of the Religious within Norfolk, 1428).

    Dean and Chapter Muniments, Box "Acta et Comperta," Rolls 1, 1a, 3, 4, 6 and 8-10 (Visitations of parishes in Norwich within the Peculiar Jurisdiction of the Cathedral Priory of Norwich, 1416-1437).

    Box "Chantries," no. 1835.

    Box "Disputes and Agreements, v Carrow, v Carmelites," nos. 939, 1582-1584, 1590, 1595, 1898, 2418, 3859, 3866 and 4081-4083.

    Box "Disputes, Ecclesiastical Courts, Norwich," nos. 573, 956, 4089 and 4124.

    Box "Papal and Archiepiscopal," no. 2388 (Churches belonging to Norwich Cathedral Priory, 1411).

    Obedientiary Rolls, nos. 210-335 (Sacrist), 1105a and 1134 (Communar and Pitancer), and 1398-1404 (Hospital of St Paul).

    Registered copies of wills proved in the court of the Dean and Chapter (then the Prior and Convent) of Norwich, Reg. 1444-1455, Reg. 1461-1559 and Reg. 1500-1530.

    Norwich City Records, Cases 1c-1d, Court Rolls 19 (1461-1483) and 20 (1483-1508).

Cases 3g-4b, Private Deeds, Box 1, "Friars Preachers in St Andrew," Box 5, "Friars Preachers in St Clement," Box 7, "Chapel Field College," Box 10, "St James" and "St John Maddermarket," Box 11, "St Mary Unbrent," and Box 12, "St Peter Hungate."

Case 8a, Presentments of Assault 1439-1441.

Case 8d, Rolls of the City Assembly, Roll 39-42 Edward III, Roll 46-47 Edward III, Roll 47 Edward III, and Roll 8 Richard II.

Cases 8e-8f, Account Rolls of the Guild of St George, 1420/1 to 1546/7.

Case 16c, Assembly Minute Books, 1 (1492-1510) and 2 (1510-1550).

Case 16d, Proceedings of the Municipal Assembly, Book 1 (1434-1491) and 2 (1491-1553).

Case 17b, Book of Pleas.

Case 17b, Domesday Book.

Case 17b, Liber Albus.

Case 17d, First Book of Worsted Weavers (1492-1504).

Case 18a, Chamberlains' Accounts, Book 2 (1470-1490).

Case 24a, Great Hospital Account Rolls, 1319/20, 1396/7, and "General" 1478/9.

Case 24b, "Writings relating to St Giles Hospital," nos. 52 and 66.

Norwich Diocesan Archives, ACT (Consistory Court Act Books) /1, Book 1 (1508-1512).

ORR (Registers of Ordinations) /1 (1531-1561).

REG (Bishop's Registers) /1, Book 1 (1299-1325) to /11, Book 17 (1536-1549), and /30 (Tanner's Index, Vol. 1).

Probate Records, Registered copies of wills proved in the Archdeacon of Norwich's Court, Reg. Fuller *alias* Roper (1469-1503) to Reg. Tarye (1519-1535).

Registered copies of wills proved in the Norwich Consistory Court, Reg. Heydon (1370-1383) to Reg. Wellman (1548-1550).

Oxford, Bodleian Library, MS Bodley 73, fol. 51v (Persons buried in the Carmelite Friary in Norwich).

MS Norfolk, Roll 18 (Visitation of Norwich Deanery in 1333).

MS Tanner 100, fols. 40r-42v (Bishop Goldwell's visitation of Norwich in 1492).

B. PRINTED WORKS

i. Primary Sources

Ancrene Riwle. Edited by Eric J. Dobson. Early English Text Society, vol. 267. London, 1972.

Andreas, Bernard. *Historia regis Henrici septimi*. Edited by James Gairdner. Rolls Series. London, 1858.

Bale, John. *Scriptorum illustrium maioris Brytannie catalogus*. Basle, 1557.

Benedict of Nursia, Saint. *Regula*. Edited by Cuthbert Butler. Sancti Benedicti Regula Monasteriorum, 2nd ed. Fribourg, 1927.

Calendar of Entries in the Papal Registers relating to Great Britain and Ireland, Papal Letters. Edited by William H. Bliss and Jesse A. Twemlow. London: Her Majesty's Stationery Office, 1893-.

Calendar of the Close Rolls Preserved in the Public Record Office. London: Her Majesty's Stationary Office, 1892-.

Calendar of the Patent Rolls Preserved in the Public Record Office. London: Her Majesty's Stationary Office, 1893-.

Calendar of Wills Proved and Enrolled in the Court of Hustings, London, A.D. 1258-A.D. 1688. Edited by Reginald R. Sharpe. 2 vols. London, 1889-1890.

The Charters of Norwich Cathedral Priory, Part One. Edited by Barbara Dodwell. Pipe Rolls Society, new series, 40. London, 1974.

Chaucer, Geoffrey. *The Canterbury Tales.* Edited by Frederick N. Robinson. The Works of Geoffrey Chaucer, 2nd ed. Oxford: Oxford University Press, 1977.

"Chronological Memoranda touching the City of Norwich." Edited by Goddard Johnson. *Norfolk Archaeology* 1 (1847) 139-166.

"The Constitution of the Hospital of St Paul (Normanspitel) in Norwich." Edited by Edward H. Carter. *Norfolk Archaeology* 25 (1933-1935) 342-353.

Corpus iuris canonici. Edited by Emil Friedberg. 2 vols. Leipzig, 1879-1881.

Councils and Synods. Edited by Frederick M. Powicke and Christopher R. Cheney. 2 vols. Oxford: Clarendon Press, 1964.

"Day-Book of John Dorne." Edited by Falconer Madan. Oxford Historical Society, *Collectanea*, 1. Oxford, 1885.

Documents Illustrating the Activities of the General and Provincial Chapters of the English Black Monks, 1215-1540. Edited by William Pantin. Royal Historical Society, Camden 3rd series, 45, 47 and 54. London, 1931, 1933 and 1937.

Domesday Book. Edited by Abraham Farley and Henry Ellis. London, 1783-1816.

Enchiridion symbolorum, definitionum et declarationum de rebus fidei et morum. Edited by Heinrich Denzinger and Adolph Schönmetzer. 35th ed. Freiburg im Breisgau: Herder, 1973.

English Guilds. Edited by Toulmin Smith. Early English Text Society, 40. London, 1870.

Erasmus, Desiderius. *Sileni Alcibiadis.* In *Opera Omnia Desiderii Erasmi Roterodami*, vol. 2.5, edited by Felix Heinimann and Emanuel Kienzle. Amsterdam: North-Holland Publishing Company, 1981.

Evidences relating to the Town Close Estate, Norwich. Editor anonymous. Norwich, 1887.

Faculty Office Registers, 1534-1549. Edited by David S. Chambers. Oxford: Clarendon Press, 1966.

The First Register of Norwich Cathedral Priory. Edited by Herbert W. Saunders. Norfolk Record Society, 11. No place, 1939.

Gascoigne, Thomas. *Loci e Libro Veritatum.* Edited by James E. Rogers. Passages Selected from Gascoigne's Theological Dictionary. Oxford: Clarendon Press, 1881.

Gregory I, Pope. *Dialogorum Libri Quatuor*. Edited by Jacques P. Migne. Patrologia Latina, 77. Paris, 1849.

Heresy Trials in the Diocese of Norwich, 1428-1431. Edited by Norman P. Tanner. Royal Historical Society, Camden 4th series, 20. London, 1977.

"The Hitherto Unpublished Certificates of Norwich Gilds." Edited by John Tingey. *Norfolk Archaeology* 16 (1905-1907) 267-305.

Inventory of Church Goods temp. Edward III. Edited by Aelred Watkin. Norfolk Record Society, 19. No place, 1947-1948.

Julian of Norwich. [*Revelations of Divine Love*]. *A Book of Showings to the Anchoress Julian of Norwich*. Edited by Edmund Colledge and James Walsh. Studies and Texts, 35. Toronto: Pontifical Institute of Mediaeval Studies, 1978.

Kempe, Margery. *The Book of Margery Kempe*. Edited by Sanford B. Meech and Hope E. Allen. Early English Text Society, 212. London, 1940.

Kent Chantries. Edited by Arthur Hussey. Kent Archaeological Society, Records Branch, 12. Ashford, 1936.

Langland, William. *Piers Plowman*. Edited by Jack A. Bennett. Oxford: Clarendon Press, 1972.

Leet Jurisdiction in the City of Norwich. Edited by William Hudson. Selden Society, 5. London, 1892.

Letters and Papers, Foreign and Domestic, of the reign of Henry VIII. Edited by John S. Brewer, James Gairdner and Robert H. Brodie. 21 vols. London: Her Majesty's Stationery Office, 1862-1910.

Lyndwood, William. *Provinciale*. Oxford, 1679.

Monumenta historica carmelitana. Edited by Benedict Zimmerman. Larino, 1905-1907.

More, Sir Thomas. *The Confutation of Tyndale's Answer*. Edited by Louis A. Schuster and others. The Complete Works of St Thomas More, 8. New Haven and London: Yale University Press, 1973.

Non-Cycle Plays and Fragments. Edited by Norman Davis. Early English Text Society, Supplementary Text 1. London, 1970.

"Norfolk Guilds." Edited by John L'Estrange and Walter Rye. *Norfolk Archaeology* 7 (1872) 105-121.

Norwich Consistory Court Depositions, 1499-1512 and 1518-1530. Edited by Edward Stone and Basil Cozens Hardy. Norfolk Record Society, 10. No place, 1938.

"Ordinationes Capituli Generalis Argentinae anno 1362 Celebrati." Edited by Gerold Fussenegger. *Archivum Franciscanum Historicum* 52 (1959) 3-11.

The Paston Letters A.D. 1422-1509. Edited by James Gairdner, 6 vols. London and Exeter, 1904.

Paston Letters and Papers of the Fifteenth Century. Edited by Norman Davis. Oxford: Clarendon Press, 1971-.

Polychronicon Ranulphi Higden. Edited by Churchill Babington and Joseph R. Lumby. Rolls Series. London, 1865-1866.

The Records of the City of Norwich. Edited by William Hudson and John Tingey. 2 vols. Norwich: Jarrold and Sons, 1906-1910.

Records of the Guild of St George in Norwich, 1389-1547. Edited by Mary Grace. Norfolk Record Society, 9. No place, 1937.

The Register of Henry Chichele, Archbishop of Canterbury, 1414-1443. Edited by Ernest F. Jacob. 4 vols. Oxford: Oxford University Press, 1938-1947.

Registrum Simonis Langham Cantuariensis archiepiscopi. Edited by Arthur C. Wood. Canterbury and York Society, 53. No place, 1956.

Religious Lyrics of the XVth Century. Edited by Carleton F. Brown. Oxford: Clarendon Press, 1939.

Taxatio ecclesiastica Angliae et Walliae auctoritate P. Nicholai IV circa A.D. 1291. Edited by Thomas Astle, Samuel Ayscough and John Caley. London, 1802.

Transcripts of Sussex Wills as far as they relate to Ecclesiological and Parochial Subjects, up to the year 1560. Edited by Robert G. Rice and Walter H. Godfrey. Sussex Record Society, 41-43 and 45. No place, 1935-1941.

Valor ecclesiasticus temp. Henr. VIII. Edited by John Caley and Joseph Hunter. 3 vols. London, 1810-1834.

"Visitation Returns of the Diocese of Hereford in 1397." Edited by Arthur T. Bannister. *English Historical Review* 44 (1929) 279-289 and 444-453, and 45 (1930) 92-101 and 444-463.

Visitations in the Diocese of Lincoln, 1517-1531. Edited by Alexander Hamilton Thompson. Lincoln Record Society, 33, 35 and 37. Lincoln, 1940-1947.

Visitations of the Diocese of Norwich, 1492-1532. Edited by Augustus Jessopp. Royal Historical Society, Camden 2nd series, 43. London, 1888.

Walsingham, Thomas. *Historia anglicana.* Edited by Henry T. Riley. Rolls Series. London, 1863-1864.

Worcestre, William. *Itineraries.* Edited by John H. Harvey. Oxford: Clarendon Press, 1969.

ii. Secondary Works

Allen, B. H. "The Administrative and Trade Structure of the Norwich Merchant Class 1485-1660." Harvard University Ph. D. thesis, 1951.

Aubenas, Roger, and Ricard, Robert. *L'Église et la Renaissance.* Histoire de l'Église, edited by Augustin Fliche and others, 15. Paris, 1951.

Beeching, Henry C., and James, Montague R. "The Library of the Cathedral Church of Norwich." *Norfolk Archaeology* 19 (1915-1917) 67-116.

Bennett, Henry S. *The Pastons and their England.* Cambridge: Cambridge University Press, 1932.

Bensly, W. T. "St Leonard's Priory, Norwich." *Norfolk Archaeology* 12 (1893-1895) 190-227.

A Bibliography of Norfolk History. Edited by Elizabeth Darrock and Barry Taylor. Norwich: University of East Anglia, 1975.

Blomefield, Francis. *An Essay towards a Topographical History of the County of Norfolk,* with a Continuation by the Rev. Charles Parkin. 5 vols. Fersfield and Lynn, 1739-1775.

——, and Parkin, Charles. *An Essay towards a Topographical History of the County of Norfolk*. 11 vols. London, 1805-1810.

Bowker, Margaret. *The Secular Clergy in the Diocese of Lincoln, 1495-1520*. Cambridge: Cambridge University Press, 1968.

Brown, Ernest H. Phelps, and Hopkins, Sheila V. "Seven Centuries of Building Wages." In *Essays in Economic History*, edited by Eleanora M. Carus-Wilson, 2: 168-178. London: Edward Arnold, 1962.

—— and ——. "Seven Centuries of the Prices of Consumables, Compared with Builders' Wages." In *Essays in Economic History*, edited by Eleanora M. Carus-Wilson, 2: 179-196. London: Edward Arnold, 1962.

Burnham, Bruce. "The Episcopal Administration of the Diocese of Norwich in the Later Middle Ages." Oxford University B. Litt. thesis, 1971.

"Calendar of Lambeth Wills." Edited by John C. Smith. *Genealogist*, new series, 34 (1917-1918) 53-64, 149-160 and 219-234, and 35 (1918-1919) 45-51 and 102-126.

Calendar of Wills and Administrations now Preserved in the Probate Registry at Canterbury, 1396-1558 and 1640-1650. Edited by Henry R. Plomer. Kent Archaeological Society, Records Branch, 6. London, 1920.

Camp, Anthony J. *Wills and their Whereabouts*. 4th ed. London, 1974.

Campbell, James. *Norwich*. Historic Towns, edited by Mary D. Lobel. London: Scolar Press, 1975.

Carter, Edward H. *Studies in Norwich Cathedral History*. Norwich: Jarrold and Sons, 1935.

Chambers, Edmund K. *The Medieval Stage*. 2 vols. Oxford: Oxford University Press, 1903.

Cheney, Christopher R. "Norwich Cathedral Priory in the Fourteenth Century." *Bulletin of the John Rylands Library* 20 (1936) 93-120.

——. "Rules for the Observance of Feast Days in Medieval England." *Bulletin of the Institute of Historical Research* 34 (1961) 117-147.

Churchill, Irene J. *Canterbury Administration*. 2 vols. London: Society for Promoting Christian Knowledge, 1933.

Clay, Rotha M. *The Hermits and Anchorites of England*. London: Methuen & Co., 1914.

——. "Further Studies on Medieval Recluses." *Journal of the British Archaeological Association*, 3rd series, 16 (1953) 74-86.

Collinson, Patrick. *The Elizabethan Puritan Movement*. London: Jonathan Cape, 1967.

Constable, Giles. "Resistance to Tithes in the Middle Ages." *Journal of Ecclesiastical History* 13 (1962) 172-185.

Craig, Hardin. *English Religious Drama of the Middle Ages*. Oxford: Clarendon Press, 1955.

Delaruelle, Étienne E., Labande, Edmond-René, and Ourliac, Paul. *L'Église au temps du Grand Schisme et de la crise conciliaire*. Histoire de l'Église, edited by Augustin Fliche and others, 14. Paris, 1962.

Delumeau, Jean. *Le Catholicisme entre Luther et Voltaire*. Nouvelle Clio, 30 bis. Paris: Presses Universitaires de France, 1971.

Dickens, Arthur G. *Lollards and Protestants in the Diocese of York, 1509-1558*. Oxford: Oxford University Press for the University of Hull, 1959.

——. *The English Reformation*. London: Batsford, 1964.

Dictionary of National Biography. Edited by Leslie Stephen and Sidney Lee. 63 vols. London: Smith, Elder and Co., 1885-1900.

Dix, Gregory. *A Detection of Aumbries*. London: Dacre Press, 1942.

Dobson, Richard B. "The Foundation of Perpetual Chantries by the Citizens of Medieval York." In *Studies in Church History*, 4, edited by Geoffrey G. Cuming. Leiden, 1967.

Dodwell, Barbara. "The Foundations of Norwich Cathedral." *Transactions of the Royal Historical Society*, 5th series, 7 (1957) 1-18.

Doucet, Victorin. "Le Studium Franciscain de Norwich en 1337." *Archivum Franciscanum Historicum* 46 (1953) 85-98.

Druery, John H. "The Erpingham House." *Norfolk Archaeology* 6 (1864) 143-148.

Dugdale, William. *Monasticon anglicanum*. 6 vols. London, 1817-1830.

Dunn, Ian, and Sutermeister, Helen. *The Norwich Guildhall*. Norwich: City of Norwich with the Norwich Survey, no date.

Emden, Arthur B. *A Biographical Register of the University of Cambridge to 1500*. Cambridge: Cambridge University Press, 1963.

——. *A Biographical Register of the University of Oxford to A.D. 1500*. 3 vols. Oxford: Clarendon Press, 1957-1959.

——. *A Biographical Register of the University of Oxford A.D. 1500 to 1540*. Oxford: Clarendon Press, 1974.

Finucane, Ronald C. *Miracles and Pilgrims: Popular Beliefs in Medieval England*. London: Dent & Sons, 1977.

Flood, R. H. *A Description of St Julian's Church, Norwich, and an Account of Dame Julian's connection with it*. Norwich, 1936.

Foxe, John. *Acts and Monuments*. Edited by Josiah Pratt. 8 vols. London, 1877.

Gasquet, Francis A. *A History of the Venerable English College, Rome*. London: Longmans, Green and Co., 1920.

Grace, Mary. "The Grey Friars in East Anglia." Typescript essay in Norwich Central Library, 1934.

Green, Alice S. *Town Life in the Fifteenth Century*. 2 vols. London: Macmillan and Co., 1894.

Haines, Roy M. "The Education of the English Clergy during the Later Middle Ages: Some Observations on the Operation of Pope Boniface viii's Constitution *Cum ex Eo*." *Canadian Journal of History* 4 (1969) 1-22.

Hammer, Carl I. "The Town-Gown Confraternity of St Thomas the Martyr in Oxford." *Mediaeval Studies* 39 (1977) 466-476.

Handbook of British Chronology, ed. Frederick M. Powicke and Edmund B. Fryde. 2nd ed. London: The Royal Historical Society, 1961.

Hardy, Basil Cozens. *The Mayors of Norwich, 1403-1835*. Norwich: Jarrold and Sons, 1938.

Harford, Dundas. "Richard of Caister, and his Metrical Prayer." *Norfolk Archaeology* 17 (1908-1910) 221-244.

Hay, George. "Pilgrims and the Hospice." *The Venerabile* 21 (1962) 99-144.

Heath, Peter. *The English Parish Clergy on the Eve of the Reformation.* London and Toronto: Routledge and Kegan Paul and University of Toronto Press, 1969.

Hefele, Charles J. and Leclerq, Henri. *Histoire des Conciles.* 11 vols. Paris: Letouzey et Ané, 1907-1952.

Hill, James W. *Medieval Lincoln.* Cambridge: Cambridge University Press, 1948.

Hoskins, William G. "English Provincial Towns in the Early Sixteenth Century." *Transactions of the Royal Historical Society,* 5th series, 6 (1956) 1-19.

Houlbrooke, Ralph. "Church Courts and People in the Diocese of Norwich, 1519-70." Oxford University D. Phil. thesis, 1970.

———. "Persecution of Heresy and Protestantism in the Diocese of Norwich under Henry viii." *Norfolk Archaeology* 35 (1970-1973) 308-326.

———. *Church Courts and the People during the English Reformation.* Oxford: Oxford University Press, 1979.

Hudson, William. *History of the Parish of St Peter Permountergate, Part 1.* Norwich, 1889.

———. "The Norwich Taxation of 1254." *Norfolk Archaeology* 17 (1908-1910) 46-157.

Hue, Nicole. "Les noms de personnes à Castres à la fin du xive siècle." In *Onzième congrès d'études de la Fédération des Sociétés Académiques et Savantes Languedoc-Pyrénées-Gascogne, 11-13 Juin 1955*, pp. 197-214. Albi, 1956.

Hughes, Philip. *The Reformation in England.* 3 vols. London: Hollis & Carter, 1950-1954.

Index of Wills in the York Registry, 1389-1514. Edited by Francis Collins. Yorkshire Archaeological and Topographical Association, Record Series, 6. No place, 1889.

Index of Wills Proved in the Consistory Court of Norwich, 1370-1550, and Wills among the Norwich Enrolled Deeds, 1298-1508. Edited by Margaret A. Farrow. Norfolk Record Society, 16. No place, 1943-1945.

Index of Wills Proved in the Prerogative Court of Canterbury, 1383-1558. Edited by John C. Smith. Index Library, 9 and 11. London, 1893 and 1895.

Index to Testamentary Records in the Commissary Court of London. Edited by Marc Fitch. Index Library, 82 and 86. London, 1969 and 1974.

Jacob, Ernest F. "English University Clerks in the Later Middle Ages: the Problem of Maintenance." *Bulletin of the John Rylands Library* 29 (1945-1946) 304-325.

———. "On the Promotion of English University Clerks during the Later Middle Ages." *Journal of Ecclesiastical History* 1 (1950) 172-186.

———. "Thomas Brouns, Bishop of Norwich, 1436-1445." In *Essays in British History Presented to Sir Keith Feiling*, edited by Hugh Trevor-Roper, pp. 61-83. London and New York: Macmillan and St Martin's Press, 1964.

——. "Two Documents Relating to Thomas Brouns, Bishop of Norwich, 1436-1445." *Norfolk Archaeology* 33 (1962-1965) 427-429.

James, Montague R. *Suffolk and Norfolk*. London and Toronto: J. M. Dent and Sons, 1930.

Jessopp, Augustus. "The Black Death in East Anglia." *The Nineteenth Century* 16 (1884) 915-934.

Jewson, Charles B. *History of the Great Hospital, Norwich*. 2nd ed. Norwich: The Great Hospital, 1966.

Jones, Douglas. *The Church in Chester, 1300-1540*. Chetham Society, 3rd series, 7. Manchester, 1957.

Jordan, William K. *Philanthropy in England, 1480-1660*. London: George Allen and Unwin, 1959.

Kemp, Eric W. "The Attempted Canonization of Robert Grosseteste." In *Robert Grosseteste, Scholar and Bishop*, edited by Daniel A. Callus, pp. 241-246. Oxford: Clarendon Press, 1955.

Kent, Ernest A. "Some Notes on the Desecrated Church of St Cuthbert, Norwich." *Norfolk Archaeology* 27 (1939-1941) 94-96.

Kirkpartick, John. *History of the Religious Orders of Norwich*. Yarmouth, 1845.

Knowles, David. *The Religious Orders in England*. 3 vols. Cambridge: Cambridge University Press, 1948-1959.

——, and Hadcock, Richard. *Medieval Religious Houses, England and Wales*. 2nd ed. London: Longman, 1971.

Kolde, Theodor. *Friedrick der Weise und die Anfänge der Reformation*. Erlangen, 1881.

Kreider, Alan. *English Chantries: The Road to Dissolution*. Cambridge Mass.: Harvard University Press, 1979.

Leach, Arthur F. *The Schools of Medieval England*. London: Methuen, 1915.

Le Bras, Gabriel. *Institutions ecclésiastiques de la Chrétienté mediévale*. Histoire de L'Église, edited by Augustin Fliche and others, 12. Paris: Bloud & Gay, 1959-1964.

Léonard, Emile G. *Histoire Générale du Protestantisme*. Paris: Presses Universitaires de France, 1961-1964. Vol. 1.

Lipman, Vivian D. *The Jews of Medieval Norwich*. London: The Jewish Historical Society of England, 1967.

Little, Andrew G. *The Grey Friars in Oxford*. Oxford Historical Society, 20. Oxford, 1891.

——. "Educational Organisation of the Mendicant Friars in England." *Transactions of the Royal Historical Society*, new series, 8 (1894) 49-70.

——. *Franciscan Papers, Lists and Documents*. Manchester: Manchester University Press, 1943.

——. "A Royal Inquiry into Property Held by the Mendicant Friars in England in 1349 and 1350." In *Historical Essays in Honour of James Tait*, edited by John G. Edwards, Vivian H. Galbraith and Ernest F. Jacob, pp. 179-188. Manchester, 1933.

McCusker, Honor. *John Bale, Dramatist and Antiquary*. Bryn Mawr, 1942.

McDonnell, Ernest W. *The Beguines and Beghards in Medieval Culture*. New Brunswick: Rutgers University Press, 1954.

McFarlane, Kenneth B. *John Wycliffe and the Beginnings of English Non-conformity*. London: English Universities Press, 1952.

——. *Lancastrian Kings and Lollard Knights*. Oxford: Clarendon Press, 1972.

——. *The Nobility of Later Medieval England*. Oxford: Clarendon Press, 1973.

McHardy, Alison. "The Crown and the Diocese of Lincoln during the Episcopate of John Buckingham, 1363-98." Oxford University D. Phil. thesis, 1972.

Mackerell, Benjamin. "Account of the Company of St George in Norwich." *Norfolk Archaeology* 3 (1852) 315-374.

Mackie, John D. *The Earlier Tudors*. Oxford: Clarendon Press, 1952.

Mason, Emma. "The Role of the English Parishioner, 1100-1500." *Journal of Ecclesiastical History* 27 (1976) 17-29.

Medieval Libraries of Great Britain. Edited by Neil Ker. 2nd ed. London: The Royal Historical Society, 1964.

Moeller, Bernd. "Frömmigkeit in Deutschland um 1500." *Archiv für Reformationsgeschichte* 56 (1965) 5-31. Translated as, "Religious Life in Germany on the Eve of the Reformation." In *Pre-Reformation Germany*, edited by Gerald Strauss, pp. 13-42. London: Macmillan, 1972.

Molinari, Paolo. *Julian of Norwich*. London: Longmans, Green and Co., 1958.

Molinier, Auguste. *Les Obituaires Français au Moyen Âge*. Paris, 1890.

Nucé, Marie Simone de. "Piété et charité publique à Toulouse de la fin du 13ᵉ au milieu du 15ᵉ siècle d'après les testaments." Toulouse University Diplôme d'Études Supérieures, 1961.

——. "Piété et charité publique à Toulouse de la fin du xiiiᵉ siècle au milieu du xvᵉ siècle d'après les testaments." *Annales du Midi* 76 (1964) 5-39.

Origo, Iris. *The Merchant of Prato*. London: Jonathan Cape, 1957.

Orme, Nicholas. *English Schools in the Middle Ages*. London: Methuen, 1973.

Owen, Dorothy M. *Church and Society in Medieval Lincolnshire*. History of Lincolnshire, edited by Joan Thirsk, 5. Lincoln, 1971.

Palliser, David M. *The Reformation in York 1534-1553*. Borthwick Papers, 40. York: St Anthony's Press, 1971.

——. "The Trade Gilds of Tudor York." In *Crisis and Order in English Towns 1500-1700*, edited by Peter Clark and Paul Slack, pp. 86-116. London: Routledge and Kegan Paul, 1972.

——. *Tudor York*. Oxford: Oxford University Press, 1979.

Pantin, William A. *The English Church in the Fourteenth Century*. Cambridge: Cambridge University Press, 1955.

——. "Instructions for a Devout and Literate Layman." In *Medieval Learning and Literature: Essays presented to Richard William Hunt*, edited by Jonathan G. Alexander and Margaret T. Gibson, pp. 398-422. Oxford: Clarendon Press, 1976.

Pearce, Ernest H. *The Monks of Westminster*. Cambridge: Cambridge University Press, 1916.

Pfaff, Richard W. *New Liturgical Feasts in Later Medieval England*. Oxford: Clarendon Press, 1970.

Phythian-Adams, Charles. "Ceremony and the Citizen: The Communal Year in Coventry." In *Crisis and Order in English Towns 1500-1700*, edited by Peter Clark and Paul Slack, pp. 57-85. London: Routledge and Kegan Paul, 1972.

Pound, John F. "The Social and Trade Structure of Norwich, 1525-1575." *Past and Present* 34 (1966) 49-69.

Powell, Edgar. *The Rising in East Anglia in 1381*. Cambridge: Cambridge University Press, 1896.

Power, Eileen E. *Medieval English Nunneries*. Cambridge: Cambridge University Press, 1922.

Prodi, Paolo. "Structure and Organisation of the Church in Renaissance Venice." In *Renaissance Venice*, edited by John R. Hale, pp. 409-430. London: Faber and Faber, 1973.

Pullan, Brian. *Rich and Poor in Renaissance Venice*. Oxford: Basil Blackwell, 1971.

Putnam, Bertha H. "Maximum Wage Laws for Priests after the Black Death, 1348-1381." *American Historical Review*, 21 (1915-1916) 12-32.

Rapp, Francis. *L'Église et la vie religieuse en Occident à la fin du Moyen Âge*. Nouvelle Clio, 25. Paris: Presses Universitaires de France, 1971.

"Report of the Summer Meeting of the Institute at Norwich, 1949." *Archaeological Journal* 106 (1949) 51-115.

Reynolds, Susan. *An Introduction to the History of English Medieval Towns*. Oxford: Clarendon Press, 1977.

Rosenthal, Joel T. *The Purchase of Paradise*. London and Toronto: Routledge and Kegan Paul and University of Toronto Press, 1972.

Russell, Josiah C. *British Medieval Population*. Albuquerque: University of New Mexico Press, 1948.

——. "The Clerical Population of Medieval England." *Traditio* 2 (1944) 177-212.

Rye, Walter. "The Riot between the Monks and Citizens of Norwich in 1272." *Norfolk Antiquarian Miscellany* 2 (1883) 17-89.

——. *Carrow Abbey*. Norwich, 1889.

——. *Norfolk Families*. 2 vols. Norwich: Goose and Son, 1911-1913.

Saunders, Herbert W. *An Introduction to the Obedientiary and Manor Rolls of Norwich Cathedral Priory*. Norwich: Jarrold and Sons, 1930.

——. *A History of the Norwich Grammar School*. Norwich: Jarrold and Sons, 1932.

Savage, William. *The Making of our Towns*. London: Eyre and Spottiswoode, 1952.

Sede Vacante Wills. Edited by Charles E. Woodruff. Kent Archaeological Society, Records Branch, 3. Canterbury, 1914.

Sheehan, Michael M. *The Will in Medieval England from the Conversion of the Anglo-Saxons to the End of the Thirteenth Century*. Studies and Texts, 6. Toronto: Pontifical Institute of Mediaeval Studies, 1963.

——. "The Influence of Canon Law on the Property Rights of Married Women in England." *Mediaeval Studies* 25 (1963) 109-124.

Sheppard, Elaine M. "The Reformation and the Citizens of Norwich." *Norfolk Archaeology* 38 (1981-) 44-58.

Southern, Richard W. *Western Society and the Church in the Middle Ages.* The Pelican History of the Church, 2. Harmondsworth: Penguin Books, 1970.

Storey, Robin L. *The End of the House of Lancaster.* London: Barrie and Rockliff, 1966.

Sumption, Jonathan. *Pilgrimage.* London: Faber and Faber, 1975.

Sutermeister, Helen. *The Norwich Blackfriars.* Norwich: City of Norwich with the Norwich Survey, 1977.

Sweet, Alfred H. "The Apostolic See and the Heads of English Religious Houses." *Speculum* 28 (1953) 468-484.

Swinburne, Henry. *A Briefe Treatise of Testaments and Last Willes.* London, 1590.

Tanner, Norman P. "Popular Religion in Norwich with special Reference to the Evidence of Wills, 1370-1532." Oxford University D. Phil. thesis, 1973.

Tanner, Thomas, and Nasmith, James. *Notitia monastica.* Cambridge, 1787.

Taylor, Richard C. *Index monasticus.* London, 1821.

Thompson, Alexander Hamilton. *The English Clergy and their Organisation in the Later Middle Ages.* Oxford: Clarendon Press, 1947.

Thomson, John A. "Clergy and Laity in London, 1376-1531." Oxford University D. Phil. thesis, 1960.

——. "Tithe Disputes in Later Medieval London." *English Historical Review* 78 (1963) 1-17.

——. "Piety and Charity in Late Medieval London." *Journal of Ecclesiastical History* 16 (1965) 178-195.

——. *The Later Lollards, 1414-1520.* Oxford: Oxford University Press, 1965.

Thrupp, Sylvia. *The Merchant Class of Medieval London.* Ann Arbor: University of Michigan Press, 1962.

Toussaert, Jacques. *Le sentiment religieux en Flandre à la fin du Moyen Âge.* Paris: Librairie Plon, 1960.

Tristram, Ernest W. *English Wall Painting of the Fourteenth Century.* London: Routledge and Kegan Paul, 1955.

Unwin, George. *The Guilds and Companies of London.* 4th ed. London: Frank Cass and Co., 1963.

Venn, John A. *Caius College.* London, 1901.

——, and others. *A Biographical History of Gonville and Caius College.* Cambridge: Cambridge University Press, 1897-. Vol. 3.

The Victoria History of London. London: Constable and Co., 1909-. Vol. 1.

The Victoria History of the County of Norfolk. London: Constable and Co., 1901-. Vol. 2.

The Victoria History of the County of York, The City of York. Oxford: Oxford University Press, 1961.

Warren, Ann K. "The English Anchorite in the Reign of Henry III, 1216-1272." *Forum* (Ball State University) 19 (1978) 21-28.

Westlake, Herbert F. *The Parish Guilds of Mediaeval England*. London: Society for Promoting Christian Knowledge, 1919.

Whitfield, Derek. "Two Unknown Seals of the Bristol Franciscans and a Canynges Deed, dated 1465." *Transactions of the Bristol and Gloucestershire Archaeological Society* 72 (1953) 67-78.

Williams, Arnold. "Relations between the Mendicant Friars and the Secular Clergy in England in the Later Fourteenth Century." *Annuale Mediaevale* 1 (1960) 22-92.

Williams, John F. "Ordination in the Norwich Diocese during the Fifteenth Century." *Norfolk Archaeology* 31 (1955-1957) 345-358.

Williamson, W. W. "Saints on Norfolk Rood-Screens and Pulpits." *Norfolk Archaeology* 31 (1955-1957) 299-346.

Wood, Anthony. *The History and Antiquities of the Colleges and Halls in the University of Oxford*. Edited by John Gutch. Oxford, 1786.

Woodforde, Christopher. *The Norwich School of Glass-Painting in the Fifteenth Century*. Oxford: Oxford University Press, 1950.

Wood-Legh, Kathleen L. *Perpetual Chantries in Britain*. Cambridge: Cambridge University Press, 1965.

Index